PERSPECTIVES IN ECONOMIC THOUGHT

PERSPECTIVES IN ECONOMIC THOUGHT

Martin C. Spechler
Indiana University

McGraw-Hill Publishing Company

New York   St. Louis   San Francisco   Auckland   Bogotá   Caracas   Hamburg

Lisbon   London   Madrid   Mexico   Milan   Montreal   New Delhi   Oklahoma City

Paris   San Juan   São Paulo   Singapore   Sydney   Tokyo   Toronto

PERSPECTIVES IN ECONOMIC THOUGHT

Copyright © 1990 by McGraw-Hill, Inc. All rights reserved. Printed in the United
States of America.
Except as permitted under the United States Copyright Act of 1976, no part of this
publication may be reproduced or distributed in any form or by any means, or stored in
a data base or retrieval system, without the prior written permission of the publisher.

1 2 3 4 5 6 7 8 9 DOC DOC 9 5 4 3 2 1 0

ISBN 0-07-060011-2

This book was set in Times Roman by Pat McCarney.
The editors were Jim Bittker and Peggy C. Rehberger;
the production supervisor was Denise L. Puryear.
The cover was designed by Karen K. Quigley.
The cover and text drawings were done by Gavriel Rosenfeld.
R. R. Donnelly & Sons Company was printer and binder.

Library of Congress Catalogue Card Number: 89-64488

Martin C. Spechler is a graduate of the Social Studies Program at Harvard, where he also earned his Ph.D. in Economics. He has taught at Harvard, the Hebrew University of Jerusalem, Tel-Aviv University, the University of Washington, and the University of Iowa.

The author or coauthor of over thirty scholarly articles on comparative economics, economic history, and economic thought, Professor Spechler is a member of the Association for Social Economics, the Association for Comparative Economic Studies, the Cliometrics Society, and the American Economics Association.

He is presently Associate Professor of Economics at Indiana University–Purdue University at Indianapolis. He also serves on the editorial board of *Comparative Economic Studies*.

To My Teachers

CONTENTS

PREFACE

This book contains classic and contemporary readings from six alternative perspectives in economic thought, as well as the neo-classical mainstream which dominates American economics today. Each chapter has an introduction identifying the principal enduring characteristics of that perspective as a mode of analysis and prescription. The readings include selections from one or two classic founders of the perspective, plus influential contemporary writings within that perspective. Limiting the number of authors and emphasizing the overall perspective should increase retention by students. My aim is that graduates in economics know what a "Keynesian" or "Marxist" line of thought is when they encounter it in a magazine, book, or news program. They should sense the assumptions, understand the argument and evidence, and even anticipate the implications of neo-Malthusian or libertarian or any other contemporary version of these perspectives.

An unusual aim of this book is to deal even-handedly with libertarian and classical perspectives—usually found to the right of mainstream—along with Marxism, Keynesianism, and institutionalism, usually to the left. Comparisons with modern neo-classical economics are made throughout. I try to identify the strengths which have made these perspectives survive; less attention is paid to shortcomings, except in the discussion questions. Critical comparisons of every perspective with others will be the natural material of group discussion and papers. Thus, while my leanings are social democratic, the book can be used by instructors of all persuasions.

Since modern and fairly sophisticated economists are included, with ample examples and policy discussion, this book may be used for a senior "capstone course," which reviews what has been learned in the economics major and shows the advantages and limitations of the mainstream paradigm. A capstone course about perspectives in economic thought would enrich the undergraduate major by putting economics into its philosophic and historical connection with other branches of social inquiry. Offering such a capstone experience has been recommended by the Carnegie Foundation for the Advancement of Teaching. Indeed, a senior course of this kind is more and more common in liberal arts colleges, even where the history of economic thought is not required.

While there are several texts in the history of thought market—the leading ones are by Ingrid Rima and by Robert Ekelund, Jr., and Robert Hebert for undergraduates and by Mark Blaug for graduate students—this is one of the few readers which can serve as a complement to them all. I include extensive selections from the major theorists and only incidental exposition of the lives of the thinkers included. Where a good textbook is assigned which details the theoretic contributions, my introductions may provide a different angle and a basis for argument. In courses where the historical background and detailed models are supplied by the instructor, *Perspectives in Economic Thought* could stand alone.

Very few readers have been published in recent years. Whether for reasons of copyright and other costs or out of concern to mention all known economists, most readers in print include only a few pages from major works. My experience with such readers has been that students remembered little after the exam. But where readings books like *Masterworks in Economics* (now out-of-print) included longer selections, most students were discouraged by extensive digressions and tedious examples. I have sought a "golden path" of reprinting considerable portions from major works yet excising unimportant materials likely to deter the non-specialist, while retaining the basic argument. Where essential points are made, of course, some difficulties are unavoidable, even desirable.

I dedicate this book to my teachers, who taught me most of what I know—and a lot I don't! Among the teachers of economic theory from whom I learned the most are Abram Bergson, Richard Gill, Albert Hirschman, and Richard Musgrave. Their broadmindedness, integrity, and scrupulous scholarship have provided me much guidance over the years. My tutors and mentors from Harvard's Social Studies committee—the late Donald Brown, the late Alexander Gerschenkron, Stanley Hoffmann, Richard Hunt, and Barrington Moore, Jr.—persuaded me to take history and theory seriously. Others from whose works I have learned, especially Mark Blaug, Samuel Hollander, and Joseph Schumpeter, are noted in the footnotes of this book. They all have my appreciation. My seniors at Indiana University–Purdue University at Indianapolis endured the first drafts of this book; their patience, comments, and even their complaints all helped more than they would think.

To my colleague Donna Kay Dial and to Gerald W. Sazama of the University of Connecticut go my thanks for reading parts of the manuscript and making many useful suggestions.

The original line drawings for this book are by Gavriel Rosenfeld of Bloomington, Indiana.

My family put up with my postponing other commitments and duties so that this manuscript could be completed on time. For this and much else, they have my love.

Martin C. Spechler

PERSPECTIVES
IN ECONOMIC
THOUGHT

CHAPTER 1

INTRODUCTION

The purpose of this book is to show that political economy has consisted of several perspectives developed in the past and continuing in the present. Beyond the neoclassical mainstream emphasized in English-speaking universities, there are other perspectives worthy of study by economists with contemporary interests. Mercantilist, Marxist, Austrian, Keynesian, and Institutionalist—these alternatives have influenced the mainstream before and may do so again. Contemporary variants of these perspectives—like neo-mercantilism, neo-institutionalism, post-Keynesianism, radical (neo-Marxist) economics—have many supporters in the United States and other parts of the world. Proponents of these alternative perspectives believe they offer true answers to pressing contemporary problems, superior to those offered by mainstream economics.

This volume presents excerpts from books and articles which illustrate these perspectives in their historical and contemporary versions. Neo-mercantilism shares the standpoint of mercantilism but without making the confusion of wealth with mere money—a fallacy known as bullionism. Radical neo-Marxism is less deterministic and rigid than classical Marxism. Austrian neo-classical economists have gone beyond the school's early contributions to marginalism and equilibrium capital theory to incorporate dynamics—how the economy moves to new equilibria—as well as libertarian precepts. Post-Keynesians and the less radical neo-Keynesians have selected and developed some parts of Keynes' critique of neo-classical economic policy, while neo-institutionalists have drawn on recent developments in psychology and anthropology to replace the dubious beliefs of Thorstein Veblen about race and instincts. Still other perspectives—for example, Thomist or Hindu—might have been included, but owing to limits of space, this volume includes only secular perspectives which persist to modern times, while recognizing that some religious thinking on economic questions retains its validity and force, particularly as guides to action for believers.

FIGURE 1-1

Historical and Contemporary Perspectives

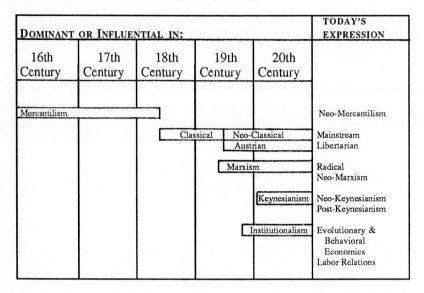

DOMINANT OR INFLUENTIAL IN:					TODAY'S EXPRESSION
16th Century	17th Century	18th Century	19th Century	20th Century	
Mercantilism					Neo-Mercantilism
			Classical	Neo-Classical	Mainstream
				Austrian	Libertarian
				Marxism	Radical Neo-Marxism
				Keynesianism	Neo-Keynesianism Post-Keynesianism
				Institutionalism	Evolutionary & Behavioral Economics Labor Relations

Recognition of several available perspectives is useful, I believe, because economics should not be viewed as an "intellectual progression from error to truth,"[1] but rather a cultural journey in which ancient sites are worth repeat visits and reappraisals in each age. The itinerary of economics from Adam Smith to Alfred Marshall and on to Paul Samuelson can be seen as progress only from a particular perspective, and then only with a loss of particular features which may be important from another point of view. Thus, architects of new perspectives often, and wisely, build up their own structures from stones of previous structures. With so many problems unsolved by present-day economists, changing our assumptions and procedures may help. Even those content to labor in the mainstream tradition will appreciate the assumptions and strengths of the neoclassical perspective better once they have viewed the alternatives.

---

[1]The "absolutist" approach, as defined by Werner Stark, *History of Economics in Its Relation to Social Development* (London, 1944), p. 1. For a contrary view to mine, see George Stigler, "Does Economics Have a Useful Past?", *History of Political Economy*, vol. I (1969), pp. 217-230. While asserting that the study of the history of economic ideas does "not provide an agenda for the professional student of the subject," the Chicago professor admits there is much to be learned in Adam Smith or Alfred Marshall on such topics as economic growth.

A PERSPECTIVE: QUESTIONS AND A FRAMEWORK FOR ANSWERS

Before turning to the perspectives and theories themselves, we must deal briefly with one or two methodological issues. First of all, what is a *perspective?* In my usage, a perspective may be defined as a complex image of the world which raises ethical and scientific questions for inquiry. Not everything that's interesting is important; not everything that's important is interesting for the social scientist. Thus, a perspective is a frame of reference which identifies important and interesting questions and points to possible explanations and solutions. It names the actors and those affected by action. Since not all aspects about a situation can normally be dealt with simultaneously, any perspective must assume much of human behavior. A perspective also implies criteria for successful causal or functional accounts of behavior. Should our theories primarily be judged by internal consistency, by their correspondence with relevant data from the real world, or by their relation to correct policy and right action?

FIGURE 1-2
What Does a Perspective Give Us?

---

1. Which problems are important?
2. Whose actions are likely to have determined the situation?
3. What can we assume about their activity? Who is affected?
4. How do we confirm or reject our hypotheses?
5. What, if anything, can be done about the situation?

Let's take an example. How would economists using different perspectives analyze the massive influx of Japanese automobiles since the early 1970s? Mainstream economists would certainly start with cost advantages which imply a comparative advantage to Japanese automakers. Neo-mercantilist writers, as we shall see, believe that Japan's comparative advantage has been created by active industrial policy in that country, while neo-Keynesians might start with an overvalued exchange rate which makes all imports too cheap in the USA. Neo-Marxists would certainly bring up the differences in working class strength, which has led to much lower wages in Japan. Neo-institutionalists might well blame the oligopolistic structure of the American auto industry which has led to uncompetitive and backward designs, particularly when energy and environmental concerns became more pressing in the mid-1970s. Finally, Austrian or libertarian economists would welcome the inevitable competition which characterizes worldwide capitalism at its best.

As this example hints, a perspective is more than a research "paradigm."[2] It also gives an agenda for ethical action and correct policy. Hence one's choice among perspectives cannot be made only on purely objective, universal grounds. Both one's philosophical (or religious) worldview and the usefulness of the theories developed from each perspective must influence one's choice. In Figure 1-3, we see that hypotheses derive from perspectives, and perspectives depend on a person's worldview. Nonetheless, a person may adopt a worldview or a perspective based on the correctness of theories implied. Natural scientists often take this pragmatic stance. Or we may adopt theories based on their compatibility with one's worldview or perspective—the stance often taken by humanists and social activists.

FIGURE 1-3
Perspectives in Economics

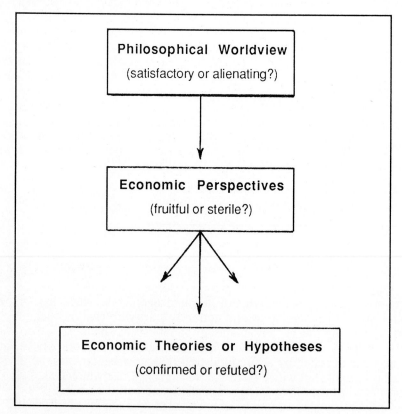

[2]Thomas Kuhn introduced the notion of a scientific "paradigm" within which most "normal science" is carried on, *The Structure of Scientific Revolutions*, 2d ed. (Chicago: University of Chicago Press, 1970); a valuable collection of articles on scientific method, including Karl Popper's opposing views and Kuhn's replies, is Imre Lakatos and Alan Musgrave, eds., *Criticism and the Growth of Knowledge* (Cambridge: Cambridge University Press, 1970).

WHY CHOOSE A CERTAIN PERSPECTIVE?

In this usage, perspectives are "meta-theories." Many different theories can and have issued from a single perspective. A very narrow theory, or hypothesis, may be refuted or confirmed according to the requirements of a perspective. Without a commitment to some definite perspective, though, it is difficult to know how social scientists could agree that a theory or hypothesis is either to be maintained (provisionally) or rejected, for there are no adequate, self-evident standards external to the community of thinkers committed to a common perspective. Consequently, a perspective remains valid as long as it generates (provisionally) true theories and explanations of social life; it fails when it no longer addresses the concerns of the contemporary world, including those of social scientists themselves.

Note that nothing so far has been said about perspectives being "economic." This is because the scope of "economics" is itself controversial and subject to change. The mainstream definition confines academic economics to the study of choices of goal made under scarcity of means. Neo-classical economists sometimes rule out alternative paradigms which have undoubtedly been influential in the past as "not economics . . . merely sociology." For my part, I would prefer we reject this dogmatism in favor of Alfred Marshall's broad definition— "economics is a study of mankind in the ordinary business of life."[3] Any perspective which makes sense of or predicts what we produce, how we produce it, and by whom, when, and how it is consumed—that is a useful sort of economics which some may legitimately wish to pursue. At the same time, it must be recognized that specialization and commitment to *one* perspective is most times the best way to progress. After all, scientific specialization has proved to be an efficient way to pursue known goals. Further, if a perspective leads to quantifiable theories, all the better. But quantification may not be possible in every area, certainly not with the same precision.

---

[3]Alfred Marshall, *Principles of Economics,* 6th ed. (London: Macmillan, 1910), p. 1. He continued, "The less we trouble ourselves with scholastic inquiries as to whether a certain consideration comes within the scope of economics, the better." *Ibid.,* Book I, ii, §7, p. 27.

CHAPTER 2

MERCANTILISM AND NEO-MERCANTILISM

EDITOR'S INTRODUCTION

Our first perspective, mercantilism, is for activists. Since its beginnings four centuries ago, mercantilist thinking—the economics of state power—has come up whenever members of a national community sense that their economic performance is inferior to that of others. In the United States today many political economists are concerned about the record American deficits in the balance of payments.[1] These deficits have accumulated over the last twenty years to the point where the United States, still the richest country in the world, has apparently become a net debtor to the citizens of other countries. Accompanying this debit balance has been the outflow of international assets from the United States and their accumulation in newly industrialized countries, notably Japan, South Korea, and Taiwan. Another aspect of international deficits has been the investment by foreigners in tangible American property, such as farm lands, office buildings, auto plants, as well as corporate property. Neo-mercantilist economists are especially concerned with these trends.

Aware of all this, mainstream economists tend to deny any adverse result from foreign ownership while affirming its benefits in technological transfer and capital formation. Deficits do, of course, imply future obligations to foreigners, and if these seem too large, then the proper remedy is depreciation

---

[1]Writers widely read in America today who might be considered "neo-mercantilist" include Ira C. Magaziner and Robert B. Reich *(Minding America's Business, The Decline and Rise of the American Economy);* Robert Kuttner *(The Economic Illusion, False Choices Between Prosperity and Social Justice);* Robert Gilpin *(U.S. Power and the Multinational Corporation* and others); and Steven Krasner *(Defending the National Interest: Raw Materials, Investments, and U.S. Foreign Policy).* Many mainstream economists, intellectually committed to free trade, have expressed neo-mercantilist thoughts, such as Robert Z. Lawrence of the liberal Brookings Institution who, in a recent book *Saving Free Trade,* calls for "pragmatic free trade," which would assist the adjustment process of industries and affected workers.

of the dollar, high real interest rates to encourage domestic saving, and a commitment throughout the advanced world to open markets.

Not reassured that such remedies have worked in recent years, however, many ordinary Americans seem troubled by the prospect of foreigners' owning their places of work. They do not believe that non-Americans will treat their communities and themselves with the same fairness and goodwill that the best American corporate bosses do. Investors fear foreigners may suddenly withdraw their support for the dollar by selling it for their own or other foreign currencies in the world market. This vulnerability to sudden collapse in the international value of the dollar and of dollar-denominated assets has become all the greater with the advent of computer-linked worldwide securities markets trading around the clock. Such distrust of foreigners beyond our control may not always be justified, but it is all too human. Distrust of outsiders has often in the past provided the emotional basis for mercantilist thinking.

Besides financial interdependence, Americans also worry that their own products will be unfairly excluded from foreign markets because of open or hidden protection, resulting in the loss of jobs upon which whole communities depend. Why should we compete freely when others do not? If manufacturing and other "good" jobs cannot be replaced, America will lose experience, human capital, and the tax base of established communities. Such worries prompted calls by neo-mercantilist writers during the 1980s for an *industrial policy,* governmental coordination of the development (or orderly shrinking) of whole industries.

Neo-mercantilist writers, not all of whom would call themselves economists, are also concerned about employment of an underclass which does not seem to be absorbed into productive, stable jobs despite fifteen years of declining real wages in this country.

Mainstream Criticisms of Mercantilism

Mercantilism, as well as its neo-mercantilist successors, has long had a bad name among mainstream economists. Mercantilism has been called "a gigantic theoretical balloon" hardly worth the time to puncture.[2] Adam Smith devoted considerable effort to debunking the "mercantile school" for its erroneous support for protection, hoarding of gold and silver, and colonialism—though he prudently allowed for Britain's Navigation Acts and retaliatory tariffs. For classical and neo-classical economists alike, mercantilism was a mere defense of the vested class or national interests, whereas enlightened men should attend to the welfare of the world as a whole.

Historical mercantilism was also condemned as primitive for confusing wealth with mere money, which in pre-modern times was gold and silver coins and bullion. Money is a means to national prosperity, say the critics, but hardly an important form of national wealth. Internationally acceptable money can be accumulated only by an export surplus, implying that consumption or

---

[2]Mark Blaug, *Economic Theory in Retrospect,* 4th ed. (Cambridge: Cambridge University Press, 1985), p. 10.

domestic investment need be sacrificed. In today's widely accepted notation for national income per year,

$$Y = C + I + G + EX - IM$$

with Y the net domestic product, C current consumption, I the net domestic investment in each year, and EX and IM, exports and imports. Thus, net exports

$$EX - IM = Y - C - G - I.$$

For the trade surplus, on the left of the equation, to be positive, national product must exceed consumption, public and private, and real investment in the productive potential of the country. The more surpluses, the less domestic uses. But consumption, present or future, constitutes the sole justifiable uses of national product. According to mainstream critics, net foreign investment $(EX - IM)$, if devoted to accumulation of sterile monetary assets like gold, absorbs national saving $(Y - C - G)$ which could otherwise be invested in real capital, leading to growth of consumption. Investing in assets which bear no interest is simply irrational.

In their condemnation of the mercantilist perspective, mainstream neoclassical economists assume that the only ethical objective of economic organization is the promotion of individual material welfare, basically present and future consumption. For these economists, national welfare is a false notion, since a nation is nothing more than the individuals who comprise it. Promoting the welfare of others may be praiseworthy, but altruism is not the ordinary motivation of men and women. Rather, individual material welfare is the chief ethical standard in a liberal society. Since individual material welfare is best promoted by personal property rights and incomes earned from productive contribution, private property is legitimate regardless of envy or inequality engendered. Personal incomes are obtained cooperatively through the division of labor, specialization, and voluntary trading in free markets. According to neoclassical thinking, therefore, any interference with this process must hurt some individuals, possibly all, and thus makes retaliation or resistance likely in the long run. Hence, the mainstream presumption in favor of free markets limits regulation to making private markets work efficiently. Neo-mercantilists see a greater scope for regulation.

What Was Mercantilism?

Though it had medieval antecedents, mercantilism has come to denote the economic thought or perspective expressing the policy concerns of the new states of Europe from the sixteenth to eighteenth centuries. The famous "enlightened despots" of that era—Elizabeth I of England, Louis XIV of France, Frederick the Great of Prussia, Maria Theresa and Joseph II of Austria, and Peter the Great of Russia—faced many similar problems. Their ambition was to build the power of newly centralized realms against erstwhile domestic, foreign, and transnational rivals. Barons, bishops, and other feudal powers had to be reduced in political influence, neighbors dominated, and the Church domesticated to serve only national interests.

Though diverse in emphasis and particular recommendations, mercantilists and the rulers they advised and counseled shared four related goals. First, mercantilists sought the *unity* of the state under a single sovereign power.[3] In economic life, this unity implied a single market, requiring a customs union without internal tolls and customs duties. Because tolls on waterways and at border crossings were a plentiful source of revenue to feudal authorities, a customs union would serve to reduce the power of the King's rivals. While all mercantilist regimes tried to remove internal tolls on commerce, few succeeded immediately. The French internal customs union promoted by J. B. Colbert, minister to Louis XIV, was only partially completed when the great mercantilist minister left office. The Russian customs union did not encompass the Empire's several dozen European provinces until 1753, despite the commands of Peter the Great and other autocrats for nearly a century before. German tolls and tariffs did not fall, even to Frederick the Great (1712-1786), until the mid-nineteenth century.

Unity would also be promoted by common weights and measures, including coinage of previous metals. This, too, would serve the sovereign's interest by prestige, seignorage (mint fees), and the possibility of debasement. Monopoly of essential goods and services and policies to provide subsistence to the whole population of the realm were also believed to promote unity, as well as public order.

To build a strong, unified state, the enlightened despots of this period found that they had to *build up a centralized government* apparatus, a bureaucracy of paid servants of the state who would be trained to carry out a single set of laws. Among these paid servants were, of course, policemen, diplomats and spies, a navy, and a standing army. All owed unqualified allegiance to the state that maintained them.

A loyal bureaucracy and professional armed forces, indispensable to defending the state against adversaries at home and abroad, required vastly increased revenues. Thus, the third common objective of mercantilists was to *raise taxes.* As Colbert wrote, "Trade is the source of [public] finance and finance is the vital nerve of war."[4] The enlightened despotisms of the period invented new types of taxes and raised the rates and yield on old ones. They levied tariffs on imports as well as exports; taxed consumption as well as liquid and real wealth. Tax collection was sometimes direct, often indirect, through the sale of tax farms or monopoly privileges, such as the sale of salt, matches, whiskey, not to mention offices of profit and prestige. By such devices, for example, Peter the Great is said to have raised the revenues of the

---

[3] Eli F. Heckscher, *Mercantilism,* rev. ed. (London: Allen and Unwin, 1955), vol. I, p. 22. Unity was the emphasis in continental Europe; where unity had already been achieved, as in England and Russia, expansion and security became the chief objectives. Those countries with considerable foreign trade emphasized the role of merchant adventurers and bullion more than those with a more closed economy.

[4] Heckscher, vol. II, p. 17.

Russian state by five times, but when he died in 1725, his giant projects—the new capital of St. Petersburg, built on the Neva marshes, a network of canals, and incessant wars—had left the Russian state destitute.

What mercantilists contributed most of all was an understanding that greater revenues would require *developing the taxable economy.* To promote economic growth, regulation of domestic production technique was adopted to assure national products met the quality required by the Court and by foreign customers. Statesmen invited foreign artisans to develop the best techniques— then tried to prohibit them from leaking out to competitors! Mercantilist ministers tried to reduce the public's consumption of expensive foreign goods, while investing in and subsidizing domestic substitutes (e.g., the famous Gobelins' tapestries), crops, and infrastructure essential to state welfare. Colonies were established abroad to provide raw materials and luxuries not obtainable at home. Building roads, ports, and canals would often be accomplished by forced labor. If not so employed, paupers were thrown into workhouses or sent to colonies to protect the public order and fill its purse, for as Cardinal Richelieu observed, "The people become ungovernable when they are idle." Foreign trade, an especially attractive source of hard cash, was favored by the chartering and protection of traders in overseas ports, as well as the cautious tolerance of foreign traders in one's own.

To make the state powerful it must be large, so mercantilists were concerned about *aggregate income,* not only *per capita,* as is true of mainstream economists. Mercantilists' concern for population size led them to favor immigration, protection of orphans, and the promotion of early marriage, the principal pro-natalist measure in the days before artificial birth control.

Mercantilism—A Set of Ideas

Mercantilism was first and always a collection of state development policies— the earliest economics of state power. To economic historians concerned with commonalities in European *practice,* the four policies outlined above expressed similar responses to similar situations, despite significant geographic and historical variation across the Continent. Historians of economic thought, by contrast, have properly asked what was the *theoretic* justification for mercantilism, and many, as mentioned above, have found that theory defective and self-serving.[5] To be sure, the enlightened despots themselves were little concerned for any deep, consistent justification of their policies, which they usually arrived at without the help of economic theorists. Our interest, however, is in the early development of a perspective that survives to this day.

---

[5]For example, as we will read below, Thomas Mun's argument for the use of gold and silver abroad by merchant trading companies may well have been prompted by his connections with the East India Company, which had little else but precious metals to offer for Asian goods desired in Europe. An extreme neoclassical condemnation of mercantilists for "bad analysis" is contained in W. R. Allen, "Modern Defenders of Mercantilist Theory," *History of Political Economy,* vol. 2 (1970), pp. 381-397.

Early mercantilist writers came from antagonistic countries and were often unaware of each other's work. They were not a unified school. The very name "mercantilist" was invented by their physiocratic opponents in the eighteenth century! Nevertheless, the mercantilist perspective has some common themes. First, the mercantilists' primary goal was secular wealth and well-being of the nation-state. Personal utility was secondary and derivative: personal interests might provide a reliable way to manipulate individuals to further state goals. Mercantilists were typically cynical about higher motivations, such as loyalty and piety. Yet the wealth of the state would not normally conflict with the prosperity of its leading citizens.[6]

National wealth had to be pursued in a cruel world of static dimensions, in which one community's gain could only come at the loss of another's. The idea of universal gain through specialization and trade or by invention and innovation would not have seemed plausible to these men living in a time of negligible economic growth. If my gain is your loss, international exchange might engender conflict and war. Even so, few mercantilists were pro-war, as open conflict hurt trade. But markets abroad were not automatically open to foreigners on equal terms with the home-born. Outside traders had to break into market towns, by force if necessary.

In this static world, most financial capital was not manifestly productive. Gold and silver are proverbially sterile; interest on loans to maintain someone else's consumption seemed wrong. The world's stock of precious metals grows slowly at all times and thus is primarily an object for redistribution among nations. Yet specie was essential to foreign trade, since few traders would accept token or paper money, however backed by sovereign promises. Christopher Columbus, who used gold to seek more gold, put it this way: "He who has gold makes and accomplishes whatever he wishes in the world and finally uses it to send souls into paradise."

Most mercantilist writers knew perfectly well that bullion was not the only form of wealth.[7] **Thomas Mun** defined wealth as lands, houses, and goods. Moreover, Mun and **William Petty**, among others, recognized that excessive monetary gold could cause a harmful rise in prices.

To obtain a significant increase in gold or silver for any national purpose, a country needed to have mines or to take the specie from those who possessed mines or hoards. That was obvious. Mercantilists made their contribution by advising the state how to accumulate treasure by a positive balance of trade, which foreigners would be expected to pay off in gold and silver. A positive balance would be achieved by exporting as much finished goods as possible, even by limiting their consumption at home through sumptuary legislation. To enhance earnings from these exports, their prices were best set according to the overseas competition. Only essentials would be imported, preferably in the

---

[6]Jacob Viner, "Power versus Plenty as Objectives of Foreign Policy in the Seventeenth and Eighteenth Centuries," *World Politics,* vol. 1, no. 1 (October, 1948), pp. 1-29.

[7]For example the prominent Austrian mercantilist Johann Joachim Becher (1625-1685) and the anonymous author of the *Discourse of the Common Weal* (1549). Charles Wilson, "Trade, Society, and the State," in *Cambridge Economic History of Europe,* vol. IV (Cambridge, 1967), pp. 508-509.

unfinished state for further processing at home. Protecting domestic manufacturing industry, in addition, would both expand exports and limit imports, thereby furnishing employment for a growing urban population. Protective tariffs would also provide revenue; they were a far more prominent tax than they are today. Essential services, such as shipping, would also be provided by taxable residents, hence the laws requiring shipping in national bottoms.

Though the mercantilists of the seventeenth and eighteenth centuries could offer only primitive, non-quantitative, and often self-serving policy advice, the perspective they adopted has recurred from time to time. In the nineteenth century, the Germans **Friedrich List** (1789-1846) and **Gustav Schmoller** (1838-1917) applauded the statecraft of the Prussian mercantilists. During the Great Depression of the 1930s, John Maynard Keynes referred to the "fragments of political wisdom" of the mercantilists, notably their concern for abundant money, low interest rates, and full employment.

Neo-Mercantilism and the Economy Today

In our own times neo-mercantilists are urging state economic policies aimed at national prosperity. A favorite of theirs is export promotion. Nowadays, of course, the trade surplus is seen as a means of state policy, not its end. The objective is no longer to build up the reserves of gold, which are not normally required to back major currencies or even to make international payments. Accumulation of interest-bearing assets is of minor interest. Neo-mercantilists do not argue for limiting the extent of foreign trade or against the consumption of foreign articles. Rather, the basic consideration is maintaining international market share in technically progressive lines of goods for the present and future.[8]

If every country tries to dominate markets for the same critical goods, though, how can a peaceful and prosperous international economic order be maintained? Without an enforceable commitment to free trade principles, there is a temptation to favor one's own industries by covertly promoting exports or blocking imports essential to national well-being. That favored sector could be agriculture (as in Japan), telecommunications systems (France), or textiles and shoes (the United States). Since free trade is unattainable and unstable in an anarchic world market, neo-mercantilists argue, negotiated flexible rules of "fair trade" are the best we can do to keep international exchange open. Let's illustrate this view.

---

[8]See H. O. Schmitt, below. Robert Gilpin has written that after World War II the USA aimed at increasing its power in relation to the USSR by controlling "the centers of industrial power and resources." *U.S. Power and the Multinational Corporation* (New York: Basic Books, 1975), p. 103.

FIGURE 1-4
Game-Theoretic Representation of "Fair Trade"

| | | **JAPAN** | |
		Free Trade	Protection
USA	Free Trade	(2, 2)	(-1, 3)
	Protection	(3, -1)	(0, 0)

In Figure 1-4 gains from trade to the USA are represented by the first number in each pair in parentheses; gains to Japan are the second. Note the *joint* gains are highest (2+2) under free trade strategies by both countries, and least under universal protection (0+0). Knowing the payoffs, though, each country might choose protection if we suppose it is trying either (1) to maximize benefits (assuming the other maintains free trade) or (2) to minimize possible losses, since in this illustration only free trade could possibly involve losses. Clearly, if both parties act in this way and choose protection, the result is the worst joint outcome (0, 0). Even limited trade with payoffs of about (1, 1) would be superior to no cooperation.

If resources were completely mobile and information costless, according to mainstream international trade theory, such worries about "chiseling" on free trade rules would have no basis. In a pure classical environment, in which competition moves resources rapidly and painlessly to successive optimal allocations, protection would only hurt. Any export subsidy would be paid by the exporting country. Cheap imports would not be disruptive, since domestic resources would shift out of import substitutes into more profitable exportables. Exchange rates would adjust to balance payments at a better position for the receiving country.[9] But if information is costly and resources are immobile, neo-mercantilist theory may have a point.

International coordination would also seem necessary to macroeconomic policy—to allow full-employment monetary and fiscal policies without fear of exchange rate pressures. One country's unilateral attempts to stimulate demand or to devalue its currency are likely to provoke destabilizing retaliation. Other countries may not accept the deficits implied by the first country's surplus. One may not accept the monetary growth implied by another's low interest rates. Wide swings of international currency values and trade flows, even among friendly governments, have stimulated policymakers and the econo-

---

[9]We ignore the exception of the "scientific tariff," in which import tariffs or export subsidies abroad improve the terms of trade to the home country. We also ignore the damage to capital rent rates in individual plants or industries, to the extent that export subsidies abroad have not been foreseen. Profits, strictly defined to be a residual over contractual charges, would not exist in equilibrium, but capital losses could occur when the equilibrium shifts away from an industry using fixed and specific capital.

mists advising them to think of new supranational institutions which would create the monetary conditions for stability and prosperity. For instance, the Tokyo summit of advanced countries in 1986 called for "multilateral surveillance" of monetary, fiscal, and exchange rate policies to be managed by the International Monetary Fund.

Some kind of bloc neo-mercantilism would have the added attraction of bolstering bargaining power in dealing with outside powers. The European Community has been dubbed the greatest mercantilist power of all time, with reason, for its goals are internal stability and prosperity, together with enhanced bargaining power in dealing with foreigners—the USA, Japan, and the Communist bloc.

READINGS: The Mercantilist Perspective

Following are several short readings on the mercantilist perspective, edited for ease of reading by the modern student.

READING 1

Thomas Mun (1571-1641) was a prosperous London merchant who could draw on wide experience in Mediterranean trade. Director of the East India Company since 1615, he had been a member of the commission which in 1622 recommended that the Dutch be deprived of supplies and that England preempt their shipping and fishing trades. During the depression of the 1620's, Mun opposed currency manipulation, preferring an expansion of exports.

Mun wrote *England's Treasure by Forraign Trade* about 1630 (it was published by his son only in 1664) to defend his view that foreign trade was profitable to England. Profitable trades abroad would expand exports and cheapen imports, hence creating a favorable balance of trade on current account. Even though merchants might ship bullion out, Mun argued, the net effect of an export surplus would be to accumulate treasure at home. No interference in mercantile affairs would be required, except perhaps to restrict the activities of "Strangers," mostly Dutchmen, who made profits from dealing in foreign currency and bills, insurance, and the like.

England's Treasure by Foreign Trade

Thomas Mun

I.   The knowledge and qualities which are required to be in a perfect merchant of foreign trade. . .

II.   The means to enrich the Kingdom, and to increase our treasure

Although a kingdom may be enriched by gifts received, or by purchase taken from some other nations, yet these are things uncertain and of small consideration when they happen. The ordinary means therefore to increase our wealth and treasure is by Foreign Trade, wherein we must ever observe this rule: to sell more to strangers yearly than we consume of theirs in value. For suppose that when this Kingdom is plentifully served with the cloth, lead, tin, iron, fish and other native commodities, we do yearly export the overplus to foreign countries to the value of twenty two hundred thousand pounds, by which means we are enabled beyond the seas to buy and bring in foreign wares for our use and consumption, to the value of twenty hundred thousand pounds. By this order duly kept in our trading, we may rest assured that the Kingdom shall be enriched yearly two hundred thousand pounds, which must be brought to us in so much treasure, because that part of our stock which is not returned to us in wares must necessarily be brought home in treasure.

For in this case it cometh to pass in the stock of a kingdom, as in the estate of a private man, who is supposed to have one thousand pounds yearly revenue and two thousand pounds of ready money in his chest. If such a man through excess shall spend one thousand five hundred pounds per annum, all his ready money will be done in four years; and in the like time his said money will be doubled if he take a frugal course to spend but five hundred pounds per annum; which rule never faileth likewise in the Commonwealth, but in some cases (of no great moment) which I will hereafter declare, when I shall show by whom and in what manner this balance of the Kingdom's account ought to be drawn up yearly, or so often as it shall please the State to discover how much we gain or lose by trade with foreign Nations. But first I will say something concerning those ways and means which will increase our exportations and diminish our importations of wares; which being done, I will then set down some other arguments both affirmative and negative to strengthen that which is here declared, and thereby to show that all the other means which are commonly supposed to enrich the Kingdom with Treasure are altogether insufficient and mere fallacies.

III. The particular ways and means to increase the exportation of our commodities, and to decrease our consumption of foreign wares

The revenue or stock of a kingdom by which it is provided of foreign wares is either natural or artificial. The natural wealth is so much only as can be spared from our own use and necessities to be exported unto strangers. The artificial consists in our manufactures and industrious trading with foreign commodities, concerning which I will set down such particulars as may serve for the cause we have in hand.

1. First, although this Realm be already exceeding rich by nature, yet might it be much increased by laying the waste grounds (which are infinite) into such employments as should no way hinder the present revenues of other manured lands, but hereby to supply ourselves and prevent the importations of hemp, flax, cordage, tobacco, and diverse other things which now we fetch from strangers to our great impoverishing.

2. We may likewise diminish our importations, if we would soberly refrain from excessive consumption of foreign wares in our diet and raiment, with such often change of fashions as is used, so much the more to increase the waste and charge, which vices at this present are more notorious amongst

us than in former ages. Yet might they easily be amended by enforcing the observation of such good laws as are strictly practiced in other countries against the said excesses, where likewise by commanding their own manufactures to be used, they prevent the coming in of others, without prohibition or offense to strangers in their mutual commerce.

3. In our exportations we must not only regard our own superfluities, but also we must consider our neighbors' necessities, that so upon the wares which they cannot want, nor yet be furnished thereof elsewhere, we may (besides the vent of the materials) gain so much of the manufacture as we can, and also endeavor to sell them dear, so far forth as the high price cause not a less vent in the quantity. But the superfluity of our commodities which strangers use and may also have the same from other nations, or may abate their vent by the use of some such like wares from other places and with little inconvenience, we must in this case strive to sell as cheap as possible we can, rather than to lose the utterance of such wares. For we have found of late years by good experience, that being able to sell our cloth cheap in Turkey, we have greatly increased the vent thereof, and the Venetians have lost as much in the utterance of theirs in those countries, because it is dearer. And on the other side a few years past, when by the excessive price of wools our cloth was exceeding dear, we lost at the least half our clothing for foreign parts, which since is no otherwise (well near) recovered again than by the great fall of price for wools and cloth. We find that twenty five in the hundred less in the price of these and some other wares, to the loss of private men's revenues, may raise above fifty upon the hundred in the quantity vented to the benefit of the public. For when cloth is dear, other nations do presently practice clothing, and we know they want neither art nor materials to this performance. But when by cheapness we drive them from this employment, and so in time obtain our dear price again, then do they also use their former remedy. So that by these alterations we learn, that it is in vain to expect a greater revenue of our wares than their condition will afford, but rather it concerns us to apply our endeavors to the times with care and diligence to help ourselves the best we may, by making our cloth and other manufactures without deceit, which will increase their estimation and use.

4. The value of our exportations likewise may be much advanced when we perform it ourselves in our own ships, for then we get only not the price of our wares as they are worth here, but also the merchants' gains, the charges of insurance, and freight to carry them beyond the seas. As for example, if the Italian merchants should come hither in their own shipping to fetch our corn, our red herrings or the like, in this case the Kingdom should have ordinarily but 25s. for a quarter of wheat, and 20s. for a barrel of red herrings, whereas if we carry these wares our selves into Italy upon the said rates, it is likely that we shall obtain fifty shillings for the first, and forty shillings for the last, which is a great difference in the utterance or vent of the Kingdom's stock. And although it is true that the commerce ought to be free to strangers to bring in and carry out at their pleasure, yet nevertheless in many places the exportation of victuals and munitions are either prohibited, or at least limited to be done only by the people and shipping of those places where they abound.

5. The frugal expending likewise of our own natural wealth might advance much yearly to be exported unto strangers; and if in our raiment we

will be prodigal, yet let this be done with our own materials and manufactures, as cloth, lace, embroideries, cutworks, and the like, where the excess of the rich may be the employment of the poor, whose labors notwithstanding of this kind, would be more profitable for the Commonwealth, if they were done to the use of strangers.

6. The fishing in His Majesty's seas of England, Scotland and Ireland is our natural wealth and would cost nothing but labor, which the Dutch bestow willingly, and thereby draw yearly a very great profit to themselves by serving many places of Christendom with our fish, for which they return and supply their wants both of foreign wares and money, besides the multitude of mariners and shipping, which hereby are maintained. . . . Our fishing plantation likewise in New-England, Virginia, Greenland, the Summer Islands and the Newfoundland, are of the like nature, affording much wealth and employments to maintain a great number of poor, and to increase our decaying trade.

7. A staple or magazine for foreign corn, indigo, spices, raw-silks, cotton wool, or any other commodity whatsoever, to be imported will increase shipping, trade, treasure, and the King's customs, by exporting them again where need shall require, which course of trading, hath been the chief means to raise Venice, Genoa, the Low-Countries, with some others; and for such a purpose England stands most commodiously, wanting nothing to this performance but our own diligence and endeavor.

8. Also we ought to esteem and cherish those trades which we have in remote or far countries, for besides the increase of shipping and mariners thereby, the wares also sent thither and received from thence are far more profitable unto the kingdom than by our trades near at hand. As for example, suppose pepper to be worth here two shillings the pound constantly, if then it be brought from the Dutch at Amsterdam, the merchant may give there twenty pence the pound, and gain well by the bargain; but if he fetch this pepper from the East-Indies, he must not give above three pence the pound at the most, which is a mighty advantage, not only in that part which serveth for our own use, but also for that great quantity which (from hence) we transport yearly unto diverse other nations to be sold at a higher price. Whereby it is plain, that we make a far greater stock by gain upon these Indian commodities, than those nations do where they grow, and to whom they properly appertain, being the natural wealth of their countries. But for the better understanding of this particular, we must ever distinguish between the gain of the Kingdom, and the profit of the merchant, for although the Kingdom payeth no more for this pepper than is before supposed, nor for any other commodity bought in foreign parts more than the stranger receiveth from us for the same, yet the merchant payeth not only that price, but also the freight, insurance, customs, and other charges which are exceeding great in these long voyages. But yet all these in the Kingdom's account are but commutations among ourselves, and no privation of the Kingdom's stock, which being duly considered, together with the support also of our other trades in our best shipping to Italy, France, Turkey, the East Countries, and other places, by transporting and venting the wares which we bring yearly from the East Indies, it may well stir up our utmost endeavors to maintain and enlarge this great and noble business, so much importing the public wealth, strength, and happiness. Neither is there

less honor and judgment by growing rich (in this manner) upon the stock of other nations, than by an industrious increase of our own means, especially when this latter is advanced by the benefit of the former, as we have found in the East Indies by sale of much of our tin, cloth, lead, and other commodities, the vent whereof doth daily increase in those countries which formerly had no use of our wares.

9. It would be very beneficial to export money as well as wares. Being done in trade only, it would increase our Treasure. But of this I write more largely in the next chapter to prove it plainly.

10. It were policy and profit for the State to suffer manufactures made of foreign materials to be exported custom-free, as velvets and all other wrought silks, fustians, thrown silks, and the like, it would employ very many poor people, and much increase the value of our stock yearly issued into other countries, and it would (for this purpose) cause the more foreign materials to be brought in, to the improvement of His Majesty's customs. I will here remember a notable increase in our manufacture of winding and twisting only of foreign raw silk, which within 35 years to my knowledge did not employ more than 300 people in the City and suburbs of London, where at this present time it doth set on work above fourteen thousand souls, as upon diligent enquiry hath been credibly reported unto His Majesty's Commissioners for Trade. And it is certain, that if the said foreign commodities might be exported from hence, free of custom, this manufacture would yet increase very much, and decrease as fast in Italy and in the Netherlands. But if any man allege the Dutch proverb, "Live and let others live," I answer that the Dutchmen, notwithstanding their own Proverb, do not only in these Kingdoms encroach upon our livings, but also in other foreign parts of our trade (where they have power) they do hinder and destroy us in our lawful course of living, hereby taking the bread out of our mouth, which we shall never prevent by plucking the pot from their nose, as of late years too many of us do practice to the great hurt and dishonor of this famous Nation. We ought rather to imitate former times in taking sober and worthy causes more pleasing to God and suitable to our ancient reputation.

11. It is needful also not to charge the native commodities with too great customs, lest by endearing them to the stranger's use, it hinder their vent. And especially foreign wares brought in to be transported again should be favored, for otherwise that manner of trading (so much importing the good of the Commonwealth) cannot prosper nor subsist. But the consumption of such foreign wares in the Realm may be the more charged, which will turn to the profit of the kingdom in the balance of the trade, and thereby also enable the King to lay up the more treasure out of yearly incomes.

12. Lastly, in all things we must endeavor to make the most we can of our own, whether it be natural or artificial, . . . forasmuch as the people which live by the art are far more in number than they who are masters of the fruits, we ought the more carefully to maintain those endeavors of the multitude, in whom doth consist the greatest strength and riches both of King and Kingdom, for where the people are many and the arts good, there the traffic must be great and the country rich. The Italians employ a greater number of people and get more money by their industry and manufactures of the raw silks of the Kingdom of Sicily than the King of Spain and his subjects have by the

revenue of this rich commodity. But what need we fetch the example so far, when we know that our own natural wares do not yield us so much profit as our industry? For iron ore in the mines is of no great worth, when it is compared with the employment and advantage it yields being digged, tried, transported, bought, sold, cast into ordnance, muskets, and many other instruments of war for offense and defense, wrought into anchors, bolts, spikes, nails and the like, for the use of ships, houses, carts, coaches, plows, and other instruments for tillage. . . .

IV. The exportation of our monies in trade of merchandise is a means to increase our treasure

This position is so contrary to the common opinion, that it will require many and strong arguments to prove it before it can be accepted of the multitudes who bitterly exclaim when they see any monies carried out of the Realm, affirming thereupon that we have absolutely lost so much treasure, and that this is an act directly against the long continued laws made and confirmed by the wisdom of this Kingdom in the High Court of Parliament, and that many places—nay Spain itself, which is the Fountain of Money—forbids the exportation thereof, some cases only excepted. To all which I might answer, that Venice, Florence, Genoa, the Low Countries, and diverse other places permit it, their people applaud it, and find great benefit by it. But all this makes a noise and proves nothing. We must therefore come to those reasons which concern the business at hand.

First, I will take that for granted which no man of judgment will deny, that we have no other means to get treasure but by foreign trade, for mines have none which do afford it, and how this money is gotten in the managing of our said trade I have already showed, that it is done by making our commodities which are exported yearly to overbalance in value the foreign wares which we consume, so that it resteth only to show how our monies may be added to our commodities, and being jointly exported may so much the more increase our treasure. . . .

When we have prepared our exportations of wares, and sent out as much of everything as we can spare or vent abroad, it is not therefore said that then we should add our money there unto to fetch in the money immediately, but rather first to enlarge our trade by enabling us to bring in more foreign wares, which being sent out again will in due time much increase our treasure.

For although in this manner we do yearly multiply our importations to the maintenance of more shipping and mariners, improvement of His Majesty's Customs and other benefits; yet our consumption of those foreign wares is no more than it was before, so that all the said increase of commodities brought in by the means of our ready money sent out as is afore written, doth in the end become an exportation unto use of a far greater value than our said monies were, which is proved by three examples. . . .

For it is in the stock of the Kingdom as in the estates of private men, who having store of wares, do not therefore say that they will not venture out or trade with their money (for this were ridiculous) but do also turn that into wares, whereby they multiply their money, and so by a continual and orderly change of one into the other grow rich, and when they please turn all their estates into treasure; for they that have wares cannot want money.

Neither is it said that money is the life of trade, as if it could not subsist without the same, for we know that there was great trading by way of commutation or barter when there was little money stirring in the world. The Italians and some other nations have such remedies against this want, that it can neither decay nor hinder their trade, for they transfer bills of debt, and have banks both public and private, wherein they do assign their credits from one to another daily for very great sums with ease and satisfaction by writings only, whilst in the mean time the mass of treasure which gave foundation to these credits is employed in foreign trade as a merchandise, and by the said means they have little other use of money in those countries more than for their ordinary expenses. It is not therefore the keeping of our money in the Kingdom, but the necessity and use of our wares in foreign countries, and our want of their commodities that causeth the vent and consumption on all sides, which makes a quick and ample trade. If we were once poor, and now having gained some store of money by trade with resolution to keep it still in the Realm, shall this cause other nations to spend more of our commodities than formerly they have done, whereby we might say that our trade is quickened and enlarged? No, verily, it will produce no such good effect, but rather according to the alteration of times by their true causes we may expect the contrary, for all men do consent that plenty of money in a Kingdom doth make the native commodities dearer, which as it is to the profit of some private men in their revenues, so is it directly against the benefit of the public in the quantity of the trade, for as plenty of money makes wares dearer, so dear wares decline their use and consumption, as hath been already plainly showed in the last chapter upon that particular of our cloth. And although this is a very hard lesson for some great landed men to learn, yet I am sure it is a true lesson for all the land to observe, lest when we have gained some store of money by trade, we lose it again by not trading with our money.

I knew a Prince in Italy (of famous memory) Ferdinando the first, great Duke of Tuscany, who being very rich in treasure, endeavored therewith to enlarge his trade by issuing out to his merchants great sums of money for very small profit. I myself had forty thousand crowns of him gratis for a whole year, although he knew that I would presently send it away in specie for the parts of Turkey to be employed in wares for this countries, he being well assured that in this course of trade it would return again (according to the old saying) with a duck in the mouth. This noble and industrious prince by his care and diligence to countenance and favor merchants in their affairs, did so increase the practice thereof, but there is scarce a nobleman or gentleman in all his dominions that doth not merchandise either by himself or in partnership with others, whereby within these thirty years the trade to his port of Leghorn is so much increased, that of a poor little town (as I myself know it) it is now become a fair and strong city, being one of the most famous places for trade in all Christendom. And yet it is worthy our observation, that the multitude of ships and wares which come thither from England, the Low Countries, and other places have little or no means to make their returns from thence but only in ready money, which they may and do carry away freely at all times, to the incredible advantage of the said great Duke of Tuscany and his subjects, who are much enriched by the continual great concourse of merchants from all the states of the neighbor princes, bringing them plenty of money daily to supply their wants of the said wares. And thus we see that the current of merchandise which carries away their treasure, becomes a flowing stream to fill them again in a greater measure with money.

There is yet an objection or two as weak as all the rest: that is, if we trade with our money we shall issue out the less wares; as if a man should say, those countries which heretofore had occasion to consume our cloth, lead, tin, iron, fish, and the like, shall now make use of our monies in the place of those necessaries, which were most absurd to affirm, or that the merchant had not rather carry out wares by which there is ever some gains expected, than to export money which is still but the same without any increase.

But on the contrary there are many countries which may yield us very profitable trade for our money, which otherwise afford us no trade at all, because they have no use of our wares, as namely the East-Indies for one in the first beginning thereof, although since by industry in our commerce with those nations we have brought them into the use of much of our lead, cloth, tin, and other things, which is a good addition to the former vent of our commodities.

Again, some men have alleged that those countries which permit money to be carried out, do it because they have few or no wares to trade withal; but we have great store of commodities, and therefore their action ought not to be our example.

To this the answer is briefly, that if we have such a quantity of wares as doth fully provide us of all things needful from beyond the seas; why should we then doubt that our moneys sent out in trade, must not necessarily come back again in treasure, together with the great gains which it may procure in such manner as is before set down? And on the other side, if those nations which send out their monies do it because they have but few wares of their own, how come they then to have so much treasure as we ever see in those places which suffer it freely to be exported at all times and by whomsoever? I answer, Even by trading with their monies, for by what other means can they get it, having no mines of gold or silver?

Thus may we plainly see, that when this weighty business is duly considered in his end as all our humane actions ought well to be weighed, it is found much contrary to that which most men esteem thereof, because they search no further than the beginning of the work, which misinforms their judgments, and leads them into error; for if we only behold the actions of the husbandman in the seed-time when he casteth away much good corn into the ground, we will rather account him a madman than a husbandman, but when we consider his labors in the harvest which is the end of his endeavors, we find the worth and plentiful increase of his actions.

V. Foreign trade is the only means to improve the price of our lands

If we melt down our plate into coin (which suits not with the majesty of so great a Kingdom, except in cases of great extremity) it would cause plenty of money for a time, yet should we be nothing the richer, but rather this treasure being thus altered is made the more apt to be carried out of the Kingdom, if we exceed our means by excess in foreign war, or maintain a war by sea or land, where we do not feed and clothe the soldier and supply the armies with our own native provisions, by which disorders our treasure will soon be exhausted.

Again, if we think to bring in store of money by suffering foreign coins to pass current at higher rates than their intrinsic value compared with our standard, or by debasing or by enhancing our own monies, all these have their several inconveniences and difficulties, but admitting that by this means plenty of money might be brought into the Realm, yet should we be nothing the richer, neither can such treasure so gotten long remain with us. For if the stranger or the English merchants bring in this money, it must be done upon a valuable consideration, either for wares carried out already, or after to be exported, which helps us nothing except the evil occasions of excess or war aforenamed be removed which do exhaust our treasure, for otherwise, what one man bringeth for gain, another man shall be forced to carry out for necessity, because there shall ever be a necessity to balance our accounts with strangers, although it should be done with loss upon the rate of the money, and confiscation also if it be intercepted by the Law.

The conclusion of this business is briefly thus. That as the treasure which is brought into the Realm by the balance of our foreign trade is that money which only doth abide with us, and by which we are enriched, so by this plenty of money thus gotten (and no otherwise) do our lands improve. For when the merchant hath a good dispatch beyond the seas for his cloth and other wares, he doth presently return to buy up the greater quantity, which raiseth the price of our wools and other commodities, and consequently doth improve the landlords' rents as the leases expire daily. And also by this means money being gained, and brought more abundantly into the Kingdom, it doth enable many men to buy lands, which will make them the dearer. But if our foreign trade come to a stop or declination by neglect at home or injuries abroad, whereby the merchants are impoverished, and thereby the wares of the Realm less issued, then do all the said benefits cease, and our lands fall of price daily.

VI. The Spanish treasure cannot be kept from other kingdoms by any prohibition made in Spain. . .

VII. The diversity of gain by foreign trade

In the course of foreign trade there are three sorts of gain, the first is that of the Commonwealth, which may be done when the merchant (who is the principal agent therein) shall lose. The second is the gain of the merchant, which he doth sometimes justly and worthily effect, although the Commonwealth be a loser. The third is the gain of the King, whereof he is ever certain, even when the Commonwealth and the merchant shall be both losers.

Concerning the first of these, we have already sufficiently showed the ways and means whereby a Commonwealth may be enriched in the course of trade, whereof it is needless here to make any repetition, only I do in this place affirm, that such happiness may be in the Commonwealth, when the merchant in his particular shall have no occasion to rejoice. As for example, suppose the

East-India Company send out one hundred thousand pounds into the East-Indies, and receive home for the same the full value of three hundred thousand pounds. Hereby it is evident that this part of the Commonwealth is trebled, and yet I may boldly say that which I can well prove, that the same Company of Merchants shall lose at least fifty thousand pounds by such an adventure if the returns be made in spice, indigo, calicoes, benjamin, refined saltpeter, and such other bulky wares in their several proportions according to their vent and use in these parts of Europe. For the freight of shipping, the insurance of the adventure, the charges of factors abroad and officers at home, the forbearance of the stock, His Majesty's Customs and Imposts, with other petty charges incident, cannot be less than two hundred and fifty thousand pounds, which being added to the principal produceth the said loss. And thus we see, that not only the Kingdom but also the King by his Customs and Imposts may get notoriously, even when the Merchant notwithstanding shall lose grievously; which giveth us good occasion here to consider, how much more the Realm is enriched by this noble trade, when all things pass so happily that the merchant is a gainer also with the King and Kingdom.

In the next place I affirm, that a merchant by his laudable endeavors may both carry out and bring in wares to his advantage by selling them and buying them to good profit, which is the end of his labors, when nevertheless the Commonwealth shall decline and grow poor by a disorder in the people, when through pride and other excesses they do consume more foreign wares in value than the wealth of the Kingdom can satisfy and pay by the exportation of our own commodities, which is the very quality of an unthrift who spends beyond his means.

Lastly, the King is ever sure to get by trade, when both the Commonwealth and merchant shall lose severally as aforewritten, or jointly, as it may and doth sometimes happen, when at one and the same time our Commodities are over-balanced by foreign wares consumed, and that the Merchants success prove no better than is before declared.

But here we must not take the King's gain in this large sense, for so we might say that His Majesty should get, although half the trade of the Kingdom were lost. We will rather suppose that whereas the whole trade of the Realm for exportations and importations is now found for to be about the yearly value of four millions and a half pounds; it may be yet increased two hundred thousand pounds per annum more by the importation and consumption of foreign wares. By this means we know that the King shall be a gainer near twenty thousand pounds, but the Commonwealth shall lose the whole two hundred thousand pounds thus spent in excess. And the merchant may be a loser also when the trade shall in this manner be increased to the profit of the King, who notwithstanding shall be sure in the end to have the greatest loss, if he prevent not such unthrifty courses as do impoverish his subjects. . . .

X. The observation of the Statute of Employments to be made by strangers, cannot increase, nor yet preserve our treasure

To keep our money in the Kingdom is a work of no less skill and difficulty than to augment our treasure, for the causes of their preservation and production are the same in nature. The statute for employment of stranger's wares into our commodities seemeth at the first to be a good and a lawful way leading to those ends, but upon the examination of the particulars, we shall find that it cannot produce such good effects.

For as the use of foreign trade is alike unto all nations, so may we easily perceive what will be done therein by strangers, when we do but observe our own proceedings in this weighty business, by which we do not only seek with the vent of our own commodities to supply our wants of foreign wares, but also to enrich ourselves with treasure. All which is done by a different manner of trading according to our own occasions and the nature of the places whereunto we do trade, as namely in some countries we sell our commodities and bring away their wares, or part in money; in other countries we sell our goods and take their money, because they have little or no wares that fits our turns. Again in some places we have need of their commodities, but they have little use of ours; so they take our money which we get in other countries. And thus by a course of traffic (which changeth according to the occurrence of time) the particular members do accommodate each other, and all accomplish the whole body of the trade, which will ever languish if the harmony of her health be distempered by the diseases of excess at home, violence abroad, charges and restrictions at home or abroad. But in this place I have occasion to speak only of restriction, which I will perform briefly.

There are three ways by which a merchant may make the returns of his wares from beyond the seas, that is to say in money, in commodities, or by exchange. But the statute of employment doth not only restrain money (in which there is a seeming providence and justice) but also the use of the exchange by bills, which doth violate the law of commerce, and is indeed an act without example in any place of the world where we have trade, and therefore to be considered, that whatsoever (in this kind) we shall impose upon strangers here, will presently be made a law for us in their countries, especially where we have our greatest trade with our vigilant neighbors, who omit no care nor occasion to support their traffic in equal privileges with other nations. And thus in the first place we should be deprived of that freedom and means which now we have to bring treasure into the Kingdom, and therewith likewise we should lose the vent of much wares which we carry to diverse places, whereby our trade and our treasure would decay together.

Secondly, if by the said Statute we thrust the exportation of our wares (more than ordinary) upon the stranger, we must then take it from the English, which were injurious to our merchants, mariners, and shipping, besides the hurt to the Commonwealth in venting the Kingdom's stock to the stranger at far lower rates here than we must do if we sold it to them in their own countries.

Thirdly, whereas we have already sufficiently showed, that if our commodities be overbalanced in value by foreign wares, our money must be carried out. How is it possible to prevent this by tying the stranger's hands, and leaving the English loose? Shall not the same reasons and advantage cause that to be done by them now, that was done by the other before? Or if we will make a statute (without example) to prevent both alike, shall we not then overthrow all at once—the King in his customs and the Kingdom in her profits? For such a restriction must of necessity destroy much trade, because the diversity of occasions and places which make an ample trade require that some men should both export and import wares; some export only, others import, some deliver out their monies by exchange, others take it up; some carry out money, others bring it in, and this in a greater or lesser quantity according to the good husbandry or excess in the Kingdom, over which only if we keep a strict law, it will rule all the rest, and without this all other statutes are no rules either to keep or procure us treasure.

Lastly, to leave no objection unanswered, if it should be said that a statute comprehending the English as well as the stranger must needs keep our money in the Kingdom. What shall we get by this, if it hinder the coming in of money by the decay of that ample trade which we enjoyed in the freedom thereof? Is not the remedy far worse than the disease? Shall we not live more like Irishmen than Englishmen, when the King's revenues, our merchants, mariners, shipping, arts, lands, riches, and all decay together with our trade?

Yea but, say some men, we have better hopes than so; for the intent of the Statute is, that as all the foreign wares which are brought in shall be employed in our commodities, thereby to keep our money in the Kingdom. So we doubt not but to send out a sufficient quantity of our own wares over and above to bring in the value thereof in ready money.

Although this is absolutely denied by the reasons afore written, yet now we will grant it, because we desire to end the dispute. For if this be true, that other nations will vent more of our commodities than we consume of theirs in value, then I affirm that the overplus must necessarily return unto us in treasure without the use of the Statute, which is therefore not only fruitless but hurtful, as some other like restrictions are found to be when they are fully discovered.

XI. It will not increase our treasure to enjoin the merchant that exporteth fish, corn or munition, to return all or part of the value in money. . .

XII. The undervaluing of our money which is delivered or received by bills of exchange here or beyond the seas, cannot decrease our treasure

The merchants exchange by bills is a means and practice whereby they that have money in one country may deliver the same to receive it again in another country at certain times and rates agreed upon, whereby the lender and the borrower are accommodated without transporting of treasure from state to state. . . .

As plenty or scarcity of money do make the price of the exchange high or low, so the over or underbalance of our trade doth effectually cause the plenty or scarcity of money. . . . Is it not then (say they) the undervaluing of our money which causeth it to be carried out of the Realm?

To this objection I will make a full and plain answer, showing that it is not the undervaluing of our money in exchange, but the overbalancing of our trade that carrieth away our treasure. . . .

XX. The order and means whereby we may draw up the balance of our foreign trade

Likewise if it happen that His Majesty doth make over any great sums of money by exchange to maintain a foreign war, where we do not feed and clothe the soldiers, and provide the armies, we must deduct all this charge out of our exportations or add it to our importations, for this expense doth either carry out or hinder the coming in of so much treasure. And here we must remember the great collections of money which are supposed to be made throughout the Realm yearly from our recusants by priests and Jesuits, who secretly convey the same unto their colleges, cloisters and nunneries beyond the seas, from whence it never returns to us again in any kind; therefore if this mischief cannot be prevented, yet it must be esteemed and set down as a clear loss to the Kingdom, except (to balance this) we will imagine that as great a value may perhaps come in from foreign princes to their pensioners here for favors or intelligence, which some states account good policy, to purchase with great liberality; the receipt whereof notwithstanding is plain treachery. . . .

XXI. The conclusion upon all that hath been said, concerning the exportation or importation of treasure

Behold then the true form and worth of foreign trade, which is *the great revenue of the King, the honor of the Kingdom, the noble profession of the merchant, the school of our arts, the supply of our arts, the employment of our poor, the improvement of our lands, the nursery of our mariners, the walls of the Kingdoms, the means of our treasure, the sinews of our wars, the terror of our enemies.* For all which great and weighty reasons, do so many well governed states highly countenance the profession, and carefully cherish the action, not only with policy to increase it, but also with power to protect it from all foreign energies, because they know it is a principle in reason of state to maintain and defend which doth support them and their estates.

QUESTIONS FOR DISCUSSION

1 What are Mun's principal objectives and how do they relate to one another? Is he a bullionist? Does he provide arguments against the accumulation of specie money?
2 How does Mun propose to achieve his objectives? Does he really show that most kinds of intervention will be useless?
3 Is Mun's theory plausible? self-serving? How does he support it?

READING 2

Jean-Baptiste Colbert (1619-1683) was a great bureaucrat, not a theorist. He served King Louis XIV as controller-general of French finances from 1665, proving a dominant force in internal affairs, as had Cardinal Richelieu a couple of decades before. Like his patron, Cardinal Mazarin, Colbert grew rich from political influence. In preparation for the wars with the wealthy maritime Dutch Republic, which Colbert considered "mortal enemies," he tried to make France self-sufficient by expanding its fleet, subsidizing and protecting industry by tariffs and monopolies, encouraging agriculture and animal husbandry for export, and building roads, canals, and harbors. Necessary imports were to be brought to France by her own merchants. To win a greater part of East Indies and Caribbean trade for France, Colbert promoted chartered companies, as had England. To assure the quality of goods wanted by court, quartermaster, and foreign customers, the King's minister issued detailed *réglements* on the specifications of goods to be produced in the realm. Such regulations also served to discipline the workforce and collect fees. A bullionist because more money would make tax collection easier, Colbert was neverthe-less willing to allow specie to be exported for trade. Initially these regulations did perhaps improve France's balance of trade, but they eventually declined into corrupt privileges.

Even if Colbert contributed nothing new to French mercantilist thought, his conception brought together many elements of that perspective. Too busy to write a treatise, Colbert's most characteristic expressions were in letters and official documents.

Letters and Instructions*

Jean-Baptiste Colbert

It is a maxim enduring and generally recognized in all states of the world that finances are the important and essential feature in them. . . . The universal rule of finances should be always to watch and use every care and all the authority of Your Majesty to attract money into the kingdom, to spread it out into all the provinces so as to make possible for the people to live and pay taxes. . . .

To maintain manufactures is to bring money back and to fill the void left by the sums which the needs of the state and our affection lead us to pay out. . . . The chief and greatest fruit that the king gets from the great expendi-tures that he is making everywhere, and especially in regard to the great num-ber of ships that he is putting on the sea for the good and advantage of his sub-jects and for the reputation of his arms, consists in exciting everywhere the industry of his subjects and in pushing into all parts of the kingdom, even the most remote, the purchases of goods, the transportation thereof, the establish-ment of new manufactures, and the employment of his subjects at sea and in every other sort of public service, so as to enable them to earn back by these means what they are obliged to give him every year through the *taille* and other taxes.

Source: Quoted in Charles W. Cole, *Colbert and a Century of French Mercantilism,* vol. I (New York: Columbia, 1939), chapter VI. Copyright © 1939 by Columbia University Press. Used by permission.

I believe this principle will be readily agreed to that it is only the abundance of money in a state which makes the difference in its greatness and power. [Spain gained] such a prodigious abundance of money through the discovery of the Indies that all Europe has seen the house of a mere archduke of Austria, which was little thought of by anyone, mount in the space of sixty or eighty years to the sovereignty of all the states of the houses of Burgundy, Aragon, Castille, Portugal, Naples, and Milan; join to this domain the crown of England and Ireland by the marriage of Philip II and Mary; make the Empire almost hereditary for its princes; contest preeminence with the crown of our kings, put, by its policies and its arms, our kingdom in imminent danger of passing into foreign hands, and finally aspire to the empire of all Europe, that is to say of all the world.

In these three points consists the greatness and the power of the state and the magnificence of the king, through all the expenditures which large revenues permit, and this magnificence is greater in that it abases, at the same time, all the neighboring states, because, there being only a given quantity of money which circulates in all Europe, and this quantity is increased from time to time by what comes into from the West Indies, it is certain and clear that if there is only 150,000,000 which circulate publicly in France that one cannot succeed in increasing it by 20,000,000, 30,000,000, and 50,000,000, without at the same time taking the same quantity from neighboring states, a fact which causes the double elevation which has been seen to progress notably in the last few years, the one augmenting the power and greatness of Your Majesty, the other abasing that of his enemies and those who are jealous of him.

In so far as one decreases the actual amount of money sent to the Levant by the people of Marseille, and in so far as one forces them to take thither our own manufactures, as the English and Dutch do, it is certain that the same advantageous return to the kingdom will be produced, and the damage of the export of money will be steadily decreased.

The commerce of all Europe is carried on by ships of every size to the number of 20,000, and it is perfectly clear that this number cannot be increased, since the number of people in all the states remains the same and consumption likewise remains the same; and that of this number of 20,000 ships, the Dutch have 15,000 to 16,000, the English have 3,000 to 4,000, and the French 500 to 600. . . . It must be added that commerce causes a perpetual combat in peace and war among the nations of Europe, as to who shall win most of it. . . . The Dutch fight at present, in this war, with 15,000 to 16,000 ships, a government of merchants, all of whose maxims and power are directed solely toward the preservation and increase of their commerce, and much more care, energy, and thrift than any other nation. . . .

The King is extremely reluctant to grant exclusive privileges for manufactures already established in the kingdom. . . . Privileges for manufactures established in the kingdom impair commerce and public liberty, but to prevent this manufacture from becoming corrupt, regulations can be made.

I am convinced that when companies themselves run manufacturing establishments they always lose thereby, and that the only means to support them and increase them is to have them go into the hands of individuals.

QUESTIONS FOR DISCUSSION

1 Does Colbert's concern for accumulating specie money seem reasonable to you? Why or why not?
2 How does Colbert appear pragmatic?

READING 3

Hans O. Schmitt (1930-   ), an economist working for the International Monetary Fund, wrote this article in a respected British journal. Some sections and footnotes have been deleted.

Mercantilism: A Modern Argument[*]

H. O. Schmitt

I. Introduction

Despite its intellectual routing by the *Wealth of Nations,* mercantilism has remained a potent force in the conduct of national policy. This paper argues that recent theoretical developments make it possible once more for economic thought to catch up with practice. It offers a new view of the desirability of running a current account surplus; examines the conditions that have made it an achievable target under fixed and flexible exchange rates; and finally, works out the policy implications for the capital account.

The traditional case against mercantilism is based on the gains from trade. If each country specializes in what it is best endowed to produce, all countries gain. The argument is most easily understood when all current transactions balance out; a country will then exchange its exports of goods and services for imports that enhance the welfare of the consumers beyond what it could have done on its own. There is no need to contradict this principle, only to note that a surplus on current transactions may bring additional benefits, enough to warrant a net shipment of goods abroad.

If mercantilism were better understood than it is, practitioners might own up to it more readily than they do. The gains from trade argue for harmonious relations among nations; if commercial rivalries nevertheless continue to be a source of conflict, they need to be better explained. Mercantilism's lack of prestige unfortunately makes its importance in modern statecraft difficult to acknowledge. A critical exercise in the history of ideas should be useful, therefore, not least for what it may contribute to a clarification of current policy.

---

[*]*Source: The Manchester School,* vol. 47 (1979), pp. 93-111. By permission of the author and editor.

II. A Surplus on Current Account

The most pervasive and more emphasized doctrine of the mercantilists has been the importance of having a current surplus. A country is of course not made better off by giving up goods but rather by receiving them; the gain from trade consists not of the things that are exported but of the things that are imported. To justify the cost of a chronic excess of exports over imports it will therefore be necessary to show an offsetting benefit. More precisely, it will be necessary to show that a current surplus can be instrumental in enhancing the total availability of goods.

The Employment Target. The traditional employment argument for a current surplus seems deficient in this respect. To be sure, other things equal, the greater a country's exports and the smaller its imports the greater will be the employment of the domestic labor force. This argument, according to Viner,[10] is to be found in the very earliest mercantilist writings, and it persists without break throughout the literature of the seventeenth and eighteenth centuries. It also provided the basis for the revival of mercantilism as a strong policy movement associated with the Great Depression of the nineteen-thirties.

In national accounting terms, a current surplus[11] can make up for a short-fall of investment and government expenditures below saving and government revenues at full employment. . . . Now, there is no obvious reason why a shortfall of exports below imports could not in turn be compensated for by altering the balance between saving and investment or between government revenues and expenditures. . . . There is then no need to obtain full employment at the cost of a current surplus. Nevertheless, self-imposed restraints on policymakers have in various countries and at various times created circumstances in which only mercantilist policies could ensure full employment. Thus the traditional aversion to inflation in Germany and Japan, combined with the inability or unwillingness to use the apparatus of fiscal policy, obliged them to rely on currency undervaluation to maintain employment, by way of the external surpluses that so vexed the United States in the next decade.

What still needs to be identified, therefore, is the benefit that causes countries, when they have a choice, to opt for a current surplus and the preferred means to achieve full employment. Rolfe and Burtle (1973) suggest that countries prefer exports to deficit spending because "exports are profitable and technologically sharpening; social expenditures less so."[12]

The Extent of the Market. We begin, first, by recalling that the original mercantilists advocated the manipulation of exports and imports for the purpose also of advancing native manufactures. . . . The expansion of manufacturing production was thus thought to yield returns that would compensate for the loss of goods through a current surplus.

---

[10]J. Viner, *Studies in the Theory of International Trade* (London: George Allen and Unwin, 1975).

[11]More goods and services exported than imported.

[12]S. E. Rolfe and J. Burtle, *The Great Wheel* (New York: Quadrangle, 1973).

A modern restatement of this argument was first proposed by Kaldor[13] who observed that the higher the rate of overall productivity growth, the greater must be the excess of the rate of growth of manufacturing production over the rate of growth of the economy as a whole. His explanation was that scale permits specialization, particularly in manufacturing, and so fosters technical progress. Thus, the faster productive resources can be moved to manufacturing from agriculture and services, the faster a country should grow. By adding to the demand for it, an export surplus in manufacturing would help to accelerate the process.

A current surplus does not necessarily ensure a surplus in manufacturing alone, of course, and when it does not, trade discrimination would have been called for. However, the reasons for associating productivity growth with manufacturing remain less clear than one might wish them to be. Though economies of scale are said to be less prominent outside the manufacturing sector, and exhausted more quickly there, Kaldor himself does not wish to suggest that they apply only to manufacturing, or even to every manufacturing activity taken separately. . . .

As imports increase with trade liberalization, the scale of output should certainly diminish in industries affected by them. To be sure, even if imports rose to match exports, the benefits of specialization would still ensure a net gain in total output, and thus a net positive incentive to invest in innovation. But the incentive from exports could surely be raised, and the disincentive from imports be reduced, by an exchange rate that allowed a current surplus to arise. Thus it is not merely exports but an export surplus that should be central to our argument. . . . By making exports and import substitutes together more profitable to produce, such an exchange rate will draw resources from the pro-duction of non-tradable to tradable goods, that from products limited to local markets to those marketable on a global scale. It is to them that scale economies apply. . . .

A shift to tradable goods production places resources directly at the disposal of producers most likely to spend on technical innovation. In normal circumstances, the flow of loan capital to an industry is contingent on the prior commitment of risk capital in the form of equity. The more risk capital is supplemented by internally generated funds in tradable goods industries, the greater the flow of loan capital to them is also likely to be. To expand their markets for this purpose, a current surplus must be made to arise.

The Savings Constraint. The stimulus to technical progress provided by a current surplus may itself provide the rationale for saving. How much of a justification depends on the social rate of time preference, and thus on the distribution of income by which it is in part determined. Countries with shorter time horizons will support a smaller current surplus and thus tend to fall behind others as regards technical progress. A political leadership that objects to this outcome may attempt to hold wages back; incomes policies are the obvious modern manifestation of such efforts. The alternative is to accept

---

[13]Nicholas Kaldor, *Causes of the Slow Rate of Economic Growth of the United Kingdom: An Inaugural Lecture* (Cambridge: Cambridge University Press, 1966).

increasing dependence on outside aid if living levels are to be kept in step with those elsewhere.

There are no soft options. A deficit that reduces incentives to invest in technical progress at home will similarly affect the incentives to purchase advanced techniques and equipment developed abroad. Likewise, any attempt to increase current surpluses beyond the limit set by the excess of public and private saving over public and private investment at full employment will succeed only in accelerating inflation. To prevent such an acceleration it will be necessary to accept a more modest current surplus. Where domestic saving falls short of domestic investment price stability will in fact require a current deficit.

A current surplus may be invested in capital assets abroad and yield a certain return there. The contribution of a current surplus to technical progress on the other hand, derives from the export surplus as such, and not from any assets accumulated abroad in consequence of it. Wider markets yield returns to scale and stimulate investment in research and development at home, not abroad. There would still be this benefit if the current surplus were not investment in income-earning assets at all, but if the whole of it were placed in idle stocks of gold instead.

III. A Self-Regulating Mechanism?

There certainly is no way a current surplus can continue if it leads to reserve accumulations in excess of a country's liquidity requirements. In practice at least, a monetary authority must eventually run out of domestic assets to sell in order to offset the effects on the domestic monetary base of a steady inflow of foreign exchange. Despite their vigorous efforts, therefore, Europe and Japan should have found their surpluses increasingly difficult to sustain over time.

The export of capital nullifies this effect. . . .

IV. A Deficit on Capital Account

A net capital export from the metropolis can, however, continue only so long as its attraction for portfolio investment (and for a return flow of investment income) does not exceed the periphery's appeal for direct investment. Europe's private long-term investment position in the United States, though still primarily of a portfolio character, now already matches the American position in Europe. To maintain the edge necessary to support a current surplus, the United States has had for some time to look farther afield. It has had to try to preserve an open door elsewhere in the world. . . .

The Present Position. New frontiers for direct investment are required whenever return flows of portfolio saving from older markets make a current surplus difficult to support. The danger of supply interruptions, which provides a major incentive for direct investment, may also pose the greatest threat to it. Following the 1973 oil embargo, for example, the foreign operations of the metropolitan oil companies have increasingly been taken over by the host countries that imposed it, reversing the earlier movement toward vertical integration. . . .

V. Conclusion

This paper has argued that a current account surplus continues to be an inducement to technical progress; that such a surplus is best supported by fostering net capital outflows; and that to secure such outflows an open door for direct investment must always be maintained abroad. International harmony is jeopardized whenever too many countries act on these principles at once.

Clearly, a market equilibrium cannot be a political equilibrium if the current balances associated with it are found unacceptable. Rival business communities will hold out for a pattern of exchange rates that guarantees them adequate access to the world market as a whole. Without a negotiated consensus among governments, therefore, no objective basis exists for determining what the world's structure of exchange rates should be. As long as no political consensus exists, any purely market equilibrium will also have to remain ephemeral at best.

In retrospect, the survival of mercantilism has certainly owed more to pressure of circumstance than to theoretical insight. It may be thought reassuring, then, that even such appealing half-truths as were launched by the *Wealth of Nations* have not invariably interfered with responsible statecraft. . . .

QUESTIONS FOR DISCUSSION

See the questions at the end of Reading 4.

READING 4

Robert Kuttner is contributing economics editor for *The New Republic*. His books include *Revolt of the Haves*.

The Economic Illusion[*]

Robert Kuttner

In the firmament of American ideological convictions, no star burns brighter than free trade. Our conviction about free trade represents ideology reinforced

[*]*Source:* Robert Kuttner, *The Economic Illusion, False Choices Between Prosperity and Social Justice* (Philadelphia: University of Pennsylvania Press, 1987), pp. 91-135. Copyright © 1984 by Robert Kuttner. Reprinted by permission of Houghton Mifflin Company.

by three decades of self-interest. During the post-war Pax Americana, the free-trade regime plainly served American interests. As the world's premier producer, we could commend the virtues of free trade to our allies the way the biggest kid on the block calls for a fair fight. Today, the ideal of free trade remains resolutely bipartisan; it is the elevation of the free-market philosophy to global scale.

If the success of the 1950s and 1960s proved to moderate Keynesians that demand management coupled with a mild welfare state "worked" domestically, it also proved to champions of free trade that market economics still reigned internationally. Among orthodox economists, one can find bitter disputes between Keynesians and monetarists, but one must look far and wide to find one who challenges the universal benefits of free trade.

The recent debate over free trade offers an instructive study of the way entrenched ideology denies changing self-interest. By the late 1970s, American interests were no longer served unequivocally by the free-trade regime. Europe and Japan had recovered from World War II; U.S. technology was easily transplanted to Third-World countries with extremely low wage rates. No longer did free trade mean cheap prices of imported raw materials and effortless exports of American manufactured goods. Instead, it meant that in industry after industry, foreign producers were making deep inroads into American domestic markets, driving American companies out of business and American workers onto the unemployment rolls.

In this new world of stiff foreign competition, the injured industries and their trade unions were not slow to clamor for relief; intellectual revisionism came much more uneasily and hesitantly. The early demands for protection were purely defensive and as a national economic strategy, largely indefensible. Nonetheless, farmers, textile manufacturers, automakers, and steel companies did get partial shelter from import competition, through an *ad hoc* assortment of subterfuges, of which more below.

From the point of a pure free trader, *any* toleration of departure from the principle opens the way to abuse. One can find plenty of cases that seem to justify that argument—oversubsidized "loser" industries that ideally should be phased out in favor of more dynamic ones. Protection of excess capacity in steel or in autos seems to be a dead-weight economic loss. But in the real world, there are so many affronts to the pure theory of free trade that the practical policy question has long since changed. It is no longer whether to manage trade, but to manage it according to which criteria and to what degree. As the different faces of industrial policy suggest, protection can be a refuge to shelter losers—or to incubate new progeny. There is no guarantee that economic planning will always be used wisely—just as there is no guarantee that "free trade" won't lead to worldwide excess capacity and a competition to batter down wages. But these issues need to be debated at the level of practical policy, and not unreal theory.

Lately, a more systematic critique of the free-trade ideology has gathered force. Characteristically, it has developed almost entirely outside the economics profession. The critics (including this writer) argued that as long as other countries were succeeding by neomercantilist methods, the "free-trade versus protection" debate was an unproductive misstatement of the practical alternatives. . . .

In principle, free trade is another area where short-run concern for equity, however well-intentioned, clashes with everyone's long-run interest in efficient use of resources. According to the free-trade orthodoxy, measures to protect the U.S. auto, steel, or textile industries and their wage earners only frustrate the emerging comparative advantage held by foreign producers like Japan, Korea, and Brazil. Protectionism, in this view, is nothing but a self-serving demand by lower industries, overpaid workers, and their political toadies to fence out superior imported goods. If Toyota makes a better car, who are we to keep it from American consumers? Protection denies American citizens the benefits of more efficient, cheaper products; it shelters declining industries that need the discipline of competition, and it retards the transition of the economy to new industries where our natural comparative advantage lies. It will raise prices, hold back economic progress, deny poor nations the fruits of their own energies; it will court stagnation, retaliation, and deeper world-wide recession. . . . The economically sound way to deal with the Japanese challenge is simply to buy their entire cornucopia—the cheaper the better. If they are superior at making autos, TVs, tape recorders, cameras, steel machine tools, baseball gloves, semiconductors, computers, and other arguably oriental products, it is irrational to shelter our own benighted industries. Far more sensible to buy their goods, let the bracing tonic of competition shake America from its torpor, and wait for the market to reveal our niche in the international division of labor.

This formulation, unfortunately, is based on multiple theoretical fallacies. Consequently, it miscasts the practical choices. As a theory, it ignores key characteristics of the modern world economy: technological dynamism and state influence. It describes a static world; it denies the possibility that competitive advantage can be created. Second, Ricardian economics presumes that the economy is operating at full-employment and full-capacity utilization. It overlooks the possibility that trade itself might have feedback effects that cause an economy to slip below full production and full employment. It fails to measure the efficiency gains of trade against the efficiency losses in output. Finally, it tends to confuse description of what is and a recommendation of what produces the best outcomes. But if we assume, by definition, that more free trade is better, we are at a loss to know how to proceed when a successful international player flourishes by defying the norms of free trade.

Ricardo in Wonderland

Consider the practical consequences of the assumption that technology is static and governments passive. Ricardo, as embellished by Heckscher-Ohlin,[14] assumes that nation's comparative advantage will be revealed by its patterns of exports, based on what economists call "factor endowments"—the nation's natural advantages of climate, minerals, location, arable land, or plentiful labor. But the theory does not fit a world of learning curves, technological

---

[14]Eli F. Heckscher and Beril Ohlin, two Swedish neoclassical economists, who showed that the pattern of free trade would follow relative endowments of factors of production.

dynamism, economies of scale, declining unit costs, and targeted industrial policies. . . .

Increasingly, comparative advantage today is not "revealed" by natural factor endowments and market forces; it is created by governments pursuing neomercantilist strategies. Even where governments do not deliberately target commercial industries, they have immense influence over where capital flows. If Boeing got a big head start on the 707 from multibillion-dollar military contracts to develop an air force transport, is that a sin against free trade? If Europe, in order to get a foothold on the civil aviation market, responds with subsidized loans to the Airbus, is that worse? If the Japanese counter by demanding coproduction agreements, requiring assembly of portions of the McDonnell-Douglas F-15 and the Boeing 767 in Japan, doesn't that distort markets?

Of course. But the planes fly. All of these are sinners against Ricardo, and it is hard to judge which sinner is the worst. By free-trade lights, the Airbus A-300 is a tainted product, because it was produced by subsidized capital. But, as it turns out, the A-300 is the most fuel-efficient plane of its generation. And it stimulated Boeing to accelerate production of its own fuel-efficient wide-body jet. Were it not for the "distortion" of capital flows and the "protectionism" of the Airbus consortium, Boeing would have dominated world markets indefinitely and the A-300 never would have flown at all. Nor is it a foregone conclusion that the subsidized capital that launched Airbus would have been better used elsewhere by the market.

Looking around the industrialized world, one can see countless offenses against the free-trade ideal, which nonetheless lead to positive-sum economic gains. According to free-trade orthodoxy, protectionism can perhaps help the protectionist country for a time, but only at the expense of the rest of the world, and ultimately at the expense of economic efficiency. In practice, however, some protectionism has served to incubate real technological breakthroughs that benefit everyone. Japan's system of public-capital allocation, research subsidies, sheltered domestic markets, and market-sharing cartels is an unequivocal violation of free-trade norms. But it has produced technological gains that benefit the Japanese and the entire world. Free-market notions of optimality may have been transgressed, but the Hondas and Sonys and steel mills are superior products nonetheless. The economists who compare the absolute gains of trade to the gains of technology tend to overlook the paradoxical link between the two: Technological advance often thrives in sheltered and subsidized markets, which defy free trade. Japan gains because its aggressive mercantilism has moved it up the product ladder; the world gains from the technological advances. Moreover, Japan acquires a comparative advantage in skilled labor thanks to the industry it developed. Conventional economics has the cause and effects backwards. It is not a productive work force that leads to the industrial dynamism, but the industrial base that allows an advanced work force to mature.

Keynesian Trade

The free-trade ideal also creates a second, quite distinct, practical dilemma: a Keynesian one. Ricardian free trade, as noted, begins with the assumption that all resources are productively deployed. The equations assume that the economy is at or very near full employment. But today's global economy is not unlike that of the 1930s. All the industrial countries are suffering high unemployment; globally, there is excess capacity in most industries. As more and more countries seek to produce advanced products for Western consumer markets, overcapacity worsens. It is reminiscent of the 1930s in the sense that the *world economy is not able to consume all that it produces*. . . . [T]he heightened game of world trade—in conditions of easily transferred technology and the entry of new, low-wage players—recreates Keynesian problems of overproduction and excess capacity, which cannot be solved by one government's pursuing Keynesian demand-management policies in isolation. . . .

The overcapacity problem arises because each producer tries to enter an established industry at the expense of all existing producers. And while there is a productivity gain because the heightened competition produces technical breakthroughs and lowers costs, there are also losses. To pursue the case of steel, one loss is that everybody except the newest, most advanced entrant is now producing at a lower fraction of total capacity. Very expensive capital equipment sits idle much of the time, which lowers productivity. The heightened competition also lowers profit margins, which means that the return on capital is depressed, which in turn depresses the market incentive to invest and discourages market-motivated producers from staying in the game. . . .

With high fixed costs, each individual producer aims to maximize production and lower price, despite worldwide overcapacity. In fact, it is even rational for a new entrant to minimize profit and perhaps to price his product below his cost for a time, in order to attract market share from established producers. . . .

Because free-trade theory assumes that the economy is operating at full-employment, most economists just take it for granted that when a Japanese supplier of, say, steel, displaces a U.S. supplier, the displaced American capital and labor will find some more useful application. . . . But suppose instead that unemployment is at 10 percent and industrial capacity use is at 75 percent. And suppose that most of the million workers displaced by import competition move not to a more productive industry, but to the fast-food business or to the unemployment rolls. During a period of high unemployment, this is surely the more realistic supposition. Research by economists Bennett Harrison and Barry Bluestone found that of 674,000 workers displaced from industrial jobs in New England between 1958 and 1975, just 18,000, or 3 percent, found jobs in high technology, and 106,000 (18 percent) ended up in service and retail jobs, generally at lower wages. Nothing in the free-trade model guarantees that workers in one economy displaced by trade will necessarily be reemployed at more productive occupations. Indeed, steel and autos, two "declining" sectors, typically have far higher value-added per worker, and in turn far higher wages, than the average job in the economy. . . .

Today, nearly half of world trade is conducted between units of multinational corporations. Just as Keynes foresaw, most basic products (steel, plastics, microprocessors, textiles, machine tools) can be produced almost anywhere, but by labor forces with vastly differing wages. And this raises another Keynesian dilemma: the tendency of open trade to depress wages.

Open trade under corporate auspices in an era of mobile capital and portable technology creates strong competitive pressures to reduce labor costs. In a world where technology and capital are highly transferable, there is a real risk that comparative advantage comes to be defined as whose labor force will work for the lowest wage. The postwar Keynesian social contract in the Western democracies—full-employment, a costly welfare state, rising real wages—suddenly comes unglued. "High labor costs" (people's jobs!) are again seen as a luxury which "we" cannot afford if we are to remain competitive.

In such a world, it is literally possible for industries to grow more productive while the national economy grows poorer. How can that be? The factors left out of the Ricardian equation are falling real wages and idle capacity. If America's autos (or steel tubes or machine tools) are manufactured more productively than a decade ago, but less productively than in Japan (or Korea or Brazil), and if we practice what we preach about open trade, then a growing share of U.S. purchasing power will go to provide jobs overseas. Even if American technology is twice as efficient, foreign producers can compensate by paying their workers one fourth the wage, which will increase pressures on American producers to lower their own pay scales. A growing share of American capital and labor will lie idle. American manufacturers, detecting soft markets and falling profits, will decline to invest. Steelmakers will buy oil companies. Consumer access to superior foreign products will not necessarily compensate for the decline in real income and the idle resources. Nor is there any guarantee that the new industries countries will necessarily use their burgeoning income from American sales to buy American capital equipment (or computers or even coal), for they are all striving to develop their own advanced, diversified economies.

Against this background of tidal change in the global economy, the conventional reverence for free trade as an ideal or as a policy guide is just not very helpful. In a world of mercantilism where none of the practical alternatives resembles pure free trade, attachment to the idea has a series of perverse consequences. It suggests that we are helpless to repair our own economy in the face of new, "revealed" foreign comparative advantages, save by increasing the rewards to capital and punishing labor. It implies that we can enrich ourselves as a society only by lowering our wages—another convenient implication for the owners of capital. And, as we shall see, our reverence for free trade assures that the form of protectionism that we do get is purely defensive, which fails to bring about constructive changes in the protected industry.

Almost any form of industrial policy requires subsidies and marketing strategies aimed at domestic industries, which by definition are departures from the free-trade ideal. If these are ruled out as ideologically impermissible, then we deny ourselves an indispensable tool for restoring a full-production economy. . . .

An Example of Managed Trade

[T]he textile industry is a fairly successful example of managed trade, which combines a measure of protection with substantial modernization. Textiles, by the common consent of the industrial nations, have been removed from the GATT[15] regime in favor of an international market-sharing agreement. . . .

Since raw cotton is the main ingredient in cotton cloth, it also follows that totally free trade in finished cotton goods would undermine the farm policy of supporting raw cotton prices—apparel makers could simply buy cheaper foreign cloth, or consumers would switch to cheaper foreign finished goods. . . .

In the mid-1950s, the American textile industry began suffering insurmountable competition from very low-wage Asian imports. The United States first imposed quotas on imports of cotton fibers, through a series of bilateral negotiations. In the early 1960s, a multilateral "long-term" agreement on cotton fibers was negotiated with other major textile producers. In 1973, broadened to cover woolens and synthetics, it became known as the Multi-Fiber Agreement. This regime effectively shelters the textile industries of Europe and the United States from runaway import penetration. Under MFA, import growth was limited to an average of 6 percent per year. Exports from one country may grow faster, but only at the expense of other exporting countries.

The consequences of this, in theory, should have been stagnation. But the result has been just the opposite. The predictability afforded by import limitation, and a climate of cooperation with the two major labor unions, encouraged the American textile industry to invest heavily in development of advanced technology. Interestingly, modernization was also stimulated by another nemesis of market economics: health and safety regulation. The cotton dust standard of the Occupational Safety and Health Administration (OSHA) devised to protect workers from byssinosis (white lung disease) served to accelerate rapid investment in cleaner, most efficient weaving and spinning machinery.

During the 1960s and 1970s, the average annual productivity growth in textiles was about twice the U.S. industrial average, second only to electronics. According to a study done for the Common Market, productivity in the most efficient American weaving operations is 130,000 stitches per worker per hour—twice as high as in France, and three times the productivity level in Britain. Thanks to this high level of productivity, textiles, surprisingly enough, have remained an export winner for the United States. In most recent years, net exports have exceeded imports.

Again, in theory, the American consumer pays the bill when the domestic market is sheltered from open foreign competition. It is possible to perform some algebraic manipulation in the spirit of Ricardo and show that textile prices would have been lower in the absence of protection. One such computation places the "cost" of each protected textile job at several hundred thousand dollars.

But these static calculations are useless as policy guides; for they leave out the several benefits: the spur to innovation, and the long-term value of maintaining a textile industry in the United States. Beyond the jobs, the benefits

---

[15]The General Agreement on Tariffs and Trade, signed in 1947, establishes the basis for non-preferential international trade, impeded only by most-favored-nation tariffs, which are to be lowered by agreement.

also include the contribution to GNP, to the balance of payments, and to the farmers who grow cotton, as well as the plain fact that investing in this generation's technology is the ticket of admission to the next.

In fact, textile "protectionism" led neither to stagnation nor to spiraling prices. Thanks to steady gains in productivity, textile prices have risen at only about half the average rate of the producer price index, both before and after the introduction of the Multi-Fiber Arrangement. Protection did not produce high-priced stagnation, in part because the domestic industry is highly competitive. . . .

New Rules of the Road

We are already well down the road toward a managed-trade regime. It would be far better to acknowledge that reality, and seek a set of reasonable rules, than to pretend that Ricardian trade is the norm and allow mercantilist states to overwhelm U.S. industry and ratchet down wages, in the name of free trade. Managed trade, on the model of the Multi-Fiber Agreement, offers an alternative regime, one that is more consistent with economic planning and distributive equity. Most economists, however, are loath to weight the practical costs and benefits of a managed trade regime, for they already "know" that the best possible trade regime is the Ricardian one.

Nonetheless, we can glean the outline of such a regime, for many of its elements already exist. Under managed trade, imports do not cease, but their market share and growth rate are explicitly limited and politically bargained. The United States, notwithstanding its protestations of free trade, has negotiated such limitations in steel, autos, textiles, televisions, and of course agriculture. The EEC has done the same for those products plus a wide range of consumer goods. . . .

Industrial policy—planning—is a necessary concomitant to assure that protection doesn't become just an umbrella under which oligopolies can stagnate, as the steel industry did. Some protection may be necessary to incubate a restructuring, but it surely is not sufficient. . . . A common element in all these devices is the principle that domestic purchasing power ought to produce domestic employment, and that the details are subject to explicit bargaining. Unlike pure protectionism based on prohibitive tariffs and tight import quotas, managed trade is quite consistent with increased trade. No doubt, this system is rather messier than the ideal of pure free trade. But free trade does not exist except as an ideal. In fairness, managed trade should be weighed against unmanaged, competitive mercantilism, for that is the practical alternative. Managed trade can be fully consistent with more trade.

QUESTIONS FOR DISCUSSION

1   Which elements of the mercantilist perspective do you see in these two modern authors? Which elements of neo-mercantilism do Schmitt and

Kuttner adopt? Do you think either author would object to being called a "neo-mercantilist?" Why?

2 Why, in Kuttner's opinion, is free trade a misleading ideal for economic policy?

3 Why is "managed trade" more than mere protectionism? Does that make it more attractive? Or possibly more dangerous?

4 How does modern industrial policy differ from the prescriptions of the first mercantilists?

CHAPTER 3

LIBERALISM AND CLASSICAL POLITICAL ECONOMY

EDITOR'S INTRODUCTION

The mercantilist writers advocated state intervention because of (1) the backward and fragmented character of their own societies, (2) endemic conflicts with outside powers, and consequently, (3) the need of the sovereign to maintain social order at a time of scarcity, brutal inequalities between classes, and incipient violence. Backwardness meant that artisans and traders were ignorant, dishonest, and impecunious, hence likely to engage in sharp practices harmful to a country's reputation. International anarchy meant that economic results could endanger a country's security, while profitable trade would enhance it. The need for stability dictated, therefore, that competition could not be allowed to bring on disturbances, as might come about if masses of vagrants and paupers were allowed to gather.

It was central to the classical perspective from **Adam Smith** to **John Stuart Mill**[1] to challenge this basis for intervention. They did so not by observing any change in social or international conditions—which was indeed difficult to perceive before the nineteenth century—but by postulating a naturally harmonious order of society enlightened by science, civilized intercourse, and Christian morality. Like liberals in politics, classical economists believed that the pursuit of *enlightened self-interest* would lead to progress, not anarchy.

What were the main elements of the classical perspective built up by this group of mainly British economists?

---

[1]Whose *Principles of Political Economy* (1848) was the distillation of classical thought. Other classical economists included James Mill (1773-1836), Robert Torrens (1780-1864), J. R. McCulloch (1789-1864), and the Frenchman Jean-Baptiste Say (1767-1832). Since many of these knew each other personally, as well as by reputation and careful reading, we are justified in calling them the first "school" of political economy.

(1) Economic actors are classified by their functions. Capitalists provide working capital stock and equipment in exchange for interest, while wage laborers have nothing to offer but time and effort. Landlords own the unimproved gifts of nature—sites and raw materials—and receive a rental from their users. Each sort of individual tries to maximize his income from the factor of production he contributes. With few people supplying more than one factor, motivations are simple. Laborers must get subsistence for themselves and if they can earn more than subsistence, they form families and have children. Consequently, the welfare and size of the working class are determined by the money wage and the price of provisions—considered together, the workers' terms of trade. To assure that wages were not squandered on debauchery and drink, education for the poor workers would be imperative, according to these middle class reformers. Capitalists reinvest their capital and net earnings to increase their holdings, so long as the returns are positive. Landlords let their land to the highest bidder and consume the surplus, providing employment for servants, craftsmen, and field hands. Capital formation, therefore, is primarily in the hands of the capitalists. Taxes could come out of their accumulations only if it could not be drawn from the idle landlords.[2]

(2) When individuals are free to act in accord with selfish material interest, such as the search for profit, they will act energetically, and, on the whole, for the benefit of their fellows. As Smith phrased it, the "invisible hand" of profit created by effective demands and costs in the marketplace would be a sufficient guide to the common good. "It is not from the benevolence of the butcher, the brewer, or the banker that we expect our dinner, but from their regard to their own self-interest."[3] Any voluntary exchange must benefit both buyer and seller; hence the society which allows all such exchanges would enjoy the best use of its resources.[4]

(3) Competition for maximum incomes would assure that any difference in returns—that is, any supernormal profits or unusually high wages—would soon be erased by eager suppliers of factors. Mobility of workers and of capital would be necessary for such competition, and that meant no monopolies or artificial restraints on the choice of occupation could be allowed.

Aside from temporary disturbances of trade, full employment of available labor would be assured provided wages were free to fall to the point where labor-using commodities or services would become attractive to capitalists. But the capitalists' increased savings from a more efficient economy would go to creating a larger wage fund and other capital stock. By what came to be

---

[2]The Physiocrats, important Continental forerunners of the classical school, were the first to see the special case for taxing the site value of land, which is fixed in aggregate supply and can neither be hidden nor readily withdrawn from production. Ricardo and his follower Henry George were the first to argue that a tax on ground rent would not affect productivity or prices and therefore could not be shifted onto consumers.

[3]*Wealth of Nations,* chapter ii, p. 43.

[4]Modern welfare economists would qualify this statement. The allocation would be optimal subject to existing skills and titles to property. For the most part, classical economists considered property rights inviolable on moral and prudential grounds. Compensating for inequality might endanger progress. Nonetheless, private charity to the orphan, the lame, and the virtuous poor were Christian duties.

known as "Say's Law of Markets," therefore, no general glut of commodities could persist.

(4) The state had the limited function of assuring a fair and open marketplace for all—primarily a matter of restraining officials, since monopolies were notoriously created by needy monarchs anxious for the proceeds and could hardly last otherwise. Any attempt to guide the allocation of capital or alter prices, wages, or interest by statute was bound to fail. The state's positive functions would be residual, much more limited than under mercantilist auspices. The state would of course guarantee the security of persons and property in peaceable exchange. To facilitate such exchange over space and time required a stable monetary unit, preferably gold and silver minted into coins.

Low taxes and limited government would together encourage private enterprise, but some public works would have to be provided to facilitate trade. Port facilities, canals, and roads could be privately provided; only legal measures would be needed to make them possible. Or public facilities might be financed with fees. The same would be true of educational institutions and even courts: charity and fees would do for the most part. Adam Smith even felt the North American colonies would be maintained by fees to Britain. If they could not or would not, then let them go free! Armies, on the other hand, must be maintained by the sovereign, lest private provision destroy the peace of the realm. Even with this modest role for government, Adam Smith and the later classical writers devoted much attention to devising efficient and just taxes for the few necessary categories of state expense.

TABLE 3-1
CLASSICAL VS. MERCANTILIST PERSPECTIVES COMPARED

Mercantilist	Classical
a. Static worldview	a. Dynamic possibilities in extending markets
b. State-oriented, holistic	b. Utilitarian, individualistic
c. Regulation needed to counter avarice, ignorance	c. Mostly laissez-faire
d. Foreign trade emphasis	d. Domestic-oriented
e. Unemployment chronic	e. Unemployment temporary only
f. Growth by borrowing	f. Growth by accumulation, some technical progress
g. Pro-natalist	g. Fearful of population growth

It is sometimes said that classical writers defended the interests of the rising bourgeoisie. No doubt some of the minor ones did. A few, notably the financier **David Ricardo**, were active businessmen. But it is more typical of the classical school, many of whom were professional clerics or teachers, to present themselves as neutral and disinterested diviners of the best scientific means to achieve the social good. Political economists aimed to discover the natural laws inherent in the social world, never to legislate them. No doubt, however, emerging capitalist and middle-class elements found the liberal economists' message in their class interest.

READINGS: The Classical Perspective

Following are five selections on the classical perspective.

READING 5

Adam Smith (1723-1790), usually regarded as the first modern economist and perhaps the greatest of all time, was in fact a rather unoriginal and bookish professor whose powers of direct observation of a rapidly changing British economy were relatively dull. His genius lay in his power to synthesize the best of available thinking and to formulate it in an enduring way. Not the first to speculate that the private pursuit of vice could conduce to the public good, Smith was the first to prove it by deductive reasoning. Bernard de Mandeville, the Dutch-born mercantilist (1670-1733) had said as much in the *Fable of the Bees; or Private Vices, Publick Benefits,* published in 1705:

> . . . luxury
> Employed a million of the poor
> And odious price a million more:
> Envy itself and vanity
> Were ministers of industry
> To such a height, the very poor
> Lived better than the rich before;
> And nothing could be added more.[5]

Unlike the cynical Mandeville, Adam Smith—himself a serene and generous soul—believed he saw a natural order in society, as Isaac Newton had in the physical universe. Smith's belief was strengthened by his contacts with the French Physiocrats during his famous trip to the Continent in 1764-1766. The Physiocrats conceptualized economic interactions as the production and distribution of the annual produce of the land. Smith also took over, with judicious amendment in Book I of his *Wealth of Nations,* the French encyclopedists' schematic account of the sources of growth: dexterity from dividing the work into simple tasks, saving time between jobs, the greater alertness from specialization, and the invention of machines. He also appreciated the French intellectuals' love of liberty and hatred of traditional prejudice.

The very organization of his great treatise was another of Smith's brilliant and discerning adaptations of works radically different from his own emerging perspective. Apparently Smith, when suddenly presented with the assignment to teach political economy at Glasgow, took his old student notes from the class of Francis Hutcheson

---

[5]pp. 11-13 of the 1705 edition, cited in the Editor's Introduction to Adam Smith, *An Inquiry into the Nature and Causes of the Wealth of Nations,* ed. by Edwin Cannan (Chicago: University of Chicago Press, 1976), pp. 1-li.

(1694-1746), the well-known mercantilist author of *A System of Moral Philosophy*. After years of reconsideration, Smith's work was published when he was already 53 and then revised continually until the author's death.

The starting point for Smithian economic theory was the Scottish professor's account of exchange value, or normal price. Any theory of allocation and distribution must begin with prices, since people are interested in money returns only for what money will buy.[6] A theory of real relative returns, therefore, requires a theory for commodity prices. Since Smith—like most classical writers—concentrated on the normal, long-run state of the economy, accidental perturbations of prices owing to temporary scarcities could be neglected. The normal price, then, would be sufficient to cover labor costs and other factors paid their normal returns. The idea of prices guiding the allocation of resources was long known.[7] Besides the role of relative prices in allocation, Smith emphasized their distributional effects, though his solutions were analytically primitive and subject to correction by later classical and neo-classical writers. The excerpts which follow are from the authoritative 1904 Cannan edition.

The Wealth of Nations

Adam Smith

Introduction and Plan of the Work

The annual labor of every nation is the fund which originally supplies it with all the necessaries and conveniences of life which it annually consumes, and which consist always either in the immediate produce of that labor, or in what is purchased with that produce from other nations.

According therefore, as this produce, or what is purchased with it, bears a greater or smaller proportion to the number of those who are to consume it, the nation will be better or worse supplied with all the necessaries and conveniences for which it has occasion.

But this proportion must in every nation be regulated by two different circumstances; first by the skill, dexterity, and judgment with which its labor is generally applied; and secondly, by the proportion between the number of those who are employed in useful labor, and that of those who are not so employed. Whatever be the soil, climate, or extent of territory of any particular nation, the abundance or scantiness of its annual supply must, in that particular situation, depend upon those two circumstances.

The abundance or scantiness of this supply too seems to depend more upon the former of those two circumstances than upon the latter. Among the savage

---

[6]The Later Scholastics and the banker-economist Richard Cantillon (c. 1680-1734), among others, had already clearly shown that value in exchange was not necessarily the same thing as value in use. Smith elaborates this point in his famous paradox of diamonds and water: diamonds were worthless, said the sober Scot, yet expensive, while water is essential but free.

[7]It has been traced to John Hales, a mercantilist writing about 1540.

nations of hunters and fishers, every individual who is able to work, is more or less employed in useful labor, and endeavors to provide, as well as he can, the necessaries and conveniences of life, for himself, or such of his family or tribe as are either too old, or too young, or too infirm to go a hunting and fishing. Such nations, however, are so miserably poor, that from mere want, they are frequently reduced, or, at least, think themselves reduced, to the necessity sometimes of directly destroying, and sometimes of abandoning their infants, their old people, and those afflicted with lingering diseases, to perish with hunger, or to be devoured by wild beasts. Among civilized and thriving nations, on the contrary, though a great number of people do not labor at all, many of whom consume the produce of ten times, frequently of a hundred times more labor than the greater part of those who work; yet the produce of the whole labor of the society is so great, that all are often abundantly supplied, and a workman, even of the lowest and poorest order, if he is frugal and industrious, may enjoy a greater share of the necessaries and conveniences of life than it is possible for any savage to acquire.

The causes of this improvement, in the productive powers of labor, and the order, according to which its produce is naturally distributed among the different ranks and conditions of men in the society, make the subject of the First Book of this Inquiry.

Whatever be the actual state of the skill, dexterity, and judgment with which labor is applied in any nation, the abundance or scantiness of its annual supply must depend, during the continuance of that state, upon the proportion between the number of those who are annually employed in useful labor, and that of those who are not so employed. The number of useful and productive laborers, it will hereafter appear, is every where in proportion to the quantity of capital stock which is employed in setting them to work, and to the particular way in which it is so employed. The Second Book, therefore, treats of the nature of capital stock, of the manner in which it is gradually accumulated, and of the different quantities of labor which it puts into motion, according to the different ways in which it is employed.

Nations tolerably well advanced as to skill, dexterity, and judgments in the application of labor, have followed very different plans in the general conduct or direction of it; and those plans have not all been equally favorable to the greatness of its produce. The policy of some nations has given extraordinary encouragement to the industry of the country; that of others to the industry of towns. Scarce any nation has dealt equally and impartially with every sort of industry. Since the downfall of the Roman empire, the policy of Europe has been more favorable to art, manufactures, and commerce, the industry of towns; than to agriculture, the industry of the country. The circumstances which seem to have introduced and established this policy are explained in the Third Book.

Though those different plans were, perhaps, first introduced by the private interests and prejudices of particular orders of men, without any regard to, or foresight of, their consequences upon the general welfare of the society; yet they have given occasion to very different theories of political economy, of which some magnify the importance of that industry which is carried on in towns, others of that which is carried on in the country. Those theories have had a considerable influence, not only upon the opinions of men of learning, but upon the public conduct of princes and sovereign states. I have endeavoured, in the Fourth Book, to explain, as fully and distinctly as I can, those different theories, and the principal effects which they have produced in different ages and nations.

To explain in what has consisted the revenue of the great body of the people, or what has been the nature of those funds, which, in different ages and nations, have supplied their annual consumption, is the object of these Four first Books. The Fifth and last Book treats of the revenue of the sovereign, or commonwealth. In this book I have endeavored to show; first, what are the necessary expenses of the sovereign, or commonwealth; which of those expenses ought to be defrayed by the general contribution of the whole society; and which of them, by that some particular part only. . . .

Book One. Of the causes of improvement in the productive powers of labor, and of the order according to which its produce is naturally distributed among the different ranks of the people

I. OF THE DIVISION OF LABOR

The greatest improvement in the productive powers of labor, and the greater part of the skill, dexterity, and judgment with which it is anywhere directed, or applied, seem to have been the effect of the division of labor.

The effects of the division of labor, in the general business of society, will be more easily understood, by considering in which manner it operates in some particular manufactures. . . . To take an example, therefore, from a very trifling manufacture; but one in which the division of labor has been very often taken notice of, the trade of the pinmaker; a workman not educated to this business (which the division of labor has rendered a distinct trade), nor acquainted with the use of the machinery employed in it (to the invention of which the same division of labor has probably given occasion), could scarce, perhaps, with his utmost industry, make one pin in a day, and certainly count not make twenty. But in the way in which this business is now carried on, not only the whole work is a peculiar trade, but it is divided into a number of branches, of which the greater part are likewise peculiar trades. One man draws out the wire, another straights it, a third cuts it, a fourth points it, a fifth grinds it at the top for receiving the head; to make the head requires two or three distinct operations; to put it on, is a peculiar business, to whiten the pins is another; it is even a trade by itself to put them into the paper; and the important business of making a pin is, in this manner, divided into about eighteen distinct operations, which, in some manufactories, are all performed by distinct hands, though in others the same man will sometimes perform two or three of them. I have seen a small manufactory of this kind where ten men only were employed, and where some of them consequently performed two or three distinct operations. But though they were very poor, and therefore but indifferently accommodated with the necessary machinery, they could, when they exerted themselves, make among them about twelve pounds of pins in a day. There are in a pound upwards of four thousand pins of a middling size. Those ten persons, therefore, could make among them upwards of forty-eight thousand pins in a day. Each person, therefore, making a tenth party of forty-eight thousand pins, might be considered as making four thousand eight hundred pins in a day. But if they had all wrought separately and independently, and without any of them having been educated to this peculiar business, they certainly could not each of them have made twenty, perhaps not one pin in a day; that is, certainly, not the two hundred and fortieth, perhaps not the four thousand eight hundredth part of what they are at present capable of performing, in consequence of a proper division and combination of their different operations.

In every other art and manufacture, the effects of the division of labor are similar to what they are in this very trifling one; though, in many of them, the labor can neither be so much subdivided, nor reduced to so great a simplicity of operation. The division of labor, however, so far as it can be introduced, occasions, in every art, a proportionable increase of the productive powers of labor. The separation of different trades and employments from one another, seems to have taken place, in consequence of this advantage. This separation too is generally carried furthest in those countries which enjoy the highest degree of industry and improvement; what is the work of one man in a rude state of society, being generally that of several in an improved one. In every improved society, the farmer is generally nothing but a farmer; the manufacturer, nothing but a manufacturer. The labor too which is necessary to produce any one complete manufacture, is almost always divided among a great number of hands. How many different trades are employed in each branch of the linen and woollen manufactures, from the growers of the flax and the wool, to the bleachers and smoothers of the linen, or to the dyers and dressers of the cloth! The nature of agriculture, indeed, does not admit of so many subdivisions of labor, nor of so complete a separation of one business from another, as manufactures. It is impossible to separate so entirely, the business of the grazier from that of the corn farmer, as the trade of the carpenter is commonly separated from that of the smith. The spinner is almost always a distinct person from the weaver; but the ploughman, the harrower, the sower of the seed, and the reaper of the corn, are often the same. The occasions for those different sorts of labor returning with the different seasons of the year, it is impossible that one man should be constantly employed in any one of them. This impossibility of making so complete and entire a separation of all the different branches of labor employed in agriculture, is perhaps the reason why the improvement of the productive powers of labor in this art, does not always keep pace with their improvement in manufactures. The most opulent nations, indeed, generally excel all their neighbors in agriculture as well as in manufactures; but they are commonly more distinguished by their superiority in the latter than in the former. Their lands are in general better cultivated, and having more labor and expense bestowed upon them, produce more in proportion to the extent and natural fertility of the ground. But this superiority of produce is seldom much more than in proportion to the superiority of labor and expense. In agriculture, the labor of the rich country is not always much more productive than that of the poor; or, at least, it is never so much more productive as it commonly is in manufactures. The corn of the rich country, therefore, will not always, in the same degree of goodness, come cheaper to market than that of the poor. The corn of Poland, in the same degree of goodness, is as cheap as that of France, notwithstanding the superior opulence and improvement of the latter country. . . .

This great increase of the quantity of work, which, in consequence of the division of labor, the same number of people are capable of performing, is owing to three different circumstances; first, to the increase of dexterity in every particular workman; secondly, to the saving of the time which is commonly lost in passing from one species of work to another; and lastly, to the invention of a great number of machines which facilitate and abridge labor, and enable one man to do the work of many.

First, the improvement of the dexterity of the workman necessarily increases the quantity of the work he can perform; and the division of labor, by reducing every man's business to some one simple operation, and by making this operation the sole employment of his life, necessarily increases very much the dexterity of the workman. A common smith, who, though accustomed to handle the hammer, has never been used to make nails, if upon some particular occasion he is obliged to attempt it, will scarce, I am assured, be able to make above two or three hundred nails in a day, and those too very bad ones. A smith who has been accustomed to make nails, but whose sole or principal business has not been that of a nailer, can seldom with his utmost diligence make more than eight hundred or a thousand nails in a day. I have seen several boys under twenty years of age who had never exercised any other trade but that of making nails, and who, when they exerted themselves, could make, each of them, upwards of two thousand three hundred nails in a day. The making of a nail, however, is by no means one of the simplest operations. The same person blows the bellows, stirs or mends the fire as there is occasion, heats the iron, and forges every part of the nail: In forging the head too he is obliged to change his tools. The different operations into which the making of a pin, or of a metal button, is subdivided, are all of them much more simple, and the dexterity of the person, of whose life it has been the sole business to perform them, is usually much greater. The rapidity with which some of the operations of those manufactures are performed, exceeds what the human hand could, by those who had never seen them, be supposed capable of acquiring.

Secondly, the advantage which is gained by saving the time commonly lost in passing from one sort of work to another, is much greater than we should at first view be apt to imagine it. It is impossible to pass very quickly from one kind of work to another, that is carried on in a different place, and with quite different tools. A country weaver, who cultivates a small farm, must lose a good deal of time in passing from his loom to the field, and from the field to his loom. When the two trades can best be carried on in the same workhouse, the loss of time is no doubt much less. It is even in this case, however, very considerable. A man commonly saunters a little in turning his hand from one sort of employment to another. When he first begins the new work he is seldom very keen and hearty; his mind, as they say, does not go to it, and for some time he rather trifles than applies to good purpose. The habit of sauntering and of indolent careless application, which is naturally, or rather necessarily acquired by every country workman who is obliged to change his work and his tools every half hour, and to apply his hand in twenty different ways almost every day of his life; renders him almost always slothful and lazy, and incapable of any vigorous application even on the most pressing occasions. Independent, therefore, of his deficiency in point of dexterity, this cause alone must always reduce considerably the quantity of work which he is capable of performing.

Thirdly, and lastly, every body must be sensible how much labor is facilitated and abridged by the application of proper machinery. It is unnecessary to give any example. I shall only observe, therefore, that the invention of all those machines by which labor is so much facilitated and abridged, seems to have been originally owing to the division of labor. Men are much more likely to discover easier and readier methods of attaining any object, when the whole attention of their minds is directed towards that single object, than when it is dissipated among a great variety of things. But in consequence of the division of labor, the whole of every man's attention comes naturally to be directed towards some one very simple object. It is naturally to be expected, therefore, that some one or other of those who are employed in each particular branch of labor should soon find out easier and readier methods of performing their own particular work, wherever the nature of it admits of such improvement. A great part of the machines made use of in those manufactures in which labor is most subdivided, were originally the inventions of common workmen, who, being each of them employed in some very simple operation, naturally turned their thoughts toward finding out easier and readier methods of performing it. Whoever has been much accustomed to visit such manufactures, must frequently have been shown very pretty machines, which were the inventions of such workmen, in order to facilitate and quicken their own particular part of the work. . . .

All the improvements in machinery, however, have by no means been the inventions of those who had occasion to use the machines. Many improvements have been made by the ingenuity of the makers of the machines, when to make them became the business of a peculiar trade; and some by that of those who are called philosophers or men of speculation, whose trade it is not to do any thing, but to observe everything; and who, upon that account, are often capable of combining together the powers of the most distant and dissimilar objects. In the progress of society, philosophy or speculation becomes, like every other employment, the principal or sole trade and occupation of a particular class of citizens. Like every other employment too, it is subdivided into a great number of different branches, each of which affords occupation to a peculiar tribe or class of philosophers; and this subdivision of employment in philosophy, as well as in every other business, improves dexterity, and saves time. Each individual becomes more expert in his own peculiar branch, more work is done upon the whole, and the quantity of science is considerably increased by it.

It is the great multiplication of the productions of all the different arts, in consequence of the division of labor, which occasions, in a well-governed society, that universal opulence which extends itself to the lowest ranks of the people. Every workman has a great quantity of his own work to dispose of beyond what he himself has occasion for; and every other workman being exactly in the same situation, he is enabled to exchange a great quantity of his own goods for a great quantity, or, what comes to the same thing, for the price of a great quantity of theirs. He supplies them abundantly with what they have occasion for, and they accommodate him as amply with what he has occasion for, and a general plenty diffuses itself through all the different ranks of the society. . . .

II. OF THE PRINCIPLE WHICH GIVES OCCASION TO THE DIVISION OF LABOR

This division of labor, from which so many advantages are derived, is not originally the effect of any human wisdom, which foresees and intends that general opulence to which it gives occasion. It is the necessary, though very slow and gradual, consequence of a certain propensity in human nature which has in view no such extensive utility; the propensity to truck, barter, and exchange one thing for another.

Whether this propensity be one of those original principles in human nature, of which no further account can be given; or whether, as seems more probable, it be the necessary consequence of the faculties of reason and speech, it belongs not to our present subject to enquire. It is common to all men, and to be found in no other race of animals, which seem to know neither this nor any other species of contracts. . . . [M]an has almost constant occasion for the help of his brethren, and it is in vain for him to expect it from their benevolence only. He will be more likely to prevail if he can interest their self-love in his favor, and show them that it is for their own advantage to do for him what he requires of them. Whoever offers to another a bargain of any kind, proposes to do this. . . . It is not from the benevolence of the butcher, the brewer, or the baker, that we expect our dinner, but from their regard to their own interest. We address ourselves, not to their humanity but to their self-love, and never talk to them of our own necessities but of their advantages. Nobody but a beggar chooses to depend chiefly upon the benevolence of his fellow citizens. Even a beggar does not depend upon it entirely. . . .

As it is by treaty, by barter, and by purchase, that we obtain from one another the greater part of those mutual good offices which we stand in need of, so it is this same trucking disposition which originally gives occasion to the division of labor. In a tribe of hunters or shepherds a particular person makes bows and arrows, for example, with more readiness and dexterity than any other. He frequently exchanges them for cattle or for venison with his companions; and he finds at last that he can in this manner get more cattle and venison, than if he himself went to the field to catch them. From a regard to his own interest, therefore, the making of bows and arrows grows to be his chief business, and he becomes a sort of armorer. . . . [T]hus the certainty of being able to exchange all that surplus part of the produce of his own labor, which is over and above his own consumption, for such parts of the produce of other men's labor as he may have occasion for, encourages every man to apply himself to a particular occupation, and to cultivate and bring to perfection whatever talent or genius he may possess for that particular species of business.

The difference of natural talents in different men is, in reality, much less than we are aware of; and the very different genius which appears to distinguish men of different professions, when grown up to maturity, is not upon many occasions so much the cause, as the effect of the division of labor. The difference between the most dissimilar characters, between a philosopher and a common street porter, for example, seems to arise not so much from nature, as from habit, custom, and education. When they came into the world, and for the first six or eight years of their existence, they were, perhaps, very much alike, and neither their parents nor play-fellows could perceive any remarkable difference. About that age, or soon after, they come to be employed in very different occupations. The difference of talents comes then to be taken notice of, and widens by degrees, till at last the vanity of the philosopher is willing to acknowledge scarce any resemblance. But without the disposition to truck, barter, and exchange, every man must have procured to himself every necessary and conveniency of life which he wanted. All must have had the same duties to perform, and the same work to do, and there could have been no such difference of employment as could alone give occasion to any great difference of talents.

III. THAT THE DIVISION OF LABOR IS LIMITED BY THE EXTENT OF THE MARKET

As it is the power of exchanging that gives occasion to the division of labor, so the extent of this division must always be limited by the extent of that power or, in other words, by the extent of the market. When the market is very small, no person can have any encouragement to dedicate himself entirely to one employment, for want of the power to exchange all that surplus part of the produce of his own labor, which is over and above his own consumption, for such parts of the produce of other men's labor as he has occasion for.

There are some sorts of industry, even of the lowest kind, which can be carried on nowhere but in a great town. A porter, for example, can find employment and subsistence in no other place. A village is by much too narrow a sphere for him; even an ordinary market town is scarce large enough to afford him constant occupation. In the lone houses and very small villages which are scattered about in so desert a country as the Highlands of Scotland, every farmer must be butcher, baker, and brewer for his own family. In such situations we can scarce expect to find even a smith, a carpenter, or a mason, within less than twenty miles of another of the same trade. The scattered families that live at eight or ten miles distance from the nearest of them, must learn to perform themselves a great number of little pieces of work, for which, in more populous countries, they would call in the assistance of those work-men. Country workmen are almost everywhere obliged to apply themselves to all the different branches of industry that have so much affinity to one another as to be employed about the same sort of materials. A country carpenter deals in every sort of work that is made of wood: a country smith in every sort of work that is made of iron. The former is not only a carpenter, but a joiner, a cabinetmaker, and even a carver in wood, as well as a wheelwright, a ploughwright, a cart and wagon maker.

As by means of water carriage a more extensive market is opened to every sort of industry than what land carriage alone can afford it, so it is upon the seacoast, and along the banks of navigable rivers, that industry of every kind naturally begins to subdivide and improve itself, and it is frequently not till a long time after that those improvements extend themselves to the inland parts of the country. The extent of their market, therefore, must for a long time be in proportion to the riches and populousness of that country, and consequently their improvement must always be posterior to the improvement of that country. In our North American colonies the plantations have constantly followed either the seacoast or the banks of navigable rivers, and have scarce any where extended themselves to any considerable distance from both.

VI. OF THE COMPONENT PARTS OF THE PRICE OF COMMODITIES

In that early and rude state of society which precedes both the accumulation of stock and the appropriation of land, the proportion between the quantities of labor necessary for acquiring different objects seems to be the only circumstance which can afford any rule for exchanging them for one another. If among a nation of hunters, for example, it usually costs twice the labor to kill a beaver which it does to kill a deer, one beaver should naturally exchange for or be worth two deer. It is natural that what is usually the produce of two days' or two hours' labor should be worth double of what is usually the produce of one day's or one hour's labor.

If the one species of labor should be more severe than the other, some allowance will naturally be made for this superior hardship; and the produce of one hour's labor in the one way may frequently exchange for that of two hours' labor in the other.

Or if the one species of labor requires an uncommon degree of dexterity and ingenuity, the esteem which men have for such talents, will naturally give a value to their produce, superior to what would be due to the time employed about it. Such talents can seldom be acquired but in consequence of long application, and the superior value of their produce may frequently be no more than a reasonable compensation for the time and labor which must be spent in acquiring them. In the advanced state of society, allowances of this kind, for superior hardship and superior skill, are commonly made in the wages of labor; and something of the same kind must probably have taken place in its earliest and rudest period.

In this state of things, the whole produce of labor belongs to the laborer; and the quantity of labor commonly employed in acquiring or producing any commodity, is the only circumstance which can regulate the quantity of labor which it ought commonly to purchase, command, or exchange for.

As soon as stock has accumulated in the hands of particular persons, some of them will naturally employ it in setting to work industrious people, whom they will supply with materials and subsistence, in order to make a profit by the sale of their work, or by what their labor adds to the value of the materials. In exchanging the complete manufacture either for money, for labor, or for other goods, over and above what may be sufficient to pay the price of the materials, and the wages of the workmen, something must be given for the profits of the undertaker of the work who hazards his stock in this adventure. The value which the workmen add to the materials, therefore, resolves itself in this case into two parts, of which the one pays their wages, the other the profits of their employer upon the whole stock of materials and wages which he advanced. He could have no interest to employ them, unless he expected from the sale of their work something more than what was sufficient to replace his stock to him; and he could have no interest to employ a great stock rather than a small one, unless his profits were to bear some proportion to the extent of his stock.

The profits of stock, it may perhaps be thought, are only a different name for the wages of a particular sort of labor, the labor of inspection and direction. They are, however, altogether different, are regulated by quite sufficient principles, and bear no proportion to the quantity, the hardship, or the ingenuity of this supposed labor of inspection and direction. They are regulated altogether by the value of the stock employed, and are greater or smaller in proportion to the extent of this stock. Let us suppose, for example, that in some particular place, where the common annual profits of manufacturing stock are ten percent there are two different manufactures, in each of which twenty workmen are employed at the rate of fifteen pounds a year each, or at the expense of three hundred a year in each manufactory. Let us suppose too, that the coarse materials annually wrought up in the one cost only seven hundred pounds, while the finer materials in the other cost seven thousand. The capital annually employed in the one will in this case amount only to one thousand pounds; whereas that employed in the other will amount to seven thousand three hundred pounds. At the rate of ten percent therefore, the undertaker of the one will expect an yearly profit of about one hundred pounds only; while that of the other will expect about seven hundred and thirty pounds. But though their profits are so very different, their labor of inspection and direction may be either altogether or very nearly the same. In many great works, almost the whole labor of this kind is committed to some principal clerk. His wages properly express the value of this labor of inspection and direction. Though in settling them some regard is had commonly, not only to his labor and skill, but to the trust which is reposed in him, yet they never bear any regular proportion to the capital of which he oversees the management; and the owner of this capital, though he is thus discharged of almost all labor, still expects that his profits should bear a regular proportion to his capital. In the price of commodities, therefore, the profits of stock constitute a component part altogether different from the wages of labor, and regulated by quite different principles.

In this state of things, the whole produce of labor does not always belong to the laborer. He must in most cases share it with the owner of the stock which employs him. Neither is the quantity of labor commonly employed in acquiring or producing any commodity, the only circumstance which can regulate the quantity which it ought commonly to purchase, command, or exchange for. An additional quantity, it is evident, must be due for the profits of the stock which advanced the wages and furnished the materials of that labor.

As soon as the land of any country has all become private property, the landords, like all other men, love to reap where they never sowed, and demand a rent even for its natural produce. The wood of the forest, the grass of the field, and all the natural fruits of the earth, which, when land was in common, cost the laborer only the trouble of gathering them, come, even to him, to have an additional price fixed upon them. He must give up to the land-lord a portion of what his labor either collects or produces. This portion, or, what comes to the same thing, the price of this portion, constitutes the rent of land, and in the price of the greater part of commodities makes a third component part.

VII. OF THE NATURAL AND MARKET PRICE OF COMMODITIES

There is in every society or neighborhood an ordinary or average rate both of wages and profit in every different employment of labor and stock. . . . These ordinary or average rates may be called the natural rates of wages, profit, and rent, at the time and place in which they commonly prevail.

When the price of any commodity is neither more nor less than what is sufficient to pay the rent of the land, the wages of the labor, and the profits of the stock employed in raising, preparing, and bringing it to market, according to their natural rates, the commodity is then sold for what may be called its natural price. . . .

Though the price, therefore, which leaves him this profit, is not always the lowest at which a dealer may sometimes sell his goods, it is the lowest at which he is likely to sell them for any considerable time; at least where there is perfect liberty, or where he may change his trade as often as he pleases.

The actual price at which any commodity is commonly sold is called its market price. It may either be above, or below, or exactly the same with its natural price.

The market price of every particular commodity is regulated by the proportion between the quantity which is actually brought to market, and the demand of those who are willing to pay the natural price of the commodity, or the whole value of the rent, labor, and profit, which must be paid in order to bring it thither. Such people may be called the effectual demanders, and their demand the effectual demand; since it may be sufficient to effectuate the bringing of the commodity to market. It is different from the absolute demand. A very poor man may be said in some sense to have a demand for a coach and six; he might like to have it; but his demand is not an effectual demand, as the commodity can never be brought to market in order to satisfy it.

When the quantity of any commodity which is brought to market falls short of the effectual demand, all those who are willing to pay the whole value of the rent, wages, and profit, which must be paid in order to bring it thither, cannot be supplied with the quantity which they want. Rather than want it altogether, some of them will be willing to give more. A competition will immediately begin among them, and the market price will rise more or less above the natural price, according as either the greatness of the deficiency, or the wealth and wanton luxury of the competitors, happen to animate more or less the eagerness of the competition. Among competitors of equal wealth and luxury the same deficiency will generally occasion a more or less eager competition, according as the acquisition of the commodity happens to be of more or less importance to them. Hence the exorbitant price of the necessaries of life during the blockade of a town or in a famine.

When the quantity brought to market exceeds the effectual demand, it cannot be all sold to those who are willing to pay the whole value of the rent, wages and profit, which must be paid in order to bring it thither. Some part must be sold to those who are willing to pay less, and the low price which they give for it must reduce the price of the whole. The market price will sink more or less below the natural price, according as the greatness of the excess increases more or less the competition of the sellers, or according as it happens to be more or less important to them to get immediately rid of the commodity. The same excess in the importation of perishable, will occasion a much greater competition than in that of durable commodities; in the importation of oranges, for example, than in that of old iron.

When the quantity brought to market is just sufficient to supply the effectual demand and no more, the market price naturally comes to be either exactly, or as nearly as can be judged of, the same with the natural price. The whole quantity upon hand can be disposed of for this price, and cannot be disposed of for more. The competition of the different dealers obliges them all to accept of this price, but does not oblige them to accept of less.

If . . . the quantity brought to market should at any time fall short of the effectual demand, some of the component parts of its price must rise above their natural rate. If it is rent, the interest of all other landlords will naturally prompt them to prepare more land for the raising of this commodity; if it is wages or profit, the interest of all other laborers and dealers will soon prompt them to employ more labor and stock in preparing and bringing it to market. The quantity brought thither will soon be sufficient to supply the effectual demand. All the different parts of its price will soon sink to their natural rate, and the whole price to its natural price. . . . The natural price, therefore, is, as it were, the central price, to which the prices of all commodities are continually gravitating.

VIII. OF THE WAGES OF LABOR

The produce of labor constitutes the natural recompense or wages of labor.

In that original state of things, which precedes both the appropriation of land and the accumulation of stock, the whole produce of labor belongs to the laborer. He has neither landlord nor master to share with him. . . . As soon as land becomes private property, the landlord demands a share of almost all the produce which the laborer can either raise, or collect from it. His rent makes the first deduction from the produce of the labor which is employed upon land.

It seldom happens that the person who tills the ground has wherewithal to maintain himself till he reaps the harvest. His maintenance is generally advanced to him from the stock of a master, the farmer who employs him, and who would have no interest to employ him, unless he was to share in the produce of his labor, or unless his stock was to be replaced to him with a profit. This profit makes a second deduction from the produce of the labor which is employed upon land.

The produce of almost all other labor is liable to the like deduction of profit. In all arts and manufactures the greater part of the workmen stand in need of a master to advance them the materials of their work, and their wages and maintenance till it be completed. He shares in the produce of their labor, or in the value which it adds to the materials upon which it is bestowed; and in this share consists his profit.

It sometimes happens, indeed, that a single independent workman has stock sufficient both to purchase the materials of his work, and to maintain himself till it be completed. He is both master and workman, and enjoys the whole produce of his own labor, or the whole value which it adds to the materials upon which it is bestowed. It includes what are usually two distinct revenues, belonging to two distinct persons, the profits of stock, and the wages of labor.

Such cases, however, are not very frequent, and in every part of Europe, twenty workmen serve under a master for one that is independent; and the wages of labor are every where understood to be, what they usually are, when the laborer is one person, and the owner of the stock which employs him another.

What are the common wages of labor, depends every where upon the contract usually made between those two parties, whose interests are by no means the same. The workmen desire to get as much, the masters to give as little as possible. The former are disposed to combine in order to raise, the latter in order to lower the wages of labor.

It is not, however, difficult to foresee which of the two parties must, upon all ordinary occasions, have the advantage in the dispute, and force the other into a compliance with their terms. The masters, being fewer in number, can combine much more easily; and the law, besides, authorizes, or at least does not prohibit their combinations, while it prohibits those of the workmen. We have no acts of parliament against combining to lower the price of work; but many against combining to raise it. In all such disputes the masters can hold out much longer. A landlord, a farmer, a master manufacturer, or merchant, though they did not employ a single workman, could generally live a year or two upon the stocks which they have already acquired. Many workmen could not subsist a week, few could subsist a month, and scarce any a year without employment. In the long run the workman may be as necessary to his master as his master is to him, but the necessity is not so immediate.

We rarely hear, it has been said, of the combinations of masters, though frequently of those of workmen. But whoever imagines, upon this account, that masters rarely combine, is as ignorant of the world as of the subject. Masters are always and every where in a sort of tacit, but constant and uniform combination, not to raise the wages of labor above their actual rate. To violate this combination is everywhere a most unpopular action, and a sort of reproach to a master among his neighbors and equals. We seldom, indeed, hear of this combination, because it is the usual, and one may say, the natural state of things which nobody ever hears of. Masters too sometimes enter into particular combinations to sink the wages of labor even below this rate. These are always conducted with the utmost silence and secrecy, till the moment of execution, and when the workmen yield, as they sometimes do, without resistance, though severely felt by them, they are never heard of by other people. Such combinations, however, are frequently resisted by a contrary defensive combination of the workmen; who sometimes too, without any provocation of this kind, combine of their own accord to raise the price of their labor. Their usual pretenses are, sometimes the high price of provisions; sometimes the great profit which their masters make by their work. But whether their combinations be offensive or defensive, they are always abundantly heard of. In order to bring the point to a speedy decision, they have always recourse to the loudest clamor, and sometimes to the most shocking violence and outrage. They are desperate, and act with the folly and extravagance of desperate men, who must either starve, or frighten their masters into an immediate compliance with their demands. The masters upon these occasions are just as clamorous upon the other side, and never cease to call aloud for the assistance of the civil magistrate, and the rigorous execution of those laws which have been enacted with so much severity against the combinations of servants, laborers, and journeymen. The workmen, accordingly, very seldom derive any advantage from the violence of those tumultuous combinations, which, partly from the interposition of the civil magistrate, partly from the superior steadiness of the masters, partly from the necessity which the greater part of the workmen are under of submitting for the sake of present subsistence, generally end in nothing, but the punishment or ruin of the ringleaders.

But though in disputes with their workmen, masters must generally have the advantage, there is however a certain rate below which it seems impossible to reduce, for any considerable time, the ordinary wages even of the lowest species of labor.

A man must always live by his work, and his wages must at least be sufficient to maintain him. They must even upon most occasions be somewhat more; otherwise it would be impossible for him to bring up a family, and the race of such workmen could not last beyond the first generation. . . .

There are certain circumstances, however, which sometimes give the laborers an advantage, and enable them to raise their wages considerably above this rate; evidently the lowest which is consistent with common humanity.

When in any country the demand for those who live by wages; laborers, journeymen, servants of every kind, is continually increasing; when every year furnishes employment for a greater number than had been employed the year before, the workmen have no occasion to combine in order to raise their wages. The scarcity of hands occasions a competition among masters, who bid against one another, in order to get workmen, and thus voluntarily break through the natural combination of masters not to raise wages. . . .

The demand for those who live by wages, therefore, necessarily increases with the increase of the revenue and stock of every country, and cannot possibly increase without it. . . . It is not the actual greatness of national wealth, but its continual increase, which occasions a rise in the wages of labor. It is not, accordingly, in the richest countries, but in the most thriving, or in those which are growing rich the fastest, that the wages of labor are highest. England is certainly, in the present times, a much richer country than any part of North America. The wages of labor, however, are much higher in North America than in any part of England.

Though North America is not yet so rich as England, it is much more thriving, and advancing with much greater rapidity to the further acquisition of riches. The most decisive mark of the prosperity of any country is the increase of the number of its inhabitants. In Great Britain, and most other European countries, they are not supposed to double in less than five hundred years. In the British colonies in North America, it has been found, that they double in twenty or five-and-twenty years. Nor in the present times is this increase principally owing to the continual importation of new inhabitants, but to the great multiplication of the species. Those who live to old age, it is said, frequently see there from fifty to a hundred, and sometimes many more, descendants from their own body. Labor is there so well rewarded that a numerous family of children, instead of being a burden, is a source of opulence and prosperity to the parents. The labor of each child, before it can leave their house, is computed to be worth a hundred pounds clear gain to them. A young widow with four or five young children, who, among the middling or inferior ranks of people in Europe, would have so little chance for a second husband, is there frequently courted as a sort of fortune. The value of children is the greatest of all encouragements to marriage. We cannot, therefore, wonder that the people in North America should generally marry very young. Notwithstanding the great increase occasioned by such early marriages, there is a continual complaint of the scarcity of hands in North America. The demand for laborers, the funds destined for maintaining them, increase, it seems, still faster than they can find laborers to employ. . . .

Is this improvement in the circumstances of the lower ranks of the [British] people to be regarded as an advantage or as an inconveniency to the society? The answer seems at first sight abundantly plain. Servants, laborers and workmen of different kinds, make up the far greater part of every great political society. But what improves the circumstances of the greater part can never be regarded as an inconveniency to the whole. No society can surely be flourishing and happy, of which the far greater part of the members are poor and miserable. It is but equity, besides, that they who feed, clothe, and lodge the whole body of the people, should have such a share of the produce of their own labor as to be themselves tolerably well fed, clothed and lodged.

Poverty, though it no doubt discourages, does not always prevent marriage. It seems even to be favorable to generation. A half-starved Highland woman frequently bears more than twenty children, while a pampered fine lady is often incapable of bearing any, and is generally exhausted by two or three. Barrenness, so frequent among women of fashion, is very rare among those of inferior station. Luxury in the fair sex, while it inflames perhaps the passion for enjoyment, seems always to weaken, and frequently to destroy altogether, the powers of generation.

But poverty, though it does not prevent the generation, is extremely unfavorable to the rearing of children. The tender plant is produced, but in so cold a soil, and so severe a climate, soon withers and dies. It is not uncommon, I have been frequently told, in the Highlands of Scotland for a mother who has borne twenty children not to have two alive. Several officers of great experience have assured me, that so far from recruiting their regiment, they have never been able to supply it with drums and fifes from all the soldiers' children that were born in it. A greater number of fine children, however, is seldom seen any where than about a barrack of soldiers. Very few of them, it seems, arrive at the age of thirteen or fourteen. In some places one half the children born die before they are four years of age; in many places before they are seven; and in almost all places before they are nine or ten. This great mortality, however, will everywhere be found chiefly among the children of the common people, who cannot afford to tend them with the same care as those of better station. Though their marriages are generally more fruitful than those of people of fashion, a smaller proportion of their children arrive at maturity. In foundling hospitals, and among the children brought up by parish charities, the mortality is still greater than among those of the common people.

Every species of animals naturally multiplies in proportion to the means of their subsistence, and no species can ever multiply beyond it. But in civilized society it is only among the inferior ranks of people that the scantiness of subsistence can set limits to the further multiplication of the human species; and it can do so in no other way than by destroying a great part of the children which their fruitful marriages produce.

The liberal reward of labor, by enabling them to provide better for their children, and consequently to bring up a greater number, naturally tends to widen and extend those limits. It deserves to be remarked too, that it necessarily does this as nearly as possible in the proportion which the demand for labor requires. If this demand is continually increasing, the reward of labor must necessarily encourage in such a manner the marriage and multiplication of laborers, as may enable them to supply that continually increasing demand by a continually increasing population. If the reward should at any time be less than what was requisite for this purpose, the deficiency of hands would soon raise it; and if it should at any time be more, their excessive multiplication would soon lower it to this necessary rate. The market would be so much understocked with labor in the one case, and so much overstocked in the other, as would soon free back its price to that proper rate which the circumstances of the society required. It is in this manner that the demand for men, like that for any other commodity, necessarily regulates the production of men; quickens it when it goes on too slowly, and stops it when it advances too fast. . . .

The liberal reward of labor, as it encourages the propagation, so it increases the industry of the common people. The wages of labor are the encouragement of industry, which, like every other human quality, improves in proportion to the encouragement it receives. A plentiful subsistence increases the bodily strength of the laborer, and the comfortable hope of bettering his condition, and of ending his days perhaps in ease and plenty, animates him to exert that strength to the utmost. . . .

IX. OF THE PROFITS OF STOCK

The rise and fall in the profits of stock depend upon the same causes with the rise and fall in the wages of labor, the increasing or declining state of the wealth of the society; but those causes affect the one and the other very differently.

The increase of stock, which raises wages, tends to lower profit. When the stocks of many rich merchants are turned into the same trade, their mutual competition naturally tends to lower its profit; and when there is a like increase of stock in all the different trades carried on in the same society, the same competition must produce the same effect in them all.

It is not easy, it has already been observed, to ascertain what are the average wages of labor even in a particular place, and at a particular time. We can, even in this case, seldom determine more than what are the most usual wages. But even this can seldom be done with regard to the profits of stock. Profit is so very fluctuating, that the person who carries on a particular trade cannot always tell you himself what is the average of his annual profit. It is affected, not only by every variation of price in the commodities which he deals in, but by the good or bad fortune both of his rivals and of his customers, and by a thousand other accidents to which goods when carried either by sea or by land, or even when stored in a warehouse, are liable. It varies, therefore, not only from year to year, but from day to day, and almost from hour to hour. To ascertain what is the average profit of all the different trades carried on in a great kingdom, must be much more difficult; and to judge of what it may have been formerly, or in remote periods of time, with any degree of precision, must be altogether impossible.

But though it may be impossible to determine with any degree of precision, what are or were the average profits of stock, either in the present, or in ancient times, some notion may be formed of them from the interest of money. It may be laid down as a maxim, that wherever a great deal can be made by the use of money, a great deal will commonly be given for the use of it; and that wherever little can be made by it, less will commonly be given for it. . . .

In a country which had acquired its full complement of riches, where in every particular branch of business there was the greatest quantity of stock that could be employed in it, as the ordinary rate of clear profit would be very small, so the usual market rate of interest which could be afforded out of it, would be so low as to render it impossible for any but the very wealthiest people to live upon the interest of their money. All people of small or middling fortunes would be obliged to superintend themselves the employment of their own stocks. It would be necessary that almost every man should be a man of business, or engage in some sort of trade. The province of Holland seems to be approaching near to this state. It is there unfashionable not to be a man of business. . . .

Book Four.   Of systems of political economy

I. OF THE PRINCIPLE OF THE COMMERCIAL OR MERCANTILE SYSTEM

That wealth consists in money, or in gold and silver, is a popular notion which naturally arises from the double function of money, as the instrument of commerce, and as the measure of value. In consequence of its being the instrument of commerce, when we have money we can more readily obtain whatever else we have occasion for, then by means of any other commodity. . . .

A rich country, in the same manner as a rich man, is supposed to be a country abounding in money; and to heap up gold and silver in any country is supposed to be the readiest way to enrich it. . . .

In consequence of these popular notions, all the different nations of Europe have studied, though to little purpose, every possible means of accumulating gold and silver in their respective countries. Spain and Portugal, the proprietors of the principal mines which supply Europe with those metals, have either prohibited their exportation under the severest penalties or subjected it to a considerable duty. . . . [T]he merchants found this prohibition, upon many occasions, extremely inconvenient. . . . They remonstrated, therefore, against this prohibition as hurtful to trade. . . .

Those arguments were partly solid and partly sophistical. They were solid so far as they asserted that the exportation of gold and silver in trade might frequently be advantageous to the country. They were solid too, in asserting that no prohibition could prevent their exportation, when private people found any advantage in exporting them. But they were sophistical in supposing, that either to preserve or to augment the quantity of those metals required more the attention of government, than to preserve or to augment the quantity of any other useful commodities, which the freedom of trade, without any such attention, never fails to supply in the proper quantity. . . [A] country that has wherewithal to buy gold and silver, will never be in want of those metals. They are to be bought for a certain price like all other commodities, and as they are the price of all other commodities, so all other commodities are the price of those metals. . . .

II. OF RESTRAINTS UPON THE IMPORTATION FROM FOREIGN COUNTRIES OF SUCH GOODS AS CAN BE PRODUCED AT HOME

The general industry of the society never can exceed what the capital of the society can employ. As the number of workmen that can be kept in employment by any particular person must bear a certain proportion to his capital, so the number of those that can be continually employed by all the members of a great society, must bear a certain proportion to the whole capital of that society, and never can exceed that proportion. No regulation of commerce can increase the quantity of industry in any society beyond what its capital can maintain. It can only divert a part of it into a direction into which it might not otherwise have gone; and it is by no means certain that this artificial direction is likely to be more advantageous to the society than that into which it would have gone of its own accord.

[E]very individual who employs his capital in the support of domestic industry, necessarily endeavors so to direct that industry, that its produce may be of the greatest possible value. The produce of industry is what it adds to the subject or materials upon which it is employed. In proportion as the value of this produce is great or small, so will likewise be the profits of the employer. But it is only for the sake of profit that any man employs a capital in the support of industry; and he will always, therefore, endeavor to employ it in the support of that industry of which the produce is likely to be of the greatest value, or to exchange for the greatest quantity either of money or of other goods.

But the annual revenue of every society is always precisely equal to the exchangeable value of the whole annual produce of its industry, or rather is precisely the same thing with that exchangeable value. As every individual, therefore, endeavors as much as he can both to employ his capital in the support of domestic industry, and so to direct that industry that its produce may be of the greatest value; every individual necessarily labors to render the annual revenue of the society as great as he can. He generally, indeed, neither intends to promote the public interest, nor knows how much he is promoting it. By preferring the support of domestic to that of foreign industry, he intends only his own security; and by directing that industry in such a manner as its produce may be of the greatest value, he intends only his own gain, and he is in this, as in many other cases, led by an invisible hand to promote an end which was no part of his intention. Nor is it always the worse for the society that it was no part of it. By pursuing his own interest he frequently promotes that of the society more effectually than when he really intends to promote it. I have never known much good done by those who affected to trade for the public good. It is an affectation, indeed, not very common among merchants, and very few words need be employed in dissuading them from it.

It is the maxim of every prudent master of a family, never to attempt to make at home what it will cost him more to make than to buy. . . . What is prudence in the conduct of every private family, can scarce be folly in that of a great kingdom. If a foreign country can supply us with a commodity cheaper than we ourselves can make it, better buy it of them with some part of the produce of our own industry, employed in a way in which we have some advantage. . . .

There seem, however, to be two cases in which it will generally be advantageous to lay some burden upon foreign, for the encouragement of domestic industry. The first is, when some particular sort of industry is necessary for the defense of the country. The defense of Great Britain, for example, depends very much upon the number of its sailors and shipping. The act of navigation, therefore, very properly endeavors to give the sailors and shipping of Great Britain the monopoly of the trade of their own country, in some cases, by absolute prohibition, and in others by heavy burdens upon the shipping of foreign countries. . . . The second case, in which it will generally be advantageous to lay some burden upon foreign for the encouragement of domestic industry, is, when some tax is imposed at home upon the produce of the latter. In this case, it seems reasonable that an equal tax should be imposed upon the like produce of the former. This would not give the monopoly of the home market to domestic industry, nor turn towards a particular employment a greater share of the stock and labor of the country, than what would naturally go to it. It would only hinder any part of what would naturally go to it from being turned away by the tax, into a less natural direction, and would leave the competition between foreign and domestic industry, after the tax, as nearly as possible upon the same footing as before it. . . .

III. CONCLUSION OF THE MERCANTILE SYSTEM

Consumption is the sole end and purpose of all production; and the interest of the producer ought to be attended to, only so far as it may be necessary for promoting that of the consumer. The maxim is so perfectly self-evident, that it would be absurd to attempt to prove it. But in the mercantile system, the interest of the consumer is almost constantly sacrificed to that of the producer; and it seems to consider production, and not consumption, as the ultimate end and object of all industry and commerce.

In the restraints upon the importation of all foreign commodities which can come into competition with those of our own growth, or manufacture, the interest of the home consumer is evidently sacrificed to that of the producer. It is altogether for the benefit of the latter, that the former is obliged to pay that enhancement of price which this monopoly almost always occasions. . . .

But in the system of laws which has been established for the management of our American and West Indian colonies, the interest of the home consumer has been sacrificed to that of the producer with a more extravagant profusion than in all our other commercial regulations. A great empire has been established for the sole purpose of raising up a nation of customers who should be obliged to buy from the shops of our different producers, all the goods with which these could supply them. For the sake of that little enhancement of price which this monopoly might afford our producers, the home consumers have been burdened with the whole expense of maintaining and defending that empire. . . .

Book Five. Of the revenue of the sovereign or commonwealth

I. OF THE EXPENSES OF THE SOVEREIGN OR COMMONWEALTH

Part One: Of the expense of defense

The first duty of the sovereign, that of protecting the society from the violence and invasion of other independent societies, can be performed only by means of a military force. . . .

Part Two: Of the expense of justice

The second duty of the sovereign, that of protecting, as far as possible, every member of the society from the injustice or oppression of every other member of it, or the duty of establishing an exact administration of justice requires two very different degrees of expense in the different periods of society. . . .

Among nations of hunters, as there is scarce any property, or at least none that exceeds the value of two or three days' labor; so there is seldom any established magistrate or any regular administration of justice. Men who have no property can injure one another only in their persons or reputations. But when one man kills, wounds, beats, or defames another, though he to whom the injury is done suffers, he who does it receives no benefit. It is otherwise with the injuries to property. The benefit of the person who does the injury is often equal to the loss of him who suffers it. Envy, malice, or resentment, are the only passions which can prompt one man to injure another in his person or reputation. But the greater part of men are not very frequently under the influence of those passions; and the very worst men are so only occasionally. As their gratification too, how agreeable soever it may be to certain characters, is not attended with any real or permanent advantage, it is in the greater part of men commonly restrained by prudential considerations. Men may live together in society with some tolerable degree of security, though there is no civil magistrate to protect them from the injustice of those passions. But avarice and ambition in the rich, in the poor the hatred of labor and the love of present ease and enjoyment, are the passions which prompt to invade property, passions much more steady in their operation, and much more universal in their influence. Wherever there is great property, there is great inequality. For one very rich man, there must be at least five hundred poor, and the affluence of the few supposes the indigence of the many. The affluence of the rich excites the indignation of the poor, who are often both driven by want, and prompted by envy, to invade his possessions. It is only under the shelter of the civil magistrate that the owner of that valuable property, which is acquired by the labor of many years, or perhaps of many successive generations, can sleep a single night in security. The acquisition of valuable and extensive property, therefore, necessarily requires the establishment of civil government.

Part Three: Of the expense of public works and public institutions

The third and last duty of the sovereign or commonwealth is that of erecting and maintaining those public institutions and those public works, which, though they may be in the highest degree advantageous to a great society, are, however, of such a nature, that the profit could never repay the expense to any individual or small number of individuals, and which it therefore cannot be expected that an individual or small number of individuals should erect or maintain. . . . [W]orks and institutions of this kind are chiefly those for facilitating the commerce of the society, and those for promoting the instruction of the people. . . .

It does not seem necessary that the expense of those public works should be defrayed from that public revenue, as it is commonly called, of which the collection and application are in most countries assigned to the executive power. The greater part of such public works may easily be so managed, as to afford a particular revenue sufficient for defraying their own expense, without bringing any burden upon the general revenue of the society. A highway, a bridge, a navigable canal, for example, may in most cases be both made and maintained by a small toll upon the carriages which make use of them. . . .

The institutions for the education of the youth may furnish a revenue sufficient for defraying their own expense. The fee or honorary which the scholar pays to the master naturally constitutes a revenue of this kind.

Even where the reward of the master does not arise altogether from this natural revenue, it still is not necessary that it should be derived from that general revenue of the society, of which the collection and application are, in most countries, assigned to the executive power. . . . The education of the common people requires, perhaps, in a civilized and commercial society, the attention of the public more than that of people of some rank and fortune. . . . [T]he common people . . . have little time to spare for education. Their parents can scarce afford to maintain them even in infancy. As soon as they are able to work, they must apply to some trade by which they can earn their subsistence. That trade too is generally so simple and uniform as to give little exercise to the understanding; while, at the same time, their labor is both so constant and so severe, that it leaves them little leisure and less inclination to apply to, or even to think of anything else.

But though the common people cannot, in any civilized society, be so well instructed as people of some rank and fortune, the most essential parts of education, however, to read, write, and account, can be acquired at so early a period of life, that the greater part even of those who are to be bred to the lowest occupations, have time to acquire them before they can be employed in those occupations. For a very small expense the public can facilitate, can encourage, and can even impose upon almost the whole body of the people, the necessity of acquiring those most essential parts of education.

QUESTIONS FOR DISCUSSION

1   What accounts for the greater wealth of nations?
2   Why is rising population a good index of prosperity?
3   Over the long run what determines exchange value of a commodity (i.e., its average price)? Why is labor value *not* the answer for Smith?
4   State in your own words the theorem of the "invisible hand." When would it be false? Is there any evidence presented to support it?
5   Can Smith's theorem of the "invisible hand" be applied to explaining wage differentials?

READING 6

The essential optimism of Adam Smith can be traced to his faith in human reason and altruism, together with the belief that widening markets would give scope for more and more specialization. While much of Smith's analysis was adopted by later classical writers, his optimism was abandoned as a consequence of two related challenges raised by **Thomas Robert Malthus** (1766-1834). Malthus asserted the tendency of human populations to grow whenever incomes exceed subsistence and the "law" of diminishing marginal returns in agriculture.[8] As a result of the first, Malthus taught, welfare or redistribution to the poor would be counterproductive, for such grants would allow improvident childbearing and would bring out the "natural indolence of mankind."[9] Paupers who receive public assistance should rather be forced to work under demeaning circumstances, like workhouses. Even in our own times, these hard attitudes have been taken over by neo-Malthusian pessimists who oppose welfare payments to the poor, population growth, and economic growth.

A curate and later the first English professor of political economy, "Parson" Malthus first published his view in 1798 in opposition to British sympathizers with the French Revolution. Like Smith, he continued to refine those famous views throughout his life.[10] The core argument is quite simple. Humankind's reproductive potential is vast; in empty, healthful lands, population would grow by three percent or more yearly, thereby doubling or more every 25 years. On the other hand, subsistence could rise only slowly on account of limited land. Consequently, if we may ignore emigration,[11] *something* must eventually limit human reproduction. Population growth may cease owing to a lower birth rate (the "preventive check") or a higher death rate ("positive check")—or both. It is simply a truism that population growth or $\delta N = BR - DR - EMIG$, when birth rates *(BR)*, death rates *(DR)* and net emigration *(EMIG)* are defined as gross yearly rates. Birth rates might fall because of misery and vice, leading to lower fecundity of adults, or abortion and contraception, condemned by Malthus as "vice" likely to "remove a necessary stimulus to industry." Just possibly, births might be reduced by late marriage ("moral restraint"), a concept added by Malthus in 1803—just a year or two before his own marriage!—provided people could be persuaded that too many children would endanger their parents' rank in society and the general standard of living. Lacking such moral restraint, though, the lower classes would be condemned to low wages, work in unwholesome occupations, and high infant mortality for their offspring. Societies which could not limit births would be subject to infanticide, famine, disease, or war.

---

[8]By this law, or theory, after all good land is exhausted, adding more labor and capital to existing (or to less fertile) land would yield less and less crops for each addition.

[9]British Prime Minister William Pitt, the Younger, is said to have withdrawn his support for an amelioration of the Poor Laws in 1800 for fear more generous welfare conditions would encourage large families.

[10]Malthus' anonymous tract *An Essay on the Principle of Population, As It Affects the Future Improvement of Society: With Remarks on the Speculations of Mr. Godwin, M. Condorcet, and Other Writers* was published in 1798, the "Second" Essay, in 1803; and the "Summary View" in the *Encyclopaedia Britannica* in 1824 and 1830.

[11]Writing at the beginning of the greatest period of intercontinental human migration on record—from the 1840s to the 1920s, Malthus considered emigration could only delay by a few years the doleful effects of population pressure.

TABLE 3-2
MALTHUS' ANALYSIS OF POSSIBLE POPULATION CONTROLS

	Preventive Checks (reduce *BR*)	**Positive Checks** (raise *DR*)
Misery & Vice	Low fertility	Poverty, infant mortality, famine, disease
	Prostitution, abortion, contraception	
	Infanticide	
Moral Restraint	Late marriage, abstinence	None mentioned

On its face, Malthus' theory is merely a classification, a list of all possible causes for the end of population growth, not a hypothesis of what will, but need not, happen. If what-ever happens confirms a theory, that theory is irrefutable and thus, by modern canons of scientific method, not a scientific theory at all.[12] If population continues to grow, it must not yet have exceeded the bounds of subsistence. If wages exceed a culture's mini-mum subsistence level, then disaster has only been postponed. If population growth ceases, one cause or another in Malthus' list can be found—or a new one invented. It is never wrong. Unless the theorist indicates which of the checks is likely to be effective in which circumstances, the Malthusian "laws" are no proper theory, though they might—as any fruitful perspective—give rise to such a theory. Indeed, some critics believe "Parson" Malthus was most interested in moral teaching.[13]

---

[12]Blaug, chapter 3; according to an influential Anglo-Saxon philosophy of science, good scientific theory is a conjecture which, though it has been subjected to severe empirical tests which might have led to its rejection, corresponds to all known facts. Karl Popper, *Conjectures and Refutations: The Growth of Scientific Knowledge* (New York: Harper, 1965), chapter 1.

[13]Donald Winch, *Malthus* (New York: Oxford, 1987), chapter 7. Yet Malthusian hypotheses have been tested empirically: George R. Boyer, "Malthus Was Right After All: Poor Relief and Birth Rates in Southeastern England," *Journal of Political Economy*, vol. 97, no. 1 (1989), pp. 93-114. Moreover, Malthus made a great effort to determine the demographic facts and to change his theories accordingly. Was this not social science?

An Essay on the Principle of Population[*]

Thomas Malthus

BOOK I. OF THE CHECKS TO POPULATION IN THE LESS CIVILIZED
PARTS OF THE WORLD AND IN PAST TIMES

Chapter I.   Statement of the subject—ratios of the increase of population and food

In an inquiry concerning the improvement of society, the mode of conducting the subject which naturally presents itself, is,

1. To investigate the causes that have hitherto impeded the progress of mankind towards happiness; and,

2. To examine the probability of the total or partial removal of these causes in future.

To enter fully into this question, and to enumerate all the causes that have hitherto influenced human improvement, would be much beyond the power of an individual. The principal object of the present essay is to examine the effects of one great cause intimately united with the very nature of man; which, though it has been constantly and powerfully operating since the commencement of society, has been little noticed by the writers who have treated this subject. . . . The cause to which I allude is the constant tendency in all animated life to increase beyond the nourishment prepared for it. . . . In plants and irrational animals, . . . wherever . . . there is liberty, the power of increase is exerted, and the superabundant effects are repressed afterwards by want of room and nourishment.

The effects of this check on man are more complicated. Impelled to the increase of his species by an equally powerful instinct, reason interrupts his career, and asks him whether he may not bring beings into the world for whom he cannot provide the means of support. If he attend to this natural suggestion, the restriction too frequently produces vice. If he hear it not, the human race will be constantly endeavouring to increase beyond the means of subsistence. But as, by that law of our nature which makes food necessary to the life of man, population can never actually increase beyond the lowest nourishment capable of supporting it, a strong check on population, from the difficulty of acquiring food, must be constantly in operation. This difficulty must fall somewhere, and must necessarily be severely felt in some or other of the various forms of misery, or the fear of misery, by a large portion of mankind.

That population has this constant tendency to increase beyond the means of subsistence, and that it is kept to its necessary level by these causes, will sufficiently appear from a review of the different states of society in which man has existed. But, before we proceed to this review, the subject will perhaps be seen in a clearer light, if we endeavour to ascertain what would be the natural

---

[*]*Source:* Thomas Malthus, Essay on the *Principle of Population,* 1799; 1803. Our abridged text follows the last edition (1826).

increase of population, if left to exert itself with perfect freedom; and what might be expected to be the rate of increase in the productions of the earth, under the most favorable circumstances of human industry. . . .

In the northern states of America, where the means of subsistence have been more ample, the manners of the people more pure, and the checks to early marriages fewer, than in any of the modern states of Europe, the population has been found to double itself, for above a century and a half successively, in less than twenty-five years. Yet, even during these periods, in some of the towns, the deaths exceeded the births, a circumstance which clearly proves that in those parts of the country which supplied this deficiency, the increase must have been much more rapid than the general average.

In the back settlements, where the sole employment is agriculture, and vicious customs and unwholesome occupations are little known, the population has been found to double itself in fifteen years. Even this extraordinary rate of increase is probably short of the utmost power of population. Very severe labor is requisite to clear a fresh country; such situations are not in general considered as particularly healthy; and the inhabitants, probably, are occasionally subject to the incursions of the Indians, which may destroy some lives, or at any rate diminish the fruits of industry. . . .

But, to be perfectly sure that we are far within the truth, we will take the slowest of these rates of increase, a rate in which all concurring testimonies agree, and which has been repeatedly ascertained to be from procreation only.

It may safely be pronounced, therefore, that population, when unchecked, goes on doubling itself every twenty-five years, or increases in a geometrical ratio.

The rate according to which the productions of the earth may be supposed to increase, will not be so easy to determine. Of this, however, we may be perfectly certain, that the ratio of their increase in a limited territory must be of a totally different nature from the ratio of the increase of population. . . .

Europe is by no means so fully peopled as it might be. In Europe there is the fairest chance that human industry may receive its best direction. The science of agriculture has been much studied in England and Scotland; and there is still a great portion of uncultivated land in these countries. Let us consider at what rate the produce of this island (Great Britain) might be supposed to increase under circumstances the most favorable to improvement.

If it be allowed that by the best possible policy, and great encouragements to agriculture, the average produce of the island could be doubled in the first twenty-five years, it will be allowing, probably, a greater increase than could with reason be expected.

In the next twenty-five years, it is impossible to suppose that the produce could be quadrupled. It would be contrary to all our knowledge of the properties of land. The improvement of the barren parts would be a work of time and labor; and it must be evident to those who have the slighest acquaintance with agricultural subjects, that in proportion as cultivation extended, the additions that could yearly be made to the former average produce must be gradually and regularly diminishing. That we may be the better able to compare the increase of population and food, let us make a supposition, which, without pretending to accuracy, is clearly more favorable to the power of production in the earth than any experience we have had of its qualities will warrant.

Let us suppose that the yearly additions which might be made to the former average produce, instead of decreasing, which they certainly would do, were to remain the same; and that the produce of this island might be increased every twenty-five years, by a quantity equal to what it at present produces. The most enthusiastic speculator cannot suppose a greater increase than this. In a few centuries it would make every acre of land in the island like a garden.

If this supposition be applied to the whole earth, and if it be allowed that the subsistence for man which the earth affords might be increased every twenty-five years by a quantity equal to what it at present produces, this will be supposing a rate of increase much greater than we can imagine that any possible exertions of mankind could make it.

It may be fairly pronounced, therefore, that, considering the present average state of the earth, the means of subsistence, under circumstances the most favorable to human industry, could not possibly be made to increase faster than in an arithmetical ratio.

The necessary effects of these two different rates of increase, when brought together, will be very striking. Let us call the population of this island eleven millions; and suppose the present produce equal to the easy support of such a number. In the first twenty-five years the population would be twenty-two millions, and the food being also doubled, the means of subsistence would be equal to this increase. In the next twenty-five years, the population would be forty-four millions, and the means of subsistence only equal to the support of thirty-three millions. In the next period the population would be eighty-eight millions, and the means of subsistence just equal to the support of half that number. And, at the conclusion of the first century, the population would be a hundred and seventy-six millions, and the means of subsistence only equal to the support of fifty-five millions, leaving a population of a hundred and twenty-one millions totally unprovided for.

Taking the whole earth, instead of this island, emigration would of course be excluded; and, supposing the present population equal to a thousand millions, the human species would increase as the numbers, 1, 2, 4, 8, 16, 32, 64, 128, 256; and subsistence as 1, 2, 3, 4, 5, 6, 7, 8, 9. In two centuries the population would be to the means of subsistence as 256 to 9; in three centuries as 4096 to 13 and in two thousand years the difference would be almost incalculable.

In this supposition no limits whatever are placed to the produce of the earth. It may increase for ever, and be greater than any assignable quantity; yet still the power of population being in every period so much superior, the increase of the human species can only be kept down to the level of the means of subsistence by the constant operation of the strong law of necessity, acting as a check upon the greater power.

Chapter II. Of the general checks to population, and the mode of their operation

The ultimate check to population appears then to be a want of food, arising necessarily from the different ratios according to which population and food increase. But this ultimate check is never the immediate check, except in cases of actual famine.

The immediate check may be stated to consist in all those customs, and all those diseases, which seem to be generated by a scarcity of the means of subsistence; and all those causes, independent of this scarcity, whether of a moral or physical nature, which tend prematurely to weaken and destroy the human frame.

These checks to population, which are constantly operating with more or less force in every society, and keep down the number to the level of the means of subsistence, may be classed under two general heads—the preventive and the positive checks.

The preventive check, as far as it is voluntary, is peculiar to man, and arises from that distinctive superiority in his reasoning faculties which enables hint to calculate distant consequences. The checks to the indefinite increase of plants and irrational animals are all either positive or, if preventive, involuntary. But man cannot look around him, and see the distress which frequently presses upon those who have large families; he cannot contemplate his present possessions or earnings, which he now nearly consumes himself, and calculate the amount of each share, when with very little addition they must be divided, perhaps, among seven or eight, without feeling a doubt whether, if he follow the bent of his inclinations, he may be able to support the offspring which he will probably bring into the world. In a state of equality, if such can exist, this would be the simple question. In the present state of society other considerations occur. Will he not lower his rank in life, and be obliged to give up in great measure his former habits? Does any mode of employment present itself by which he may reasonably hope to maintain a family? Will he not at any rate subject himself to greater difficulties, and more severe labor, than in his single state? Will he not be unable to transmit to his children the same advantages of education and improvement that he had himself possessed? Does he even feel secure that, should he have a large family, his utmost exertions can save them from rags and squalid poverty, and their consequent degradation in the community? And may he not be reduced to the grating necessity of forfeiting his independence, and of being obliged to the sparing hand of charity for support?

These considerations are calculated to prevent, and certainly do prevent, a great number of persons in all civilized nations from pursuing the dictate of nature in an early attachment to one woman.

If this restraint do not produce vice, it is undoubtedly the least evil that can arise from the principle of population. Considered as a restraint on a strong natural inclination, it must be allowed to produce a certain degree of temporary unhappiness; but evidently slight, compared with the evils which result from any of the other checks to population; and merely of the same nature as many other sacrifices of temporary to permanent gratification, which it is the business of a moral agent continually to make.

When this restraint produces vice, the evils which follow are but too conspicuous. A promiscuous intercourse to such a degree as to prevent the birth of children, seems to lower, in the most marked manner, the dignity of human nature. It cannot be without its effect on men, and nothing can be more obvious than its tendency to degrade the female character, and to destroy all its most amiable and distinguishing characteristics. Add to which, that among those unfortunate females with which all great towns abound, more real distress and aggravated misery are, perhaps, to be found, than in any other department of human life.

When a general corruption of morals, with regard to the sex, pervades all the classes of society, its effects must necessarily be to poison the springs of domestic happiness, to weaken conjugal and parental affection, and to lessen the united exertions and ardor of parents in the care and education of their children; effects which cannot take place without a decided diminution of the general happiness and virtue of society; particularly as the necessity of art in the accomplishment and conduct of intrigues, and in the concealment of their consequences, necessarily leads to many other vices.

The positive checks to population are extremely various, and include every cause, whether arising from vice or misery, which in any degree contribute to shorten the natural duration of human life. Under this head, therefore, may be enumerated all unwholesome occupations, severe labor and exposure to the seasons, extreme poverty, bad nursing of children, large towns, excesses of all kinds, the whole train of common diseases and epidemics, wars, plague, and famine.

On examining these obstacles to the increase of population which are classed under the heads of preventive and positive checks, it will appear that they are all resolvable into moral restraint, vice, and misery.

Of the preventive checks the restraint from marriage which is not followed by irregular gratifications may properly be termed moral restraint.

Promiscuous intercourse, unnatural passions, violations of the marriage bed, and improper arts to conceal the consequences of irregular connections, are preventive checks that clearly come under the head of vice.

Of the positive checks, those which appear to arise unavoidably from the laws of nature, may be called exclusively misery; and those which we obviously bring upon ourselves, such as wars, excesses, and many others which it would be in our power to avoid, are of a mixed nature. They are brought upon us by vice, and their consequences are misery.

The sum of all these preventive and positive checks, taken together, forms the immediate check to population; and it is evident that, in every country where the whole of the procreative power cannot be called into action, the preventive and the positive checks must vary inversely as each other; that is, in countries either naturally unhealthy, or subject to a great mortality, from whatever cause it may arise, the preventive check will prevail very little. In those countries, on the contrary, which are naturally healthy, and where the preventive check is found to prevail with considerable force, the positive check will prevail very little, or the mortality be very small.

In every country some of these checks are, with more or less force, in constant operation; yet, notwithstanding their general prevalence, there are few states in which there is not a constant effort in the population to increase beyond the means of subsistence. This constant effort as constantly tends to subject the lower classes of society to distress, and to prevent any great permanent melioration of their condition.

These effects, in the present state of society, seem to be produced in the following manner. We will suppose the means of subsistence in any country just equal to the easy support of its inhabitants.The constant effort towards population, which is found to act even in the most vicious societies, increases the number of people before the means of subsistence are increased. The food, therefore, which before supported eleven millions, must now be divided among eleven millions and a half. The poor consequently must live much worse, and many of them be reduced to severe distress. The number of laborers also being above the proportion of work in the market, the price of labor must tend to fall, while the price of provisions would at the same time tend to rise. The laborer therefore must do more work to earn the same as he did before. During this season of distress, the discouragements to marriage and the difficulty of rearing a family are so great, that the progress of population is retarded. In the meantime, the cheapness of labor, the plenty of laborers, and the necessity of an increased industry among them, encourage cultivators to employ more labor upon their land, to turn up fresh soil, and to manure and improve more completely what is already in tillage, till ultimately the means of subsistence may become in the same proportion to the population as at the period from which we set out. The situation of the laborer being then again tolerably comfortable, the restraints to population are in some degree loosened; and, after a short period, the same retrograde and progressive movements with respect to happiness are repeated. . . .

One principal reason why this oscillation has been less remarked, and less decidedly confirmed by experience than might naturally be expected, is, that the histories of mankind which we possess are, in general, histories only of the higher classes. We have not many accounts that can be depended upon, of the manners and customs of that part of mankind where these retrograde and progressive movements chiefly take place. . . .

BOOK II. OF THE CHECKS TO POPULATION IN THE DIFFERENT STATES OF MODERN EUROPE

Chapter XIII. General deductions from the preceding view of society

That the checks which have been mentioned are the immediate causes of the slow increase of population, and that these checks result principally from an insufficiency of subsistence, will be evident from the comparatively rapid increase which has invariably taken place, whenever, by some sudden enlargement in the mean of subsistence, these checks have in any considerable degree been removed.

It has been universally remarked that all new colonies settled in healthy countries, where room and food were abundant, have constantly made a rapid progress in population. . . . But the English North American colonies, now the powerful people of the United States of America, far outstripped all the others in the progress of their population. To the quantity of rich land which they possessed in common with the Spanish and Portuguese colonies, they added a greater degree of liberty and equality. . . . The consequence of these favorable circumstances united was a rapidity of increase almost without parallel in history. Throughout all the northern provinces the population was found to double itself in 25 years. . . .

Whatever was the original number of British emigrants which increased so fast in North America, let us ask, Why does not an equal number produce an equal increase in the same time in Great Britain? The obvious reason to be assigned is the want of food; and that this want is the most efficient cause of the three immediate checks to population, which have been observed to prevail in all societies, is evident from the rapidity with which even old states recover the desolations of war, pestilence, famine, and the convulsions of nature. They are then for a short time placed a little in the situation of new colonies, and the effect is always answerable to what might be expected. If the industry of the inhabitants be not destroyed, subsistence will soon increase beyond the wants of the reduced numbers; and the invariable consequence will be that population, which before perhaps was nearly stationary, will begin immediately to increase, and will continue its progress till the former population is recovered. . . .

It has appeared from the registers of different countries that the progress of their population is checked by the periodical though irregular returns of plagues and sickly seasons. . . . How far these "terrible correctives to the redundance of mankind" have been occasioned by the too rapid increase of population, is a point which it would be very difficult to determine with any degree of precision. The causes of most of our diseases appear to us to be so mysterious, and probably are really so various, that it would be rashness to lay too much stress on any single one; but it will not perhaps be too much to say that among these causes we ought certainly to rank crowded houses and insufficient or unwholesome food, which are the natural consequences of an increase of population faster than the accommodations of a country with respect to habitations and food will allow.

Almost all the histories of epidemics which we possess tend to confirm this supposition, by describing them in general as making their principal ravages among the lower classes of people. . . .

Of the other great scourge of mankind, famine, it may be observed that it is not in the nature of things that the increase of population should absolutely produce one. This increase though rapid is necessarily gradual; and as the human frame cannot be supported even for a very short time without food, it is evident that no more human beings can grow up than there is provision to maintain. But though the principle of population cannot absolutely produce a famine, it prepares the way for one, and by frequently obliging the lower classes of people to subsist nearly on the smallest quantity of food that will support life, turns even a slight deficiency from the failure of the seasons into a severe dearth, and may be fairly said therefore to be one of the principal causes of famine.

It also appears that when the increasing produce of a country and the increasing demand for labor so far meliorate the condition of the laborer as greatly to encourage marriage, the custom of early marriages is generally continued till the population has gone beyond the increased produce, and sickly seasons appear to be the natural and necessary consequence. . . .

BOOK IV. OF OUR FUTURE PROSPECTS RESPECTING THE REMOVAL
OR MITIGATION OF THE EVILS ARISING FROM THE PRINCIPLE OF
POPULATION

Chapter I.   Of moral restraint, and our obligation to practice this virtue

In the first edition of this essay I observed that as from the laws of nature it
appeared that some check to population must exist, it was better that this check
should arise from a foresight of the difficulties attending a family and the fear
of dependent poverty than from the actual presence of want and sickness. . . .

It is clearly the duty of each individual not to marry till he has a prospect of
supporting his children; but it is at the same time to be wished that he should
retain undiminished his desire of marriage, in order that he may exert himself
to realize this prospect, and be stimulated to make provision for the support of
greater numbers. . . . The interval between the age of puberty and the period at
which each individual might venture on marriage must, according to the
supposition, be passed in strict chastity, because the law of chastity cannot be
violated without producing evil. The effect of anything like a promiscuous
intercourse, which prevents the birth of children, is evidently to weaken the
best affections of the heart, and in a very marked manner to degrade the female
character; and any other intercourse would, without improper arts, bring as
many children into the society as marriage, with a much greater probability of
their becoming a burden to it. [from Chapter II]

Chapter III.   Of the only effectual mode of improving the condition of the poor

If we be really serious in what appears to be the object . . . of essentially and
permanently bettering the condition of the poor, we must explain to them the
true nature of their situation, and show them that the withholding of the
supplies of labor is the only possible way of really raising its price, and that
they themselves being the possessors of this commodity have alone the power
to do this. . . .

The first grand requisite to the growth of prudential habit is the perfect
security of property, and the next perhaps is that respectability and importance
which are given to the lower classes by equal laws and the possession of some
influence in the framing of them. The more excellent therefore is the
government, the more does it tend to generate that prudence and elevation of
sentiment by which alone in the present state of our being poverty can be
avoided. [from Chapter VI]

Chapter XIV.   Of our rational expectations respecting the future improvement of society

Among the higher and middle classes of society the effect of this knowledge
will I hope be to direct without relaxing their efforts in bettering the condition
of the poor; to show them what they can and what they cannot do; and that

although much may be done by advice and instruction, by encouraging habits of prudence and cleanliness, by discriminate charity, and by any mode of bettering the present condition of the poor which is followed by an increase of the preventive cheek; yet that without this last effect all the former efforts would be futile; and that in any old and well-peopled state to assist the poor in such a manner as to enable them to marry as early as they please and rear up large families, is a physical impossibility. . . . Among the poor themselves its effects would be still more important. That the principal and most permanent cause of poverty has little or no direct relation to forms of government or the unequal division of property; and that as the rich do not in reality possess the power of finding employment and maintenance for the poor, the poor cannot in the nature of things possess the right to demand them, are important truths flowing from the principle of population. . .

On the whole, . . . though our future prospects respecting the mitigation of the evils arising from the principle of population may not be so bright as we would wish, yet they are far from being entirely disheartening, and by no means preclude that gradual and progressive improvement in human society, which before the late wild speculations on this subject was the object of rational expectation. To the laws of property and marriage, and to the apparently narrow principle of self-interest which prompts each individual to exert himself in bettering his condition, we are indebted for all the noblest exertions of human genius, for everything that distinguishes the civilized from the savage state. . . . The structure of society in its great features will probably always remain unchanged. We have every reason to believe that it will always consist of a class of proprietors and a class of laborers; but the condition of each and the proportion which they bear to each other may be so altered as greatly to improve the harmony and beauty of the whole.

QUESTIONS FOR DISCUSSION

1 Malthus is known as the first great economist to "test" his theories with empirical evidence, using the "comparative method." Based on passages in this selection, how does Malthus test his theories?
2 If the evidence had turned out otherwise, should he have withdrawn his theory?
3 What factors for human improvement have been ignored by Malthus?

READING 7

Neo-Malthusian writings have stressed the superabundance of human population relative to the supply of natural resources, not necessarily food, and to available gainful employment. One finds the neo-Malthusian perspective informing much discussion of unemployment during the Great Depression, less developed countries since World War II, and the underclass in contemporary America. One celebrated example is the report of the influential Club of Rome, a group of prominent businessmen and statesmen from several countries formed in 1968 to foster "understanding of the varied but interdependent components—economic, political, natural, and social—that make up the global system." Their Project on the Predicament of Mankind adopted the systems dynamics model of Jay Forrester,[14] and a large research team at the Massachusetts Institute of Technology was set to work. Their report prompted much public discussion It is excerpted below.

The neo-Malthusian perspective has been opposed by neoclassical economists, such as Robert Solow (also of MIT), who stress the likely reactions in open markets to any emerging shortage. Should demand for any material or energy source exceed its supply at current prices, they predict, rising prices would lead firms to economize, by substituting other materials or sources, or to develop more expensive and hitherto unprofitable supplies. For example, no sooner had the Club of Rome's report appeared than OPEC's quadrupling of the oil price led car buyers, homeowners, and factory managers around the world to conserve energy to a remarkable extent. Opponents of the neo-Malthusians also appeal to the record of technological progress over the time since Malthus wrote, especially in producing food and fiber. According to Julian Simon, an influential anti-Malthusian, more people would mean more ingenuity, hence more progress.[15]

Present-day opponents of the American welfare system have also adopted neo-Malthusian ideas. According to Thomas Sowell[16] and others, easy welfare has corrupted the poor, leading to illegitimacy and welfare dependency through several generations. Only self-help, religious values, parental responsibility, and delay of gratification will restore the American underclass to self-respecting and productive life, according to this view. Critics of this neo-Malthusian argument counter that the poor need meaningful jobs near their homes, and these have been lacking because of insufficient aggregate demand, public transportation, and international competition.

The following article shows what might be called a neo-Malthusian approach to world economic problems.

The Limits to Growth[*]

Donella H. Meadows
Dennis L. Meadows
Jørgen Randers
William H. Behrens III

I do not wish to seem overdramatic, but I can only conclude from the information that is available to me as Secretary-General, that Members of the United Nations have perhaps ten years left in which to sub-

---

[14]The model has been published in Jay W. Forrester, *World Dynamics* (Cambridge, Mass.: Wright-Allen Press, 1971). The method assumes that any complex system has many circular and interacting relationships with different time lags—for example, positive or negative feedback loops. This complex structure is crucial in determining the model's behavior.

[15]Julian Simon, *The Ultimate Resource* (Princeton, N.J.: Princeton University Press, 1981).

[16]Thomas Sowell, *Markets and Minorities* (New York: Basic Books, 1975), p. 123.

[*]Source: *The Limits to Growth: A Report for The Club of Rome's Project on the Predicament of Mankind,* by Donella H. Meadows, Dennis L. Meadows, Jørgen Randers, William W. Behrens, III (New York: Universe Books, 1972), A Potomac Associates book published by Universe Books, New York, 1972. Graphics by Potomac Associates. By permission.

ordinate their ancient quarrels and launch a global partnership to curb the arms race, to improve the human environment, to defuse the population explosion, and to supply the required momentum to development efforts. If such a global partnership is not forged within the next decade, then I very much fear that the problems I have mentioned will have reached such staggering proportions that they will be beyond our capacity to control.

—U Thant, 1969

The problems U Thant mentions—the arms race, environmental deterioration, the population explosion, and economic stagnation—are often cited as the central, long-term problems of modern man. Many people believe that the future course of human society, perhaps even the survival of human society, depends on the speed and effectiveness with which the world responds to these issues. And yet only a small fraction of the world's population is actively concerned with understanding these problems or seeking their solutions. . . .

Are the implications of these global trends actually so threatening that their resolution should take precedence over local, short-term concerns? Is it true, as U Thant suggested, that there remains less than a decade to bring these trends under control? If they are not brought under control, what will the consequences be? What methods does mankind have for solving global problems, and what will be the results and the costs of employing each of them?

PROBLEMS AND MODELS

Every person approaches his problems . . . with the help of models. A model is simply an ordered set of assumptions about a complex system. It is an attempt to understand some aspect of the infinitely varied world by selecting from perceptions and past experience a set of general observations applicable to the problem at hand. A farmer uses a mental model of his land, his assets, market prospects, and past weather conditions to decide which crops to plant each year. . . . Decision-makers at every level unconsciously use mental models to choose among policies that will shape our future world. These mental models are, of necessity, very simple when compared with the reality from which they are abstracted. The human brain, remarkable as it is, can only keep track of a limited number of the complicated, simultaneous interactions that determine the nature of the real world.

We, too, have used a model. Ours is a formal, written model of the world. It constitutes a preliminary attempt to improve our mental models of long-term, global problems by combining the large amount of information that is already in human minds and in written records with the new information-processing tools that mankind's increasing knowledge has produced—the scientific method, systems analysis, and the modern computer.

Our world model was built specifically to investigate five major trends of global concern—accelerating industrialization, rapid population growth, widespread malnutrition, depletion of nonrenewable resources, and a deteriorating environment. These trends are all interconnected in many ways, and their development is measured in decades or centuries, rather than in months or years. With the model we are seeking to understand the causes of these trends, their interrelationships, and their implications as much as one hundred years in the future.

The model we have constructed, is, like every other model, imperfect, oversimplified, and unfinished. We are well aware of its shortcomings, but we believe that it is the most useful model now available for dealing with problems far out on the space-time graph. To our knowledge it is the only formal model in existence that is truly global in scope, that has a time horizon longer than thirty years, and that includes important variables such as population, food production, and pollution, not as independent entities, but as dynamically interacting elements, as they are in the real world.

Since ours is a formal, or mathematical model it also has two important advantages over mental models. First, every assumption we make is written in a precise form so that it is open to inspection and criticism by all. Second, after the assumptions have been scrutinized, discussed, and revised to agree with our best current knowledge, their implications for the future behavior of the world system can be traced without error by a computer, no matter how complicated they become. . . .

Decisions are being made every day, in every part of the world, that will affect the physical, economic, and social conditions of the world system for decades to come. These decisions cannot wait for perfect models and total understanding. They will be made on the basis of some model, mental or written, in any case. We feel that the model described here is already sufficiently developed to be of some use to decision-makers. Furthermore, the basic behavior models we have already observed in this model appear to be so fundamental and general that we do not expect our broad conclusions to be substantially altered by further revisions. . . .

The following conclusions have emerged from our work so far. We are by no means the first group to have stated them. For the past several decades, people who have looked at the world with a global, long-term perspective have reached similar conditions. Nevertheless, the vast majority of policymakers seems to be actively pursuing goals that are inconsistent with these results.

Our conclusions are:

1. If the present growth trends in world population, industrialization, pollution, food production, and resource depletion continue unchanged, the limits to growth on this planet will be reached sometime within the next one hundred years. The most probable result will be a rather sudden and uncontrollable decline in both population and industrial capacity.

2. It is possible to alter these growth trends and to establish a condition of ecological and economic stability that is sustainable far into the future. The state of global equilibrium could be designed so that the basic material needs of each person on earth are satisfied and each person has an equal opportunity to realize his individual human potential.

3. If the world's people decide to strive for this second outcome rather than the first, the sooner they begin working to attain it, the greater will be their chances of success. . . .

It is a simple matter of arithmetic to calculate extrapolated values for gross national production (GNP) per capita from now until the year 2000 on the assumption that relative growth rates of population and GNP will remain roughly the same in these ten countries. The result of such a calculation . . . will almost certainly not actually be realized. They are not predictions. The values merely indicate the general direction our system, as it is currently structured, is taking us. *They demonstrate that the process of economic growth, as it is occurring today, is inexorably widening the absolute gap between the rich and the poor nations of the world.*

If extrapolations do not actually come to pass, it will be because the balance between the positive and negative feedback loops determining the growth rates of population and capital in each nation has been altered. . . .

Even with the optimistic assumption that all possible land is utilized, there will still be a desperate land shortage before the year 2000 if per capita land requirements and population growth rates remain as they are today. . . . Exponential growth in a limited space . . . shows how one can move within a very few years from a situation of great abundance to one of great scarcity. There has been an o verwhelming excess of potentially arable land for all of history, and now, within 30 years (or about one population doubling time), there may be a sudden and serious shortage. . . Precise numerical assumptions about the limits of the earth are unimportant when viewed against the inexorable progress of exponential growth. We might assume, for example, that *no* arable land is taken for citizens, roads, or other nonagricultural uses. . . . Or we can suppose that it is possible to double, or even quadruple, the productivity of the land through advances in agricultural technology and investments in capital, such as tractors, fertilizers, and irrigation systems. . . . Each doubling of productivity gains about 30 years. . . .

Of course, society will not be suddenly surprised by the "crisis point" at which the amount of land needed becomes greater than that available. Symptoms of the crisis will begin to appear long before the crisis point is reached. Food prices will rise so high that some people will starve; others will be forced to decrease the effective amount of land they use and to shift to lower quality diets. These symptoms are already apparent in many parts of the world. . . . Perhaps 10 to 20 million deaths each year can be attributed directly or indirectly to malnutrition.[17]

The earth is finite. The closer any human activity comes to the limit of the earth's ability to support that activity, the more apparent and unresolvable the trade-offs become. When there is plenty of unused arable land, there can be more people and also more food per person. When all the land is already used, the trade-off between more people or more food per person becomes a choice between absolutes.

In general, modern society has not learned to recognize and deal with these trade-offs. The apparent goal of the present world system is to produce more people with more (food, material goods, clean air and water) for each person. If society continues to strive for that goal, it will eventually reach one of the many early limitations. . . . It is not possible to foretell exactly which limitation

---

[17]Paul R. Ehrlich and Anne H. Ehrlich, *Population, Resources, Environment* (San Francisco: W. H. Freeman and Co., 1970), p. 72.

will occur first or what the consequences will be, because there are many conceivable, unpredictable human responses to such a situation.

QUESTIONS FOR DISCUSSION

1 In a response to the world systems approach, Robert Solow says that the "doomsday" prediction comes from the assumption that natural resources, including waste disposal capacity, are finite, but are consumed at an increasing rate, without any mechanism to turn off that consumption as exhaustion approaches.[18] What mechanisms do you think could defuse the population-resource doomsday bomb?
2 The Club of Rome report recognizes that industrialization has cut birth rates in the advanced countries nearly to the replacement level but argues that increased discretionary incomes would raise the desired birth rate. Considering that most of the world's families have below-average incomes—far below present American levels—and birth rates of 35 to 50 per thousand people per year, what do you think of the dangers of over-population?
3 The MIT group acknowledges their debt to Malthus, among others. What Malthusian elements do you see in their reasoning? Do they improve on Malthus in any way?

READING 8

The analytic high point of classical economics was undoubtedly the work of **David Ricardo** (1772-1823). A Sephardic Jew who converted to Unitarianism, he made a fortune as a stockbroker in the City of London before retiring to writing and politics. Like his friend Malthus, Ricardo was an avid reader of Smith's, but more pessimistic, owing to the pressure of population on available resources. As pamphleteer and later Member of Parliament, Ricardo attacked the effect of Napoleon's blockade and the protectionist Corn Law after that. According to Ricardo, limitation of grain imports pushed up food prices, as well as land rents—a pernicious effect aggravated by the quickening of population growth.

Turning to theoretical work, which eventually led to his treatise *On the Principles of Political Economy of Taxation* (1817), Ricardo redirected the aim of political economy away from growth, upon which he despaired of any scientific propositions, to questions of the functional or class distribution of the product. For this purpose he believed his analytic method—actually some arithmetic examples constructed on special assumptions—would yield valid conclusions about the effect of accumulation and population growth on the rates of return to the three factors of production and their shares in total product. Later commentators have concluded that Ricardo was successful in deducing rates of return and suggestive, though not quite conclusive, about the likely trend of functional shares. Ricardo's fundamental theorem remains central to the classical achievement: subsistence wages and the law of diminishing marginal returns to labor and capital on the land will

---

[18]Robert M. Solow, "Is the End of the World at Hand?" *Challenge* (March-April, 1973), pp. 39-50.

mean that rent increases with accumulation while the rate of profit declines until further accumulation is choked off ("the stationary state"). Note that the pattern of output, which would suit demand, plays little or no role in this long-run theory of distribution.

Ricardian theory begins as Smith and Malthus did. Relative normal price *(p)* must cover costs:

$$p = \hat{w}l + ik + rt$$

where $\hat{w}$ is the minimum subsistence wage per unit labor, determined by "habit and custom." As the supply of laborers is elastic in the long run, wages for unskilled labor cannot long be above $\hat{w}$.[19]

l　is the units of ordinary labor per unit output
i　is the rate of interest on units of capital per unit output, denoted as k
r　is the rental rate per unit land used per unit output, denoted as t

All prices are considered relative to a standard commodity, say gold, produced with average labor/capital intensity. Other commodities' relative prices are thus sensitive to the income distribution. In general, as Ricardo realized, commodities which employ more capital (or employ it longer) must carry higher relative prices if rates of return are to be equal in all industries.

Such is the microeconomic theory of price under competitive conditions. Each producer and industry takes the wage, interest rate, and rental rate for each grade of land as given in determining price. At the macroeconomic level, however, Ricardo and Malthus realized that this would not be adequate. In particular, land has no opportunity cost to society at large; if rental rates fell, or if they rose—as they did in the years immediately preceding their work—the amount of raw land available in the country would be unchanged. On the other hand, a lower wage would eventually destroy part of the working class and a lower interest rate impair the rate of accumulation. Hence it may be said that rent, and also interest, are price-determined for Ricardo, rather than price-determining. This was to be the core of Ricardo's answer to why the corn price and the rent on corn land moved up together before 1815, then fell together after Waterloo in spite of the Corn Laws.

Ricardo developed this theory by assuming that the economy was one huge farm with fixed supply of land of varying fertility. With L_0 workers currently willing to work for subsistence, the competitive return to workers, who bring their own tools, is determined by their (marginal) contribution. The interest rate is thus this return less subsistence divided by the (working) capital applied: $i = MP - \hat{w}l/k$ where MP is the marginal product of labor and tools together.

---

[19]Together with the assumption that wages must be paid out of "stock," circulating capital devoted to this purpose, the Ricardo-Malthus theory was called the "iron law of wages."

FIGURE 3-1
Ricardo's Theory of Distribution

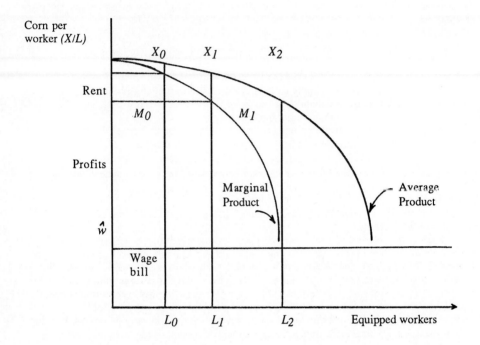

In Figure 3-1, as more and more labor is applied to a given farm by the capitalist farmer, the marginal product of labor-plus-equipment falls, though the worker must be paid at least $\hat{w}$, the subsistence in corn terms. The landlord receives the surplus after paying the farmer the competitive profits on his investment of equipment, seed, and wages advanced. With L_0 workers employed, the rent is $(X_0 - M_0)$ times L_0; the farmer's profits are $(M_0 - \hat{w})$ times L_0 after paying the subsistence wage w to each of L_0 workers. But as population and the labor force grow, producing more food on this and other farms, the rent per worker rises, while the profits per equipped worker must fall. With the amount of land fixed but necessary capital rising, this implies that the rental rate rises and the profit or interest rate falls, until at labor force L_2, profits are squeezed down to nothing.

Thus increased accumulation in circulating capital, to pay more workers, which temporarily might increase real wages above subsistence, must eventually reduce the rate of profit in terms of corn even if the competition of laborers cut their wages to subsistence. With competition of capital, the profit rates must do likewise in any other sector of the economy. Eventually, the interest rate becomes so low that all capitalists will no longer agree to accumulate.

On the basis of his arithmetical examples, Ricardo believed that accumulation also dictated a rise in the *share* of rent to the landlords, but this appears to depend on his special (and unsupported) assumptions about the elasticity of output on marginal (no-rent) land, relative to its elasticity on inframarginal (rent-bearing) land.[20]

---

[20]See the model of Luigi Pasinetti in Blaug, ch. 3.

that England would be better off trading manufactured goods for agricultural ones, even if its own productivity were superior to its trading partners in both products. This "law of comparative advantage" is no doubt one of the signal achievements of English classical economics. Nevertheless, despite Ricardo's enormous authority, the repeal of grain tariffs (the Corn Laws) would not be accomplished until 1846, when the pressure on living standards and the persuasiveness of the classical perspective were practically irresistible.

On the Principles of Political Economy and Taxation

David Ricardo

Preface

The produce of the earth—all that is derived from its surface by the united application of labor, machinery, and capital, is divided among three classes of the community, namely, the proprietor of the land, the owner of the stock or capital necessary for its cultivation, and the laborers by whose industry it is cultivated.

But in different stages of society, the proportions of the whole produce of the earth which will be allotted to each of these classes, under the names of rent, profit, and wages, will be essentially different; depending mainly on the actual fertility of the soil, on the accumulation of capital and population, and on the skill, ingenuity, and instruments employed in agriculture.

To determine the laws which regulate this distribution is the principal problem in Political Economy: much as the science has been improved by the writing of Turgot, Stuart, Smith, Say, Sismondi, and others, they afford very little satisfactory information respecting the natural course of rent, profit, and wages.

In 1815, Mr. Malthus . . . presented to the world . . . the true doctrine of rent; without a knowledge of which it is impossible to understand the effect of the progress of wealth on profits and wages, or to trace satisfactorily the influence of taxation on different classes of the community; particularly when the commodities taxed are the productions immediately derived from the surface of the earth. . . .

I. ON VALUE

i. The value of a commodity, or the quantity of any other commodity for which it will exchange, depends on the relative quantity of labor which is necessary for its production, and not on the greater or less compensation which is paid for that labor. . . .

Possessing utility, commodities derive their exchangeable value from two sources: from their scarcity, and from the quantity of labor required to obtain them.

There are some commodities, the value of which is determined by their scarcity alone. No labor can increase the quantity of such goods, and therefore their value cannot be lowered by an increased supply. Some rare statues and pictures, scarce books, and coins, wines of a peculiar quality, which can be made only from grapes grown on a particular soil, of which there is a very limited quantity, are all of this description. Their value is wholly independent of the quantity of labor originally necessary to produce them, and varies with the varying wealth and inclinations of those who are desirous to possess them.

These commodities, however, form a very small part of the mass of commodities daily exchanged in the market. By far the greatest part of those goods which are the object of desire are produced by labor; and they may be multiplied, not in one country alone, but in many, almost without any assignable limit, if we are disposed to bestow the labor necessary to obtain them.

In speaking, then of commodities, of their exchangeable value, and of the laws which regulate their relative prices, we mean always such commodities only as can be increased in quantity by the exertion of human industry, and on the production of which competition operates without restraint.

In the early stages of society, the exchangeable value of these commodities, or the rule which determines how much shall be given in exchange for another, depends almost exclusively on the comparative quantity of labor expended on each. . . .

ii. Labor of different qualities differently rewarded. This no cause of variation in the relative value of commodities.

The estimation in which different qualities of labor are held comes soon to be adjusted in the market with sufficient precision for all practical purposes, and depends much on the comparative skill of the laborer and intensity of the labor performed. The scale, once formed, is liable to little variation. . . . In comparing, therefore, the values of the same commodity at different periods of time, the consideration of the comparative skill and intensity of labor required for that particular commodity needs scarcely to be attended to, as it operates equally at both periods. . . .

If a piece of cloth be now of the value of two pieces of linen, and if, in ten years hence, the ordinary value of a piece of cloth should be four pieces of linen, we may safely conclude, that either more labor is required to make the cloth, or less to make the linen, or that both causes have operated. . . .

iii. Not only the labor applied immediately to commodities affects their value, but the labor also which is bestowed on the implements, tools, and buildings, with which such labor is assisted

Even in that early state to which Adam Smith refers, some capital, though possibly made and accumulated by the hunter himself, would be necessary to enable him to kill his game. Therefore, the value of these animals would be regulated, not solely by the time and labor necessary to their destructions, but also by the time and labor necessary for providing the hunter's capital, the weapon. . . .

If we look to a state of society in which greater improvements have been made, and in which arts and commerce flourish, we shall still find that commodities vary in value conformably with this principle; in estimating the exchangeable value of stockings, for example, we shall find that their value, comparatively with other things, depends on the total quantity of labor necessary to manufacture them and bring them to market. First, there is the labor necessary to cultivate the land on which the raw cotton is grown; secondly, the labor of conveying the cotton to the country where the stockings are to be manufactured, which includes a portion of the labor bestowed in building the ship in which it is conveyed, and which is charged in the freight of the goods; thirdly, the labor of the spinner and weaver; fourthly, a portion of the labor of the engineer, smith, and carpenter, who erected the buildings and machinery, by the help of which they are made; fifthly, the labor of the retail dealer, and of many others, whom it is unnecessary further to particularize. The aggregate sum of these various kinds of labor determines the quantity of other things for which these stockings will exchange, while the same consideration of the various quantities of labor which have been bestowed on those other things will equally govern the portion of them which will be given for the stockings.

To convince ourselves that this is the real foundation of exchangeable value, let us suppose any improvement to be made in the means of abridging labor in any one of the various processes through which the raw cotton must pass before the manufactured stockings come to the market to be exchanged for other things, and observe the effects which will follow. If fewer men were required to cultivate the raw cotton, or if fewer sailors were employed in navigating, or shipwrights in constructing the ship, in which it was conveyed to us; if fewer hands were employed in raising the building and machinery, or if these, when raised, were rendered more efficient, the stockings would inevitably fall in value, and consequently command less of other things. They would fall, because a less quantity of labor was necessary to their production, and would therefore exchange for a smaller quantity of those things in which no such abridgment of labor had been made. . . .

iv. The principle that the quantity of labor bestowed on the production of commodities regulates their relative value considerably modified by the employment of machinery and other fixed and durable capital

In the former section we have supposed the implements and weapons necessary to kill the deer and salmon to be equally durable, and to be the result of the same quantity of labor, and we have seen that the variations in the relative value of deer and salmon depended solely on the varying quantities of labor necessary to obtain them, but in every state of society, the tools, implements, buildings, and machinery employed in different trades may be of various degrees of durability, and may require different portions of labor to produce them. The proportions, too, in which the capital that is to support labor, and the capital that is invested in tools, machinery, and buildings may be variously combined. This difference in the degree of durability of fixed capital, and this variety in the proportions in which the two sorts of capital may be combined, introduce another cause, besides the greater or less quantity of labor necessary to produce commodities, for the variations in their relative value—this cause is the rise or fall in the value of labor.

The food and clothing consumed by the laborer, the buildings in which he works, the implements with which his labor is assisted, are all of a perishable nature. There is, however, a vast difference in the time for which these different capitals will endure: a steam engine will last longer than a ship, a ship than the clothing of the laborer, and the clothing of the laborer longer than the food which he consumes. According as capital is rapidly perishable, and require to be frequently reproduced, or is of slow consumption, it is classed under the heads of circulating or of fixed capital. . . .

Suppose two men employ one hundred men each for a year in the construction of two machines, and another man employs the same number of men in cultivating corn, each of the machines at the end of the year will be of the same value as the corn, for they will each be produced by the same quantity of labor. Suppose one of the owners of one of the machines to employ it, with the assistance of one hundred men, the following year in making cloth, and the owner of the other machine to employ his also, with the assistance likewise of one hundred men, in making cotton goods, while the farmer continues to employ one hundred men as before in the cultivation of corn. During the second year they will all have employed the same quantity of labor, but the goods and machine together of the clothier, and also of the cotton manufacturer, will be the result of the labor of two hundred men employed for a year; or, rather, of the labor of one hundred men for two years; whereas the corn will be produced by the labor of one hundred men for one year, consequently if the corn be of the same value of £500, the machine and cloth of the clothier together ought to be of the value of £1000, and the machine and cotton goods of the cotton manufacturer ought to be also of twice the value of the corn. But they will be of more than twice the value of the corn, for the profit on the clothier's and cotton manufacturer's capital for the first year has been added to their capitals, while that of the farmer has been expended and enjoyed. On account then of the different degrees of durability of their capitals, or, which is the same thing, on account of the time which must elapse before one set of commodities can be brought to market, they will be valuable, not exactly in proportion to the quantity of labor bestowed on them—they will not be as two to one, but something more, to compensate for the greater length of time which must elapse before the most valuable can be brought to market. . . .

But how will their relative value be affected by a rise in the value of labor? It is evidence that the relative values of cloth and cotton goods will undergo no change, for what affects one must equally affect the other under the circumstances supposed; neither will be relative values of wheat and barley undergo any change, for they are produced under the same circumstances as far as fixed and circulating capital are concerned; but the relative value of corn to cloth, or to cotton goods, must be altered by the rise of labor.

There can be no rise in the value of labor without a fall of profits. If the corn is to be divided between the farmer and the laborer, the larger the proportion that is given to the latter the less will remain for the former. So, if cloth or cotton goods be divided between the workman and his employer, the larger the proportion given to the former the less remains for the latter. . . . The manufactured goods in which more fixed capital was employed would fall relatively to corn or to any other goods which a less portion of fixed capital entered. The degree of alteration in the relative value of goods, on account of a rise or fall of labor, would depend on the proportion which the fixed capital bore to the whole capital employed. All commodities which are produced by very valuable machinery, or in very valuable buildings, or which require a great length of time before they can be brought to market, would fall in relative value, while all those which were chiefly produced by labor, or which would be speedily brought to market, would rise in relative value.

The reader, however, should remark that this cause of the variation of commodities is comparatively slight in its effects. . . . The greatest effects which could be produced on the relative prices of these goods from a rise of wages could not exceed 6 or 7 per cent; for profits could not, probably, under any circumstances, admit of a greater general and permanent depression than to that amount. . . .

> v. The principle that value does not vary with the rise or fall of wages, modified also by the unequal durability of capital, and by the unequal rapidity with which it is returned to its employer. . . .

But a rise in the wages of labor would not equally affect commodities produced with machinery quickly consumed, and commodities produced with machinery slowly consumed. In the production of the one, a great deal of labor would be continually transferred to the commodity produced—in the other very little would be so transferred. Every rise of wages, therefore, or, which is the same thing, every fall of profits, would lower the relative value of those commodities which were produced with a capital of a durable nature, and would proportionally elevate those which were produced with capital more perishable. A fall of wages would have precisely the contrary effect. . . .

If therefore the maker of the machine should raise the price of it in consequence of a rise of wages, an unusual quantity of capital would be employed in the construction of such machines, till their price afforded only the common rate of profits. We see then that machines would not rise in price in consequence of a rise of wages.

The manufacturer, however, who in a general rise of wages can have recourse to a machine which shall not increase the charge of production on his commodity, would enjoy peculiar advantages if he could continue to charge the same price for his goods; but he, as we have already seen, would be obliged to lower the price of his commodities, or capital would flow to his trade till his profits had sunk to the general level. Thus then is the public benefited by machinery: these mute agents are always the produce of much less labor than that which they displace, even when they are of the same money value. Through their influence an increase in the price of provisions which raises wages will affect fewer persons; . . . and the saving which is the consequence shows itself in the reduced price of the commodity manufactured. Neither machines, nor the commodities made by them, rise in real value, but all commodities made by machines fall, and fall in proportion to their durability. . . .

vii. Different effects from the alteration in the value of money, the medium in which PRICE is always expressed. . .

Money being a variable commodity, the rise of money wages will be frequently occasioned by a fall in the value of money. A rise in wages from this cause will, indeed, be invariably accompanied by a rise in the price of commodities; but in such cases it will be found that labor and all commodities have not varied in regard to each other, and that the variation has been confined to money. . . .

It is according to the division of the whole produce of the land of any particular farm, between the three classes, of landlord, capitalist, and laborer, that we are to judge the rise or fall of rent, profit, and wages, and not according to the value at which that produce may be estimated in a medium which is confessedly variable.

It is not by the absolute quantity of produce obtained by either class that we can correctly judge of the rate of profit, rent, and wages, but by the quantity of labor required to obtain that produce. By improvements in machinery and agriculture the whole produce may be doubled; but if wages, rent and profit be also doubled, these three will bear the same proportions to one another as before, and neither could be said to have relatively varied. But if wages partook not of the whole of this increase; if they, instead of being doubled, were only increased one half; if rent, instead of being doubled, were only increased three fourths, and the remaining increase went to profit, it would, I apprehend, be correct for me to say that rent and wages had fallen while profits had risen. . . .

II. ON RENT

Rent is that portion of the produce of the earth which is paid to the landlord for the use of the original and indestructible powers of the soil. . . . A portion only of the money annually to be paid for the improved farm would be given for the original and indestructible powers of the soil; the other portion would be paid for the use of the capital which had been employed in ameliorating the quality of the land, and in erecting such buildings as were necessary to secure and preserve the produce. . . .

On the first settling of a country in which there is an abundance of rich and fertile land, a very small proportion of which is required to be cultivated for the support of the actual population, or indeed can be cultivated with the capital which the population can command, there will be no rent; for no one would pay for the use of land when there was an abundant quantity not yet appropriated, and, therefore, at the disposal of whosoever might choose to cultivate it.

On the common principles of supply and demand, no rent could be paid for such land, for the reason stated why nothing is given for the use of air and water, or for any other of the gifts of nature which exist in boundless quantity. . . .

If all land had the same properties, if it were unlimited in quantity, and uniform in quality, no charge could be made for its use, unless where it possessed peculiar advantages of situation. It is only, then because land is not unlimited in quantity and uniform in quality, and because, in the progress of population, land of an inferior quality, or less advantageously situated, is called into cultivation that rent is ever paid for the use of it. When, in the progress of society land of the second degree of fertility is taken into cultivation, rent immediately commences on that of the first quality and the amount of that rent will depend on the difference in the quality of these two portions of land.

When land of the third quality is taken into cultivation, rent immediately commences on the second, and it is regulated as before by the difference in their productive powers. At the same time, the rent of the first quality will rise, for that must always be above the rent of the second by the difference between the produce which they yield with a given quantity of capital and labor. With every step in the progression of population, which shall oblige a country to have recourse to land of a worse quality, to enable it to raise its supply of food, rent, on all the more fertile land, will rise.

Thus suppose land—No. 1, 2, 3—to yield, with an equal employment of capital and labor, a net produce of 100, 90, and 80 quarters of corn. In a new country, where there is an abundance of fertile land compared with the population, and where therefore it is only necessary to cultivate No. 1, the whole net produce will belong to the cultivator, and will be the profits of the stock which he advances. As soon as population had so far increased as to make it necessary to cultivate No. 2, from which ninety quarters only can be obtained after supporting the laborers, rent would commence on No. 2; for either there must be two rates of profit on agricultural capital, or ten quarters, or the value of ten quarters must be withdrawn from the produce of No. 1 for some other purpose. Whether the proprietor of the land, or any other person cultivated No. 1, these ten quarters would equally constitute rent; for the cultivator of No. 2 would get the same result with his capital whether he cultivated No. 1, paying ten quarters for rent, or continued to cultivate No. 2 paying no rent. In the same manner it might be shown that when No. 3 is brought into cultivation, the rent of No. 2 must be ten quarters, or the value of ten quarters, whilst the rent of No. 1 would rise to twenty quarters; for the cultivator of No. 3 would have the same profits whether he paid twenty quarters for the rent of No. 1, ten quarters for the rent of No. 2, or cultivated No. 3 free of all rent.

It often, and, indeed, commonly happens, that before No. 2, 3, 4, or 5, or the inferior lands are cultivated, capital can be employed more productively on those lands which are already in cultivation. It may perhaps be found that by doubling the original capital employed in No. 1, though the produce will not be doubled, will not be increased by 100 quarters, it may be increased by eighty-five quarters, and that this quantity exceeds what could be obtained by employing the same capital on land No. 3.

In such case, capital will be preferably employed on the old land, and equally create a rent; for rent is always the difference between the produce obtained by the two equal quantities of capital and labor. If, with a capital of £1000 a tenant obtain 100 quarters of wheat from his land, and by the employment of a second capital of £1000 he obtain a further return of eighty-five, his landlord would have the power, at the expiration of his lease, of obliging him to pay fifteen quarters or an equivalent value for additional rent;

for there cannot be two rates of profit. If he is satisfied with a diminution of fifteen quarters in the return for his second £1000, it is because no employment more profitable can be found for it. The common rate of profit would be in that proportion, and if the original tenant refused, some other person would be found willing to give all which exceeded that rate of profit to the owner of the land from which he derived it.

In this case, as well as in the other, the capital last employed pays no rent. For the greater productive powers of the first £1000, fifteen quarters, is paid for rent, for the employment of the second £1000 no rent whatever is paid. If a third £1000 be employed on the same land, with a return of seventy-five quarters, rent will then be paid for the second £1000, and will be equal to the difference between the produce of these two, or ten quarters; and at the same time the rent for the first £1000 will rise from fifteen to twenty-five quarters; while the last £1000 will pay no rent whatever.

If, then, good land existed in a quantity much more abundant than the production of food for an increasing population required, or if capital could be indefinitely employed without a diminished return on the old land, there could be no rise of rent; for rent invariably proceeds from the employment of an additional quantity of labor with a proportionally less return.

The most fertile and most favorably situated land will be first cultivated, and the exchangeable value of its produce will be adjusted in the same manner as the exchangeable value of all other commodities, by the total quantity of labor necessary in various forms, from first to last, to produce it and bring it to market. When land of an inferior quality is taken into cultivation, the exchangeable value of raw produce will rise, because more labor is required to produce it.

The exchangeable value of all commodities, whether they be manufactured, or the produce of the mines, or the produce of land, is always regulated, not by the less quantity of labor that will suffice for their production under circumstances highly favorable, and exclusively enjoyed by those who have peculiar facilities of production; but by the greater quantity of labor necessarily bestowed on their production by those who have no such facilities; by those who continue to produce them under the most unfavorable circumstances; meaning—by the most unfavorable circumstances, the most unfavorable under which the quantity of produce required renders it necessary to carry on the production.

Thus, in a charitable institution, where the poor are set to work with the funds of benefactors, the general prices of the commodities, which are the produce of such work, will not be governed by the peculiar facilities afforded to these workmen, but by the common, usual, and natural difficulties which every other manufacturer will have to encounter. The manufacturer enjoying none of these facilities might indeed by driven altogether from the market if the supply afforded by these favored workmen were equal to all the wants of the community; but if he continued the trade, it would be only on condition that he should derive from it the usual and general rate of profits on stock; and that could only happen when his commodity sold for a price proportioned to the quantity of labor bestowed on its production.

It is true, that on the best land the same produce would still be obtained with the same labor as before, but its value would be enhanced in consequence of the diminished returns obtained by those who employed fresh labor and stock on the less fertile land. Notwithstanding, then, that the advantages of fertile over inferior lands are in no case lost, but only transferred from the cultivator or consumer to the landlord, yet, since more labor is required on the inferior lands, and since it is from such land only that we are enabled to furnish ourselves with the additional supply of raw produce, the comparative value of that produce will continue permanently above its former level, and make it exchange for more hats, cloth, shoes, etc., etc. in the production of which no such additional quantity of labor is required.

The reason, then, why raw produce rises in comparative value is because more labor is employed in the production of the last portion obtained, and not because a rent is paid to the landlord. The value of corn is regulated by the quantity of labor bestowed on its production on that quality of land, or with that portion of capital, which pays no rent. Corn is not high because a rent is paid, but a rent is paid because corn is high; and it has been justly observed that no reduction would take place in the price of corn although landlords should forego the whole of their rent. Such a measure would only enable some farmers to live like gentlemen, but would not diminish the quantity of labor necessary to raise raw produce on the least productive land in cultivation.

Nothing is more common than to hear of the advantages which the land possesses over every other source of useful produce, on account of the surplus which it yields in the form of rent. Yet when land is most abundant, when most productive, and most fertile, it yields no rent; and it is only when its powers decay, and less is yielded in return for labor, that a share of the original produce of the more fertile portions is set apart for rent. It is singular that this quality in the land, which should have been noticed as an imperfection compared with the natural agents by which manufactures are assisted, should have been pointed out as constituting its peculiar preeminence. If air, water, the elasticity of steam, and the pressure of the atmosphere were of various qualities; if they could be appropriated, and each quality existed only in moderate abundance, they, as well as the land, would afford a rent, as the successive qualities were brought into use. . . .

The rise of rent is always the effect of the increasing wealth of the country, and of the difficulty of providing food for its augmented population. It is a symptom, but it is never a cause of wealth; for wealth often increases most rapidly while rent is either stationary or even falling. Rent increases most rapidly as the disposable land decreases in its productive powers. Wealth increases most rapidly in those countries where the disposable land is most fertile, where importation is least restricted, and where, through agricultural improvements, production can be multiplied without any increase in the proportional quantity of labor, and where consequently the progress of rent is slow. . . .

It follows from the same principles that any circumstances in the society which should make it unnecessary to employ the same amount of capital on the land, and which should therefore make the portion last employed more productive, would lower rent. Any great reduction in the capital of a country which should materially diminish the funds destined for the maintenance of labor would naturally have this effect. Population regulates itself by the funds which are to employ it, and therefore always increases or diminishes with the increase or diminution of capital. Every reduction of capital is therefore necessarily followed by a less effective demand for corn, by a fall of price, and by diminished cultivation. In the reverse order to that in which the accumulation of capital raises rent will the diminution of it lower rent. Land of a less unproductive quality will be in succession relinquished, the exchangeable value of produce will fall, and land of a superior quality will be the land last cultivated, and that which will then pay no rent.

The same effects may, however, be produced when the wealth and population of a country are increased, if that increase is accompanied by such marked improvements in agriculture as shall have the same effect of diminishing the necessity of cultivating poorer lands, or of expending the same amount of capital on the cultivation of the more fertile portions. . . .

It is undoubtedly true that the fall in the relative price of raw produce, in consequence of the improvement in agriculture, or rather in consequence of less labor being bestowed on its production, would naturally lead to increased accumulation; for the profits of stock would be greatly augmented. This accumulation would lead to an increased demand for labor, to higher wages, to an increased population, to a further demand for raw produce, and to an increased cultivation. It is only, however, after the increase in the population that rent would be as high as before; that is to say, after No. 3 was taken into cultivation. A considerable period would have elapsed, attended with a positive diminution of rent.

But improvements in agriculture are of two kinds: those which increase the productive powers of the land and those which enable us, by improving our machinery, to obtain its produce with less labor. They both lead to a fall in the price of raw produce; they both affect rent, but they do not affect it equally. If they did not occasion a fall in the price of raw produce they would not be improvements; for it is the essential quality of an improvement to diminish the quantity of labor before required to produce a commodity; and this diminution cannot take place without a fall of its price or relative value.

The improvements which increase the productive powers of the land are such as the more skillful rotation of crops or the better choice of manure. These improvements absolutely enable us to obtain the same produce from a smaller quantity of land. If, by the introduction of a course of turnips, I can feed my sheep besides raising my corn, the land on which the sheep were before fed becomes unnecessary, and the same quantity of raw produce is raised by the employment of a less quantity of land. If I discover a manure which will enable me to make a piece of land produce 20 per cent more corn, I may withdraw at least a portion of my capital from the most unproductive part of my farm. But, as I before observed, it is not necessary that land should be thrown out of cultivation in order to reduce rent: to produce this effect, it is sufficient that successive portions of capital are employed on the same land with different results, and that the portion which gives the least results should be withdrawn. If, by the introduction of the turnip husbandry, or by the use of a more invigorating manure, I can obtain the same produce with less capital, and without disturbing the difference between the productive powers of the successive portions of capital, I shall lower rent, for a different and more productive portion will be that which will form the standard from which every other will be reckoned. . . .

But there are improvements which may lower the relative value of produce without lowering the corn rent, though they will lower the money rent of land. Such improvements do not increase the productive powers of the land, but they enable us to obtain its produce with less labor. They are rather directed to the formation of the capital applied to the land than to the cultivation of the land itself. Improvements in agricultural implements, such as the plow and the threshing machine, economy in the use of horses employed in husbandry, and a better knowledge of the veterinary art, are of this nature. Less capital, which is the same thing as less labor, will be employed on the land; but to obtain the same produce, less land cannot be cultivated. Whether improvements of this kind, however, affect corn rent must depend on the question whether the difference between the produce obtained by the employment of different portions of capital be increased, stationary, or diminished. If four portions of capital, 50, 60, 70, 80, be employed on the land, giving each the same results, and any improvement in the formation of such capital should enable me to withdraw 5 from each, so that they should be 45, 55, 65, and 75, no alteration would take place in the corn rent; but if the improvements were such as to enable me to make the whole saving on that portion of capital which is least productively employed, corn rent would immediately fall, because the difference between the capital most productive and the capital least productive would be diminished; and it is this difference which constitutes rent.

Without multiplying instances, I hope enough has been said to show that whatever diminishes the inequality in the produce obtained from successive portions of capital employed on the same or on new land tends to lower rent; and that whatever increases that inequality necessarily produces an opposite effect, and tends to raise it.

In speaking of the rent of the landlord, we have rather considered it as the proportion of the produce, obtained with a given capital on any given farm, without any reference to its exchangeable value; but since the same cause, the difficulty of production, raises the exchangeable value of raw produce, and raises also the proportion of raw produce paid to the landlord for rent, it is obvious that the landlord is doubly benefited by difficulty of production. First, he obtains a greater share, and, secondly, the commodity in which he is paid is of greater value. . . .

V. ON WAGES

The natural price of labor is that price which is necessary to enable the laborers, one with another, to subsist and to perpetuate their race, without either increase or diminution.

The power of the laborer to support himself, and the family which may be necessary to keep up the number of laborers, does not depend on the quantity of money which he may receive for wages, but on the quantity of food, necessaries, and conveniences become essential to him from habit which that money will purchase. The natural price of labor, therefore, depends on the price of the food, necessaries, and conveniences required for the support of the laborer and his family. With a rise in the price of food and necessaries, the natural price of labor will rise; with the fall in their price, the natural price of labor will fall.

With the progress of society the natural price of labor has always a tendency to rise, because one of the principal commodities by which its natural price is regulated has a tendency to become dearer from the greater difficulty of producing it. As, however, the improvements in agriculture, the discovery of new markets, whence provisions may be imported, may for a time counteract the tendency to a rise in the price of necessaries, and may even occasion their natural price to fall, so will the same causes produce the correspondent effects on the natural price of labor.

The natural price of all commodities, excepting raw produce and labor, has a tendency to fall in the progress of wealth and population, for though, on one hand, they are enhanced in real value, from the rise in the natural price of the raw material of which they are made, this is more than counterbalanced by the improvement in machinery, by the better division and distribution of labor, and by the increasing skill, both in science and art, of the producers. . . .

It is when the market price of labor exceeds its natural price that the condition of the laborer is flourishing and happy, that he has it in his power to command a greater proportion of the necessaries and enjoyments of life, and therefore to rear a healthy and numerous family. When, however, by the encouragement which high wages give to the increase of population, the number of laborers is increased, wages again fall to their natural price, and indeed from a reaction sometimes fall below it.

When the market price of labor is below its natural price, the condition of the laborers is most wretched; then poverty deprives them of those comforts which custom renders absolute necessaries. It is only after their privations have reduced their number, or the demand for labor has increased, that the market price of labor will rise to its natural price, and that the laborer will have the moderate comforts which the natural rate of wages will afford.

Notwithstanding the tendency of wages to conform to their natural rate, their market rate may, in an improving society, for an indefinite period, be constantly above it; for no sooner may the pulse which an increased capital gives to a new demand for labor be obeyed, than another increase of capital may produce the same effect; and thus, if the increase of capital be gradual and constant, the demand for labor may give a continued stimulus to an increase of people. . . .

It is not to be understood that the natural price of labor, estimated even in food and necessaries, is absolutely fixed and constant. It varies at different times in the same country, and very materially differs in different countries. It essentially depends on the habits and customs of the people. An English laborer would consider his wages under their natural rate, and too scanty to support a family, if they enabled him to purchase no other food than potatoes, and to live in no better habitation than a mud cabin; yet these moderate demands of nature are often deemed sufficient in countries where "man's life is cheap" and his wants easily satisfied. Many of the conveniences now enjoyed in an English cottage would have been thought luxuries at an earlier period of our history. . . .

It has been calculated that under favorable circumstances population may be doubled in twenty-five years; but under the same favorable circumstances the whole capital of a country might possibly be doubled in a shorter period.

In that case, wages during the whole period would have a tendency to rise, because the demand for labor would increase still faster than the supply.

In new settlements, where the arts and knowledge of countries far advanced in refinement are introduced, it is probable that capital has a tendency to increase faster than mankind; and if the deficiency of laborers were not supplied by more populous countries, this tendency would very much raise the price of labor. In proportion as these countries become populous, and land of a worse quality is taken into cultivation, the tendency to an increase of capital diminishes; for the surplus produce remaining, after satisfying the wants of the existing population, must necessarily be in proportion to the facility of production, viz. to the smaller number of persons employed in production. Although, then, it is probable that, under the most favorable circumstances, the power of production is still greater than that of population, it will not long continue so; for the land being limited in quantity, and differing in quality, with every increased portion of capital employed on it there will be a decreased rate of production, whilst the power of population continues always the same.

In those countries where there is abundance of fertile land, but where, from the ignorance, indolence, and barbarism of the inhabitants, they are exposed to all the evils of want and famine, and where it has been said that population presses against the means of subsistence, a very different remedy should be applied from that which is necessary in long settled countries, where, from the diminishing rate of the supply of raw produce, all the evils of a crowded population are experienced. In one case, the evil proceeds from bad government, from the insecurity of property, and from a want of education in all ranks of the people. To be made happier they require only to be better governed and instructed, as the augmentation of capital, beyond the augmentation of people, would be the inevitable result. No increase in the population can be too great, as the powers of production are still greater. In the other case, the population increases faster than the funds required for its support. Even exertion of industry, unless accompanied by a diminished rate of increase in the population, will add to the evil, for production cannot keep pace with it.

With a population pressing against the means of subsistence, the only remedies are a reduction of people or a more rapid accumulation of capital. In rich countries, where all the fertile land is already cultivated, the latter remedy is neither very practicable nor very desirable, because its effect would be, if pushed very far, to render all classes equally poor. But in poor countries, where there are abundant means of production in store, from fertile land not yet brought into cultivation, it is the only safe and efficacious means of removing the evil, particularly as its effect would be to elevate all classes of the people. . . .

In the natural advance of society, the wages of labor will have a tendency to fall, as far as they are regulated by supply and demand; for the supply of laborers will continue to increase at the same rate, whilst the demand for them will increase at a slower rate. . . . ; but we must not forget that wages are also regulated by the prices of the commodities on which they are expended.

As population increases, these necessaries will be constantly rising in price, because more labor will be necessary to produce them. If, then, the money wages of labor should fall, whilst every commodity on which the wages of labor were expended rose, the laborer would be double affected, and would be soon totally deprived of subsistence. Instead, therefore, of the money wages of labor falling, they would rise; but they would not rise sufficiently to enable the laborer to purchase as many comforts and necessaries as he did before the rise in the price of those commodities. . . .

Notwithstanding, then, that the laborer would be really worse paid, yet this increase in his wages would necessarily diminish the profits of the manufacturer; for his goods would sell at no higher price, and yet the expense of producing them would be increased.

It appears, then, that the same cause which raises rent, namely, the increasing difficulty of providing an additional quantity of food with the same proportional quantity of labor, will also raise wages; and therefore if money be of unvarying value, both rent and wages will have a tendency to rise with the progress of wealth and population.

But there is this essential difference between the rise of rent and the rise of wages. The rise in the money value of rent is accompanied by an increased share of the produce; not only is the landlord's money rent greater, but his corn rent also; he will have more corn, and each defined measure of that corn will exchange for a greater quantity of all other goods which have not been raised in value. The fate of the laborer will be less happy; he will receive more money wages, it is true, but his corn wages will be reduced; and not only his command of corn, but his general condition will be deteriorated, by his finding it more difficult to maintain the market rate of wages above their natural rate. . . .

In proportion as corn became dear, he would receive less corn wages, but his money wages would always increase, whilst his enjoyments, on the above supposition, would be precisely the same. But as other commodities would be raised in price in proportion as raw produce entered into their composition, he would have more to pay for some of them. Although his tea, sugar, soap, candles, and house rent would probably be no dearer, he would pay more for his bacon, cheese, butter, linen, shoes, and cloth; and therefore, even with the above increase of wages, his situation would be comparatively worse. . . .

VI. ON PROFITS

We have seen that the price of corn is regulated by the quantity of labor necessary to produce it, with that portion of capital which pays no rent. We have seen, too, that all manufactured commodities rise and fall in price in proportion as more or less labor becomes necessary to their production. Neither the farmer who cultivates that quantity of land which regulates price, nor the manufacturer who manufactures goods, sacrifices any portion of the produce for rent. The whole value of their commodities is divided into two portions only: one constitutes the profits of stock, the other the wages of labor.

Supposing corn and manufactured goods always to sell at the same price, profits would be high or low in proportion as wages were low or high. But suppose corn to rise in price because more labor is necessary to produce it; that cause will not raise the price of manufactured goods in the production of which no additional quantity of labor is required. If, then, wages continued the same, the profit of manufacturers would remain the same; but if, as is absolutely certain, wages should rise with the rise of corn, then their profits would necessarily fall. . . .

It is to be understood that I am speaking of profits generally. I have already remarked that the market price of a commodity may exceed its natural or necessary price, as it may be produced in less abundance than the new demand for it requires. This, however, is but a temporary effect. The high profits on capital employed in producing that commodity will naturally attract capital to that trade and as soon as the requisite funds are supplied, the quantity of the commodity is duly increased, its price will fall, and the profits of the trade will conform to the general level. A fall in the general rate of profits is by no means incompatible with a partial rise of profits in particular employments. It is through the inequality of profits that capital is moved from one employment to another. . . .

The natural tendency of profits then is to fall; for, in the progress of society and wealth, the additional quantity of food required is obtained by the sacrifice of more and more labor. This tendency, this gravitation as it were of profits, is happily checked at repeated intervals by the improvements in machinery connected with the production of necessaries, as well as by dis-coveries in the science of agriculture, which enable us to relinquish a portion of labor before required, and therefore to lower the price of the prime neces-sary of the laborer. The rise in the price of necessaries and in the wages of labor is, however, limited; for as soon as wages should be equal to . . . the whole receipts of the farmer, there must be an end of accumulation; for no capital can then yield any profit whatever, and no additional labor can be demanded, and consequently population will have reached its highest point. Long, indeed, before this period, the very low rate of profits will have arrested all accumulation, and almost the whole produce of the country, after paying the laborers, will be the property of the owners of land and the receivers of tithes and taxes. . . .

I have already said that long before this state of prices was become permanent there would be no motive for accumulation; for no one accumulates but with a view to make his accumulation productive, and it is only when so employed that it operates on profits. Without a motive there could be no accumulation and consequently such a state of prices never could take place. The farmer and manufacturer can no more live without profit than the laborer without wages. Their motive for accumulation will diminish with every diminution of profit, and will cease altogether when their profits are so low as not to afford them an adequate compensation for their trouble, and the risk which they must necessarily encounter in employing their capital productively. . . .

In all countries, and all times, profits depend on the quantity of labor requisite to provide necessaries for the laborers on that land or with that capital which yields no rent. The effects then of accumulation will be different in dif-ferent countries, and will depend chiefly on the fertility of the land. However extensive a country may be where the land is of a poor quality, and where the importation of food is prohibited, the most moderate accumulations of capital will be attended with great reductions in the rate of profit and a rapid rise in rent; and on the contrary a small but fertile country, particularly if it freely permits the importation of food, may accumulate a large stock of capital without any great diminution in the rate of profits, or any great increase in the rent of land. . . .

VII. ON FOREIGN TRADE

No extension of foreign trade will immediately increase the amount of value in a country, although it will very powerfully contribute to increase the mass of commodities, and therefore the sum of enjoyments. As the value of all foreign goods is measured by the quantity of the produce of our land and labor which is given in exchange for them, we should have no greater value if, by the discovery of new markets, we obtained double the quantity of foreign goods in exchange for a given quantity of ours. If by the purchase of English goods to the amount of £1000 a merchant can obtain a quantity of foreign goods, which he can sell in the English market for £1200, he will obtain 20 per cent. profit by such an employment of his capital; but neither his gains, nor the value of the commodities imported, will be increased or diminished by the greater or small quantity of foreign goods obtained. Whether, for example, he imports twenty-five or fifty pipes of wine, his interest can be no way affected if at one time the twenty-five pipes, and another the fifty pipes, equally sell for £1200. In either case his profit will be limited to £200, the profits of this individual merchant would exceed the general rate of profits, and capital would naturally flow into their advantageous trade, till the fall of the price of wine had brought everything to the former level. . . .

If more of the produce of the land and labor of England be employed in the purchase of foreign commodities, less can be employed in the purchase of other things, and therefore fewer hats, shoes, etc., will be required. At the same time that capital is liberated from the production of shoes, hats, etc., more must be employed in manufacturing those commodities with which foreign commodities are purchased; and, consequently, in all cases the demand for foreign and home commodities together, as far as regards value, is limited by the revenue and capital of the country. If one increases the other must diminish. If the quantity of wine imported in exchange for the same quantity of English commodities be doubled, the people of England can either consume double the quantity of wine that they did before or the same quantity of wine and a greater quantity of English commodities. . . .

It is not, therefore, in consequence of the extension of the market that the rate of profit is raised, although such extension may be equally efficacious in increasing the mass of commodities, and may thereby enable us to augment the funds destined for the maintenance of labor, and the materials on which labor may be employed. It is quite as important to the happiness of mankind, that our enjoyments should be increased by the better distribution of labor, by each country producing those commodities for which by its situation, its climate, and its other natural or artificial advantages, it is adapted, and by their exchanging them for the commodities of other countries, as that they should be augmented by a rise in the rate of profits.

It has been my endeavor to show throughout this work that the rate of profits can never be increased but by a fall in wages, and that there can be no permanent fall of wages but in consequence of a fall of the necessaries on which wages are expended. If, therefore, by the extension of foreign trade, or by improvements in machinery, the food and necessaries of the laborer can be brought to market, at a reduced price, profits will rise. If, instead of growing our own corn, or manufacturing the clothing and other necessaries of the laborer, we discover a new market from which we can supply ourselves with these commodities at a cheaper price, wages will fall and profits rise; but if the commodities obtained at a cheaper rate, by the extension of foreign commerce, or by the improvement of machinery, be exclusively the commodities consumed by the rich, no alteration will take place in the rate of profits. The rate of wages would not be affected, although wine, velvets, silks, and other expensive commodities should fall 50 per cent., and consequently profits would continue unaltered.

Foreign trade, then, though highly beneficial to a country, as it increases the amount and variety of the objects on which revenue may be expended, and affords, by the abundance and cheapness of commodities, incentives to saving, and to the accumulation of capital, has no tendency to raise the profit of stock unless the commodities imported be of that description on which the wages of labor are expended. . . .

VIII. ON TAXES

Taxes are a portion of the produce of the land and labor of a country placed at the disposal of the government, and are always ultimately paid either from the capital or from the revenue of the country. . . .

If the consumption of the government when increased by the levy of additional taxes be met either by an increased production or by a diminished consumption on the part of the people, the taxes will fall upon revenue, and the national capital will remain unimpaired; but if there be no increased production or diminished unproductive consumption on the part of the people, the taxes will necessarily fall on capital, that is to say, they will impair the fund allotted to productive consumption.

In proportion as the capital of a country is diminished, its productions will be necessarily diminished; and, therefore, if the same unproductive expenditure on the part of the people and of the government continue, with a constantly diminishing annual reproduction, the resources of the people and the state will fall away with increasing rapidity, and distress and ruin will follow.

Notwithstanding the immense expenditure of the English government during the last twenty years, there can be little doubt but that the increased production on the part of the people has more than compensated for it. The national capital has not merely been unimpaired, it has been greatly increased, and the annual revenue of the people, even after the payment of their taxes, is probably greater at the present time than at any former period of our history. . . .

Still, however, it is certain that but for taxation this increase of capital would have been much greater. There are no taxes which have not a tendency to lessen the power to accumulate. . . . Some taxes will produce these effects in a much greater degree than others; but the great evil of taxation is to be found, not so much in any selection of its objects as in the general amount of its effects taken collectively. . . .

QUESTIONS FOR DISCUSSION

1   Two types of wine are produced with the same amount of labor and the same machine. But the first takes twice as long to bring to market. By Ricardo's reckoning, would the two types sell for the same price? Why or why not?

2   Can Ricardo successfully explain the wage differentials which appear in the market by his cost theory?

3   Why does Ricardo's proof that the rate (and share) of interest must fall with continued accumulation not also prove that the *share* of rent must rise, assuming that wages are set at their subsistence level?

READING 9

Henry George (1839-1897) has been one of the most widely influential followers of Ricardo around the world. A journalist and gold prospector in California, George was impressed by the phenomenon of land speculation. In George's opinion, the increase in land values in urban areas represented an "unearned increment" to the owners unrelated to productive contribution to society. After all, as Ricardo had taught, the development of population and society is what makes land scarce. Land prices, of course, are merely the capitalized value of rent, which depends on the (actual or expected) locational or agricultural advantages of any plot over free land at the margin of cultivation. Land held vacant for speculation hinders rational development, in George's view. High and rising rents, moreover, increase the prices for urban services, concentrate wealth, and aggravate poverty.

More radical than the English classical writers, George felt property in unimproved land was also immoral. Hence, he campaigned for a confiscatory tax on land site values. Henry George's *Progress and Poverty* (1879) has gone through many printings and translations. It remains the revered text of the Single Tax Movement, which has had some influence in the United States and New Zealand. His basic ideas continue to have wider influence.

A columnist for the liberal *The New Republic,* noting the rise in the real cost of homes in America, recently wrote:

The bloated prices of existing houses may make the owners feel rich, but they add nothing to the nation's wealth. A house is exactly the same house after it doubles in "value." In fact, as my favorite economist, Henry George, pointed out a century ago, inflated land values make the economy less efficient. They operate like a tax on the truly productive factors, labor and capital. Housing inflation has depressed our economy, frenzied our psyches, divided our society. A turnaround would be nerve-wracking but no bad thing.[21]

---

[21]TRB, "Blow Your House Down," *The New Republic,* October 10, 1988, pp. 4, 41.

In George's times one could conceive of a single tax covering all necessary state expenses. Late nineteenth century government consumption took only 6% of the American national product; rent was a larger share (about 7% in 1899-1908) of national income than it is today (around 4%); hence a tax of 100% on rentals, with exemptions for the value of structures and improvements, might have gone a long way in financing the Federal and state budgets. Not so today, when government consumption takes nearly a quarter of GNP. A single tax would merely cover the budget deficit!

Any single tax on land values also raises the question of fairness. If people have bought land in good faith for its income and appreciation, could a democratic government justifiably expropriate their income and capital gains? Even if site values could be appraised accurately—hardly an easy matter, even when such large taxes are being contemplated—a tax on land would create allocational distortions where other factors of production (e.g., commercial structures) are complementary to land.

Progress and Poverty

Henry George

Introductory

THE PROBLEM

The present century has been marked by a prodigious increase in wealth-producing power. . . . At the beginning of this marvelous era it was natural to expect, and it was expected, that labor-saving inventions would lighten the toil and improve the condition of the laborer; that the enormous increase in the power of producing wealth would make real poverty a thing of the past. . . .

Now, however, we are coming into collision with facts which there can be no mistaking. From all parts of the civilized world come complaints of industrial depression; of labor condemned to involuntary idleness; of capital massed wasting; of pecuniary distress among business men; of want and suffering and anxiety among the working classes. . . .

The phenomena we class together and speak of as industrial depression are but intensifications of phenomena which always accompany material progress, and which show themselves more clearly and strongly as material progress goes on. Where the conditions to which material progress everywhere tends are most fully realized—that is to say, where population is densest, wealth greatest, and the machinery of production and exchange most highly developed—we find the deepest poverty, the sharpest struggle for existence, and the most of enforced idleness. . . .

I propose in the following pages to attempt to solve by the methods of political economy the great problem I have outlined. I propose to seek the law which associates poverty with progress, and increases want with advancing wealth; and I believe that in the explanation of this paradox we shall find the explanation of those recurring seasons of industrial and commercial paralysis which, viewed independently of their relations of more general phenomena, seen, so inexplicable. . . .

BOOK III: THE LAWS OF DISTRIBUTION

. . . There must be land before labor can be exerted, and labor must be exerted before capital can be produced. Capital is a result of labor, and is used by labor to assist it in further production. Labor is the active and initial force, and labor is therefore the employer of capital. . . . Capital is not a necessary factor in production. Labor exerted upon land can produce wealth without the aid of capital, and in the necessary genesis of things must so produce wealth before capital can exist. Therefore the law of rent and the law of wages must correlate each other and form a perfect whole without reference to the law of capital, as otherwise these laws would not fit the cases which can readily be imagined, and which to some degree actually exist, in which capital takes no part in production. . . . [Chapter I]

Chapter 2. Rent and the Law of Rent

No matter what are its capabilities, land can yield no rent and have no value until some one is willing to give labor or the results of labor for the privilege of using it; and what any one will thus give depends not upon the capacity of the land, but upon its capacity as compared with that of land that can be had for nothing. . . .

This law, which of course applies to land used for other purposes than agriculture, and to all natural agencies, such as mines, fisheries, etc., has been exhaustively explained and illustrated by all the leading economists since Ricardo. But its mere statement has all the force of a self-evident proposition, for it is clear that the effect of competition is to make the lowest reward for which labor and capital will engage in production, the highest that they can claim; and hence to enable the owner of more productive land to appropriate in rent all the return above that required to recompense labor and capital at the ordinary rate—that is to say, what they can obtain upon the least productive land in use, or at the least productive point, where, of course, no rent is paid. . . .

The increase of rent which goes on in progressive countries is at once seen to be the key which explains why wages and interest fail to increase with increase of productive power. For the wealth produced in every community is divided into two parts by what may be called the rent line, which is fixed by the margin of cultivation, or the return which labor and capital could obtain from such natural opportunities as are free to them without the payment of rent. From the part of the produce below this line wages and interest must be paid. All that is above goes to the owners of land. Thus, where the value of land is low, there may be a small production of wealth, and yet a high rate of wages and interest, as we see in new countries. And, where the value of land is high, there may be a very large production of wealth, and yet a low rate of wages and interest, as we see in old countries. And, where productive power increases, as it is increasing in all progressive countries, wages and interest will be affected, not by the increase, but by the manner in which rent is affected. If the value of land increases proportionately, all the increased production will be swallowed up by rent, and wages and interest will remain as before. If the value of land increases in greater ratio than productive power, rent will swallow up even more than the increase; and while the produce of labor and capital will be much larger, wages and interest will fall. It is only when the value of land fails to increase as rapidly as productive power, that wages and interest can increase with the increase of productive power. All this is exemplified in actual fact. . .

BOOK IV: EFFECT OF MATERIAL PROGRESS UPON THE DISTRIBUTION OF WEALTH

Chapter 2. The Effect of Increase of Population upon the Distribution of Wealth

The manner in which increasing population advances rent . . . is that the increased demand for subsistence forces production to inferior soil or to inferior productive points. . . . The effect of increasing population upon the distribution of wealth is to increase rent, and consequently to diminish the proportion of the produce which goes to capital and labor, in two ways: First, By lowering the margin of cultivation. Second, by bringing out in land special capabilities otherwise latent, and by attaching special capabilities to particular lands. I am disposed to think that the latter mode, to which little attention has been given by political economists is really the most important.

BOOK V: THE PROBLEM SOLVED

Chapter 2. The Persistence of Poverty Amid Advancing Wealth

. . . The reason why, in spite of the increase of productive power, wages constantly tend to a minimum which will give but a bare living, is that, with increase in productive power, rent tends to even greater increase, thus producing a constant tendency to the forcing down of wages. . . .
Look over the world today, comparing different countries with each other, and you will see that it is not the abundance of capital or the productiveness of labor that makes wages high or low; but the extent to which the monopolizers of land can, in rent, levy tribute upon the earnings of labor. Is it not a notorious fact, known to the most ignorant, that new countries, where the aggregate wealth is small, but where land is cheap, are always better countries for the laboring classes than the rich countries, where land is dear? Wherever you find land relatively low, will you not find wages relatively high? And wherever land is high, will you not find wages low? As land increases in value, poverty deepens and pauperism appears. In the new settlements, where land is cheap, you will find no beggars and the inequalities in condition are very slight. In the great cities where land is so valuable that it is measured by the foot, you will find the extremes of poverty and of luxury. And this disparity in

condition between the two extremes of the social scale may always be measured by the price of land. . . .

It is not in the relations of capital and labor; it is not in the pressure of population against subsistence that an explanation of the unequal development of our civilization is to be found. The great cause of inequality in the distribution of wealth is inequality in the ownership of land. The ownership of land is the great fundamental fact which ultimately determines the social, the political, and consequently the intellectual and moral condition of a people. . . .

BOOK VI: Chapter 2. The True Remedy

There is but one way to remove an evil—and that is, to remove its cause. Poverty deepens as wealth increases, and wages are forced down while productive power grows, because land, which is the source of all wealth and the field of all labor, is monopolized. To extirpate poverty, to make wages what justice commands they should be, the full earnings of the laborer, we must therefore substitute for the individual ownership of land a common ownership. Nothing else will go to the cause of the evil—in nothing else is there the slightest hope. . . .

We must make land common property.

Book VIII: Chapter 2. How Equal Rights to the Land May be Asserted and Secured

But a question of method remains. How shall we do it? . . . I do not propose either to purchase or to confiscate private property in land. The first would be unjust; the second, needless. . . . *It is not necessary to confiscate land; it is only necessary to confiscate rent.*

We already take some rent in taxation. We have only to make some changes in our modes of taxation to take it all. . . . In this way the state may become the universal landlord without calling herself so, and without assuming a single new function. In form, the ownership of land would remain just as now. No owner of land need be dispossessed, and no restriction need be placed upon the amount of land anyone could hold. For, rent being taken by the state in taxes, land, no matter in whose name it stood, or in what parcels it was held, would be really common property, and every member of the community would participate in the advantages of its ownership.

Now, insomuch as the taxation of rent, or land values, must necessarily be increased just as we abolish other taxes, we may put the proposition into practical form by proposing—

To abolish all taxation save that upon land values. . . .

BOOK IX: Chapter 1. Of the Effect upon the Production of Wealth

To abolish the taxation which . . . now hampers every wheel of exchange and presses upon every form of industry would be like removing an immense weight from a powerful spring. . . . And to shift the burden of taxation from production and exchange to the value or rent of land would not merely be to give new stimulus to the production of wealth; it would be to open new opportunities. For under this system no one would care to hold land unless to use it, and land now withheld from use would everywhere be thrown open to improvement.

The selling price of land would fall; land speculation would receive its death blow; land monopolization would no longer pay. Millions and millions of acres from which settlers are now shut out by high prices would be abandoned by their present owners or sold to settlers upon nominal terms. And this not merely on the frontiers, but within what are now considered well-settled districts. . . .

Consider the effect of such a change upon the labor market. Competition would no longer be one-sided as now. Instead of laborers competing with each other for employment, and in their competition cutting down wages to the point of bare subsistence, employers would everywhere be competing for laborers, and wages would rise to the fair earnings of labor. . . . The employers of labor would not have merely to bid against other employers, all feeling the stimulus of greater trade and increased profits, but against the ability of laborers to become their own employers upon the natural opportunities freely opened to them by the tax which prevented monopolization. . . .

Chapter 2. Of the Effect upon Distribution and thence upon Production

To relieve land and capital from all taxation, direct and indirect, and to throw the burden upon rent, would be, as far as it went, to counteract [the constant] tendency to inequality, and, if it went so far as to take in taxation the whole of rent, the cause of inequality would be totally destroyed. Rent, instead of causing inequality, as now, would then promote equality. Labor and capital would then receive the whole produce, minus that portion taken by the state in the taxation of land values, which, being applied to public purposes, would be equally distributed in public benefits. . . .

QUESTIONS FOR DISCUSSION

1   Wouldn't a tax on the value of central business district real estate simply raise the price of hotel rooms, clothing, and restaurant meals bought there?
2   Do you think that private ownership of land improves the income distribution in our society? How about the preservation of the environment?
3   In what sense is *The New Republic* writer correct in saying that high housing values are a tax on truly productive factors?

Karl Marx

CHAPTER 4

MARXISM AND NEO-MARXISM

EDITOR'S INTRODUCTION

The great revolutionary theorist **Karl Marx** (1818-1883) consciously constructed his doctrine in opposition to the bourgeois (traditional middle-class) society. Marx criticized the doctrines of previous political economists, who he said justified the privileges of that society. Nevertheless, he drew elements from a number of Western intellectual traditions, giving these prior ideas a revolutionary twist, as well as a coherence, that no opposition perspective has had before or since. Marx combined German idealistic philosophy in the tradition of **G. W. F. Hegel** (1770-1831) with French leftist politics as well as Ricardian economics. These influences can be traced sequentially to Marx's own stays in several Western European cities.

A radical German-Jewish student who resided in Berlin and the Rhineland until 1843, Marx absorbed the Left Hegelian dialectic materialism of **Ludwig Feuerbach** (1804-1872) and others. This mode of philosophical speculation provided him with a stage theory of history, according to which society progresses from lower to higher stages of human freedom, with correspondingly greater ability to control the material environment. But Marx transformed this conservative Hegelian tradition into a revolutionary activism: "The philosophers have only *interpreted* the world, in various ways. The point, however, is to *change* it."[1]

Each successive stage is identified by Marx with an ever more numerous social class of people who assume a ruling position—first slave-holders, then feudal lords who have control over land and serfs, then capitalists who control

---

[1]Karl Marx, "Theses on Feuerbach" (1845), translated by Friedrich Engels in the appendix to *Ludwig Feuerbach and the End of Classical German Philosophy* in Karl Marx and Frederick Engels, *Selected Works,* vol. 1 (Moscow: Progress, 1969), p. 15.

the physical means of production, and finally "communism," in which the workers would rule without class antagonists.[2] With the advent of communism, since scarcity would still prevail, the dictatorship of the proletariat would follow the socialist principle of distribution according to labor contribution.[3] Eventually, this "lower" stage of communist development would give way to a higher stage of "full communism"—in which people would work according to their abilities and interests and would consume according to their needs.[4]

The logical and rational progression of these stages is a strong reminder of the Hegelian motto: "All that is real is rational, all that is rational is real." Like Hegel's version of history, which culminated in the Prussian monarchy, Marx's version of history proceeds by thesis-antithesis-synthesis, a logical dialectic in which conceptual "contradictions" express themselves in real conflict. In other words, violent clashes between the groups representing the incompatible concepts or principles—the exploiters and exploited of each stage—punctuate the stepwise progression of human history.

The second important influence on Marx came during his residence in Paris and Brussels in the years surrounding the famous 1848 revolutions. About then Marx assumed the intellectual leadership of a clandestine political group by writing the *Communist Manifesto* (1848). This short tract made far-reaching demands upon the new parliamentary democracies of the West to prepare the way for an inclusive social democracy well beyond anything then existent. By demanding a progressive income tax, nationalizations, and free public education, the Communist League and allied Social-Democrats in France extended the program of even the most liberal-democratic element of the French Revolution.

Marx and his collaborator Friedrich Engels adopted some themes of French socialist criticism: that the artisans and peasants were being ruined by modern industry, that the rich-poor gap was growing, that the bourgeoisie was incapable of managing a modern economy, and that competing industrialists would bring on a war of extermination between nations. From the anarchistic socialism of **P. J. Proudhon** (1809-1865) Marx also grudgingly adopted his condemnation of all private property. To replace it, Marx and Engels called for social ownership, rational planning, and public works—all measures associated with the writings and followers of **Henri Comte de Saint-Simon** (1760-1825). As we shall see, however, Marx was impatient with the "petit bourgeois" (small-scale, anti-modern), pacifist, reformist, and "utopian" characteristics of many of the socialist blueprints which were well known in France (such as that of **Charles Fourier**, 1772-1837). These socialist reformers preferred to address their blueprints to the ruling and middle classes, rather than the proletariat:

---

[2]A primeval tribal form, the "Asiatic mode of production," and two other variants of peasant production may be ignored here. If they be included, the possibility of multiple paths of development must be conceded. F. L. Pryor, "Classification and Analysis of Precapitalist Economic Systems by Marx and Engels," *History of Political Economy* 14:4 (1982), pp. 521-542.

[3]See Marx's *Critique of the Gotha Program* (1875).

[4]*The German Ideology* (1846).

> Economists, philanthropists, . . . temperance fanatics, hole-and-corner reformers of every imaginable kind desire the existing state of society without its revolutionary elements . . . to lessen the cost of bourgeois government for the benefit of the working class,

wrote Marx ironically in the *Communist Manifesto*. Instead of marshalling ethical arguments, which Marx considered insufferably sentimental and hopeless, he sought to prove that actual historical forces would impress the truths of "scientific socialism" upon the minds of humankind.

Finally—and most important for his economic perspective—during his long exile in London from 1849 until his death, Marx studied and adapted Ricardian classical political economy. Like the classical school, Marx provisionally adopted the labor theory of value—not as an approximation as in Ricardo, nor as a theory of primitive distribution, as in Smith—but as a statement about the ultimate source of value and justification for labor ownership of the fruits of production.

For his theory of exchange value (relative price), Marx essentially adopted Ricardo's notion of the long-run equilibrium cost of production (see Chapter 3), which implies that goods with different capital intensities will *not* be traded according to labor embodied. In addition, monopoly and short-run forces would, as Ricardo and Smith understood, draw price away from average cost. As for wages, Marx supposes they will be paid by the wage fund available (termed *"v"* for variable capital). Average wages could temporarily diverge from the customary subsistence level in booms or busts. Wage differentials among skill grades are also dealt with similarly in Marx and Ricardo, and Ricardo is actually praised by the radical Marx for admitting that the introduction of machinery could harm the employment prospects of the workers. Moreover, Marx adopted the Ricardo-Malthus analysis of differential rent. Unlike Ricardo, though, Marx emphasized that bargaining by employers could lengthen hours and reduce real wages to the working class.

Marx was well aware of these borrowings but claimed a certain degree of originality, too. In a letter to his publisher, Josef Weydemeyer, dated March 5, 1852, Marx wrote that his innovation consisted in conceiving of classes as bound up with particularly historical phases in the development of production and in proving that the class struggle would "necessarily" lead to the "dictatorship of the proletariat" as a transition to the "abolition of all classes."

As an economic perspective, Marxism is characterized by:

1 The effort to find a *class-based* conceptualization—the "mode of production"—for each society at every period in its history. The sequence is universal: every society ought to go through feudal and capitalist stages, since then the "forces of production" (skills, capital, and specialization) would be prepared for the next, higher stage of development. All the associated legal, political, and cultural institutions are integrated by this class-based conception, "the relations of production," essentially the means by which economic surplus above subsistence is extracted from the ultimate producers for the purposes of the privileged classes. Under feudalism, for example, legal, customary, and religious obligations combined to authorize political, military, and ecclesiastical exploitation. Capitalism, a more progressive if less stable mode, also has a supportive ideology, of which the core is the notions of property rights and impersonal market forces. Despite these supports, Marx sees elements in capitalism which are certain eventually to bring its overthrow—concentration of workers and the replacement of small capitalists by hired managers running enormous enterprises.

2 The latest stage is characterized by the decline of preexisting gradations and classes and the *polarization* of the class structure between two principal antagonists, bourgeoisie and proletariat. Thus, for Marx, the landlords, the old middle classes, and the artisans must disappear during the capitalist stage because of the superior competitive strength of modern industry in supplying a world market. Oddly, Marx comes to this un-Ricardian conclusion through some Ricardian assumptions. Capitalists are forced by competition to accumulate and to move into sectors with the highest return, thereby driving all returns down to zero. Their accumulation drives wages temporarily above long-run subsistence. Despite higher worker incomes, the capitalists' inability to sell output profitably leads to crisis and eventual revolt, even if war and famine are avoided.

3 Historical change comes from *conflict* between class-based groups, like unions on the workers' side or corporations, trusts, or interlocking directorates on the side of capital. The most important organization supporting the capitalist side is the state. According to the *Communist Manifesto,* "The executive of the modern State is but a committee for managing the common affairs of the whole bourgeoisie." Thus in contrast to the neoclassical mainstream, the Marxist perspective concedes the state little real independence.[5]

The capitalist state may channel funds into accumulation, suppress worker radicalism, mobilize paupers for manual work in factories, and moderate competition. It can also enforce laws (e.g., the British Factory Acts) designed to prevent individual employers from overexploiting the working class. Yet such reforms, however beneficial to the working class when and if enforced, are supported only so long as they reinforce capitalist class control over the system. Because of this stress on control, the state probably would retard overall economic progress. Less and less able to assure economic development, it must be overthrown by the workers, joined perhaps by paid managers and revolutionary intellectuals.

Within this Marxist perspective, Marx, Engels, and later Marxists advanced several different, even contradictory, theories of capitalist breakdown. Since Marx edited for publication only volume I of *Das Kapital* (1867), we do not know to what extent the distinct and even contradictory materials of vols. II and III (edited by Engels and published in 1885 and 1894), not to mention other unedited earlier and later manuscripts, would have been altered by Marx had he lived on. Marx has three theories of "crisis":

1 (Relative) impoverishment and underconsumption. According to this theory, capitalists' power and technological change create a vast "reserve army

---

5The exception is those transitional periods of divided upper classes when a military leader may take charge. Cf. Marx's *The Eighteenth Brumaire of Louis Napoleon* (1853).

of the unemployed," surplus labor who compete among themselves to drive the wages down to or even below subsistence.

> The price of a commodity, and therefore also of labor, is equal to its cost of production. In proportion, therefore, as the repulsiveness of labor increases, the wage decreases. Nay more, in proportion as the use of machinery and division of labor increases . . . the burden of toil also increases, whether by prolongation of working hours or by the increase of the work exacted in a given time or by the increased speed of the machinery.[6]

Because of insufficient purchasing power in the hands of consumers, capitalist industry suffers continual stagnation. Prosperity can be restored temporarily only by greater exploitation of markets or conquest of new ones.

2 The "law" of declining profit. Technological change, thought Marx and most of his contemporaries, would ordinarily be labor-saving and capital-using. In value terms, the profit rate (p') equals the surplus (s) of value over wages paid, divided by the flow of capital invested in materials and depreciation (c) and wages advanced (v):

$$p' = s / (c + v) = s / (c + v) \times v / v = [s / v] \times [v / (c + v)]$$

Defining Marx's "organic composition of capital," his expression for the capital intensity of production, as $q' = c / (c + v) = 1 - [v / (c + v)]$, we obtain a new expression for the profit rate:

$$p' = [s / v] \times (1 - q')$$

meaning that the profit rate is the product of the rate of exploitation $[s/v]$ times one minus the organic composition of capital. If the rate of exploitation is determined in the workplace bargaining over the length of the working day and does not vary over the short period, then any increase in capital intensity owing to technological change will *lower* the profit rate.[7]

If the new technology raises the rate of surplus value by permitting workers to earn their subsistence in less time, then there would be some offset

---

[6]Inaugural Address to the International Workingmen's Association (1864).

[7]The innovating capitalists, of course, may raise their profit rates temporarily; the expectation of higher or more stable profits is the principal incentive to innovate. But eventually greater output or lower prices to reduce profits for everyone.

to this tendency.[8] Similarly, if food and raw materials can be obtained cheaper abroad, that too would lower *"v"* and sustain profits. Cheaper raw materials is the principal objective of imperialist wars, says Marx in volume III.

3 Anarchy of the market. Noting the uncertainties of individual lines of trade, Marx was one of the first economists to realize that demand for investment goods generally would have to be sufficient to absorb available saving (surplus) if capitalist production and growth were to continue. Marx doubted the unguided market could assure "realization"—i.e., full use of capacity in investment goods—though he occasionally alludes to the role of wages in affecting the demand for machines. If wages are high, there is an incentive to substitute machines; if wages are low, the incentive would be less. Beyond Marx's real theory of business cycles, he added a great deal of verbiage about the role of money and credit, which are seen as additional destabilizing elements of the anarchic capitalist system.

Primarily a revolutionary perspective, Marxism has given rise to many theories and predictions, true and false, without losing its appeal as an organizing synthesis with unique appeal for radical socialists in many countries.

READING 10

Capital **and Other Writings**

Karl Marx

Man and Society[*]

In their social production human beings enter into definite relations that are indispensable and independent of their wills, relations of production which correspond to definite stages of development of their material productive forces. The sum total of these relations of production constitutes the economic structure of society, the real foundation upon which legal and political superstructures rise and to which correspond definite forms of social consciousness. The mode of production of material life determines the social, political and intellectual life process in general. It is not the consciousness of humankind which determines their existence, but rather their social existence which determines their consciousness. At a certain stage of development, the productive forces of society come into conflict with the existing relations of production,

---

[8]If technological change raises surplus value without raising wages, as envisioned in the theory of impoverishment and underconsumption, then profit rates may not fall at all. Theories #1 and #2 appear to be alternatives; both cannot be true at the same time. High wages in an expansion could indeed be the cause of a crisis and recession for Marx, but they hardly are consistent with absolute or relative immiseration.

[*]*Source:* Preface to *A Contribution to the Critique of Political Economy*, 1859, translated by the editor.

or—to put the same thing in legal language—with the property relations within which they had worked before. These relations turn from forms of development of the productive forces into fetters upon them. Then a period of social revolution will begin. With the change of its economic foundations, the entire immense superstructure is more or less rapidly transformed. In considering such transformations the distinction should always be drawn between the material transformation of the economic conditions of production, which can be determined with the precision of natural science, and the legal, political, religious, aesthetic, or philosophic—in short, ideological—forms in which men become conscious of this conflict and fight it out. Just as our opinion of an individual is not based on what he thinks of himself, so we cannot judge of such a period of transformation by its consciousness of itself. On the contrary, this consciousness must rather be explained from the contradictions of material life, from the existing conflict between the social productive forces and the relations of production. No social order ever disappears before all the productive forces for which it has room have developed; and new, higher relations of production never appear before the material conditions of their existence have matured in the womb of the old society. Therefore, humankind always engages itself only in such tasks as it can solve since, looking at the matter more closely, it will always be found that the task arises only when the material conditions for its resolution already exist or at least are in the process of formation. In broad outlines we can designate the Asiatic, ancient, feudal, and modern bourgeois modes of production as progressive epochs in the economic formation of society. The bourgeois relations of production are the last antagonistic form of social process of production . . . at the same time the productive forces developing in the womb of bourgeois society create the material conditions for the resolution of that antagonism.

Role of the Revolutionary Intellectual[*]

When a society has got upon the right track for the discovery of the natural laws of its movement—and it is the ultimate aim of this work, to lay bare the economic law of motion of modern society—it can neither clear by bold leaps, nor remove by legal enactments, the obstacles offered by the successive phases of its normal development. But it can shorten and lessen the birth pangs.

Bourgeois and Proletarians[*]

The history of all hitherto existing society is the history of class struggles.

Freeman and slave, patrician and plebeian, lord and serf, guild-master and journeyman, in a word, oppressor and oppressed, stood in constant opposition to one another, carried on an uninterrupted, now hidden, now open fight, a fight that each time ended, either in a revolutionary re-constitution of society at large or in the common ruin of the contending classes. . . .

---

[*]*Source:* Preface to the first German edition of *Capital*, 1867, translated by Samuel Moore.

[*]*Source: The Communist Manifesto*, 1848, translated by Friedrich Engels.

The modern bourgeois society that has sprouted from the ruins of feudal society has not done away with class antagonisms. It has but established new classes, new conditions of oppression, new forms of struggle in place of the old ones.

Our epoch, the epoch of the bourgeoisie, possesses, however, this distinctive feature: it has simplified the class antagonisms. Society as a whole is more and more splitting up into two great hostile camps, into two great classes directly facing each other: Bourgeoisie and Proletariat. . . .

Modern industry, the place of the industrial middle class, industrial millionaires, the leaders of whole industrial armies, the modern bourgeois . . . has established the world-market, for which the discovery of America paved the way. This market has given an immense development to commerce, to navigation, to communication by land. This development has, in its turn, reacted on the extension of industry, and in proportion as industry, commerce, navigation, railways extended, in the same proportion the bourgeoisie developed, increased its capital, and pushed into the background every class handed down from the Middle Ages.

We see, therefore, how the modern bourgeoisie is itself the product of a long course of development of a series of revolutions in the modes of production and of exchange.

Each step in the development of the bourgeoisie was accompanied by a corresponding political advance of that class. An oppressed class under the sway of the feudal nobility . . . the bourgeoisie has at least, since the establishment of Modern Industry of the world-market, conquered for itself, in the modern representative State, exclusive political sway. The executive of the modern State is but a committee for managing the common affairs of the whole bourgeoisie.

The bourgeoisie, historically, has played a most revolutionary part. The bourgeoisie, wherever it has got the upper hand, has put an end to all feudal, patriarchal, idyllic relations. It has pitilessly torn asunder the motley feudal ties that bound man to his "natural superiors," and has left remaining no other nexus between man and man than naked self-interest, than callous "cash payment." It has drowned the most heavenly ecstasies of religious fervor, of chivalrous enthusiasm, of philistine sentimentalism, in the icy water of egotistical calculation. It has resolved personal worth into exchange value, and in place of the numberless indefeasible chartered freedoms, has set up that single, unconscionable freedom—Free Trade. In one word, for exploitation, veiled by religious and political illusions, it has substituted naked, shameless, direct, brutal exploitation.

The bourgeoisie has stripped of its halo every occupation hitherto honored and looked up to with reverent awe. It has converted the physician, the lawyer, the priest, the poet, the man of science, into its paid wage-laborers.

The bourgeoisie has torn away from the family its sentimental veil, and has reduced the family relation to a mere money relation. . . .

It has been the first to show what man's activity can bring about. It has accomplished wonders far surpassing Egyptian pyramids, Roman aqueducts, and Gothic cathedrals. . . . The bourgeoisie cannot exist without constantly revolutionizing the instruments of production, and thereby the relations of production, and with them the whole relations of society. Conservation of the old modes of production in unaltered form, was, on the contrary, the first condition of existence for all earlier industrial classes. Constant revolutionizing of production, uninterrupted disturbance of all societal conditions, everlasting uncertainty and agitation distinguish the bourgeois epoch from all earlier ones. . . .

The bourgeoisie has through its exploitation of the world-market given a cosmopolitan character to production and consumption in every country. . . . All old-established national industries have been destroyed or are daily being destroyed. . . . In place of the old wants, satisfied by the productions of the country, we find new wants, requiring for their satisfaction the products of distant lands and climes. In place of the old local and national seclusion and self-sufficiency, we have intercourse in every direction, universal interdependence of nations. And as in material, so also in intellectual production. The intellectual creations of individual nations become common property. . . .

The bourgeoisie, by the rapid improvement of all instruments of production, by the immensely facilitated means of communication, draws all, even the most barbarian, nations into civilization. The cheap prices of its commodities are the heavy artillery with which it batters down all Chinese walls, with which it forces the barbarians' intensely obstinate hatred of foreigners to capitulate. It compels all nations, on pain of extinction, to adopt the bourgeois mode of production; it compels them to introduce what it calls civilization into their midst, i.e., to become bourgeois themselves. In one word, it creates a world after its own image.

The bourgeoisie has subjected the country to the rule of the towns. It has created enormous cities, has greatly increased the urban population as compared with the rural, and has thus rescued a considerable part of the population from the idiocy of rural life. . . . It has agglomerated population, centralized means of production, and has concentrated property in a few hands. The necessary consequence of this was political centralization. . . .

Modern bourgeois society . . . is like the sorcerer, who is no longer able to control the powers of the nether world whom he has called up by his spells. For many a decade past the history of industry and commerce is but the history of the revolt of modern productive forces against modern conditions of production, against property relations that are the conditions for existence of the bourgeoisie and of its rule. It is enough to mention the commercial crises that by their periodical return put on its trial, each time more threateningly, the existence of the entire bourgeois society. In these crises a great part not only of the existing products, but also of the previously created productive forces, are periodically destroyed. In these crises there breaks out an epidemic that, in all earlier epochs, would have seemed an absurdity—the epidemic of overproduction. . . . The productive forces at the disposal of society no longer tend to further the development of the conditions of bourgeois property; on the contrary, they have become too powerful for these conditions, by which they are fettered, and so soon as they overcome these fetters, they bring disorder into the whole of bourgeois society. . . . And how does the bourgeoisie get over these crises? On the one hand by enforced destruction of a mass of productive forces; on the other, by the conquest of new markets and by the more thorough exploitation of the old ones. That is to say, by paving the way for more extensive and more destructive crises, and by diminishing the means whereby crises are prevented. . . .

But not only has the bourgeoisie forged the weapons that bring death to itself; it has also called into existence the men who are to wield those weapons—the modern working class—the proletarians.

In proportion as the bourgeoisie, i.e., capital, is developed, in the same proportion is the proletariat, the modern working class, developed—a class of laborers, who live only so long as they find work, and who work only so long as their labor increases capital. These laborers, who must sell themselves piecemeal, are a commodity, like every other article of commerce, and are consequently exposed to all the vicissitudes of competition, to all the fluctuations of the market.

Owing to the extensive use of machinery and to division of labor, the work of the proletarians has lost all its individual character, and, consequently, all charm for the workman. He becomes an appendage of the machine, and it is only the most simple, most monotonous, and most easily acquired knack, that is required of him. Hence, the cost of production of a workman is restricted, almost entirely, to the means of subsistence that he requires for his maintenance, and for the propagation of his race. But the price of a commodity, and therefore also of labor, is equal to its cost of production. In proportion, therefore, as the repulsiveness of the work increases, the wage decreases. Nay more, in proportion as the use of machinery and division of labor increases, in the same proportion the burden of toil also increases, whether by prolongation of the working hours, by increase of the work exacted in a given time or by increased speed of the machinery, etc. . . .

The less the skill and exertion of strength implied in manual labor, in other words, the more modern industry becomes developed, the more is the labor of men superseded by that of women. Differences of age and sex have no longer any distinctive social validity for the working class. All are instruments of labor, more or less expensive to use, according to their age and sex.

No sooner is the exploitation of the labor by the manufacturer, so far, at an end, and he receives his wages in cash, than he is set upon by the other portions of the bourgeoisie, the landlord, the shopkeeper, the pawnbroker, etc.

The lower strata of the middle class—the small tradespeople, shopkeepers, and retired tradesmen generally, the handicraftsmen and peasants—all these sink gradually into the proletariat, partly because their diminutive capital does not suffice for the scale on which Modern Industry is carried on, and is swamped in the competition with the large capitalists, partly because their specialized skill is rendered worthless by new methods of production. Thus the proletariat is recruited from all classes of the population. . . .

With the development of industry the proletariat not only increases in number; it becomes concentrated in greater masses, its strength grows, and it feels that strength more. The various interests and conditions of life within the ranks of the proletariat are more and more equalized, in proportion as machinery obliterates all distinctions of labor, and nearly everywhere reduces wages to the same low level. The growing competition among the bourgeois, and resulting commercial crises, make the wages of the workers ever more fluctuating. The unceasing improvement of machinery, ever more rapidly developing, makes their livelihood more and more precarious; the collisions between individual workmen and individual bourgeois take more and more the character of collisions between two classes. Thereupon the workers begin to form combinations (Trades' Unions) against the bourgeois; they club together in order to keep up the rate of wages; they found permanent associations in order to make provision beforehand for these occasional revolts. Here and there the contest breaks out into riots.

Now and then the workers are victorious, but only for a time. The real fruit of their battle lies, not in the immediate result, but in the ever-expanding union of the workers. The union is helped on by the improved means of communication that are created by modern industry and that place the workers of different localities in contact with one another. . . .

This organization of the proletarians into a class, and consequently into a political party, is continually being upset again by the competition between the workers themselves. But it ever rises up again, stronger, firmer, mightier. It compels legislative recognition of particular interests of the workers, by taking advantage of the divisions among the bourgeoisie itself. Thus the ten-hours' bill in England was carried.

Altogether collisions between the classes of the old society further, in many ways, the course of development of the proletariat. The bourgeoisie finds itself involved in a constant battle. At first with the aristocracy; later on, with those portions of the bourgeoisie itself whose interests have become antagonistic to the progress of industry; at all times, with the bourgeoisie of foreign countries. In all these battles it sees itself compelled to appeal to the proletariat, to ask for its help, and thus, to drag it into the political arena. The bourgeoisie itself, therefore, supplies the proletariat with its own elements of political and general education, in other words it furnishes the proletariat with weapons for fighting the bourgeoisie. . . .

Finally, in times when the class struggle nears the decisive hour, the process of dissolution going on within the ruling class, in fact within the whole range of old society, assumes such a violent, glaring character, that a small section of the ruling class cuts itself adrift, and joins the revolutionary class, the class that holds the future in its hands. Just as, therefore, at an earlier period, a section of the nobility went over to the bourgeoisie, so now a portion of the bourgeoisie goes over to the proletariat, and in particular, a portion of the bourgeois ideologists, who have raised themselves to the level of comprehending theoretically the historical movement as a whole.

Of all the classes that stand face to face with the bourgeoisie today, the proletariat alone is a really revolutionary class. The other classes decay and finally disappear in the face of modern industry; the proletariat is its special and essential product.

The lower middle class, the small manufacturer, the shopkeeper, the artisan, the peasant, all these fight against the bourgeoisie, to save from extinction their existence as fraction of the middle class. They are therefore not revolutionary, but conservative. Nay more, they are reactionary, for they try to roll back the wheel of history. If by chance they are revolutionary, they are so only in view of their impending transfer into the proletariat, they thus defend not their present, but their future interests, they desert their own standpoint to place themselves at that of the proletariat.

The "dangerous class," the social scum, that passively rotting mass thrown off by the lowest layers of old society, may here and there, be swept into the movement by a proletarian revolution, its conditions of life, however, prepare if far more for the part of a bribed tool of reactionary intrigue. . . .

The proletarians cannot become masters of the productive forces of society, except by abolishing their own previous mode of appropriation, and thereby also every other previous mode of appropriation. They have nothing of their own to secure, and to fortify; their mission is to destroy all previous securities for, and insurances of, individual property.

All previous historical movements were movements of minorities, or in the interest of minorities. The proletarian movement is the self-conscious, independent movement of the immense majority, in the interests of the immense majority. . . .

The Process of Capitalist Accumulation[*]

The wealth of those societies in which the capitalist mode of production prevails presents itself as "an immense accumulation of commodities," its unit being a single commodity. Our investigation must therefore begin with the analysis of a commodity.

A commodity is, in the first place, an object outside us, a thing that by its properties satisfies human wants of some sort or another. The nature of such wants, whether, for instance, they spring from the stomach or from fancy, makes no difference. Neither are we here concerned to know how the object satisfies these wants, whether directly as means of subsistence, or indirectly as means of production. . . .

The utility of a thing makes it a use-value. . . . This property of a commodity is independent of the amount of labor required to appropriate its useful qualities. When treating of use-value, we always assume to be dealing with definite quantities, such as dozens of watches, yards of linen, or tons of iron. The use-values of commodities furnish the material for a special study, that of the commercial knowledge of commodities. Use-values become a reality only by use or consumption: they also constitute the substance of all wealth, whatever may be the social form of that wealth. In the form of society we are about to consider, they are, in addition, the material depositories of exchange value.

Exchange value, at first sight, presents itself as a quantitative relation, as the proportion in which values in use of one sort are exchanged for those of another sort, a relation constantly changing with time and place. Hence exchange value appears to be something accidental and purely relative; and consequently an intrinsic value, i.e., an exchange value that is inseparable connected with, inherent in, commodities seems a contradiction in terms. Let us consider the matter a little more closely.

A given commodity, e.g., a quarter of wheat, is exchanged for x blacking, y silk, or z gold, etc.—in short, for other commodities in the most different

---

*Source: Karl Marx, Capital: A Critique of Political Economy, vols. 1-3, translated by Samuel Moore. Copyright by Charles H. Kerr and Co., 1906-1909.

proportions. Instead of one exchange value, the wheat has, therefore, a great many. But since x blacking, y silk, or z gold, etc., each represent the exchange value of one quarter of wheat, x blacking, y silk, z gold, etc., must as exchange values be replaceable by each other or equal to each other. Therefore, first: the valid exchange values of a given commodity express something equal; secondly, exchange value, generally, is only the mode of expression, the phenomenal form, of something contained in it, yet distinguishable from it. . . . The exchange values of commodities must be capable of being expressed in terms of something common to them all, of which thing they represent a greater or less quantity.

If then we leave out of consideration the use-value of commodities, they have only one common property left, that of being products of labor. But even the product of labor itself has undergone a change in our hands. If we make abstraction from its use-value, we make abstraction at the same time from the material elements and shapes that make the product a use-value; we see in it no longer a table, a house, yarn, or any other useful thing. Its existence as a material thing is put out of sight. Neither can it any longer be regarded as the product of the labor of the joiner, the mason, the spinner, or of any other definite kind of productive labor. Along with the useful qualities of the products themselves, we put out of sight both the useful character of the various kinds of labor embodied in them and the concrete forms of that labor; there is nothing left but what is common to them all; all are reduced to one and the same sort of labor, human labor in the abstract. . . .

We have seen that when commodities are exchanged, their exchange value manifests itself as something totally independent of their use-value. But if we abstract from their use-value, there remains their Value as defined above. Therefore, the common substance that manifests itself in the exchange-value of commodities, whenever they are exchanged, is their value. . . .

A use-value, or useful article, therefore, has value only because human labor in the abstract has been embodied or materialized in it. How, then, is the magnitude of this value to be measured? Plainly, by the quantity of the value-creating substance, the labor, contained in the article. The quantity of labor, however, is measured by its duration, and labor time in its turn finds its standard in weeks, days, and hours.

Some people might think that if the value of a commodity is determined by the quantity of labor spent on it, the more idle and unskillful the laborer, the more valuable would his commodity be, because more time would be required in its production. The labor, however, that forms the substance of value is homogeneous human labor, expenditure of one uniform labor-power. The total labor-power of society, which is embodied in the sum total of the values of all commodities produced by that society, counts here as one homogeneous mass of human labor-power, composed though it be of innumerable individual units. Each of these units is the same as any other, so far as it has the character of the average labor-power of society, and takes effect as such; that is, so far as it requires for producing a commodity no more time than is needed on an average, no more than is socially necessary. The labor time socially necessary is that required to produce an article under the normal conditions of production, and with the average degree of skill and intensity prevalent at the time. The introduction of power looms into England probably reduced by one half the labor required to weave a given quantity of yarn into cloth. The hand-loom weavers, as a matter of fact, continued to require the same time as before; but for all that, the product of one hour of their labor represented after the change only half an hour's social labor, and consequently fell to one-half its former value. . . .

The value of a commodity would therefore remain constant, if the labor time required for its production also remained constant, But the latter changes with every variation in the productiveness of labor. This productiveness is determined by various circumstances, amongst others, by the average amount of skill of the workmen, the state of science, and the degree of its practical application, the social organization of production, the extent and capabilities of organization of the means of production, and by physical conditions. For example, the same amount of labor in favorable seasons is embodied in 8 bushels of corn, and in unfavorable, only in four. The same labor extracts from rich mines more metal than from poor mines. Diamonds are of very rare occurrence on the earth's surface, and hence their discovery costs, on an average, a great deal of labor time. Consequently much labor is represented in a small compass. . . .

A thing can be a use-value without having value. This is the case whenever its utility to man is not due to labor. Such are air, virgin soil, natural meadows, etc. A thing can be useful, and the product of human labor, without being a commodity. Whoever directly satisfies his wants with the produce of his own labor, creates, indeed, use-values, but not commodities. In order to produce the latter, he must not only produce use-values, but use-values for others, social use-values. . . . Lastly, nothing can have value, without being an object of utility. If the thing is useless, so is the labor contained in it; the labor does not count as labor, and therefore creates no value. . . .

Two-Fold Character of Labor Embodied in Commodities

Productive activity, if we leave out of sight its special form, viz., the useful character of the labor, is nothing but the expenditure of human labor-power. Tailoring and weaving, though qualitatively different productive activities, are each a productive expenditure of human brains, nerves, and muscles, and in this sense are human labor. They are but two different modes of expending human labor-power. Of course this labor-power, which remains the same under all its modifications, must have attained a certain pitch of development before it can be expended in a multiplicity of modes. But the value of a commodity represents human labor in the abstract, the expenditure of human labor in general. And just as in society a general or a banker plays a great part, but mere man, on the other hand, a very shabby part, so here with mere human labor. It is the expenditure of simple labor-power, i.e., of the labor-power which, on an average, apart from any special development, exists in the organism of every ordinary individual. Simple average labor, it is true, varies in character in different countries and at different times, but in a particular society it is given. Skilled labor counts only as simple labor intensified, or rather, as multiplied simple labor, a given quantity of skilled being considered equal to a greater quantity of simple labor. Experience shows that this reduction is constantly being made. A commodity may be the product of the most skilled labor, but its value, by equating it to the product of simple unskilled labor, represents a definite quantity of the latter labor alone. The different proportions in which different sorts of labor are reduced to unskilled labor as their standard are established by a social process that goes on behind the backs of the producers and, consequently, appear to be fixed by custom. For simplicity's sake we shall henceforth account every kind of labor to be unskilled, simple labor; by this we do no more than save ourselves the trouble of making the reduction. . . . [Chapter I]

Exchange

It is plain that commodities cannot go to market and make exchanges of their own account. We must, therefore, have recourse to their guardians, who are also their owners. . . . In order that these objects may enter into relation with each other as commodities, their guardians must place themselves in relation to one another, as persons whose will resides in those objects, and must behave in such a way that each does not appropriate the commodity of the other, and part with his own, except by means of an act done by mutual consent. They must, therefore, mutually recognize in each other the right of private proprietors. This juridical relation, which thus expresses itself in a contract, whether such contract be part of a developed legal system or not, is a relation between two wills, and is but the reflex of the real economical relation between the two. It is this economical relation that determines the subject matter comprised in each such juridical act. The persons exist for one another merely as representatives of, and, therefore, as owners of, commodities. . . .

[A] particular commodity cannot become the universal equivalent except by a social act. . . . Thereby the bodily form of this commodity becomes the form of the socially recognized universal equivalent. . . . Thus it becomes—money. [Chapter II]

Money

Throughout this work, I assume, for the sake of simplicity, gold as the money commodity.

The first chief function of money is to supply commodities with the material for the expression of their values, or to represent their values as magnitudes of the same denomination, qualitatively equal and quantitatively comparable. It thus serves as a *universal measure of value*. . . .

It is not money that renders commodities commensurable. Just the contrary. It is because all commodities, as values, are realized human labor, and therefore commensurable, that their values can be measured by one and the same special commodity, and the latter be converted into the common measure of their values, i.e., into money. . . .

Price is the money name of the labor realized in a commodity. . . . [Chapter III]

The General Formula for Capital

If we abstract from the material substance of the circulation of commodities, that is, from the exchange of the various use-values, and consider only the economic forms produced by this process of circulation, we find its final result to be money: this final product of the circulation of commodities is the first form in which capital appears.

As a matter of history, capital, as opposed to landed property, invariably takes the form at first of money; it appears as moneyed wealth, as the capital of the merchant and of the usurer. . . .

The simplest form of the circulation of commodities is *C-M-C,* the transformation of commodities into money, and the change of the money back again into commodities; or selling in order to buy. But alongside of this form we find another specifically different form: *M-C-M,* the transformation of money into commodities, and the change of commodities back again into money; or buying in order to sell. Money that circulates in the latter manner is thereby transformed into, becomes capital, and is already potentially capital. [Chapter IV]

The Buying and Selling of Labor-Power

[I]n order that our owner of money may be able to find labor-power offered for sale as a commodity, various conditions must first be fulfilled. The exchange of commodities of itself implies no other relations of dependence than those which result from its own nature. On this assumption labor-power can appear upon the market as a commodity only if, and so far as, its possessor, the individual whose labor-power it is, offers it for sale, or sells it, as a commodity. In order that he may be able to do this, he must have it at his disposal, must be the untrammelled owner of his capacity for labor, *i.e.,* of his person. He and the owner of money meet in the market, and deal with each other as on the basis of equal rights, with this difference alone, that one is buyer, the other seller; both, therefore, equal in the eyes of the law. The continuance of this relation demands that the owner of the labor-power should sell it only for a definite period, for if he were to sell it rump and stump, once for all, he would be selling himself, converting himself from a free man into a slave. . . .

The second essential condition to the owner of money finding labor-power in the market as a commodity is this—that the laborer instead of being in the position to sell commodities in which his labor is incorporated, must be obliged to offer for sale as a commodity that very labor-power which exists only in his living self. . . .

Nature does not produce on the one side owners of money or commodities, and on the other men possessing nothing but their own labor-power. This relation has no natural basis, neither is its social basis one that is common to all historical periods. It is clearly the result of a past historical development, the product of many economical revolutions, of the extinction of a whole series of older forms of social production. . . .

We must now examine more closely this peculiar commodity, labor-power. Like all others it has a value. How is that value determined?

The value of labor-power is determined, as in the case of every other commodity, by the labor time necessary for the production, and consequently also the reproduction, of this special article. So far as it has value, it represents no more than a definite quantity of the average labor of society incorporated in it. Labor-power exists only as a capacity, or power of the living individual. Its production consequently presupposes his existence. Given the individual, the production of labor-power consists in his reproduction of himself or his maintenance. For his maintenance he requires a given quantity of the means of subsistence. Therefore, the labor time requisite for the production of labor-power reduces itself to that necessary for the reproduction of those means of subsistence; in other words, the value of labor-power is the value of the means of subsistence necessary for the maintenance of the laborer. Labor-power, however, becomes a reality only by its exercise; it sets itself in action only by working. But thereby a definite quantity of human muscle, nerve, brain, etc., is wasted, and these require to be restored. This increased expenditure demands a larger income. If the owner of labor-power works today, tomorrow he must again be able to repeat the same process in the same conditions as regards health and strength. His means of subsistence must therefore be sufficient to maintain him in his normal state as a laboring individual. His natural wants, such as food, clothing, fuel, and housing, vary according to the climatic and other physical conditions of his country. On the other hand, the number and extent of his so-called necessary wants, as also the modes of satisfying them, are themselves the product of historical development and depend therefore to a great extent on the degree of civilization of a country, more particularly on the conditions under which, and consequently on the habits and degree of comfort in which, the class of free laborers has been formed. In contradistinction therefore to the case of other commodities, there enters into the determination of the value of labor-power a historical and moral element. Nevertheless—in a given country, at a given period, the average quantity of the means of subsistence necessary for the laborer is practically known.

The owner of labor-power is mortal. If then his appearance in the market is to be continuous, and the continuous conversion of money into capital assumes this, the seller of labor-power must perpetuate himself. . . . Hence the sum of the means of subsistence necessary for the production of labor-power must include the means necessary for the laborer's substitutes, *i.e.,* his children, in order that this race of peculiar commodity owners may perpetuate its appearance in the market.

In order to modify the human organism, so that it may acquire skill and handiness in a given branch of industry, and become labor-power of a kind, a special education or training is requisite, and this, on its part, costs an equivalent in commodities of a greater or less amount. This amount varies according to the more or less complicated character of the labor-power. The expenses of this education (excessively small in the case of ordinary labor-power) enter *pro tanto* into the total value spent in its production. . . . [Chapter VI]

The Labor Process and Surplus Value

Our capitalist has two objects in view; in the first place, he wants to produce a use-value that has a value in exchange, that is to say, an article destined to be sold, a commodity; and secondly, he desires to produce a commodity whose value shall be greater than the sum of the values of the commodities used in its production, that is, of the means of production and the labor-power that he purchased with his good money in the open market. His aim is to produce not only a use-value, but a commodity also; not only use-value, but value; not only value, but at the same time surplus-value. . . .

The labor required for the production of the cotton, the raw material of the yarn, is part of the labor necessary to produce the yarn, and is therefore contained in the yarn. The same applies to the labor embodied in the spindle, without whose wear and tear the cotton could not be spun.

Hence, in determining the value of the yarn, or the labor-time required for its production, all the special processes carried on at various times and in different places, which were necessary, first to produce the cotton and the wasted portion of the spindle, and then with the cotton and spindle to spin the yarn, may together be looked on as different and successive phases of one and the same process. The whole of the labor in the yarn is past labor and it is a matter of no importance that the operations necessary . . . are more remote than the final operation of spinning. . . .

We assumed, on the occasion of its sale, that the value of a day's labor-power is 3 shillings, and that 6 hours' labor are incorporated in that sum; and consequently that this amount of labor is requisite to produce the necessaries of life daily required on an average by the laborer. If now our spinner by working for one hour can convert 1 2/3 lbs. of cotton into 1 2/3 lbs. of yarn, it follows that in 6 hours he will convert 10 lbs. of cotton into 10 lbs. of yarn. Hence, during the spinning process, the cotton absorbs 6 hours' labor. The same quantity of labor is also embodied in a piece of gold of the value of 3 shillings. Consequently by the mere labor of spinning a value of 3 shillings is added to the cotton.

Let us now consider the total value of the product, the 10 lbs. of yarn. Two and a half days' labor have been embodied in it, of which two days were contained in the cotton and in the substance of the spindle worn away, and half a day was absorbed during the process of spinning. This 2 1/2 days' labor is also represented by a piece of gold of the value of 15 shillings. . . .

Our capitalist stares in astonishment. The value of the product is exactly equal to the value of the capital advanced. The value so advanced has not expanded, no surplus-value has been created, and consequently money has not been converted into capital. The price of the yarn is 15 shillings, and 15 shillings were spent in the open market upon the constituent elements of the product, or, what amounts to the same thing, upon the factors of the labor process; 10 shillings were paid for the cotton, 2 shillings for the substance of the spindle worn away, and 3 shillings for the labor-power. The swollen value of the yarn is of no avail, for it is merely the sum of the values formerly existing in the cotton, the spindle, and the labor-power; out of such a simple addition of existing values, no surplus-value can possibly arise. These separate values are now all concentrated in one thing; but so they were also in the sum of 15 shillings, before it was split up into three parts, by the purchase of the commodities.

There is in reality nothing very strange in this result. The value of one pound of yarn being eighteen pence, if our capitalist buys 10 lbs. of yarn in the market, he must pay 15 shillings for them. It is clear that, whether a man buys his house ready built or gets it built for him, in neither case will the mode of acquisition increase the amount of money laid out on the house.

Our capitalist, who is at home in his vulgar economy, exclaims: "Oh! but I advanced my money for the express purpose of making more money." The way to Hell is paved with good intentions, and he might just as easily have intended to make money without producing at all. He threatens all sorts of things. He won't be caught flapping again. In future he will buy the commodities in the market, instead of manufacturing them himself. But if all his brother capitalists were to do the same, where would he find his commodities in the market? And his money he cannot eat. He tries persuasion, "Consider my abstinence; I might have played ducks and drakes with the 15 shillings; but instead of that I consumed it productively, and made yarn with it." Very well, and by way of reward he is now in possession of good yarn instead of a bad conscience; and as for playing the part of a miser, it would never do for him to relapse into such bad ways as that; we have seen before to what results such asceticism leads. Besides, where nothing is, the king has lost his rights: whatever may be the merit of his abstinence, there is nothing wherewith specially to remunerate it, because the value of the product is merely the sum of the values of the commodities that were thrown into the process of production. Let him therefore console himself with the reflection that virtue is its own reward. . . .

Let us examine the matter more closely. The value of a day's labor-power amounts to 3 shillings, because on our assumption half a day's labor is embodied in that quantity of labor-power, *i.e.,* because the means of subsistence that are daily required for the production of labor-power cost half a day's labor. But the past labor that is embodied in the labor-power and the living labor that it can call into action; the daily cost of maintaining it and its daily expenditure in work, are two totally different things. The former determines the exchange-value of the labor-power, the latter is its use-value. The fact that half a day's labor is necessary to keep the laborer alive during 24 hours does not in any way prevent him from working a whole day. Therefore, the value of labor-power and the value which that labor-power creates in the labor process are two entirely different magnitudes; and this difference of the two values was what the capitalist had in view, when he was purchasing the labor-power. The useful qualities that labor-power possesses, and by virtue of which it makes yarn or boots, were to him nothing more than a *conditio sine qua non;* for in order to create value, labor must be expended in a useful manner. What really influenced him was the specific use-value which this commodity possesses of being *a source not only of value, but of more value than it has itself.* This is the special service that the capitalist expects from labor-power, and in this transaction he acts in accordance with the "eternal laws" of the exchange of commodities. The seller of labor-power, like the seller of any other commodity, realizes its exchange-value and parts with its use-value. He cannot take the one without giving the other. The use-value of labor-power, or in other words, labor, belongs just as little to its seller as the use-value of oil after it has been sold belongs to the dealer who has sold it. The owner of the money has paid the value of a day's labor-power; his, therefore, is the use of it for a day; a day's labor belongs to him. The circumstance that on the one hand the daily sustenance of labor-power costs only half a day's labor, while on the other hand the very same labor-power can work during a whole day, that consequently the value which its use during one day creates, is double what he pays for that use, this circumstance is, without doubt, a piece of good luck for the buyer, but by no means an injury to the seller.

Our capitalist foresaw this state of things, and that was the cause of his laughter. The laborer therefore finds, in the workshop, the means of production necessary for working, not only during six, but during twelve hours. Just as during the six hours' process our 10 lbs. of cotton absorbed six hours' labor, and became 10 lbs. of yarn, so now 20 lbs. of cotton will absorb 12 hours' labor and be changed into 20 lbs. of yarn. Let us now examine the product of this prolonged process. There is now materialized in this 20 lbs. of yarn the labor of five days, of which four days are due to the cotton and the lost steel of the spindle, the remaining day having been absorbed by the cotton during the spinning process. Expressed in gold, the labor of five days is 30 shillings. This is therefore the price of the 20 lbs. of yarn, giving, as before, eighteen pence as the price of a pound. But the sum of the value of the commodities that entered into the process amounts to 27 shillings. The value of the yarn is 30 shillings. Therefore the value of the product is 1/9 greater than the value advanced for its production; 27 shillings have been transformed into 30 shillings; a surplus-value of 3 shillings has been created. The trick has at last succeeded; money has been converted into capital.

Every condition of the problem is satisfied, while the laws that regulate the exchange of commodities have been in no way violated. Equivalent has been exchanged for equivalent. For the capitalist as buyer paid for each commodity, for the cotton, the spindle, and the labor-power, its full value. He then did what is done by every purchaser of commodities; he consumed their use-value. The consumption of the labor-power, which was also the process of producing commodities, resulted in 20 lbs. of yarn, having a value of 30 shillings. The capitalist, formerly a buyer, now returns to market as a seller, of commodities. He sells his yarn at eighteen pence a pound, which is its exact value. Yet for all that he withdraws 3 shillings more from circulation than he originally threw into it. This metamorphosis, this conversion of money into capital, takes place both within the sphere of circulation and also outside it; within the circulation, because conditioned by the purchase of the labor-power in the market; outside the circulation, because what is done within it is only a stepping-stone to the production of surplus-value, a process which is entirely confined to the sphere of production. . . . [Chapter VII]

That part of capital then, which is represented by the means of production, by the raw material, auxiliary material, and the instruments of labor does not, in the process of production, undergo any quantitative alteration of value. I therefore call it the constant part of capital, or, more shortly, constant capital.

On the other hand, that part of capital represented by labor-power does, in the process of production, undergo an alteration of value. It both reproduces the equivalent of its own value and also produces an excess, a surplus-value, which may itself vary, may be more or less according to circumstances. This part of capital is continually being transformed from a constant into a variable magnitude. I therefore call it the variable part of capital, or, shortly, variable capital. [Chapter VIII]

The Rate of Surplus Value

The method of calculating the rate of surplus-value is, shortly, as follows. We take the total value of the product and put the constant capital which merely reappears in it equal to zero. What remains is the only value that has, in the process of producing the commodity, been actually created. If the amount of surplus-value be given, we have only to deduct it from this remainder, to find the variable capital. And *vice versa,* if the latter be given and we require to find the surplus-value. If both be given, we have only to perform the concluding operation, viz., to calculate s/v the ratio of the surplus-value to the variable capital. . . . [Chapter IX]

The Working Day

The capitalist has bought the labor-power at its day rate. . . . But what is a working day?

We see then that, apart from extremely elastic bounds, the nature of the exchange of commodities itself imposes no limit to the working day, no limit to surplus-labor. The capitalist maintains his rights as a purchaser when he tries to make the working day as long as possible and to make, whenever possible, two working days out of one. On the other hand, the peculiar nature of the commodity sold implies a limit to its consumption by the purchaser, and the laborer maintains his right as a seller when he wishes to reduce the working day to one of definite normal duration. There is here, therefore, an antinomy, right against right, both equally bearing the seal of the law of exchanges. Between equal rights force decides. Hence is it that in the history of capitalist production, the determination of what is a working day, presents itself as the result of a struggle, a struggle between collective capital, *i.e.,* the class of capitalists, and collective labor, *i.e.,* the working class.

Capital has not invented surplus-labor. Wherever a part of society possesses the monopoly of the means of production, the laborer, free or not free, must add to the working time necessary for his own maintenance an extra working time in order to produce the means of subsistence for the owners of the means of production, whether this proprietor be . . . Norman baron, American slave owner, Wallachian Boyard, modern landlord or capitalist. It is, however, clear that in any given economic formation of society, where not the exchange value but the use-value of the product predominates, surplus-labor will be limited by a given set of wants which may be greater or less, and that here no boundless thirst for surplus-labor arises from the nature of the production itself. . . . But as soon as people, whose production still moves within the lower forms of slave labor, corvée labor, etc., are drawn into the whirlpool of an international market dominated by the capitalistic mode of production, the sale of their products for export becoming their principal interest, the civilized horrors of overwork are grafted on the barbaric horrors of slavery, serfdom, etc. Hence the Negro labor in the Southern States of the American Union preserved something of a patriarchal character, so long as production was chiefly directed to immediate local consumption. But in proportion as the export of cotton became of vital interest to these states, the overworking of the Negro and sometimes the using up of his life in 7 years' labor became a factor in a calculated and calculating system. It was no longer a question of obtaining from him a certain quantity of useful products. It was now a question of production of surplus labor itself. . . . [Chapter X]

Machinery and Modern Industry

Like every other increase in the productiveness of labor, machinery is intended to cheapen commodities, and, by shortening that portion of the working day in which the laborer works for himself, to lengthen the other portion that he gives, without an equivalent, to the capitalist. In short, it is a means for producing surplus-value. . . .

The productive forces resulting from cooperation and division of labor cost capital nothing. They are natural forces of social labor. . . . Machinery, like every other component of constant capital, creates no new value, but yields up its own value to the product that it serves to beget. In so far as the machine has value, and, in consequence, parts with value to the product, it forms an element in the value of that product. Instead of being cheapened, the product is made dearer in proportion to the value of the machine. . . . The productiveness of a machine is . . . measured by the human labor-power it replaces. . . .

In so far as machinery dispenses with muscular power, it becomes a means of employing laborers of slight muscular strength, and those whose bodily development is incomplete, but whose limbs are all the more supple. The labor of women and children was, therefore, the first thing sought for by capitalists who used machinery. That mighty substitute for labor and laborers was forthwith changed into a means for increasing the number of wage laborers by enrolling, under the direct sway of capital, every member of the workman's family, without distinction of age or sex. Compulsory work for the capitalist usurped the place not only of the children's play, but also of free labor at home within moderate limits for the support of the family.

Machinery also revolutionizes out and out the contract between the laborer and the capitalist, which formally fixes their mutual relations. Taking the exchange of commodities as our basis, our first assumption was that capitalist and laborer met as free persons, as independent owners of commodities; the one possessing money and means of production, the other labor-power. But now the capitalist buys children and young persons under age. Previously, the workman sold his own labor-power, which he disposed of nominally as a free agent. Now he sells wife and child. He has become a slave dealer. . . .

If machinery be the most powerful means for increasing the productiveness of labor—i.e., for shortening the working time required in the production of a commodity, it becomes in the hands of capital the most powerful means, in those industries first invaded by it, for lengthening the working day beyond all bounds set by human nature. It creates, on the one hand, new conditions by which capital is enabled to give free scope to this its constant tendency and, on the other hand, new motives with which to whet capital's appetite for the labor of others.

In the first place, in form of machinery, the implements of labor become automatic, things moving and working independent of the workman. They are thenceforth an industrial *perpetuum mobile,* that would go on producing forever, did it not meet with certain natural obstructions in the weak bodies and the strong wills of its human attendants. The automaton, as capital and because it is capital, is endowed, in the person of the capitalist, with intelligence and will; it is therefore animated by the longing to reduce to a minimum the resistance offered by that repellant yet elastic natural barrier, man. This resistance is moreover lessened by the apparent lightness of machine work, and by the more pliant and docile character of the women and children employed on it.

If, then, the capitalistic employment of machinery, on the one hand, supplies new and powerful motives to an excessive lengthening of the working day, and radically changes as well the methods of labor, as also the character of the social working organism, in such a manner as to break down all opposition to this tendency, on the other hand it produces, partly by opening out to the capitalist new strata of the working class, previously inaccessible to him, partly by setting free the laborers it supplants, a surplus working population, which is compelled to submit to the dictation of capital. Hence that remarkable phenomenon in the history of Modern Industry, that machinery sweeps away every moral and natural restriction on the length of the working day. Hence, too, the economical paradox, that the most powerful instrument for shortening labor time becomes the most unfailing means for placing every moment of the laborer's time and that of his family at the disposal of the capitalist for the purpose of expanding the value of his capital. . . .

The immoderate lengthening of the working day, produced by machinery in the hands of capital, leads to a reaction on the part of society, the very sources of whose life are menaced, and thence to a normal working day whose length is fixed by law. Thenceforth a phenomenon that we have already met with, namely, the intensification of labor, develops into great importance. Our analysis of absolute surplus-value had reference primarily to the extension or duration of the labor, its intensity being assumed as given. We now proceed to consider the substitution of a more intensified labor for labor of more extensive duration, and the degree of the former. . . .

At the same time that factory work exhausts the nervous system to the uttermost, it does away with the many-sided play of the muscles, and confiscates every atom of freedom, both in bodily and intellectual activity. The lightening of the labor, even, becomes a sort of torture, since the machine does not free the laborer from work, but deprives the work of all interest. Every kind of capitalist production, in so far as it is not only a labor process but also a process of creating surplus-value, has this in common, that it is not the workman that employs the instruments of labor, but the instruments of labor that employ the workman. But it is only in the factory system that this inversion for the first time acquires technical and palpable reality. By means of its conversion into an automaton, the instrument of labor confronts the laborer, during the labor process, in the shape of capital, of dead labor, that dominates, and pumps dry, living labor power.

We shall here merely allude to the material conditions under which factory labor is carried on Every organ of sense is injured in an equal degree by artificial elevation of the temperature, by the dust-laden atmosphere, by the deafening noise, not to mention danger to life and limb among the thickly crowded machinery, which, with the regularity of the seasons, issues its list of the killed and wounded in the industrial battle. Economy of the social means of production, matured and forced as in a hothouse by the factory system, is turned, in the hands of capital, into systematic robbery of what is necessary for the life of the workman while he is at work, robbery of space, light, air, and of protection to his person against the dangerous and unwholesome accompaniments of the productive process, not to mention the robbery of appliances for the comfort of the workman. . . .

The contest between the capitalist and the wage laborer dates back to the very origin of capital. It raged on throughout the whole manufacturing period. But only since the introduction of machinery has the workman fought against the instrument of labor itself, the material embodiment of capital. . . . [Chapter XV]

The General Law of Capitalist Accumulation

If we suppose that, all other circumstances remaining the same, the composition of capital also remains constant (i.e., that a definite mass of means of production constantly needs the same mass of labor-power to set in motion), then the demand for labor and the subsistence fund of the laborers clearly increase in the same proportion as the capital, and the more rapidly, the more rapidly the capital increases. Under special stimulus to enrichment, such as the opening of new markets or of new spheres for the outlay of capital in consequence of newly developed social wants, etc., the scale of accumulation may be suddenly extended, merely by a change in the division of the surplus-value or surplus product into capital and revenue, the requirements of accumulating capital may exceed the increase of labor-power or of the number of laborers; the demand for laborers may exceed the supply and, therefore, wages may rise. . . . [Chapter XXV, §1]

The Industrial Reserve Army

In all spheres the increase of the variable part of capital, and therefore of the number of laborers employed by it, is always connected with violent fluctuations and transitory production of surplus population, whether this takes the more striking form of the repulsion of laborers already employed or the less evident but not less real form of the more difficult absorption of the additional laboring population through the usual channels. With the magnitude of social capital already functioning, and the degree of its increase, with the extension of the scale of production, and the mass of the laborers set in motion, with the development of the productiveness of their labor, with the greater breadth and fullness of all sources of wealth, there is also an extension of the scale on which greater attraction of laborers by capital is accompanied by their greater repulsion; the rapidity of the change in the organic composition of capital and in its technical form increases, and an increasing number of spheres of production becomes involved in this change. . . , now simultaneously, now alternatively. The laboring population therefore produces, along with the accumulation of capital produced by it, the means by which itself is made relatively superfluous, is turned into a relative surplus population; and it does this to an always increasing extent. This is a law of population peculiar to the capitalist mode of production; and in fact every special historic mode of production has its own special laws of population, historically valid within its limits alone. An abstract law of population exists for plants and animals only, and only in so far as man has not interfered with them.

But if a surplus laboring population is a necessary product of accumulation or of the development of wealth on a capitalist basis, this surplus population becomes, conversely, the lever of capitalistic accumulation, nay, a condition of existence of the capitalist mode of production. It forms a disposable industrial reserve army that belongs to capital quite as absolutely as if the latter had bred it at its own cost. Independently of the limits of the actual increase of population, it creates, for the changing needs of the self-expansion of capital, a mass of human material always ready for exploitation. With accumulation, and the development of the productiveness of labor that accompanies it, the power of sudden expansion of capital grows also; it grows, not merely because the elasticity of the capital already functioning increases, not merely because the absolute wealth of society expands, of which capital only forms an elastic part, not merely because credit, under every special stimulus, at once places an unusual part of this wealth at the disposal of production in the form of additional capital; it grows, also, because the technical conditions of the process of production themselves—machinery, means of transport, etc.—now admit of the rapidest transformation of masses of surplus product into additional means of production. The mass of social wealth, overflowing with the advance of accumulation and transformable into additional capital, thrusts itself frantically into old branches of production, whose market suddenly expands, or into newly formed branches, such as railways, etc., the need for which grows out of the development of the old ones. In all such cases there must be the possibility of throwing great masses of men suddenly on the decisive points without injury to the scale of production in other spheres. Overpopulation supplies these masses. The course characteristic of modern industry, viz., a decennial cycle (interrupted by smaller oscillations) of periods of average activity, production at high pressure, crisis and stagnation, depends on the constant formation, the greater or less absorption, and the re-formation of the industrial reserve army of surplus population. In their turn, the varying phases of the industrial cycle recruit the surplus population and become one of the most energetic agents of its reproduction. . . . The whole form of the movement of modern industry depends, therefore, upon the constant transformation of a part of the laboring population into unemployed or half-employed hands. The superficiality of Political Economy shows itself in the fact that it looks upon the expansion and contraction of credit, which is a mere symptom of the periodic changes of the industrial cycle, as their cause. [Chapter XXV, §3]

Primitive Accumulation

The accumulation of capital presupposes surplus-value; surplus-value presupposes capitalistic production; capitalistic production presupposes the pre-existence of considerable masses of capital and of labor-power in the hands of producers of commodities. The whole movement, therefore, seems to turn into a vicious circle, out of which we can only get by supposing a primitive accumulation . . . an accumulation not the result of the capitalist mode of production, but its starting point. . . .

The historical movement which changes the producers into wage workers appears, on the one hand, as their emancipation from serfdom and from the fetters of the guilds, and this side alone exists for our bourgeois historians. But, on the other hand, these new freedmen became sellers of themselves only after they had been robbed of all their own means of production and of all the guarantees of existence afforded by the old feudal arrangements. And the history of this, their expropriation, is written in the annals of mankind in letters of blood and fire.

The industrial capitalists, these new potentates, had on their part not only to displace the guild masters of handicrafts, but also the feudal lords, the possessors of the sources of wealth. In this respect their conquest of social power appears as the fruit of a victorious struggle both against feudal lordship and its revolting prerogatives, and against the guilds and the fetters they laid on the free development of production and the free exploitation of man by man. . . . The starting point of the development that gave rise to the wage laborer as well as to the capitalist was the servitude of the laborer. The advance consisted in a change of form of this servitude, in the transformation of feudal exploitation into capitalist exploitation. To understand its march we need not go back very far. Although we come across the first beginnings of capitalist production as early as the 14th or 15th century, sporadically, in certain towns of the Mediterranean, the capitalistic era dates from the 16th century. . . .

In the history of primitive accumulation all revolutions are epoch-making that act as levers for the capitalist class in course of formation; but, above all, those moments when great masses of men are suddenly and forcibly torn from their means of subsistence and hurled as free and "unattached" proletarians on the labor market. The expropriation of the agricultural producer, of the peasant, from the soil is the basis of the whole process. [Chapter XXVI]

Expropriation of Agricultural Population from the Land

The prelude of the revolution that laid the foundation of the capitalist mode of production was played in the last third of the 15th and the first decade of the 16th century. A mass of free proletarians was hurled on the labor market by the breaking up of the bands of feudal retainers, who, as Sir James Steuart well says, "everywhere uselessly filled house and castle." Although the royal power, itself a product of bourgeois development, in its strike after absolute sovereignty forcibly hastened on the dissolution of these bands of retainers, it was by no means the sole cause of it. In insolent conflict with king and parliament, the great feudal lords created an incomparably larger proletariat by the forcible driving of the peasantry from the land, to which the latter had the same feudal right as the lord himself, and by the usurpation of the common lands. The rapid rise of the Flemish wool manufactures, and the corresponding rise in the price of wool in England, gave the direct impulse to these evictions. The old nobility had been devoured by the great feudal wars. The new nobility was the child of its time, for which money was the power of all powers. Transformation of arable land into sheepwalks was, therefore, its cry. . . . The dwellings of the peasants and the cottages of the laborers were razed to the ground or doomed to decay. [Chapter XXVII]

The Genesis of the Industrial Capitalist

The genesis of the industrial capitalist did not proceed in such a gradual way as that of the farmer. Doubtless many small guild masters, and yet more independent small artisans, or even wage laborers, transformed themselves into small capitalists, and (by gradually extending exploitation of age labor and corresponding accumulation) into full-blown capitalists. . . . The snail's pace of this method corresponded in no wise with the commercial requirements of the new world market that the great discoveries of the end of the 15th century created. But the middle age had handed down two distinct forms of capital, which mature in the most different economic social formations and which, before the era of the capitalist mode of production, are considered as capital— usurer's capital and merchant's capital. . . .

The money capital formed by means of usury and commerce was prevented from turning into industrial capital, in the country by the feudal constitution, in the town by the guild organization. These fetters vanished with the dissolution of feudal society, with the expropriation and partial eviction of the country population. The new manufacturers were established at seaports or in inland points beyond the control of the old municipalities and their guilds. Hence in England an embittered struggle of the corporate towns against these new industrial nurseries.

The discovery of gold and silver in America, the extirpation, enslavement, and entombment in mines of the aboriginal population, the beginning of the conquest and looting of the East Indies, the turning of Africa into a warren for the commercial hunting of black-skins, signalized the rosy dawn of the era of capitalist production. These idyllic proceedings are the chief moments of primitive accumulation. . . .

The different momenta of primitive accumulation distribute themselves now, more or less in chronological order, particularly over Spain, Portugal, Holland, France, and England. In England at the end of the 17th century, they arrive at a systematical combination, embracing the colonies, the national debt, the modern mode of taxation, and the protectionist system. These methods depend in part on brute force, e.g., the colonial system. But they all employ the power of the State, the concentrated and organized force of society, to hasten, hothouse fashion, the process of transformation of the feudal mode of production into the capitalist mode, and to shorten the transition. Force is the midwife of every old society pregnant with a new one. It is itself an economic power. . . .

The treatment of the aborigines was, naturally, most frightful in plantation colonies destined for export trade only, such as the West Indies, and in rich and well-populated countries, such as Mexico and India, that were given over to plunder. But even in the colonies properly so-called, the Christian character of primitive accumulation did not belie itself. Those sober virtuosi of Protestantism, the Puritans of New England, in 1703 by decrees of their assembly set a premium of £40 on every Indian scalp and every captured redskin: in 1720 a premium of £100 on every scalp; in 1744, after Massachusetts-Bay had proclaimed a certain tribe as rebels, the following prices: for a male scalp of 12 years and upwards £100 (new currency), for a male prisoner £105, for women and children prisoners £50, for scalps of women and children £50. . . .

The colonial system ripened, like a hothouse, trade and navigation. . . . Powerful levers for concentration of capital, the colonies secured a market for the budding manufactures and, through the monopoly of the market, an increased accumulation. The treasures captured outside Europe by undisguised looting, enslavement, and murder floated back to the mother country and were there turned into capital. . . .

The public debt becomes one of the most powerful levers of primitive accumulation. . . . The state creditors actually give nothing away, for the sum lent is transformed into public hands, just as so much hard cash would. But further, apart from the class of lazy annuitants thus created, and from the improvised wealth of the financiers, middlemen between the government and the nation—as also apart from the tax farmers, merchants, private manufacturers, to whom a good part of every national loan renders the service of a capital fallen from heaven—the national debt has given rise to joint-stock companies, to dealings in negotiable effects of all kinds, and to agiotage, in a word to stock-exchange gambling and the modern bankocracy.

At their birth the great banks, decorated with national titles, were only associations of private speculators, who placed themselves by the side of governments and, thanks to the privileges they received, were in a position to advance money to the state. Hence the accumulation of the national debt has no more infallible measure than the successive rise in the stock of these banks, whose full development dates from the founding of the Bank of England in 1694. The Bank of England began with lending its money to the Government at 8 per cent.; at the same time it was empowered by Parliament to coin money out of the same capital, by lending it again to the public in the form of bank notes. It was allowed to use these notes for discounting bills, making advances on commodities, and for buying the precious metals. It was not long ere this credit money, made by the bank itself, became the coin in which the Bank of England made its loans to the state and paid, on account of the state, the interest on the public debt. . . . [Chapter XXXI]

Historical Tendency of Capitalist Accumulation

The private property of the laborer in his means of production is the foundation of petty industry, whether agricultural, manufacturing, or both; petty industry, again, is an essential condition for the development of social production and of the free individuality of the laborer himself. . . . This mode of production presupposes parcelling of the soil and scattering of the other means of production. As it excludes the concentration of these means of production, so also it excludes cooperation, division of labor within each separate process of production, the control over and the productive application of the forces of nature by society, and the free development of the social productive powers. It is compatible only with a system of production and a society moving within narrow and more or less primitive bounds. . . . At a certain stage of development it brings forth the material agencies for its own dissolution. From that moment new forces and new passions spring up in the bosom of society; but the old social organization fetters them and keeps them down. It must be annihilated; it is annihilated. Its annihilation, the transformation of the individualized and scattered means of production into socially concentrated ones, of the pygmy property of the many into the huge property of the few, the expropriation of the great mass of the people from the soil, from the means of subsistence, and from the means of labor, this fearful and painful expropriation of the mass of the people forms the prelude to the history of capital. . . .

As soon as this process of transformation has sufficiently decomposed the old society from top to bottom, as soon as the laborers are turned into proletarians, their means of labor into capital, as soon as the capitalist mode of production stands on its own feet, then the further socialization of labor and further transformation of the land and other means of production into socially exploited and, therefore, common means of production, as well as the further expropriation of private proprietors, takes a new form. That which is now to be expropriated is no longer the laborer working for himself, but the capitalist exploiting many laborers. This expropriation is accomplished by the action of the immanent laws of capitalistic production itself, by the centralization of capital. One capitalist always kills many. Hand in hand with this centralization, or this expropriation of many capitalists by few, develop, on an ever-extending scale, the cooperative form of the labor process, the conscious technical application of science, the methodical cultivation of the soil, the transformation of the instruments of labor into instruments of labor only usable in common, the economizing of all means of production by their use as the means of production of combined, socialized labor, the entanglement of all peoples in the net of the world market, and with this, the international character of the capitalistic regime. Along with the constantly diminishing number of the magnates of capital, who usurp and monopolize all advantages of this process of transformation, grows the mass of misery, oppression, slavery, degradation, exploitation; but with this too grows the revolt of the working class, a class always increasing in numbers, and disciplined, united, organized by the very mechanism of the process of capitalist production itself. The monopoly of capital becomes a fetter upon the mode of production, which has sprung up and flourished along with, and under it. Centralization of the means of production and socialization of labor at least reach a point where they become incompatible with their capitalist integument. This integument is burst asunder. The knell of capitalist private property sounds. The expropriators are expropriated. . . .

The transformation of scattered private property, arising from individual labor, into capitalist private property is, naturally, a process, incomparably more protracted, violent, and difficult, than the transformation of capitalistic private property, already practically resting on socialized production, into socialized property. In the former case, we had the expropriation of the mass of the people by a few usurpers; in the latter, we have the expropriation of a few usurpers by the mass of the people. [Chapter XXXII]

Wages, Underconsumption, and Crises

It is purely a tautology to say that crises are caused by the scarcity of solvent consumers, or of a paying consumption. The capitalist system does not know any other modes of consumption but a paying one. . . . But if one were to attempt to clothe this tautology with a semblance of a profounder justification by saying that the working class receive too small a portion of their own product, and the evil would be remedied by giving them a larger share of it, or raising their wages, we should reply that crises are precisely always preceded by a period in which wages rise generally and the working class actually get a larger share of the annual product intended for consumption. From the point of view of the advocates of "simple" (!) common sense, such a period should rather remove a crisis. It seems, then, that capitalist production comprises certain conditions which are independent of good or bad will and permit the working class to enjoy that relative prosperity only momentarily, and at that always as a harbinger of a coming crisis. [Vol. II, Chapter XX]

The General Rate of Profit and Equilibrium Prices of Production

The average profit is but accidentally determined by the unpaid labor absorbed in the sphere of the individual capitalist. Only in this crude and meaningless form are we still reminded of the fact that value of the commodities is determined by the labor contained in them. [Vol. III, Chapter IX]

Equalization of Profit through Competition and Market Prices

The price of production of the produced commodities coincides exactly or approximately with their values as expressed in money. . . . competition distributes the social capital in such a way between the various spheres of production that the prices of production of each sphere are formed after the model of the prices of production in those spheres of average composition, which is $k + kp'$, cost-price plus the average rate of profit multiplied by the cost-price. Now, this average rate of profit is nothing else but the percentage of profit in that sphere of average composition, in which the profit is identical with the surplus-value. Hence the rate of profit is the same in all spheres of production, for it is apportioned according to that one of the average spheres of production in which the average composition of capitals prevails. Consequently the sum of the profits of all spheres of production must be equal to the sum of surplus-values, and the sum of the prices of production of the total social product equal to the sum of its values. . . . In this way the tendency necessarily prevails to make of the prices of production merely changed forms of value, or to make of profits but mere portions of surplus-value produced in each special sphere of production, but in proportion to the mass of capital employed in each sphere of production. . . .

Now, if the commodities are sold at their values, then, as we have shown, considerably different rates of profit arise in various spheres of production, according to the different organic composition of the masses of capital invested in them. But capital withdraws from spheres with low rates of profit and invades others which yield a higher rate. By means of this incessant emigration and immigration, in one word, by its distribution among the various spheres in accord with a rise of the rate of profit here, and its fall there, it brings about such a proportion of supply to demand that the average profit in the various spheres of production becomes the same, so that values are converted into prices of production. This equilibration is accomplished by capital in a more or less perfect degree to the extent that capitalist development is advanced in a certain nation, in other words, to the extent that conditions in the respective countries are adapted to the capitalist mode of production. . . .

The incessant equilibration of the continual differences is accomplished so much quicker, (1) the more movable capital is, the easier it can be shifted from one sphere and one place to another; (2) the quicker labor-power can be transferred from one sphere to another and from one local point of production to another. The first condition implies complete freedom of trade in the interior of society and the removal of all monopolies with the exception of those which naturally arise out of the capitalist mode of production. It implies, furthermore, the development of the credit-system, which concentrates the inorganic mass of the disposable social capital instead of leaving it in the hands of individual capitalists. Finally it implies a subordination of the various spheres of production to the control of capitalists. . . . This equilibration meets great obstacles, whenever numerous and large spheres of production, which are not operated on a capitalistic basis (such as farming by small farmers) are interpolated between the capitalist spheres and interrelated with them. . . [Vol. III, Chapter X]

The Tendency of the Rate of Profit to Fall

The same rate of surplus-value, with the same degree of labor exploitation, would express itself in a falling rate of profit, because the material growth of the constant capital, and consequently of the total capital, implies their growth in value, although not in the same proportion.

If it is further assumed that this gradual change in the composition of capital is not confined to some individual spheres of production, but occurs more or less in all, or at least in the most important ones, so that they imply changes in the organic average composition of the total capital of a certain society, then the gradual and relative growth of the constant over the variable capital must necessarily lead to a *gradual fall of the average rate of profit [s/C]*, so long as the rate of surplus-value *[s/v]*, or the intensity of exploitation of labor by capital, remain the same. . . . It is, in another way, but an expression of the progressive development of the productive powers of society, which is manifested by the fact that the same number of laborers, in the same time, convert an ever growing quantity of raw and auxiliary materials into products, thanks to the growing application of machinery and fixed capital in general, so that less labor is needed for the production of the same, or of more, commodities. . . .

The law of the falling tendency of the rate of profit . . . does not argue in any way against the fact that the absolute mass of the employed and exploited labor set in motion by the social capital, and consequently the absolute mass of the surplus value appropriated by it, may grow. . . . Accumulation itself, however, and the concentration of capital that goes with it, is a material means of increasing the productive power. Now, this growth of the means of production includes the increase of the laboring population, the creation of a laboring population which corresponds to the surplus-capital or even exceeds its general requirements, leading to an overpopulation of working people. A momentary excess of the surplus-capital over the laboring population controlled by it would have a twofold effect. It would, on the one hand, mitigate the conditions, which decimate the offspring of the laboring class and would facilitate marriages among them, by raising wages. This would tend to increase the laboring population. On the other hand, it would employ the methods by which relative surplus-value is increased (introduction and improvement of machinery) and thereby create still more rapidly an artificial relative overpopulation, which in its turn would be a hothouse for the actual propagation of its numbers, since under capitalist production poverty propagates its kind. . . .

The development of capitalist production and accumulation lifts the processes of labor to a higher scale and gives them greater dimensions, which imply larger investments of capital for each individual establishment. A growing concentration of capitals (accompanied by a growing number of capitalists, though not to the same extent) is therefore one of the material requirements of capitalist production as well as one of the results produced by it. Hand in hand with it, and mutually interacting, goes a progressive expropriation of the more or less direct producers. It is, then, natural for the capitalists that they should control increasing armies of laborers (no matter how much the variable capital may relatively decrease in comparison to the constant capital), and that the mass of surplus-value, and of profit, appropriated by them, should grow simultaneously with the fall of the rate of profit, and in spite of it. . . .

Given a certain laboring population, the mass of surplus-value, and therefore the absolute mass of profit, must grow if the rate of surplus-value increases by a prolongation or intensification of the working day, or by a lowering of the value of wages through a development of the productive power of labor, and must do so in spite of the relative decrease of the variable capital compared with the constant. . . . [Vol. III, Chapter XIII]

Counteracting Causes Which May Offset the Falling Rate of Profit

If we consider the enormous development of the productive powers of labor ... the enormous mass of fixed capital ... how is it that this fall is not greater and more rapid? There must be some counteracting influences at work, which thwart and annul the effects of this general law, leaving to it merely the character of a tendency.

1. Raising the Intensity of Exploitation. There are many ways of intensifying labor, which imply an increase of the constant capital as compared to the variable, and consequently a fall in the rate of profit, for instance, setting a laborer to watch a larger number of machines. In such cases—and in the majority of manipulations serving to produce relative surplus-value—the same causes, which bring about an increase in the rate of surplus-value, may also imply a fall in the mass of surplus-value, looking upon the matter from the point of view of the total quantities of invested capital. But there are other means of intensification, such as increasing the speed of machinery, which, although consuming more raw materials, and, so far as the fixed capital is concerned, wearing out the machinery so much faster, nevertheless do not affect the relation of its value to the price of labor set in motion by it. It is particularly the prolongation of the working day, this invention of modern industry, which increases the mass of appropriated surplus-labor without essentially altering the proportion of the employed labor-power to the constant capital. . . .

2. Depression of Wages Below Their Value. This is mentioned only empirically at this place, since it, like many other things, which might be enumerated here has nothing to do with the general analysis of capital, but belongs in a presentation of competition. . . .

3. Cheapening of the Elements of Constant Capital. From the point of view of the total capital, the value of the constant capital does not increase in the same proportion as its material volume. For instance, the quantity of cotton, which a single European spinning operator works up in a modern factory, has grown in a colossal degree compared to the quantity formerly worked up by a European operator with a spinning wheel. But the value of the worked-up cotton has not grown in proportion to its mass. The same holds good of machinery and other fixed capital . . . as a result of the increased productivity of labor. . . .

4. Relative Overpopulation. The relative overpopulation becomes so much more apparent in a certain country, the more the capitalist mode of production is developed in it. This, again, is on the one hand a reason, which explains why the imperfect subordination of labor to capital continues in many lines of production, and continues longer than seems at first glance compatible with the general stage of development. This is due to the cheapness and mass of the disposable or unemployed wage laborers, and to the greater resistance, which some lines of production, by their nature, oppose to a transformation of manufacture into machine production. . . .

5. Foreign Trade. To the extent that foreign trade cheapens partly the elements of constant capital, partly the necessities of life for which the variable capital is exchanged, it tends to raise the rate of profit by raising the rate of surplus-value and lowering the value of the constant capital. It exerts itself generally in this direction by permitting an expansion of the scale of production. But by this means it hastens on the one hand the process of accumulation, on the other the reduction of the variable as compared to the constant capital, and thus a fall in the rate of profit. . . .

Is the average rate of profit raised by the higher rate of profit, which capital invested in foreign, and particularly in colonial trade, realizes? Capitals invested in foreign trade are in a position to yield a higher rate of profit, because, in the first place, they come in competition with commodities produced in other countries with lesser facilities of production, so that an advanced country is enabled to sell its goods above their value even when it sells them cheaper than the competing countries. To the extent that the labor of the advanced countries is here exploited as a labor of a higher specific weight, the rate of profit rises, because labor which has not been paid as being of a higher quality is sold as such. The same condition may obtain in the relations with a certain country, into which commodities are exported and from which commodities are imported. This country may offer more materialized labor in goods than it receives, and yet it may receive in return commodities cheaper than it could produce them. In the same way a manufacturer, who exploits a new invention before it has become general, undersells his competitors and yet sells his commodities above their individual values, that is to say, he exploits the specifically higher productive power of the labor employed by him as surplus-value. By this means he secures a surplus-profit. On the other hand, capitals invested in colonies, etc., may yield a higher rate of profit for the simple reason that the rate of profit is higher there on account of the backward development, and for the added reason, that slaves, coolies, etc., permit a better exploitation of labor. . . [Vol. III, Chapter XIV]

Internal Contradictions of the Law

So far as the rate of self-expansion of the total capital, the rate of profit, is the incentive of capitalist production . . . its fall checks the formation of new independent capitals and thus seems to threaten the develop of the process of capitalist production. It promotes overproduction, speculation, crises, surplus-capital along with surplus-population. . . .

But this production of surplus-value is but the first act of the capitalist process of production, it merely terminates the act of direct production. . . . Now comes the second act of the process. The entire mass of commodities, the total product, which contains a portion which is to reproduce the constant and variable capital as well as a portion representing surplus value, must be sold. If this is not done, or only partly accomplished, or only at prices which are below the prices of production, the laborer has been none the less exploited, but his exploitation does not realize as much for the capitalist. It may yield no surplus-value at all for him, or only realize a portion of the produced surplus-value, or it may even mean a partial or complete loss of his capital. The conditions of direct exploitation and those of the realization of surplus-value are not identical. They are separated logically as well as by time and space. The first are only limited by the productive power of society, the last by the proportional relations of the various lines of production and by the consuming power of society. This last-named power is not determined either by the absolute productive power nor by the absolute consuming power, but by the consuming power based on antagonistic conditions of distribution, which reduces the consumption of the great mass of the population to a variable minimum within more or less narrow limits. The consuming power is furthermore restricted by the tendency to accumulate, the greed for an expansion of capital and production of surplus-value on an enlarged scale. This is a law of capitalist production imposed by incessant revolutions in the methods of production themselves, the resulting depreciation of existing capital, the general competitive struggle and the necessity of improving the product and expanding the scale of production, for the sake of self-preservation and on penalty of failure. The market must, therefore, be continually extended, so that its interrelations and the conditions regulating them assume more and more the form of a natural law independent of the producers and become very more uncontrollable. . . . But to the extent that the productive power develops, it finds itself at variance with the narrow basis on which the conditions of consumption rest. . . . [Vol. III, Chapter XV]

The Falling Rate of Profit and Crises

Together with the fall of the rate of profit grows the mass of capitals, and hand in hand with it goes a depreciation of the existing capital, which checks this fall and gives an accelerating push to the accumulation of capital-values. . . . Periodically the conflict of antagonistic agencies seeks vent in crises. The crises are always but momentary and forcible solutions of the existing contradictions, violent eruptions, which restore the disturbed equilibrium for a while. . . .

   With the fall of the rate of profit grows the lowest limit of capital required in the hands of the individual capitalist for the productive employment of labor, required both for the exploitation of labor and for bringing the consumed labor time within the . . . limits of the average social labor time required for the production of the commodities. Simultaneously with it grows the concentration, because there comes a certain limit where large capital with a small rate of profit accumulates faster than small capital with a large rate of profit. This increasing concentration in its turn brings about a new fall in the rate of profit at a certain climax. The mass of the small divided capitals is thereby pushed into adventurous channels, speculation, fraudulent credit, fraudulent stocks, crises. . . .

   The equilibrium is restored by making more or less capital unproductive or destroying it. . . . The principal work of destruction would show its most dire effects in a slaughtering of the *values* of capitals. That portion of the value of capital which exists only in the form of claims on future shares of surplus-value of profit, which consists in fact of creditor's notes on production in its various forms, would be immediately depreciated by the reduction of the receipts on which it is calculated. . . . One portion of the commodities on the market can complete its process of circulation and reproduction only by means of an immense contraction of its prices, which means a depreciation of the capital represented by it. In the same way the elements of fixed capital are more or less depreciated. Then there is the added complication that the process of reproduction is based on definite assumptions as to prices, so that a general fall in prices checks and disturbs the process of reproduction. This interference and stagnation paralyzes the function of money as a medium of payment, which is conditioned on the development of capital and the resulting price relations. The chain of payments due at certain times is broken in a hundred places, and the disaster is intensified by the collapse of the credit-system. Thus violent and acute crises are brought about, sudden and forcible depreciations, an actual stagnation and collapse of the process of reproduction, and finally a real falling off in reproduction. . . .

The fall in prices and the competitive struggle would have given to every capitalist an impulse to raise the individual value of his total product above its average value by means of new machines, new and improved working methods, new combinations, which means, to increase the productive power of a certain quantity of labor, to lower the proportion of the variable to the constant capital, and thereby to release some laborers, in short, to create an artificial over-population. The depreciation of the elements of constant capital itself would be another factor tending to raise the rate of profit. . . . The present stagnation of production would have prepared an expansion of production later on, within capitalistic limits. And in this way the cycle would be run once more. . . .

The barrier of the capitalist mode of production becomes apparent:

(1) In the fact that the development of the productive power of labor creates in the falling rate of profit a law which turns into an antagonism of this mode of production at a certain point and requires for its defeat periodical crises.

(2) In the fact that the expansion or contraction of production is determined by the appropriation of unpaid labor and . . . by a definite rate of profit, instead of being determined by the relations of production to . . . the wants of socially developed human beings. [Vol. III, Chapter XV]

Financial Capital and Real Capital

Let us furthermore make exceptions of fluctuations of prices, which prevent large portions of the total capital from reproducing themselves under average conditions and which, owing to the general interrelations of the entire process of reproduction, such as are developed particularly by credit, must always call forth general stoppages of a transient nature. Let us also make abstraction of the bogus transactions and speculations, which the credit system favors. In that case, a crisis could be explained only by a disproportion of the consumption of the capitalists and the accumulation of their capitals. But as matters stand, the reproduction of the capitals invested in production depends largely upon the consuming power of the non-producing classes; while the consuming power of the laborers is handicapped partly by the laws of wages, partly by the fact that it can be exerted only so long as the laborers can be employed at a profit for the capitalist class. The last cause of all real crises always remains the poverty and restricted consumption of the masses as compared to the tendency of capitalist production to develop the productive forces in such a way, that only the absolute power of consumption of the entire society would be their limit. [Vol. III, Chapter XXX]

QUESTIONS FOR DISCUSSION

1 What are the strongest *radical* or revolutionary elements in Marx's economic theory?
2 How does Marx use facts of economic history to support his perspective or theory of capitalism? Is he testing economic predictions? If one or another of his economic "predictions" were to fail—as many have—would his perspective or theory have to be rejected?
3 What might prevent the profit rate from falling?

READING 11

Neo-Marxist economic theories have generally followed the lines taken in one or another part of the master's legacy. Which theory is adopted often depends on the political orientation of the writer. The Russian leader **V. I. Lenin** (1870-1924) was principally interested in revolution in a semi-developed country; hence he developed Marx's theory of imperialism. According to Lenin's theory, highly developed capitalist powers come into conflict with each other as they seek markets, cheap resources and labor, and control in less developed areas. Imperialists' competition may allow worker and peasant states to emerge, as in Russia.

The American economy suffered from low growth and high unemployment during the 1930s and late 1950s. Accordingly, it was natural for neo-Marxist authors such as **Paul Baran** (1909-1964) and **Paul Sweezy** (born 1910) to pursue the notion of insufficient aggregate demand—what amounts to underconsumption, another Marxist theory of capitalist breakdown.

It is said that Prof. Baran of Stanford was the only Marxist professor of economics at a major American university during the anti-communist McCarthy era. His *The Political Economy of Growth* (1957) is still read by students of economic development and international political economy. Sweezy had written a brilliant Marxist treatise, *The Theory of Capitalist Development* (1942), in which many have seen the influence of Keynes, too. As editor of the independent *Monthly Review,* Sweezy has been interested in various attempts to establish socialism in China, Cuba, and the USSR on the ground that the international class struggle of the late 20th century now extends to the Third World.

According to *Monopoly Capital* (1966), excerpted below, the "surplus" (defined as potential production at full employment less "socially necessary" costs) has been rising in the Western capitalist countries for decades. Monopolistic competition aggravates the gap between what the economy could produce and what workers can purchase. Wasteful selling expenses and domestic investment in new capacity are inadequate to absorb the growing surplus, say these neo-Marxist authors. Only imperialist military spending can absorb the surplus without adversely affecting the interests of the corporate capitalist class.

Monopoly Capital[*]

Paul Baran and Paul Sweezy

Important works of Marxian social science have been rare in recent years. Marxists have too often been content to repeat familiar formulations, as though nothing really new had happened since the days of Marx and Engels—or of Lenin at the latest. As a result Marxists have failed to explain important developments, or sometimes even to recognize their existence. The Great Depression of the 1930s accorded admirably with Marxian theory, and its occurrence of course greatly strengthened the belief that similar catastrophic economic breakdowns were inevitably in the future. And yet, much to the surprise of many Marxists, two decades have passed since the end of the Second World War without the recurrence of severe depression. Nor have Marxists contributed significantly to our understanding of some of the major characteristics of the "affluent society"—particularly its colossal capacity to generate private and public waste and the profound economic, political, and cultural consequences which flow from this feature of the system. . . .

There is one important factor which we believe can be identified and isolated and hence (at least in principle) remedied: the Marxian analysis of capitalism still rests in the final analysis on the assumption of a competitive economy. . . .

We believe that the time has come to remedy this situation and to do so in an explicit and indeed radical fashion. . . . Today the typical economic unit in the capitalist world is not the small firm producing a negligible fraction of a homogeneous output for an anonymous market but a large-scale enterprise producing a significant share of the output of an industry, or even several industries, and able to control its prices, the volume of its production, and the types and amounts of its investments. . . .

We also believe that the modes of utilization of surplus constitute the indispensable mechanism linking the political, cultural, and ideological superstructure. . . . The economic surplus, in the briefest possible definition, is the difference between what a society produces and the costs of producing it. . . . The magnitude of the surplus in the United States amounted to 46.9 percent of Gross National Product in 1929. This figure declined in the early years of the Great Depression and of course rose sharply during the Second World War. Apart from these interludes, the trend has been steadily upward, reaching 56.1 percent in 1963. . . . The portion of the surplus which is usually identified with surplus value (profits + interest + rent = Phillips's "property

[*]*Source:* Selections from chapters 1-4 and 7 of Paul Baran and Paul M. Sweezy, *Monopoly Capital, An Essay on the American Economic and Social Order* (New York and London: Monthly Review Press, 1966). Copyright © 1966 by Paul M. Sweezy. Reprinted by permission of Monthly Review Foundation.

income") declined sharply in the same period.[9] In 1929 property income was 57.5 percent of total surplus, and in 1963 it was only 31.9 percent. . . .

The Giant Corporation

We start . . . with an analysis of the typical unit of Big Business, the modern giant corporation. . . . The corporate paradigm on which we wish to focus attention has a number of characteristic features of which we may single out the following:

(1) Control rests in the hands of management, that is to say, the board of directors plus the chief executive officers. Outside interests are often (but not always) represented on the board to facilitate the harmonization of the interests and policies of the corporation with those of customers, suppliers, bankers, etc.; but real power is held by the insiders, those who devote full time to the corporation and whose interests and careers are tied to its fortunes.

(2) Management is a self-perpetuating group. Responsibility to the body of stockholders is for all practical purposes a dead letter. Each generation of managers recruits its own successors and trains, grooms, and promotes them according to its own standards and values. The corporate career recognizes two characteristic forms of advance: rising from lower to higher positions within a given company and moving from a smaller company to a larger one. The acme of success is the presidency or board chairmanship of one of the biggest corporations.

(3) Each corporation aims at and normally achieves financial independence through the internal generation of funds which remain at the disposal of management. The corporation may still, as a matter of policy, borrow from or through financial institutions, but it is not normally forced to do so and hence is able to avoid the kind of subjection to financial control which was so common in the world of Big Business fifty years ago.

Before we investigate the behavior of giant corporations of this type, a few words of explanation and clarification may be useful.

In the first place, there is no implication in our description of the corporate paradigm that great wealth, or family connections, or large personal or family stockholdings are unimportant in the recruiting and promotion of management personnel—that, for example, the chances of a David Rockefeller's getting a job at the Chase Manhattan Bank and rising to the top position are the same as those of anyone else with similar personal and intellectual attributes. On the contrary, wealth and connections are of the utmost importance, and it may indeed be taken for granted that they are normally decisive. What we are implying is something quite different: that stock ownership, wealth, connections, etc., do not as a rule enable a man to control or exercise great influence on a giant corporation from the outside. They are rather tickets of admission to the inside, where real corporate power is wielded. . . .

What needs to be emphasized is that the location of power inside rather than outside the typical giant corporation renders obsolete the conception of the

---

[9]Joseph D. Phillips prepared the estimates of the surplus and it components for the United States, 1929-1963, which are presented in the Appendix.

"interest group" as a fundamental unit in the structure of capitalist society. In traditional usage, an interest group is a number of corporations under common control, the locus of power being normally an investment or commercial bank or a great family fortune. Thus a Morgan company was one under the control of the investment banking firm of J. P. Morgan & Company, a Rockefeller company one under the control of the Rockefeller family, and so on. The members of an interest group would naturally coordinate their policies; and in the case of conflicts, the interests of the controlling power (or of the whole group as interpreted by the controlling power) would prevail.

A whole series of developments have loosened or broken the ties that formerly bound the great interest groups together. . . . This does not of course mean that each giant corporation operates in isolation, that there are no alliances and alignments, no agreements and groupings. On the contrary, these forms of action—like their opposites, competition and struggle—are of the very essence of monopoly capitalism. All that we are asserting is that the relevant line-ups are determined not by ties to outside control centers but by the rational calculations of inside management. . . .

Behavior of the Large Corporation

What pattern of behavior can be expect from huge, management-controlled, financially independent corporations?

Formal economic theory has largely ignored this question, continuing to operate with the assumption of the profit-maximizing individual entrepreneur who has occupied the central role in theories of the capitalist system since well before the time of Adam Smith. Retaining this assumption amounts in effect to making another: that in all respects that matter to the functioning of the system the corporation acts like an individual entrepreneur. . . .

In practice, the search for "maximum" profits can only be the search for the greatest *increase* in profits which is possible in the given situation, subject of course to the elementary proviso that the exploitation of today's profit opportunities must not ruin tomorrow's. This is all there is to the profit maximization principle, but it also happens to be all that is necessary to validate the economizing behavior patterns which have been the very backbone of all serious economic theory for the last two centuries. . . . The big corporation, if not more profit-oriented than the individual entrepreneur . . . is at any rate better equipped to pursue a policy of profit maximization. The result is much the same: the economy of large corporations is more, not less, dominated by the logic of profit-making than the economy of small entrepreneurs ever was.[10] . . .

---

[10]Baran and Sweezy base their characterization on the research of James S. Earley, "Marginal Policies of 'Excellently Managed' Companies," *The American Economic Review* (March, 1956), together with an untitled paper in the *Papers and Proceedings* of the American Economic Association (May, 1957), pp. 333-335.

Motivation of Corporate Managers

Big corporations, then, are run by company men. What kind of people are they? What do they want and why? What position do they hold in the class structure of American society?

The fact is that the managerial stratum is the most active and influential part of the propertied class. All studies show that its members are largely recruited from the middle and upper reaches of the class structure; they overlap with what C. Wright Mills calls the "very rich"; with few and negligible exceptions, they are wealthy men in their own right, quite apart from the large incomes and extensive privileges which they derive from their corporate connections. It is of course true, as we have emphasized, that in the typical big corporation the management is not subject to stockholder control, and in this sense the "separation of ownership from control" is a fact. But there is no justification for concluding from this that managements in general are divorced from ownership in general. Quite the contrary, managers are among the biggest owners; and because of the strategic positions they occupy, they function as the protectors and spokesmen for all large-scale property. Far from being a separate class, they constitute in reality the leading echelon of the property-owning class. This is not to argue that managers have no distinctive interests *qua* managers. Like other segments of the propertied class, they do. But the conflicts of interest that arise in this way are between managers and small property owners rather than between managers and large property owners. The clearest case in point has to do with dividend policy.

It is generally assumed that the desire of managers, noted earlier, to generate the largest feasible volume of internal corporate funds leads to an interest in a low dividend payout rate, while stockholders' concern to maximize their disposable cash income leads to an interest in a high payout rate. Actually, this is much too simple. Most managers are themselves big owners of stock (in their own and other companies) and as such have the same interest in dividends as other big stockholders. This interest is neither in a minimum nor a maximum payout rate but somewhere in between: stockholdings should yield a reasonable cash income (for managers this is particularly important as a guarantee of family security after they retire or die); on the other hand, they should also steadily appreciate in value. The first requirement calls for dividends, the second for plowing back of earnings. Nevertheless, the special managerial interest in a low payout rate does exist and is undoubtedly important. But the point to be emphasized is that this makes managers the allies of the very largest stockholders for whom a minimum payout rate is "also a desideratum." The reason of course is that the very rich save a large part of their incomes in any case, and it is to their advantage for the corporations in which they own stock to do the saving for them rather than pay out dividends from which to do their own saving. Corporate saving results in an increase in the value of their stock. If at any time they need the cash, either to spend or for some other investment, they can sell part or all of their shares, realizing the increment of value in the form of a capital gain taxable at the maxi-mum rate of 25 percent. On the other hand, if they receive more in the form of dividends they have to pay taxes at the much higher rates applicable to their brackets, which of course cuts down their effective rate of saving.

Pressure for higher payout rates generally comes from small stockholders. Only rarely is it effectively exerted on managements via the formal corporate voting machinery, but this does not mean that the small stockholder is without influence. Socially the seven million or so small stockholders in the United States are an important group: they are quite likely to be solid citizens, leaders of public opinion with local political influence. Since the tiny upper echelon of the propertied class (including its leading element, the managers of the big corporations) is always politically vulnerable, it naturally wants to have the support and loyalty of the small stockholder. A moderate, and perhaps even more important a steady, dividend policy is the most effective way of insuring this support. . . .

The company man is dedicated to the advancement of his company This does not mean, however, that he is any more or less *homo economicus,* any more or less selfish, any more or less altruistic than either the tycoon or the individual owner-entrepreneur before him. All of these conceptions are at best irrelevant and at worst misleading. The problem is not one of "psychology" of any kind but of the selective and molding effects of institutions on the personnel that operates them. It might seem that this is too elementary to require mention, but unfortunately it is not possible to take for granted such a degree of enlightenment among economists. Economic theory is still heavily permeated by the "psychologizing" tradition of nineteenth-century utilitarianism, and economists need continually to be reminded that this tradition leads only to confusion and obscurantism.

To be a going concern, a social order must instill in its members the ambition to be a success in its own terms. Under capitalism the highest form of success is business success and under monopoly capitalism the highest form of business is the big corporation. In this system the normal procedure for an ambitious young man must be to work himself up to as near the top as possible of as big a corporation as possible. Once he enters a given corporation, he devotes himself to two ends: ascending the managerial ladder and advancing the relative status of his company in the corporate world. In practice these two ends are indistinguishable: the young man's rise in the company depends on his contribution to improving the position of the company. . . .

This remains true even after he has reached the top of a given company. If he makes a good record, he may be "called" to a larger company. And even if he is not, or has no hope of being, he is still just as much interested in improving the position of the company he leads; for standing, prestige, and power in the business world are not personal attributes but rather are conferred on the individual businessman by the standing, prestige, and power of his company and by his position in that company. . . .

But size is not the only index of corporate status: this is an oversimplification. Other important indexes are rate of growth and "strength" as measured by such standards as credit rating and the price of a company's securities. Thus, assuming equal size, one company will rank ahead of others if it is stronger and growing more rapidly; and strength and rapid growth may even offset a big size differential if the larger company is stagnant or declining.

The primary objectives of corporate policy—which are at the same time and inevitably the personal objectives of the corporate managers—are thus strength, rate of growth, and size. There is no general formula for quantifying or combining these objectives—nor is there any need for one. For they are reducible to the single common denominator of profitability. Profits provide the internal funds for expansion. Profits are the sinew and muscle of strength, which in turn gives access to outside funds if and when they are needed. Internal expansion, acquisition, and merger are the ways in which corporations grow, and growth is the road to size. Thus profits, even though not the ultimate goal, are the necessary means to all ultimate goals. As such, they become the immediate, unique, unifying, quantitative aim of corporate policies, the touchstone of corporate rationality, the measure of corporate success. . . .

The replacement of the individual capitalist by the corporate capitalist constitutes an institutionalization of the capitalist function. The heart and core of the capitalist function is accumulation: accumulation has always been the prime mover of the system, the locus of its conflicts, the source of both its triumphs and its disasters. But only in the infancy of the system could accumulation be said to exhaust the obligations of the capitalist: With success came also responsibilities. . . .

Advertising and Public Relations

Expenses of representation have traditionally taken the form of conspicuous waste on the one hand and philanthropy on the other. Both have always had what would nowadays be called a public-relations purpose: the one to dazzle and overawe the public, the other to secure its loyalty and affection. Both have been borne by the capitalist in his private capacity.

One of the most striking changes in the American scene in recent years has been a marked decline of both types of expenditure by the aristocracy of the business world. The great estates of Newport and Southampton, the regal yachts of the Morgans and the Astors, the debutante parties costing half a million dollars or more—one now reads more about these things in history books than in the society pages of the daily paper. The Big Businessman of today (Texas oilmen excepted, as they should be) lives if not modestly at least in decent obscurity: the last thing he wants is to make a big splash with his wealth. Similarly, individual philanthropy seems to play a decreasingly prominent role. . . . These developments do not mean, however, that capital's expenses of representation have somehow been abolished. Like other aspects of the capitalist function, responsibility for meeting capital's expenses of representation has been institutionalized. Nowadays it is the corporation itself that has to maintain a high standard of living before the public, and it does so by erecting grandiose headquarters providing its functionaries with offices which grow plushier by the year, transporting them in fleets of company-owned jet planes and Cadillacs, granting them unlimited expense accounts, and so on and on. Most of this is the sheerest kind of conspicuous waste, correlated negatively, if at all, with productive efficiency; yet no corporation with serious claims to Big Business standing would dream of neglecting this aspect of its operations. . . .

We have tried to show that the giant corporation of today is an engine for maximizing profits and accumulating capital to at least as great an extent as the individual enterprise of an earlier period. But it is not merely an enlarged and institutionalized version of the personal capitalist. There are major differences between these types of business enterprise, and at least two of them are of key importance to a general theory of monopoly capitalism: the corporation has a longer time horizon than the individual capitalist, and it is a more rational calculator. Both differences are fundamentally related to the incomparably larger scale of the corporation's operations.

The corporation is in principle immortal and inculcates in its functionaries a long time horizon, not because of its special legal form (after all, a corporation can be wound up just as easily as a proprietorship) but because what it "incorporates" is a vast and complex capital investment the value of which depends on its being maintained as a going concern. Similarly, the size of the corporation's operations enforces a far-reaching specialization and rationalization of the managerial function . . . cost accounting, budgeting, data processing, management consulting, operations research, and much else besides. . . .

The corporation, being under no pressure to realize quick returns and disposing over ample resources, approaches a new development with care and circumspection and does not make a final commitment until the relevant investigations and preparations have been carried out. Finally, and in a sense ironically, the corporation knows how to use for its own ends the very weaknesses of the small enterprise which it has outgrown. When a new industry or field of operations is being opened up, the big corporation tends to hold back deliberately and to allow individual entrepreneurs or small businesses to do the vital pioneering work. Many fail and drop out of the picture, but those which succeed trace out the most promising lines of development for the future. It is at this stage that the big corporations move to the center of the stage. Referring to the electric appliance field which he knew from long experience, T. K. Quinn, formerly a Vice President of General Electric, wrote: "I know of no original product invention, not even electric shavers or heating pads, made by any of the giant laboratories or corporations, with the possible exception of the household garbage grinder. . . . The record of the giants is one of moving in, buying out and absorbing the smaller creators."[11]. . .

The Tendency of the Surplus to Rise

The study of monopoly capitalism, like that of competitive capitalism, must begin with the workings of the price mechanism.

---

[11]T. K. Quinn, *Giant Business: Threat to Democracy,* New York, 1953, p. 117. [Even the kitchen garbage disposal was probably invented and perfected by a smaller company! —Ed.]

The crucial difference between the two is well known and can be summed up in the proposition that under competitive capitalism the individual enterprise is a "price taker," while under monopoly capitalism the big corporation is a "price maker.". . .

When we say that giant corporations are price makers, we mean that they can and do choose what prices to charge for their products. There are of course limits to their freedom of choice: above and below certain prices it would be preferable to discontinue production altogether. But typically the range of choice is wide. . . .

The typical giant corporation . . . is one of several corporations producing commodities which are more or less adequate substitutes for each other. When one of them varies its price, the effect will immediately be felt by the others. If firm A lowers its price, some new demand may be tapped, but the main effect will be to attract customers away from firms B, C, and D. Those not willing to give up their business to A will retaliate by lowering their prices, perhaps even undercutting A. While A's original move was made in the expectation of increasing its profit, the net result may be to leave all the firms in a worse position.

Under these circumstances, it is impossible for a single corporation, even if it has the fullest information about the demand for the products of the industry as a whole and about its own costs, to tell what price would maximize its profits. What it can sell depends not only on its own price but also on the prices charged by its rivals, and these it cannot know in advance. A firm may thus make ever so careful an estimate of the profit-maximizing price, but in the absence of knowledge about rivals' reactions it will be right only by accident. A wrong guess about rivals' reactions would throw the whole calculation off and necessitate readjustments which in turn would provoke further moves by rivals, and, so on, the whole process quite possibly degenerating into mutually destructive price warfare.

Unstable market situations of this sort were very common in the earlier phases of monopoly capitalism, and still occur from time to time, but they are not typical of present-day monopoly capitalism. And clearly they are anathema to the big corporations with their penchant for looking ahead, planning carefully, and betting only on the sure thing. To avoid such situations therefore becomes the first concern of corporate policy, the *sine qua non* of orderly and profitable business operations.

This objective is achieved by the simple expedient of banning price cutting as a legitimate weapon of economic warfare. Naturally this has not happened all at once or as a conscious decision. Like other powerful taboos, that against price cutting has grown up gradually out of long and often bitter experience, and it derives its strength from the fact that it serves the interests of powerful forces in society. As long as it is accepted and observed, the dangerous uncertainties are removed from the rationalized pursuit of maximum profits.

With price competition banned, sellers of a given commodity or of close substitutes have an interest in seeing that the price or prices established are such as to maximize the profits of the group as a whole. They may fight over the division of these profits . . . but none can wish that the total to be fought over should be smaller rather than larger. This is the decisive fact in determining the price policies and strategies of the typical large corporation.

And it means that the appropriate general price theory for an economy dominated by such corporations is the traditional monopoly price theory of classical and neo-classical economics. What economists have hitherto treated as a special case turns out to be, under conditions of monopoly capitalism, the general case. . . .

If maximization of the profits of the group constitutes the content of the pricing process under monopoly capitalism, its form can differ widely according to specific historical and legal conditions. In some countries, sellers are permitted or even encouraged to get together for the purpose of coordinating their policies. Resulting arrangements can vary all the way from tight cartels regulating both prices and outputs (a close approach to the pure monopoly case) to formal agreements to abide by certain price schedules (as exemplified by the famous "Gary dinners" in the American steel industry in the early years of the century). In the United States, where for historical reasons the ideology of competition has remained strong in spite of the facts of monopolization, antitrust laws effectively prevent such open collusion among sellers. Secret collusion is undoubtedly common, but it has its drawbacks and risks, and can hardly be described as the norm toward which a typical oligopolistic industry tends. That norm, it seems clear, is a kind of tacit collusion which reaches its most developed form in what is known as "price leadership."

As defined by Burns, "price leadership exists when the price at which most of the units in an industry offer to sell is determined by adopting the price announced by one of their number."[12] The leader is normally the largest and most powerful firm in the industry—such as U.S. Steel or General Motors—and the others accept its dominant role not only because it profits them to do so but also because they know that if it should come to price warfare the leader would be able to stand the gaff better than they could. . . .

But there are many other situations in which no such regularity is discernible: which firm initiates price changes seems to be arbitrary. This does not mean that the essential ingredient of tacit collusion is absent. The initiating firm may simply be announcing to the rest of the industry, "We think time has come to raise (or lower) price in the interest of all of us." If the others agree, they will follow. If they do not, they will stand pat, and the firm that made the first move will rescind its initial price change. It is this willingness to rescind if an initial change is not followed which distinguishes the tacit-collusion situation from a price-war situation. So long as all firms accept this convention—and it is really nothing but a corollary of the ban on price competition—it becomes relatively easy for the group as a whole to feel its way toward the price which maximizes the industry's profit. . . .

A qualification of the foregoing analysis seems called for. In the "pure" monopoly case, prices move upward or downward with equal ease, in response to changing conditions, depending entirely on whether a hike or a cut will improve the profit position. In oligopoly this is no longer quite the case. If one seller raises his price, this cannot possibly be interpreted as an aggressive move. The worst that can happen to him is that the others will

---

[12]Arthur R. Burns, *The Decline of Competition: A Study of the Evolution of American Industry* (New York, 1936), p. 76.

stand pat and he will have to rescind (or accept a smaller share of the market). In the case of a price cut, on the other hand, there is always the possibility that aggression is intended, that the cutter is trying to increase his share of the market by violating the taboo on price competition. If rivals do interpret the initial move in this way, a price war with losses to all may result. Hence everyone concerned is likely to be more circumspect about lowering than raising prices. Under oligopoly, in other words, prices tend to be stickier on the downward side than on the upward side, and this fact introduces a significant upward bias into the general price level in a monopoly capitalist economy. . . .

Regulation of "Natural Monopolies" and State Intervention

The common affairs of the entire bourgeois class include concern that no industries which play an important role in the economy and in which large property interests are involved should be either too profitable or too unprofitable. Extra large profits are gained not only at the expense of consumers but also of other capitalists (electric power and telephone service, for example, are basic costs of all industries), and in addition they may, and at times of political instability do, provoke demands for genuinely effective anti-monopoly action. Abnormally low profits in a major branch of the economy, such as agriculture, on the other hand, damage the interest of a large and powerful group of property owners who are able through pressure and bargaining with the other capitalists to enlist the necessary support for remedial action. It therefore becomes a state responsibility under monopoly capitalism to insure, as far as possible, that prices and profit margins in the deviant industries are brought within the range prevailing among the general run of giant corporations.

This is the background and explanation of the innumerable regulatory schemes and mechanisms which characterize the American economy today—commission regulation of public utilities, prorationing of oil production price supports and acreage controls in agriculture, and so on. In each case of course some worthy purpose is supposed to be served—to protect consumers, to conserve natural resources, to save the family-size farm—but only the naive believe that these fine sounding aims have any more to do with the case than the flowers that bloom in the spring. There is in fact a vast literature, based for the most part on official documents and statistics, to prove that regulatory commissions protect investors rather than consumers, that oil prorationing wastes rather than conserves natural resources, that the family-size farm is declining faster than in any previous period of American history.[13] All of this is fully understandable once the basic principle is grasped that under monopoly capitalism the function of the state is to serve the interests of monopoly capital. . . .

---

[13]A considerable body of the relevant material is conveniently assembled and summarized in Walter Adams and Horace M. Gray, *Monopoly in America: The Government as Promoter,* New York, 1955. [Footnote in original.]

The abandonment of price competition does not mean the end of all competition: it takes new forms and rages on with ever increasing intensity. Most of these new forms of competition come under the heading of what we call the sales effort. . . . Here we confine attention to those forms of competition which have direct bearing on costs of production and hence on the magnitude of the surplus.

If it is true, as we have argued, that oligopolies succeed in attaining a close approximation to the theoretical monopoly price and if their never ceasing efforts to cut costs, so much stressed by James Earley, are generally successful, then it follows with inescapable logic that surplus must have a strong and persistent tendency to rise. . . .

The firm with lower costs and higher profits enjoys a variety of advantages over higher-cost rivals in the struggle for market shares. . . . it can afford to be aggressive even to the point of threatening, and in the limiting case precipitating, a price war. It can get away with tactics (special discounts, favorable credit terms, etc.) which if adopted by a weak firm would provoke retaliation. It can afford the advertising, research, development of new product varieties, extra services, and so on, which are the usual means of fighting for market shares and which tend to yield results in proportion to the amount spent on them. . . . The lower-cost, higher-profit company acquires a special reputation which enables it to attract and hold customers, bid promising executive personnel away from rival firms, and recruit the ablest graduates of engineering and business schools. . . .

The whole motivation of cost reduction is to increase profits, and the monopolistic structure of markets enables the corporations to appropriate the lion's share of the fruits of increasing productivity directly in the form of higher profits. This means that under monopoly capitalism, declining costs imply continuously widening profit margins. And continuously widening profit margins in turn imply aggregate profits which rise not only absolutely but as a share of national product. If we provisionally equate aggregate profits with society's economic surplus, we can formulate as a law of monopoly capitalism that the surplus tends to rise both absolutely and relatively as the system develops. . . .

Profits which are neither invested nor consumed are no profits at all. It may be legitimate to speak of the potential profits which would be reaped if there were more investment and capitalists' consumption, but such potential profits cannot be traced in the statistical record—or rather they leave their traces in the statistical record in the paradoxical form of unemployment and excess capacity. . . .

The Absorption of Surplus:
Capitalists' Consumption and Investment

Does capitalist consumption tend to rise as a share of surplus? If not, the investment-seeking part of surplus must rise relative to total income, and the possibility that capitalists' consumption might provide a solution to the problem is excluded. . . .

The problem is now quite simply whether there is in fact a tendency for the distributed share of surplus (dividends) to rise, remain constant, or fall as surplus itself expands. And here the evidence leaves no doubt about the answer. Most large companies have a target dividend payout rate which remains remarkably constant over long periods of time (50 percent seems to be the most common figure). When profits rise, however, they do not immediately adjust dividends to maintain the target rate. . . . If this pattern is adhered to—and there is every indication that it is a deeply rooted aspect of corporate behavior—it follows that a continuous rise in earnings would be accompanied by an equally continuous decline in the payout rate.

Under these circumstances capitalists' consumption would increase absolutely, which of course is to be expected, but it would decline as a proportion of surplus and even more as a proportion of total income. Since these conclusions hold *a fortiori* to the extent that capitalists save out of their dividend incomes, it is clear that no solution of the problem of surplus absorption can be expected from this quarter. . . .

Can Investment Absorb Rising Saving?

The actual investment of an amount of surplus which rises relative to income must mean that the economy's capacity to produce grows more rapidly than its output. Such an investment pattern is certainly not impossible; indeed, it has frequently been observed in the history of capitalism. But what is impossible is that it should persist indefinitely. Sooner or later, excess capacity grows so large that it discourages further investment. When investment declines, so do income and employment and hence also surplus itself. In other words, this investment patten is self-limiting and ends in an economic downturn—the beginning of a recession or depression. . . .

As soon as we admit the possibility of less-than-capacity production, certain further points need to be made. . . . Any decline in the operating rate, through either a reduction in output or an increase in capacity or some combination of the two, will result in a decline in profits as well. . . . Surplus decreases relatively rapidly whenever production falls below capacity. Moreover, since the rate of dividend payout lags in the downward as well as in the upward direction, the investment-seeking part of surplus shrinks even faster. . . . On the downswing, in other words, the ratio of consumption to both surplus and total output rises, and this sooner or later puts a stop to the contraction. The lower turning point is reached when the amount of surplus seeking investment is exactly absorbed by available investment outlets. At this point, a temporary equilibrium is reached which is characterized by the existence of excess productive capacity and unemployed workers. . . .

Exogenous Sources of Investment Not Sufficient

But not all investment is endogenous. There is also "exogenous" investment, which may be defined as all investment which takes place independently of the demand factors generated by the normal workings of the system. . . . Three types of exogenous investment have figured prominently in economic literature: (1) investment to meet the needs of an expanding population; (2) investment in new methods of production and new products; and (3) foreign investment. To what extent can they be expected, singly or in combination, to provide the investment outlets needed to absorb a rising surplus?

(1) Population. . . . While there is no reason to deny that population growth per se does create some investment outlets, neither is there any case for assigning great importance to this factor. The experience of the United States during the 1940's and 1950's, when the rate of population growth rose sharply as compared to the depressed rate of the 1930's, strongly supports the theory—which was held by the classical economists—that population growth is a dependent, not an independent, variable. . . .

(2) New Methods and New Products. . . . Whereas in the competitive case no one, not even the innovating firms themselves, can control the rate at which new technologies are generally adopted, this ceases to be true in the monopolistic case. It is clear that the giant corporation will be guided not by the profitability of the new method considered in isolation, but by the net effect of the new method on the overall profitability of the firm. And this means that in general there will be a slower rate of introduction of innovations than under competitive criteria. . . . The introduction of new techniques in a manner which involves adding to productivity capacity (demand being assumed unchanged) will normally be avoided. The monopolist will prefer to wait until his existing capital is ready for replacement anyway before installing the new equipment. . . . Under monopoly capitalism there is no necessary correlation, as there is in a competitive system, between the rate of technological progress and the volume of investment outlets. Technological progress tends to determine the *form* which investment takes at any given time rather than its amount. . . .

Where the amount of depreciation is very large, as in present-day monopoly capitalism, it is quite possible that business can finance from this source alone all the investment it considers profitable to make in innovations (both new products and new processes), leaving no "innovational" outlets to help absorb investment-seeking surplus. . . .

(3) Foreign Investment. . . . As an outlet for investment-seeking surplus generated in the corporate sector of the monopoly capitalist system, . . . it neither does nor can be expected to play an important role. Indeed, except possibly for brief periods of abnormally high capital exports from the advanced countries, foreign investment must be looked upon as a method of pumping surplus out of underdeveloped areas, not as a channel through which surplus is directed into them. . . .

In 1963, United States corporations (nearly all giants) had foreign direct investments amounting to $40.6 billion. But a large proportion of this—probably the majority—was acquired without any outflow of capital from the United States [by providing patents and reinvestment of profits] . . . .

Even in cases where substantial sums of capital are exported, subsequent expansion commonly takes place through plowing back of profits; and the return flow of interest and dividends (not to mention remittances disguised in the form of payment for services and the like) soon repays the original investment many times over—and still continues to pour capital into the coffers of the parent corporation in the United States. . . . Under these circumstances, it is of course obvious that foreign investment aggravates rather than helps to solve the surplus absorption problem. . . . Monopoly capitalism is a self-contradictory system. It tends to generate ever more surplus, yet it fails to provide the consumption and investment outlets required for absorption of a rising surplus and hence for the smooth working of the system. Since surplus which cannot be absorbed will not be produced, it follows that the normal state of the monopoly capitalist economy is stagnation. . . . This means chronic underutilization of available human and material resources. . . .

How Can a Capitalist Society Stimulate Demand?

There are many conceivable ways of stimulating demand. If a socialist society, for example, should find that through some planning error more consumer goods were being produced than could be sold, given the existing structure of prices and incomes, the simplest and most direct remedy would clearly be to cut prices. This would reduce the amount of surplus at the disposal of the planning authorities and correspondingly raise the purchasing power of consumers. The threatened glut could be quickly and painlessly averted: everyone would be better off, no one worse off. Such a course of action is obviously not open to a monopoly capitalist society, in which the determination of prices is the jealously guarded prerogative of the giant corporations. . . .

[An alternative way of stimulating demand is] advertising. . . . Every giant corporation is driven by the logic of its situation to devote more and more attention and resources to the sales effort. And monopoly capitalist society as a whole has every interest in promoting rather than restricting and controlling this method of creating new markets and expanding old ones.

The Absorption of Surplus: Militarism and Imperialism

Why does the United States oligarchy need and maintain such a huge military machine nowadays when it used to get along with such a little one? In order to answer this question, we must first consider the role of armed force in capitalist society. . . . It would be quite impossible to understand the role of armed force in capitalist society without placing the international character of the system at the very center of the analytic focus. It is not that armed force under capitalism is used only in the international sphere. In every capitalist country it is used to dispossess, repress, and otherwise control the domestic labor force. But in relation to the problem which concerns us—the absorption of surplus by the military machine in the United States today—this aspect is of negligible importance and can be abstracted from. We can concentrate on the international uses of armed force.

The hierarchy of nations which make up the capitalist system is characterized by a complex set of exploitative relations. Those at the top exploit in varying degrees all the lower layers, and similarly those at any given level exploit those below them until we reach the very lowest layer which has no one to exploit. . . . Now it is obvious that all nations—except the dependent and defenseless ones at the bottom—have a need for armed force to maintain and if possible improve their positions in the exploitative hierarchy. How much a given nation needs at a given time depends on its position in the hierarchy and on the pattern of relations in the hierarchy as a whole at that particular time. Leading nations will always require most, and the magnitude of their needs will vary according to whether there is or is not an active struggle going on among them for the top position. . . .

The Purpose of American Military Imperialism

The American oligarchy's need for a huge military machine must be sought elsewhere than in a non-existent threat of Soviet aggression. Once we recognize this and free our minds of the cant and confusion generated by the oligarchy's ideological and propagandistic distortions, we shall soon discover what we are looking for: the same implacable hatred of socialism, the same determination to destroy it, that has dominated the leading nations of the capitalist world from the time the Bolsheviks seized power in November, 1917. The central purpose has always been the same: to prevent the expansion of socialism, to compress it into as small an area as possible, and ultimately to wipe it off the face of the earth. . . .

Most trade in the capitalist world is carried on by private enterprises, mainly by large corporations. What these corporations are interested in is not trade as such but profits: the reason they and the governments they control are opposed to the spread of socialism is not that it necessarily reduces their chances of importing or exporting (though of course it may), but that it does necessarily reduce their opportunities to profit from doing business with and in the newly socialized area. And when account is taken of the fact that for corporations in the leading capitalist countries, profit rates from doing business with and in the less developed and underdeveloped countries are generally higher than domestic profit rates, the reason for the vehemence of opposition to the spread of socialism in precisely those areas will be appreciated. . . . If we look ahead, we find that American corporate business, far from regarding its expansion abroad as having come to an end, is relying heavily for its future prosperity on the continued penetration of other countries' economies. . . .

What really interests the giant multinational corporations which dominate American policy[?] What they really want is *monopolistic control* over foreign sources of supply and foreign markets, enabling them to buy and sell on specially privileged terms, to shift orders from one subsidiary to another, to favor this country or that depending on which has the most advantageous tax, labor, and other policies—in a word, they want to do business on their own terms and wherever they choose. And for this what they need is not trading partners but "allies" and clients willing to adjust their laws and policies to the requirements of American Big Business. . . .

The Effect of American Militarism

So much for the American oligarchy's <u>need</u> for a military establishment. We must next examine the effect of satisfying this need on the private interests of the members of the oligarchy, and on the stability and cohesiveness of the country's class structure. . . . Most governmental activities designed to satisfy collective needs involve either competition with private interests or injury to the class position and privileges of the oligarchy and . . . for these reasons opposition is quickly aroused and rapidly reinforced as these activities are extended. The result is that roadblocks are encountered long before socially rational and desirable goals have been attained. How is it with government activities in the military sphere?

To begin with, it is obvious that the building up of a gigantic military establishment neither creates nor involves competition with private enterprise. There are no private military establishments with a vested interest in keeping the government out of their preserves; and the military plays the role of an ideal customer for private business, spending billions of dollars annually on terms that are most favorable to the sellers. Since a large part of the required capital equipment has no alternative use, its cost is commonly included in the price of the end product. The business of producing arms is therefore virtually risk-free, in spite of which the allowable profit rates include a generous margin for a mythical risk factor. . . . And the fact that military procurement officers often look forward to lucrative employment with arms manufacturers after retirement from the service hardly makes for strictness in their dealings with suppliers. . . . Supplying the military is universally regarded as good business: all corporations, big and little, bid for as large a share as they can get. The private interests of the oligarchy, far from generating opposition to military spending, encourage its continuous expansion.

The class interests of the oligarchy work in the same direction. Whereas massive government spending for education and welfare tends to undermine its privileged position, the opposite is true of military spending. The reason is that militarization fosters all the reactionary and irrational forces in society, and inhibits or kills everything progressive and humane. Blind respect is engendered for authority; attitudes of docility and conformity are taught and enforced; dissent is treated as unpatriotic and even treasonable. In such an atmosphere, the oligarchy feel that its moral authority and material position are secure. . . .

It would be misleading to leave the impression that only the oligarchy has favored the steady increase in military spending during these years. If one assumes the permanence of monopoly capitalism with its proved incapacity to make rational use for peaceful and humane ends of its enormous productive potential, one must decide whether one prefers the mass unemployment and hopelessness characteristic of the Great Depression or the relative job security and material well-being provided by the huge military budgets of the 1940's and 1950's. Since most Americans, workers included, still do assume without question the permanence of the system, it is only natural that they should prefer the situation which is personally and privately more advantageous. And in order to rationalize this preference, they have accepted the official ideology of anti-Communism which appears to justify an unlimited expansion of the military establishment as essential to national survival. . . .

Limitations to Using Military Spending to Assure Prosperity

Limitations on the effectiveness of arms spending as an instrument of economic control stem from the nature of the new weapons created by modern science and technology. These limitations are of two kinds, the first economic and second military.

The economic limitation is quite simply, that the new technology of warfare has reduced the power of arms spending to stimulate the economy.

It is commonplace that warfare is becoming more and more a matter of science and technology, less and less a matter of masses of men and weapons. Rockets and missiles are replacing bombers and rendering fighter planes largely purposeless; huge fleets of surface vessels are obsolete; massed armies are giving way to highly specialized troops wielding an array of fantastically destructive weapons. As a consequence of these changes, there has been a sharp shift in the character of goods and services purchased by military outlays. A much larger proportion goes for research and development, engineering, supervision, and maintenance; a much smaller proportion for the kind of mass-produced military hardware (artillery, tanks, planes, trucks, jeeps, ships) that played the decisive role in two world wars. This change in the composition of military demand means that a given amount of military spending employs far fewer persons today than it used to. . . . Given the present nature of military demand, it might be wholly impossible to reach a level of full employment by simple increases in the military budget: a bottleneck of specialized scientific and engineering skills could prove to be an insuperable obstacle to further expansion long before the indirect effects of the increased spending had reached the unemployed steel workers of Pittsburgh, the coal miners of Kentucky and West Virginia, the school dropouts in the slums and ghettos of the big cities all over the country. . . .

The second limitation on the use of arms spending as an economic stimulant derives from the logic of the military situation itself. The piling up of modern weapons of total destruction in an arms race between two evenly matched powers not only has no rational military purpose—that would perhaps matter too much—but actually reduces the chances that the country could survive a full-scale war. . . .

QUESTIONS FOR DISCUSSION OR PAPERS

1   Would you agree that Baran and Sweezy present a Marxist theory which depends mainly on overproduction/underconsumption? If so, what qualifications would you add? If not, what sort of Marxist theory is it? How does it see the capitalist order breaking down?

2   What influences of "mainstream" economic theory can you observe in Baran and Sweezy?

3   What is the particular role of monopolistic market structure in this book?

4   Do you think the evidence presented in these excerpts confirms the basic argument? (Much more evidence is available in the book itself which has many more examples and tables than could be reproduced here. If you are writing a critical essay, you may want to check it out.)

Alfred Marshall

CHAPTER 5

THE MAINSTREAM
NEO-CLASSICAL PERSPECTIVE

EDITOR'S INTRODUCTION

Mainstream microeconomics and general equilibrium theory, as taught in most American universities, is a refined version of English and Franco-Swiss neo-classical theory, which was first developed between about 1866-1871 and 1930. This version of neo-classical economics developed within a familiar liberal and utilitarian perspective, little changed from the time of **Jeremy Bentham** and **John Stuart Mill.**[1]

Neo-classical economics is first of all a set of technical improvements to classical economics. Early neoclassical writers like **William Stanley Jevons** (1835-1882) in England, **Léon Walras** (1834-1910) in Lausanne, and **Carl Menger** (1840-1921) in Vienna applied mathematical concepts to the idea of subjective utility. They envisioned a utility-maximizing individual who would experience diminishing marginal utility as his consumption of each commodity increased, just as Ricardo and Malthus' farmer experienced diminishing marginal product on the land. If our consumer is fully rational, his demand for each commodity would be that amount where the marginal utility of the good or service—roughly, the utility of the last unit purchased—just equals the price, or the marginal disutility of labor or other sacrifice in purchasing it.

Since in equilibrium the ratio of marginal utilities of any two consumer goods must equal the ratio of their prices, it could be shown that a falling price would stimulate additional demand—the familiar demand curve later popularized by **Alfred Marshall** (1842-1924). In the simple case where supply is given, market demand determines the price at which that supply is disposed of.

---

[1] The utilitarian philosophy justifies the notion that people's welfare depends on their enjoyments or consumption and that levels of utility can be compared, on the assumption of equality, and even summed to yield a judgment about social policy. Since Sir **John Hicks** (1903-   ) and **Abram Bergson's** (1914-   ) contributions in the 1930s, however, interpersonal comparisons are not so readily made. Instead, there has been an effort to divorce positive economics from welfare economics.

Where, more generally, both supply and demand respond to price, then both supply and demand schedules determine the price, as well as the amount supplied and demanded in each period. This is the essence of *partial equilibrium* analysis—the market situation for each commodity or factor taken separately. While requiring the assumption of *ceteris paribus* ("all other things equal"), which is risky to make, Marshall's simple supply and demand curves have shown their power in developing quantitative predictions and welfare implications in many applications. On the other hand, the consideration of all varieties of consumer goods, capital equipment, and labor as separate entities deprives the neoclassical theory of the macroeconomic conclusions to which classical economics was driving.

Léon Walras was the first to insist, in his *Elements of Pure Economics* (published in French in two parts in 1874-1877), that prices of any commodity or factor would be affected by the prices in all other markets. For example, the demand for tea would be increased if the price of sugar were to fall or the price of coffee were to rise. For *general equilibrium* Walras required that supply equal demand in each and every market simultaneously, requiring perfectly flexible prices through *tâtonnement,* a form of trial-and-error in which excess demand would somehow stimulate rising prices and excess supply, falling prices. As is understood by today's neo-classical theorists, there may be a set of prices which will equate supply and demand for all commodities and factors at any one time, but this (static) equilibrium may not be stable or readily achieved.

Walras' disciples **Vilfredo Pareto** (1848-1923) and **Enrico Barone** (1859-1924) extended the concept of general equilibrium. Pareto stated that a fully competitive general equilibrium outcome, which of course would be influenced by existing property rights and the resultant inequality of incomes, could be unanimously accepted. By this Pareto meant that no other set of prices and outcomes could improve someone's utility without making another person worse off—the definition of efficiency we now call "Pareto optimality." An efficient outcome is better than an inefficient one, particularly if the income distribution could be rectified. Barone was the first to suggest that a socialist planning agency could in principle establish the same efficient equilibrium result by establishing what we now call market-clearing "shadow prices."

Neo-classical economists for the most part treated the pricing of all factors symmetrically. Both labor and all kinds of capital would receive the market value of their marginal product in production. Thus the value of already existing capital goods would be *imputed* to them by their marginal contribution to the production of consumer goods; if that value is greater than the cost of production, the difference is a quasi-rent, which provides an incentive for further production.

To achieve theoretical simplicity, the early neo-classical economists were willing to restrict the scope of their analysis, at least temporarily. For example, they developed their theories on the assumption of fixed supplies of capital and labor. This simplification put aside the dynamic factors of population growth and technological change, which the classical writers had included. As the work of Alfred Marshall excerpted below shows, however, mainstream neoclassical writers have had a theory of growth, however rudimentary and sometimes implicit.

TABLE 1
PRESENT-DAY NEO-CLASSICAL PERSPECTIVE

---

a. Competitive market equilibrium prevails. Imperfect competition exceptional.
b. Factors are paid the value of their marginal contribution to production. Bilateral monopoly, group, and power considerations generally ignored.
c. Tastes are assumed fixed and universal.
d. Organizational and management factors negligible.
e. Political or social influences minimal—or should be.
f. Equity considerations are separable from efficiency.

Present-day neo-classical writers, such as **George Stigler** (1911-   ) and **Gary Becker** (1930-   ) of the University of Chicago, continue to work under the assumption that people's tastes do not change and that everywhere they are identical.[2] Organization and management style are irrelevant because competitive processes will eliminate inefficient forms.[3] The political and legal structure is assumed unchanging, except perhaps when "rent-seeking" individuals buy off politicians or bureaucrats to advance special interests.[4] The few analytical attempts to vary one or another of the elements of the neo-classical perspective usually assume the others remain in place.[5]

---

[2]George Stigler and Gary Becker, "De Gustibus Non Est Disputandum," *American Economic Review* (March, 1977), pp. 76-90. Several other examples and a response are contained in Martin C. Spechler, "Taste Variability Is Indisputable," in *The Forum for Social Economics* (Fall/Winter, 1982-1983), pp. 15-30.

[3]This neo-classical assumption is examined and challenged in M. C. Spechler, "Organization and Economic Behavior: An Interpretation of Recent Findings," *Weltwirtschäftliches Archiv: Review of World Economics* Band 118 (1982), pp. 366-380.

[4]"Public choice" economists like **James Buchanan, Anthony Downs,** and **Gordon Tullock** have applied neo-classical precepts to politicians and bureaucrats and to the process of institutional change. See Robert Tollison, "Rent Seeking: A Survey," *Kyklos,* vol. 35 (1982), pp. 575-602; George Stigler, *The Citizen and the State: Essays on Regulation* (Chicago: University of Chicago Press, 1975); Mancur Olson, *The Rise and Decline of Nations* (New Haven: Yale University Press, 1982); and Douglass North and Lance Davis, *Institutional Change and American Economic Growth* (Cambridge, England: Cambridge University Press, 1971).

[5]For a good account of neo-classical economics from a neo-Marxian point of view, see Richard D. Wolff and Stephen A. Resnick, *Economics: Marxian versus Neoclassical* (Baltimore: Johns Hopkins, 1987).

READING 12

Alfred Marshall (1842-1924), professor of political economy at Cambridge most of his academic career, was a man of curious contradictions. Son of a clerical family and himself once a candidate for holy orders, Marshall remained personally committed to Christian morals. Yet he insisted that as an economist he had no special insights on ethical matters.

> I had doubts as to the propriety of inequalities of opportunity, rather than of material comfort. Then, in my vacations I visited the poorest quarters of several cities and walked through one street after another, looking at the faces of the poorest people. Next, I resolved to make as thorough a study as I could of Political Economy.[6]

Marshall devoted much thought and time to advising his government about currency and trade matters, sympathized with trade unions, and was not entirely adverse to socialist ideals. Yet despite Marshall's impulse to public service and his belief that truths in economics were relative to their historical situation, he is remembered as a technical innovator who developed the theory of static equilibrium, the essence of neo-classical "price theory" taught in English and American universities today. His distinction of the short period (when capital stock cannot be changed) from the long (when all is variable) is part of the modern economist's basic vocabulary, as are the notions of consumer and producer's surplus, quasi-rents, and internal economies of scale, which he distinguished from the external economies arising from local development of an industrial branch. His rigorous mathematical training led him to conceptualize the price elasticity of demand, the stability conditions for equilibrium (still known by his name in international trade), and other refinements of marginalism. But Marshall frequently disparaged and minimized the role of mathematics in economics!

Rigorous in his use of scientific method to analyze problems and the founder of economics as a separate discipline, he nevertheless urged that his students learn from evolutionary biology, psychology, history, and of course the great political economists of the past. Science requires the isolation of problems with surrounding issues provisionally held in abeyance, he taught. Accordingly, Marshall's treatment of quasi-mechanical partial equilibrium in the short run and his predominant attention to normal conditions held many developmental forces inactive for the sake of simplicity. Lest readers believe him uninterested in "the main concern of economics . . . human beings who are impelled, for good and evil, to change and progress," Marshall wrote in the preface to the 1920 edition:

> The Mecca of the economist lies in economic biology rather than in economic dynamics. But biological concepts are more complex than those of mechanics.[7]

Despite this aspiration, most scholars would agree that Marshall's long period does not really furnish us with a theory of economic development, though his analytical tools have been useful in more recent attempts at such a theory.

---

[6]Quoted by John Maynard Keynes, *Essays in Biography,* vol. X in *The Collected Writings of John Maynard Keynes* (London: Macmillan, 1972), p. 171.

[7]Preface to the Eighth Edition (London: Macmillan, 1920), p. xv. Marshall goes on to say that while new lands and cheap transportation had suspended the effect of Malthusian and Ricardian theories of diminishing returns, continued high rates of population increase would tend once again to increase rent relative to other forms of property income.

Marshall's comprehensive *Principles of Economics,* first published in 1890 when he was 48 years old, went through many editions and printings. These selections are taken from one of the last.[8]

Principles of Economics

Alfred Marshall

Competition: Pros and Cons

When competition is arraigned, its anti-social forms are made prominent; and care is seldom taken to inquire whether there are not other forms of it, which are so essential to the maintenance of energy and spontaneity, that their cessation might probably be injurious on the balance to social well-being. The traders or producers, who find that a rival is offering goods at a lower price than will yield them a good profit, are angered at his intrusion, and complain of being wronged, even though it may be true that those who buy the cheaper goods are in greater need than themselves; and that the energy and resourcefulness of their rival is a social gain. . . . A privileged class of producers . . . often use their combined force to frustrate the attempts of an able man to rise from a lower class than their own. Under the pretext of repressing anti-social competition, they deprive him of the liberty of carving out for himself a new career, where the services rendered by him to the consumers of the commodity would be greater than the injuries which he inflicts on the relatively small group which objects to his competition.

If competition is contrasted with energetic cooperation in unselfish work for the public good, then even the best forms of competition are relatively evil; while its harsher and meaner forms are hateful. And in a world in which all men were perfectly virtuous, competition would be out of place; but so also would be private property and every form of private right. Men would think only of their duties; and no one would desire to have a larger share of the comforts and luxuries of life than his neighbors. . . . Such is the Golden Age to which poets and dreamers may look forward. But in the responsible conduct of affairs, it is worse than folly to ignore the imperfections which still cling to human nature.

History in general, and especially the history of socialistic ventures, shows that ordinary men are seldom capable of pure ideal altruism for any considerable time together; and that the exceptions are to be found only when the masterful fervor of a small bank of religious enthusiasts makes material concerns to count for nothing in comparison with the higher faith.

---

[8]Keynes' judgment of Marshall's great treatise is also true of the other masterpieces abridged in this volume: "It needs much study and independent thought on the reader's own part before he can know the half of what is contained in the concealed crevices of that rounded globe of knowledge which is Marshall's *Principles of Economics.*" Keynes, *Essays in Biography,* p. 212. The reader of these excerpts is encouraged to read more deeply into the originals.

No doubt men, even now, are capable of much more unselfish service than they generally render; and the supreme aim of the economist is to discover how this latent social asset can be developed most quickly, and turned to account most wisely. But he must not decry competition in general, without analysis: he is bound to retain a neutral attitude towards any particular manifestation of it until he is sure that, human nature being what it is, the restraint of competition would not be more anti-social in its working than the competition itself. . . . We need a term that does not imply any moral qualities, whether good or evil. but which indicates the undisputed fact that modern business and industry are characterized by more self-reliant habits, more forethought, more deliberate and free choice. . . . *Economic Freedom* points in the right direction. . . . [Book I, i, §4]

If we take averages sufficiently broad to cause the personal peculiarities of individuals to counterbalance one another, the money which people of equal incomes will give to obtain a benefit or avoid an injury is a good measure of the benefit or injury. . . . Next we must take account of the fact that a stronger incentive will be required to induce a person to pay a given price for anything if he is poor than if he is rich. A shilling is the measure of less pleasure, or satisfaction of any kind, to a rich man than to a poor one. . . . By far the greater number of the events with which economics deals affect in about equal proportions all the different classes of society; so that if the money measures of the happiness caused by two events are equal, it is reasonable and in accordance with common usage to regard the amounts of happiness in the two cases as equivalent. . . . [Book I, ii, §3]

When the motive to a man's action is spoken of as supplied by the money which he will earn, it is not meant that his mind is closed to all other considerations save those of gain. For even the most purely business relations of life assume honesty and good faith. . . . Much of the work by which people earn their living is pleasurable in itself; and there is truth in the contention of socialists that more of it might be made so. [§5]

The tendency of careful economic study is to base the rights of private property not on any abstract principle, but only the observation that in the past they have been inseparable from solid progress; and that therefore it is the part of responsible men to proceed cautiously and tentatively in abrogating or modifying even such rights as may seem to be inappropriate to the ideal conditions of social life. [§6]

Theory of Consumer Demand

There is an endless variety of wants, but there is a limit to each separate want. . . . The *total utility* of a thing to anyone (that is, the total pleasure or other benefit it yields him) increases with every increase in his stock of it, but not as fast as his stock increases. . . . [Book III, iii, §1]

The larger the amount of a thing that a person has the less, other things being equal (i.e., the purchasing power of money, and the amount of money at his command being equal) will be the price which he will pay for a little more of it. . . . [§3] In large markets, then—where rich and poor, old and young, men and women, persons of all varieties of tastes, temperaments, and occupations are mixed together,—the peculiarities in the wants of individuals will compen-sate one another in a comparatively regular gradation of total demand. . . . There is then one general law of demand: The greater the amount to be sold, the smaller must be the price at which it is offered to find purchasers; or, in other words, the amount demanded increases with a fall in price. . . . [§5]

Internal Economies

An able man, assisted perhaps by some strokes of good fortune, gets a firm footing in the trade, he works hard and lives sparely, his own capital grows fast, and the credit that enables him to borrow more capital grows still faster; he collects around him subordinates of more than ordinary zeal and ability; as his business increases they rise with him, they trust him and he trusts them, each of them devotes himself with energy to just that work for which he is specially fitted, so that no high ability is wasted on easy work, and no difficult work is entrusted to unskillful hands. Corresponding to this steadily increasing economy of skill, the growth of his business brings with it similar economies of specialized machines and plant of all kinds; every improved process is quickly adopted and made the basis of further improvements; success brings credit and credit brings success; credit and success help to retail old customers and to bring new ones; the increase of his trade gives him great advantages in buying; his goods advertise one another and thus diminish his difficulty in finding a vent for them. The increase in the scale of his business increases rapidly the advantages which he has over his competitors, and lowers the price at which he can afford to sell. This process may go on as long as his energy and enterprise, his inventive and organizing power retain their full strength and freshness and so long as the risks which are inseparable from business do not cause him exceptional losses; and if it could endure for a hundred years, he and one or two others like him would divide between them the whole of that branch of industry in which he is engaged. The large scale of their production would put great economies within their reach; and provided they competed to their utmost with one another, the public would derive the chief benefit of these economies, and the price of the commodity would fall very low. . . . As with the growth of trees, so was it with the growth of businesses as a general rule before the great recent development of vast joint-stock companies, which often stagnate, but do not readily die. Now that rule is far from universal, but it still holds in many industries and trades. Nature still presses on the private business by limiting the length of the life of its original founders, and by limiting even more narrowly that part of their lives in which their faculties retain full vigor. And so, after a while, the guidance of the business falls into the hands of people with less energy and less creative genius, if not with less active interest in its prosperity. If it turned into a joint-stock company, it may retain the advantages of division of labor, of specialized skill and machinery; it may even increase them by a further increase of its capital; and under favorable conditions it may secure a permanent and prominent place in the work of production. But it is likely to have lost so much of its elasticity and progressive force, that the advantages are no longer exclusively on its side in its competition with younger and smaller rivals. . . . [Book IV, xiii, §1]

The Representative Firm and the Supply Price

When we come to discuss the causes which govern the supply price of a commodity, we shall have to analyze carefully the normal cost of producing a commodity, relative to a given aggregate volume of production; and for this purpose we shall have to study *the expenses of a representative producer* for that aggregate volume. On the one hand we shall not want to select some new producer just struggling into business, who works under many disadvantages, and has to be content for a time with little or no profits, but who is satisfied with the fact that he is establishing a connection and taking the first steps towards building up a successful business; nor on the other hand shall we want to take a firm which by exceptionally long-sustained ability and good fortune has got together a vast business, and huge well-ordered workshops that give it a superiority over almost all its rivals. But our representative firm must be one which has had a fairly long life, and fair success, which is managed with normal ability, and which has normal access to the economies, external and internal, which belong to that aggregate volume of production.

An increase in the aggregate volume of production of anything will generally increase the size, and therefore the internal economies possessed by such a representative firm; . . . it will always increase the external economies to which the firm has access; and thus will enable it to manufacture at a less proportionate cost of labor and sacrifice than before. . . . While the part which nature plays in production shows a tendency to diminishing return, the part which man plays shows a tendency to increasing return. . . . [Book IV, xiii, §2]

Equilibrium of Demand Price and Supply Price

We are investigating the equilibrium of normal demand and normal supply in their most general form. . . . We assume that the forces of demand and supply have free play; that there is no close combination among dealers on either side, but each acts for himself, and there is much free competition; that is, buyers generally compete freely with sellers. But though everyone acts for himself, his knowledge of what others are doing is supposed to be generally sufficient to prevent him from taking a lower or paying a higher price than others are doing. . . . We assume that there is only one price in the market, at one and the same time; it being understood that separate allowance is made, when necessary for differences in the expense of delivering goods to dealers in different parts of the market; including allowance for the special expenses of retailing.

In such a market there is a demand price for each amount of the commodity, that is, a price at which each particular amount of the commodity can find purchasers in a day or week or year. . . . The unit of time may be chosen according to circumstances of each particular problem: it may be a day, a month, a year, or even a generation: but in every case it must be short relatively to the period of the market under discussion. It is to be assumed that the general circumstances of the market remain unchanged throughout this period; that there is, for instance, no change in fashion or taste, no new substitute which might affect the demand, no new invention to disturb the supply. [Book V, iii, §4]

When . . . the amount produced (in a unit of time) is such that the demand price is greater than the supply price, then sellers receive more than is sufficient to make it worth their while to bring goods to market to that amount; and there is at work an active force tending to increase the amount brought forward for sale. On the other hand, when the amount produced is such that the demand price is less than the supply price, sellers receive less than is sufficient to make it worth their while to bring goods to market on that scale; so that those who were just on the margin of doubt as to whether to go on producing are decided not to do so, and there is an active force at work tending to diminish the amount brought forward for sale. When the demand price is equal to the supply price, the amount produced has no tendency either to be increased or to be diminished; it is in equilibrium. . . .

Such an equilibrium is *stable,* that is, the price, if displaced a little from it, will tend to return, as a pendulum oscillates about its lowest point; and it will be found to be a characteristic of stable equilibria that in them the demand price is greater than the supply price for amounts just less than the equilibrium amount, and *vice versa.* [Book V, iii, §6]

We might as reasonably dispute whether it is the upper or the under blade of a pair of scissors that cuts a piece of paper, as whether value is governed by utility or by cost of production. . . . [Book V, iii, §7]

In a rigidly stationary state in which supply could be perfectly adjusted to demand in every particular, the normal expenses of production, the marginal expenses, and the average expenses (rent being counted in) would be one and the same thing, for long periods and for short. . . .

When the period under survey is long enough to enable the investment of capital in building up a new business to complete itself and to bear full fruits; then the marginal supply price is that, the expectation of which in the long run just suffices to induce capitalists to invest their material capital, and workers of all grades to invest their personal capital in the trade.

On the other side of the line of division are periods of time long enough to enable producers to adapt their production to changes in demand, in so far as that can be done with the existing provision of specialized skill, specialized capital, and industrial organization; but not long enough to enable them to make any important changes in the supplies of these factors of production. . . . If trade is brisk all energies are strained to their utmost, overtime is worked, and then the limit to production is given by want of power rather than by want of will to go further or faster. But if trade is slack every producer has to make up his mind how near to prime cost it is worth his while to take fresh orders And here there is no definite law, the chief operative force is the fear of spoiling the market; and that acts in different ways and different strengths on different individuals and different industrial groups. For the chief motive of all open combinations and of all informal silent and "customary" understandings whether among employers or employed is the need for preventing individuals from spoiling the common market by action that may bring them immediate gains, but at the cost of a greater aggregate loss to the trade. [Book V, xv, §1]

This leads to the consideration of some difficulties of a technical character connected with the marginal expenses of production of a commodity that obeys the law of increasing return. The difficulties arise from the temptation to represent supply price as dependent on the amount produced, without allowing for the length of time that is necessarily occupied by each individual business in extending its internal, and still more its external organization; and in consequence they have been most conspicuous in mathematical and semi-mathematical discussions of the theory of value. For when changes of supply price and amount produced are regarded as dependent exclusively on one another without any reference to gradual growth, it appears reasonable to argue that the marginal supply price for each individual producer is the addition to this aggregate expense of production made by producing his last element; that this marginal price is likely in many cases to be diminished by an increase in his output much more than the demand price in the general market would be by the same cause.

The statical theory of equilibrium is therefore not wholly applicable to commodities which obey the law of increasing return. . . .

For short periods, the difficulties of adjusting the internal and external organization of a business to rapid changes in output are so great that the supply price must generally be taken to rise with an increase, and to fall with a diminution in the amount produced.

But in long periods both the internal and external economies of production on a large scale have time to develop themselves. The marginal supply price is not the expenses of production of any particular bale of goods; but it is the whole expenses (including insurance, and gross earnings of management) of a marginal increment in the aggregate process of production and marketing. [Book V, xv, §4]

QUESTIONS FOR DISCUSSION

1   What is the normative basis to intervene in the free workings of the market, according to Marshall?
2   If economies to scale (or "increasing returns") are the rule, why do we not see an increasing degree of monopoly in modern capitalist economies?
3   Why would increasing returns—long-run falling average costs—pose a difficulty for the static theory of equilibrium value? Drawing a diagram

with a fairly elastic demand curve, such as might be confronted by a single producer, may help you think this one out.

4   Could a certain price be a short-run equilibrium but above or below the long-run equilibrium value? If so, what would happen and how? If not, does the distinction have any practical value?

Joseph Schumpeter

CHAPTER 6

AUSTRIAN NEO-CLASSICAL ECONOMICS AND THE LIBERTARIAN PERSPECTIVE

EDITOR'S INTRODUCTION

The Austrian version of neo-classical economics developed about the same time as the English version but because of the difficult German texts and the libertarian, radical right-wing associations of many of its proponents, this version has had little circulation in the United States until recent years. In this book we give the Austrian school greater emphasis because of its profound challenge to mainstream economics and its relative neglect in American economics texts.

Marshall's idea of growth resembled that of Charles Darwin in biology. Like evolutionary mutations, small innovations might be introduced by individuals or firms. If buyers feel the changes are worth their cost, they will survive and spread, gradually replacing older products and processes. Business firms will similarly rise and fall like biological individuals in a species subject to much slower forces of change. Neo-classical growth models since Marshall have incorporated much of this perspective of gradual adjustment to the environment.[1] Instead of developing the notion of equilibrium on the model of mechanics or evolutionary biology as had Marshall and his followers, the Austrian school of neo-classical economics

---

[1]Robert M. Solow, "A Contribution to the Theory of Economic Growth," *Quarterly Journal of Economics,* vol. 70 (February, 1956) and others, as surveyed in F. H. Hahn and R. C. O. Matthews, "The Theory of Economic Growth: A Survey" in *Surveys of Economic Theory,* vol. II (London: Macmillan, 1965), pp. 1-124.

emphasized disequilibrium and the conditions for dynamic progress, as we shall see below in the work of Schumpeter.

Unlike the English neo-classical economists, who often found merits in government intervention to correct competition, the Austrian school was strongly anti-socialist and opposed to state intervention, possibly in reaction to the heavy bureaucracies which had long encumbered the German states.[2] Carl Menger's great student **Eugen von Böhm-Bawerk** (1851-1914) advanced a famous critique of Marx[3] and rigorously developed a productivity theory of interest—which had an obvious ideological interest. According to Böhm-Bawerk, capital permitted more roundabout methods, more productive than direct transformation of original inputs into output, hence permitted the payment of an agio, interest per unit time, to impatient lenders who would advance the funds only for such a premium.[4]

Contemporary Austrian economics, which has been revived in the United States since about 1970, owes most to the thinking of **Ludwig von Mises** (1881-1973) and **Friedrich A. Hayek** (1899-   ). Mises and Hayek were typical of the Austrian school in analyzing business cycles as a result of the subjective demand for credit and the effect of nominal prices on investment. Hayek also taught that attempting artificially to sustain wages during a downturn would inevitably cause low wages or unemployment for more workers, a misallocation of investment, and inflation. Attempting to maintain employment levels, such as by Keynesian demand management, could bring on accelerating inflation; the only solution would be for workers to seek new jobs, possibly at lower wages.

To these neo-classical elements, Mises and Hayek added a libertarian perspective.[5] Philosophically, this means the *sanctity of individual choices*. Obligations come only from an individual's express consent. Aside from preventing violence, government is therefore an imposition and cannot be legitimate without unanimous consent.[6]

To this libertarianism or liberal individualism, Hayek has linked an influential analysis of information. According to him, complicated and often inarticulate knowledge is essential to the proper working of a modern economy. No central authority could ever assemble all the particular and local

---

[2]Not all of them, however. **Friedrich von Wieser** (1851-1926), Menger's other famous student, believed government intervention would be useful in an economy marked by big business and labor unions.

[3]*The Close of the Marxian System* (1896).

[4]Böhm-Bawerk's foreign disciples **Knut Wicksell** (1851-1926) of Sweden and **Irving Fisher** (1867-1947) of Yale University made clear that the real rate of interest is simply the price which equates the demand for consumption and productive loans with the supply of savings.

[5]Friedrich von Hayek, *Individualism and Economic Order* (1948). Hayek identifies his individualism with Smith, Edmund Burke, and Alexis de Tocqueville. Like traditional conservatives, Hayek believes men are "very irrational and fallible," as well as uninformed, but not necessarily selfish. They are constrained by competition.

[6]It is doubtful that Hayek, the urbane European, ever pressed what we Americans would call "libertarian" doctrine to the point some philosophical anarchists have in the USA—for example, Ayn Rand, Robert Nozick, and the Individualist Society.

information necessary to create a rational allocation of resources. On the other hand, Hayek insisted, an "extended order" can arise as an *unintended* consequence of many wills interacting in the free market. Even a stable monetary unit could come about through free and unregulated banking—a position for which there is some historical basis. Prices are a parsimonious way in which necessary but incomplete information is tested and communicated through the market to the firms and households who need to make decisions. A succession of individual decisions, imperfectly coordinated by prices, evolves in the right direction without ever reaching equilibrium. To generate and utilize price information, the market must have risk-takers and capitalists with a personal stake in success, not hired bureaucrats. For this and other reasons, both Mises and Hayek were potent critics of socialism on theoretic and political grounds.[7]

A second element of Austrian economics is the role of the *entrepreneur*. In the work of **Joseph A. Schumpeter** (1883-1950), another Austrian who emigrated to the USA in middle age, the entrepreneur is portrayed as a creative leader who innovates a "new combination"—a new product, method of production, a new market or source of supply for a country's industry, or even a new financial or organizational technique. For instance, as Schumpeter might have said today, "junk" bonds or leveraged management buyouts are innovations created by entrepreneurs, who persuade capitalists to risk their funds for new purposes.

In the process of "creative destruction" entrepreneurs also bid resources away from less productive uses through the use of bank credit. Since their efforts attract clusters of imitators, entrepreneurial initiatives account for booms and even long (Kondratieff) cycles. But such discontinuous bursts of growth also mean mistakes and speculation, which bring on depression.

Entrepreneurs seek to make and protect profits through monopoly and non-price competition, including education of consumers if necessary. Despite its static inefficiency, Schumpeter argued, some monopoly power is in fact necessary for technical progress. Profits finance the research labs needed to conduct the routinized scientific research of the future. With their superior financial resources, Schumpeter taught, large firms have been responsible for remarkable growth in the past. Eventually all monopoly profits from innovation are competed away, unless guaranteed by state power. Moreover, monopolies may lend stability to the market which small, competitive firms could not.

Many of these Austrian[8] themes have been amplified by **Israel M. Kirzner**, a disciple of Mises, who has broadened the concept of entrepreneur-

---

[7]Mises' *Socialism: An Economic and Sociological Analysis* (1922) denied Barone's idea that rational prices could exist under socialism. Schumpeter's *Capitalism, Socialism, and Democracy* (1942) can be read as predicting the downfall of capitalism through the misguided and pusillanimous influence of democratic intellectuals.

[8]Schumpeter differed somewhat from other Austrians in his guarded admiration for Marx's economic sociology and schema of historical development. Schumpeter also admired the mathematical concept of equilibrium developed by the Lausanne School and, unlike the later Austrians, favored the use of mathematics. Although Schumpeter did not consider himself an "Austrian"—possibly because of his famous dispute with Böhm-

ship to mean any agent who alertly takes advantage of opportunity in the market—arbitrage, profit from disequilibrium, or the application of new, but still risky and untested, knowledge.[9] An entrepreneur may literally identify new needs, employing advertising to convince customers of them For Kirzner, as for Schumpeter, most anti-monopoly policy is misguided, except perhaps to disperse the concentrated hold on an essential economic resource. Any penalty on "monopolization," as in Section 2 of the Sherman Anti-trust Act, discourages alertness for opportunities. The apparent monopolist may turn out to be the most effective competitor in improving quality and cutting price.

READING 13

Joseph Schumpeter was a versatile genius. He served briefly as the Minister of Finance in post-World War I Austria, president of a small bank, and then professor of public finance in Germany. In his essays on imperialism (*Imperialism and Social Classes* [1919]), which are still widely read, Schumpeter wrote that war and imperialism were social atavisms, throwbacks of pre-capitalist ages, and that only monopolistic export cartels would bring one country's capitalists into conflict with another's. After coming to Harvard University in the early 1930s, he showed himself a brilliant teacher and researcher. His empirical *Business Cycles* (1939) and his posthumous *History of Economic Analysis* (1954), edited by his widow, are monuments of scholarship, though often highly idiosyncratic. Few economists, for example, even among those who agree that business cycles come from clusters of innovations, would agree that these cycles are periodic, as Schumpeter believed.

Following are excerpts from his classic *Theorie der Wirtschäftlichen Entwicklung,* first published in Leipzig in 1912 and revised for the 1926 edition, from which the English translation was made. Schumpeter's *Capitalism, Socialism and Democracy* (1942), from which the second selections have been taken, argued that capitalism was becoming endangered by the routinization of entrepreneurship and the failure of Western intellectuals to appreciate the virtues of capitalism.

The Fundamental Phenomenon of Economic Development[*]

Joseph A. Schumpeter

The theory of the first chapter describes economic life from the standpoint of a "circular flow," running on in channels essentially the same year after year— similar to the circulation of the blood in an animal organism. Now this circular

---

Bawerk over the possibility of interest without development—and disparaged the idea of a "school," the similarities to the Austrian economists are decisive.

[9]I. M. Kirzner, *Competition and Entrepreneurship* (1973).

[*]*Source:* Excerpted from *The Theory of Economic Development,* translated by Redvers Opie (Cambridge, Massachusetts: Harvard University Press, 1961), chapter II. Copyright © 1934 by Joseph Schumpeter. Reprinted by permission of Harvard University Press.

flow and its channels do alter in time, and here we abandon the analogy with the circulation of the blood. For although the latter also changes in the course of the growth and decline of the organism, yet it only does so continuously, that is by steps which one can choose smaller than any assignable quantity, however small, and always within the same framework. Economic life experiences such changes too, but it also experiences others which do not appear continuously and which change the framework, the traditional course itself. They cannot be understood by means of any analysis of the circular flow, although they are purely economic and although their explanation is obviously among the tasks of pure theory. Now such changes and the phenomena which appear in their train are the object of our investigation. But we do not ask: what changes of this sort have actually made the modern economic system what it is? nor: what are the conditions of such changes? We only ask, and indeed in the same sense as theory always asks: how do such changes take place and to what economic phenomena do they give rise?

The same thing may be put somewhat differently. The theory of the first chapter describes economic life from the standpoint of the economic system's tendency towards an equilibrium position, which tendency gives us the means of determining prices and quantities of goods, and may be described as an adaptation to data existing at any time. In contrast to the conditions of the circular flow this does not mean in itself that year after year "the same" things happen; for it only means that we conceive the several processes in the economic system as partial phenomena of the tendency towards an equilibrium position, but not necessarily towards the same one. The position of the ideal state of equilibrium in the economic system, never attained, continually "striven after" (of course not consciously), changes, because the data change. And theory is not weaponless in the face of these changes in data. It is constructed so as to be able to deal with the consequences of such changes; it has special instruments for the purpose (for example, the instrument called quasi-rent). If the change occurs in the non-social data (natural conditions) or in non-economic social data (here belong the effects of war, changes in commercial, social, or economic policy), or in consumers' tastes, then to this extent no fundamental overhaul of the theoretical tools seems to be required. These tools only fail—and here this argument joins the preceding—where economic life itself changes its own data by fits and starts. The building of a railway may serve as an example. Continuous changes, which may in time, by continual adaptation through innumerable small steps, make a great department store out of a small retail business, come under the "static" analysis. But "static" analysis is not only unable to predict the consequences of discontinuous changes in the traditional way of doing things; it can neither explain the occurrence of such productive revolutions nor the phenomena which accompany them. It can only investigate the new equilibrium position after the changes have occurred. It is just this occurrence of the "revolutionary" change that is our problem, the problem of economic development in a very narrow and formal sense The reason why we so state the problem and turn aside from traditional theory lies not so much in the fact that economic changes, especially, if not solely, in the capitalist epoch, have actually occurred thus and not by continuous adaptation, but more in their fruitfulness.

By "development," therefore, we shall understand only such changes in economic life as are not forced upon it from without but arise by its own initiative, from within. Should it turn out that there are no such changes arising in the economic sphere itself, and that the phenomenon that we call economic development is in practice simply founded upon the fact that the data change and that the economy continuously adapts itself to them, then we should say that there is no economic development. By this we should mean that economic development is not a phenomenon to be explained economically, but that the economy, in itself without development, is dragged along by the changes in the surrounding world, that the causes and hence the explanation of the development must be sought outside the group of facts which are described by economic theory.

Nor will the mere growth of the economy, as shown by the growth of population and wealth, be designated here as a process of development. For it calls forth no qualitatively new phenomena, but only processes of adaptation of the same kind as the changes in the natural data. Since we wish to direct our attention to other phenomena, we shall regard such increases as changes in data.[10] . . .

These spontaneous and discontinuous changes in the channel of the circular flow and these disturbances of the center of equilibrium appear in the sphere of industrial and commercial life, not in the sphere of the wants of the consumers of final products. Where spontaneous and discontinuous changes in consumers' tastes appear, it is a question of a sudden change in data with which the businessman must cope, hence possibly a question of a motive or an opportunity for other than gradual adaptations of his conduct, but not of such other conduct itself. Therefore this case does not offer any other problems than a change in natural data or require any new method of treatment; wherefore we shall neglect any spontaneity of consumers' needs that may actually exist, and assume tastes as "given." This is made easy for us by the fact that the spontaneity of wants is in general small. To be sure, we must always start from the satisfaction of wants, since they are the end of all production, and the given economic situation at any time must be understood from this aspect. Yet innovations in the economic system do not as a rule take place in such a way that first new wants arise spontaneously in consumers and then the productive apparatus swings round through their pressure. We do not deny the presence of this nexus. It is, however, the producer who as a rule initiates economic change, and consumers are educated by him if necessary; they are, as it were, taught to want new things, or things which differ in some respect or other from those which they have been in the habit of using. Therefore, while it is permissible and even necessary to consider consumers' wants as an independent and indeed the fundamental force in a theory of the circular flow, we must take a different attitude as soon as we analyze change. . . .

---

[10]The problems of capital, credit, entrepreneurial profit, interest on capital, and crises (or business cycles) are the ones in which this fruitfulness will be demonstrated here. Yet it is not thereby exhausted. For the expert theorist I point, for example, to the difficulties which surround the problem of increasing return, the question of multiple points of intersection between supply and demand curves, and the element of time, which even Marshall's analysis has not overcome. [footnote in original]

Development Is Introducing Major New Combinations

Development in our sense is then defined by the carrying out of new combinations.

This concept covers the following five cases: (1) The introduction of a new good—that is one with which consumers are not yet familiar—or of a new quality of a good. (2) The introduction of a new method of production, that is one not yet tested by experience in the branch of manufacture concerned, which need by no means be founded upon a discovery scientifically new, and can also exist in a new way of handling a commodity commercially. (3) The opening of a new market, that is a market into which the particular branch of manufacture of the country in question has not previously entered, whether or not this market has existed before. (4) The conquest of a new source of supply of raw materials or half-manufactured goods, again irrespective of whether this source already exists or whether it has first to be created. (5) The carrying out of the new organization of any industry, like the creation of a monopoly position (for example through trustification) or the breaking up of a monopoly position. . . .

[I]t is not essential to the matter—though it may happen—that the new combinations should be carried out by the same people who control the productive or commercial process which is to be displaced by the new. On the contrary, new combinations are, as a rule, embodied, as it were, in new firms which generally do not arise out of the old ones but start producing beside them; to keep to the example already chosen, in general it is not the owner of stage-coaches who builds railroads. This fact not only puts the discontinuity which characterizes the process we want to describe in a special light, and creates so to speak still another kind of discontinuity in addition to the one mentioned above, but it also explains important features of the course of events. Especially in a competitive economy, in which new combinations mean the competitive elimination of the old, it explains on the one hand the process by which individuals and families rise and fall economically and socially and which is peculiar to this form of organization, as well as a whole series of other phenomena of the business cycle, of the mechanism of the formation of private fortunes, and so on. In a non-exchange economy, for example a socialist one, the new combinations would also frequently appear side by side with the old. But the economic consequences of this fact would be absent to some extent, and the social consequences would be wholly absent. And if the competitive economy is broken up by the growth of great combines, as is increasingly the case today in all countries, then this must become more and more true of real life, and the carrying out of new combinations must become in ever greater measure the internal concern of one and the same economic body. The difference so made is great enough to serve as the watershed between two epochs in the social history of capitalism.

Credit and the Reallocation of Resources

We must notice secondly, only partly in connection with this element, that whenever we are concerned with fundamental principles, we must never assume that the carrying out of new combinations takes place by employing means of production which happen to be unused. In practical life, this is very often the case. There are always unemployed workmen, unsold raw materials, unused productive capacity, and so forth. This certainly is a contributory circumstance, a favorable condition and even an incentive to the emergence of new combinations; but great unemployment is only the consequence of non-economic events—as for example the World War—or precisely of the development which we are investigating. In neither of the two cases can its existence play a fundamental role in the explanation, and it cannot occur in a well balanced circular flow from which we start. Nor would the normal yearly increment meet the case, as it would be small in the first place, and also because it would normally be absorbed by a corresponding expansion of production within the circular flow, which, if we admit such increments, we must think of as adjusted to this rate of growth. As a rule, the new combinations must draw the necessary means of production from some old combinations—and for reasons already mentioned we shall assume that they always do so, in order to put in bold relief what we hold to be the essential contour line. The carrying out of new combinations means, therefore, simply the different employment of the economic system's existing supplies of productive means—which might provide a second definition of development in our sense. That rudiment of a pure economic theory of development which is implied in the traditional doctrine of the formation of capital always refers merely to saving and to the investment of the small yearly increase attributable to it. In this it asserts nothing false, but it entirely overlooks much more essential things. The slow and continuous increase in time of the national supply of productive means and of savings is obviously an important factor in explaining the course of economic history through the centuries, but it is completely overshadowed by the fact that development consists primarily in employing existing resources in a different way, in doing new things with them, irrespective of whether those resources increase or not. . . .

The next step in our argument is also self-evident: command over means of production is necessary to the carrying out of new combinations. . . . [As a rule] the possessor of wealth, even if it is the greatest combine, must resort to credit if he wishes to carry out a new combination, which cannot like an established business be financed by returns from previous production. To provide this credit is clearly the function of that category of individuals which we call "capitalists." It is obvious that this is the characteristic method of the capitalist type of society—and important enough to serve as its *differentia specifica*—for forcing the economic system into new channels. . . .

The Entrepreneur Carries Out New Combinations

The carrying out of new combinations we call "enterprise"; the individuals whose function it is to carry them out we call "entrepreneurs." . . .[W]e call entrepreneurs not only those "independent" businessmen in an exchange economy who are usually so designated, but all who actually fulfil the function by which we define the concept, even if they are, as is becoming the rule, "dependent" employees of a company, like managers, members of boards of directors, and so forth. . . .

Economic leadership in particular must hence be distinguished from "invention." As long as they are not carried into practice, inventions are economically irrelevant. And to carry any improvement into effect is a task entirely different from the inventing of it. . . .

[I]n *no* sense is his characteristic motivation of the hedonist kind. . . . Experience teaches . . . that typical entrepreneurs retire from the arena only when and because their strength is spent and they feel no longer equal to their task. This does not seem to verify the picture of the economic man, balancing probable results against disutility of effort and reaching in due course a point of equilibrium beyond which he is not willing to go. . . . And activity of the entrepreneurial type is obviously an obstacle to hedonist enjoyment of those kinds of commodity which are usually acquired by incomes beyond a certain size, because their "consumption" presupposes leisure. . . .

First of all, there is the dream and the will to found a private kingdom, usually, though not necessarily, also a dynasty. . . . The sensation of power and independence loses nothing by the fact that both are largely illusions. . . . Then there is the will to conquer: the impulse to fight, to prove oneself superior to others, to succeed for the sake, not of the fruit of success, but of success itself. From this aspect, economic action becomes akin to sport. . . . Finally, there is the joy of creating, of getting things done, or simply exercising one's energy and ingenuity. . . . Our type seeks out difficulties, changes in order to change, delights in ventures. This group of motives is the most distinctly anti-hedonist of the three.

Only with the first group of motives is private property as the result of entrepreneurial activity an essential factor in making it operative. With the other two it is not. Pecuniary gain is indeed a very accurate expression of success, especially of *relative* success, and from the standpoint of the man who strives for it, it has the additional advantage of being an objective fact and largely independent of the opinion of others. These and other peculiarities incident to the mechanism of "acquisitive" society make it very difficult to replace it as a motor of industrial development, even if we would discard the importance it has for creating a fund for investment. . . .

READING 14

The Theory of Economic Development*

Joseph A. Schumpeter

The Process of Creative Destruction

The theories of monopolistic and oligopolistic competition and their popular variants may in two ways be made to serve the view that capitalist reality is unfavorable to maximum performance in production. One may hold that it always has been so and that all along output has been expanding in spite of the secular sabotage perpetrated by the managing bourgeoisie. Advocates of this proposition would have to produce evidence to the effect that the observed rate of increase can be accounted for by a sequence of favorable circumstances unconnected with the mechanism of private enterprise and strong enough to overcome the latter's resistance. This is precisely the question which we shall discuss in Chapter IX. However, those who espouse this variant at least avoid the trouble about historical fact that the advocates of the alternative proposition have to face. This avers that capitalist reality once tended to favor maximum productive performance, or at all events productive performance so considerable as to constitute a major element in any serious appraisal of the system; but that the later spread of monopolist structures, killing competition, has by now reversed that tendency.

First, this involves the creation of an entirely imaginary golden age of perfect competition that at some time somehow metamorphosed itself into the monopolistic age, whereas it is quite clear that perfect competition has at no time been more of a reality than it is at present. Secondly, it is necessary to point out that the rate of increase in output did not decrease from the nineties from which, I suppose, the prevalence of the largest-side concerns, at least in manufacturing industry, would have to be dated; that there is nothing in the behavior of the time series of total output to suggest a break in trend and, most important of all, that the modern standard of life of the masses evolved during the period of relatively unfettered "big business." If we list the items that enter the modern workman's budget and from 1899 on observe the course of their prices not in terms of money but in terms of the hours of labor that will buy them—i.e., each year's money prices divided by each year's hourly wage rates—we cannot fail to be struck by the rate of the advance which, considering the spectacular improvement in qualities, seems to have been greater and not smaller than it ever was before. If we economists were given less to wishful thinking and more to the observation of fact doubts would immediately arise as to the realistic virtues of a theory that would have led us to

---

*Source: Excerpted from *Capitalism, Socialism and Democracy* (Third Edition; New York: Harper & Row Torchbooks, 1962), chapters VII and VIII, pp. 81-107. Copyright 1942, 1947 by Joseph A. Schumpeter. Reprinted by permission of Harper & Row, Publishers, Inc.

expect a very different result. Nor is this all. As soon as we go into details and inquire into the individual items in which progress was most conspicuous, the trail leads not to the door of those firms that work under conditions of comparatively free competition but precisely to the doors of the large concern—which, as in the case of agricultural machinery, also account for much of the progress in the competitive sector—and a shocking suspicion dawns upon us that big business may have had more to do with creating that standard of life than with keeping it down. . . .

The essential point to grasp is that in dealing with capitalism we are dealing with an evolutionary process. It may seem strange that anyone can fail to see so obvious a fact which moreover was long ago emphasized by Karl Marx. Yet that fragmentary analysis which yields the bulk of our propositions about the functioning of modern capitalism persistently neglects it. Let us restate the point and see how it bears upon our problem.

Capitalism, then, is by nature a form or method of economic change and not only never is but never can be stationary. And this evolutionary character of the capitalist process is not merely due to the fact that economic life goes on in a social and natural environment which changes and by its change alters the data of economic action; this fact is important and these changes (wars, revolutions and so on) often condition industrial change, but they are not its prime movers. Nor is this evolutionary character due to a quasi-automatic increase in population and capital or to the vagaries of monetary systems of which exactly the same thing holds true. The fundamental impulse that sets and keeps the capitalist engine in motion comes from the new consumers' goods, the new methods of production or transportation, the new markets, the new forms of industrial organization that capitalist enterprise creates.

As we have seen in the preceding chapter, the contents of the laborer's budget, say from 1760 to 1940, did not simply grow on unchanging lines but they underwent a process of qualitative change. Similarly, the history of the productive apparatus of a typical farm, from the beginnings of the rationalization of crop rotation, plowing and fattening to the mechanized thing of today—linking up with elevators and railroads—is a history of revolutions. So is the history of the productive apparatus of the iron and steel industry from the charcoal furnace to our own type of furnace, or the history of the apparatus of power production from the overshot water wheel to the modern power plant, or the history of transportation from the mailcoach to the airplane. The opening up of new markets, foreign or domestic, and the organizational development from the craft shop and factory to such concerns as U.S. Steel illustrate the same process of industrial mutation—if I may use that biological term—that incessantly revolutionizes[11] the economic structure from within, incessantly destroying the old one, incessantly creating a new one. This process of Creative Destruction is the essential fact about capitalism. It is what

---

[11]Those revolutions are not strictly incessant; they occur in discrete rushes which are separated from each other by spans of comparative quiet. The process as a whole works incessantly however, in the sense that there always is either revolution or absorption of the results of revolution, both together forming what are known as business cycles.

capitalism consists in and what every capitalist concern has got to live in. This fact bears upon our problem in two ways.

First, since we are dealing with a process whose every element takes considerable time in revealing its true features and ultimate effects, there is no point in appraising the performance of that process *ex visu* of a given point in time; we must judge its performance over time, as it unfolds through decades or centuries. A system—any system, economic or other—that at *every* given point of time fully utilizes its possibilities to the best advantage may yet in the long run be inferior to a system that does so at no given point of time, because the latter's failure to do so may be a condition for the level or speed of long-run performance.

Second, since we are dealing with an organic process, analysis of what happens in any particular part of it—say, in an individual concern or industry—may indeed clarify details of mechanism but is inconclusive beyond that. Every piece of business strategy acquires its true significance only against the background of that process and within the situation created by it. It must be seen in its role in the perennial gale of creative destruction; it cannot be understood irrespective of it, or, in fact, on the hypothesis that there is a perennial lull.

But economists who, *ex visu* of a point of time, look for example at the behavior of an oligopolist industry—an industry which consists of a few big firms—and observe the well-known moves and countermoves within it that seem to aim at nothing but high prices and restrictions of output are making precisely that hypothesis. They accept the data of the momentary situation as if there were no past or future to it and think that they have understood what there is to understand if they interpret the behavior of those firms by means of the principle of maximizing profits with reference to those data. . . . In other words, the problem that is usually being visualized is how capitalism administers existing structures, whereas the relevant problem is how it creates and destroys them. . . . But in capitalist reality as distinguished from its textbook picture, it is not that kind of competition which counts but the competition from the new commodity, the new technology, the new source of supply, the new type of organization (the largest-scale unit of control for instance)—competition which commands a decisive cost or quality advantage and which strikes not at the margins of the profits and the outputs of the existing firms but at their foundations and their very lives. . . . It is hardly necessary to point out that competition of the kind we now have in mind acts not only when in being but also when it is merely an ever-present threat. It disciplines before it attacks. The businessman feels himself to be in a competitive situation even if he is alone in his field or if, though not alone, he holds a position such that investigating government experts fail to see any effective competition between him and any other firms in the same or a neighboring field and in consequence conclude that his talk, under examination, about his competitive sorrows is all make-believe. In many cases, though not in all, this will in the long run enforce behavior very similar to the perfectly competitive pattern. . . .

Monopolistic Practices

Restrictive practices of this kind, as far as they are effective, acquire a new significance in the perennial gale of creative destruction, a significance which they would not have in a stationary state or in a state of low and balanced growth. In either of these cases restrictive strategy would produce no result other than an increase in profits at the expense of buyers except that, in the case of balanced advance, it might still prove to be the easiest and most effective way of collecting the means by which to finance additional investment. But in the process of creative destruction, restrictive practices may do much to steady the ship and to alleviate temporary difficulties. . . . Practically any investment entails, as a necessary complement of entrepreneurial action, certain safeguarding activities such as insuring or hedging. Long-range investing under rapidly changing conditions, especially under conditions that change or may change at any moment under the impact of new commodities and technologies, is like shooting at a target that is not only indistinct but moving—and moving jerkily at that. Hence it becomes necessary to resort to such protecting devices as patents or temporary secrecy of processes or, in some cases, long-period contracts secured in advance. . . . [I]f a patent cannot be secured or would not, if secured, effectively protect, other means may have to be used in order to justify the investment. Among them are a price policy that will make it possible to write off more quickly than would otherwise be rational, or additional investment in order to provide excess capacity to be used only for aggression or defense. . . .

Largest-scale plans could in many cases not materialize at all if it were not known from the outset that competition will be discouraged by heavy capital requirements or lack of experience, or that means are available to discourage or checkmate it so as to gain the time and space for further developments. Even the conquest of financial control over competing concerns in otherwise unassailable positions . . . move, as far as long-run effects on total output alone are envisaged, into a different light; they *may* be methods for removing obstacles that the institution of private property puts in the path of progress. . . . Enterprise would in most cases be impossible if it were not known from the outset that exceptionally favorable situations are likely to arise which if exploited by price, quality and quantity manipulation will produce profits adequate to tide over exceptionally unfavorable situations provided these are similarly managed. Again this requires strategy that in the short run is often restrictive. In the majority of successful cases this strategy just manages to serve its purpose. In some cases, however, it is so successful as to yield profits far above what is necessary in order to induce the corresponding investment. These cases then provide the baits that lure capital on to untried trails. . . .

Pure cases of long-run monopoly must be of the rarest occurrence . . . even tolerable approximations to the requirements of the concept must be still rarer than are cases of perfect competition. The power to exploit at pleasure a given pattern of demand . . . can under the conditions of intact capitalism hardly persist for a period long enough to matter for the analysis of total output, unless buttressed by public authority, for instance, in the case of fiscal monopolies. . . . Outside the field of public utilities, the position of a single seller can in general be conquered—and retained for decades—only on the condition that he does not behave like a monopolist. . . .

The theory of simple and discriminating monopoly teaches that, excepting a limiting case, monopoly price is higher and monopoly output smaller than competitive price and competitive output. This is true provided that the method and organization of production—and everything else—are exactly the same in both cases. Actually however there are superior methods available to the monopolist which either are not available at all to a crowd of competitors or are not available to them so readily: for there are advantages which, though not strictly unattainable on the competitive level of the enterprise, are as a matter of fact secured only on the monopoly level, for instance, because monopolization may increase the sphere of influence of the better, and decrease the sphere of influence of the inferior, brains, or because the monopoly enjoys a disproportionately higher financial standing. . . .

Perfectly free entry into a *new* field may make it impossible to enter it at all. The introduction of new methods of production and new commodities is hardly conceivable with perfect—and perfectly prompt—competition from the start. And this means that the bulk of what we call economic progress is incompatible with it. As a matter of fact, perfect competition is and always has been temporarily suspended whenever anything new is being introduced— automatically or by measures devised for the purpose. . . .

What we have got to accept is that [the large scale establishment] has come to be the most powerful engine of progress and in particular of the long-run expansion of total output not only in spite of, but to a considerable extent through, this strategy which looks so restrictive when viewed in the individual case and from the individual point of time. In this respect perfect competition is not only impossible, but inferior, and has no title to being set up as a model of ideal efficiency. It is hence a mistake to base the theory of government regulation of industry on the principle that big business should be made to work as the respective industry would work in perfect competition.

QUESTIONS FOR DISCUSSION

1 Summarize Schumpeter's attack on the neo-classical theory of competition. Do you agree that monopoly might have some useful purpose in a modern economy? What would be its disadvantages?

2 Schumpeter taught that interest would be necessary to induce capitalists to lend their money to entrepreneurs for the purpose of financing innovations. In the "circular flow" no such incentive would be needed, hence no positive interest. Do you agree? What would happen if the real interest rate were to fall to zero?

3 Does Schumpeter's theory support the necessity of capitalism if we are to have economic progress?

4 What are the "Austrian" elements in Schumpeter's work? Which are not?

READING 15

In the early 1930s **Friedrich A. Hayek** (born 1899) left Vienna, where he had been a student of law and economics, to go to Great Britain, where he taught many years at the London School of Economics. Though a reform socialist as a youth, he soon came under the influence of Ludwig von Mises, who regarded the socialist solution to economic problems as impossible. Hayek's *Collectivist Economic Planning: Critical Studies on the Possibilities of Socialism* (1935) is a penetrating review of early models of market socialism by Oskar Lange, Abba Lerner, and others.

The Austrian Catholic's anti-collectivist *The Road to Serfdom* (1944) is a powerful polemic against communism, fascism, and creeping socialism. A "liberal individualist" with a conservative's esteem for private property, the family, and religion, Hayek has said, "A society which is efficient cannot be just."[12] Quite consistently, then, he also criticized income or inheritance taxation. Altruism is an "instinct" appropriate for face-to-face communities, but to help the needy whom one doesn't know one would do best to follow market signals and seek profits.

Hayek has opposed much of modern macroeconomics, even the monetarism pursued by conservatives like Milton Friedman. According to Hayek, no statistical regularities between *average* prices and money should be relied on. No one has even produced a satisfactory definition of money. Though Hayek would prefer zero inflation—itself an average, of course—the important signals are *individual* prices, not some statistical construct. Because he believes that governments cannot resist monetary manipulation, Hayek would prefer to allow private concerns to issue money on a competitive basis. Let the public decide whose money best suits them.

During the last decades of his long life, much of which was spent in the United States, Hayek has turned to the study of political philosophy, producing a number of distinguished works.

The Use of Knowledge in Society[*]

Friedrich A. Hayek

1. What is the problem we wish to solve when we try to construct a rational economic order? On certain familiar assumptions the answer is simple enough. *If* we possess all the relevant information, *if* we can start out from a given system of preferences, and *if* we command complete knowledge of available means, the problem which remains is purely one of logic. That is, the answer to the question of what is the best use of the available means is implicit in our assumptions. The conditions which the solution of this optimum problem must satisfy have been fully worked out and can be stated best in mathematical form: put at their briefest, they are that the marginal rates of substitution between any two commodities or factors must be the same in all their different uses.

---

[12]"Hayek—His Life and Thought" (Princeton, New Jersey: Films for the Humanities, Inc., 1984).

[*]*Source:* First published in *American Economic Review*, 35, no. 4 (September, 1945), pp. 519-530, and reprinted in Friedrich A. Hayek, *Individualism and Economic Order* (Chicago: University of Chicago Press, 1948). Sections 1-6 are reprinted by permission.

This, however, is emphatically not the economic problem which society faces. And the economic calculus which we have developed to solve this logical problem, though an important step toward the solution of the economic problem of society, does not yet provide an answer to it. The reason for this is that the "data" from which the economic calculus starts are never for the whole "given" to a single mind which could work out the implication and can never be so given.

The peculiar character of the problem of a rational economic order is determined precisely by the fact that the knowledge of the circumstances of which we must make use never exists in concentrated or integrated form but solely as the dispersed bits of incomplete and frequently contradictory knowledge which all the separate individuals possess. The economic problem of society is thus not merely a problem of how to allocate given resources—if given is taken to mean given to a single mind which deliberately solves the problem set by these "data." It is rather a problem of how to secure the best use of resources known to any of the members of society, for ends whose relative importance only these individuals know. Or, to put it briefly, it is a problem of the utilization of knowledge which is not given to anyone in its totality.

This character of the fundamental problem has, I am afraid, been obscured rather than illuminated by many of the recent refinements of economic theory, particularly by many of the uses made of mathematics. Though the problem with which I want primarily to deal in this paper is the problem of a rational economic organization, I shall in its course be led again and again to point to its close connections with certain methodological questions. Many of the points I wish to make are indeed conclusions toward which diverse paths of reasoning have unexpectedly converged. But, as I now see these problems, this is no accident. It seems to me that many of the current disputes with regard to both economic theory and economic policy have their common origin in a misconception about the nature of the economic problem of society. This misconception in turn is due to an erroneous transfer to social phenomena of the habits of thought we have developed in dealing with the phenomena of nature.

2. In ordinary language we describe by the word "planning" the complex of interrelated decisions about the allocation of our available resources. All economic activity is in this sense planning; and in any society in which many people collaborate, this planning, whoever does it, will in some measure have to be based on knowledge which, in the first instance, is not given to the planner but to somebody else, which somehow will have to be conveyed to the planner. The various ways in which the knowledge on which people base their plans is communicated to them is the crucial problem for any theory explaining the economic process, and the problem of what is the best way of utilizing knowledge initially dispersed among all the people is at least one of the main problems of economic policy—or of designing an efficient economic system.

The answer to this question is closely connected with that other question which arises here, that of *who* is to do the planning. It is about this question that all the dispute about economic planning centers. This is not a dispute about whether planning is to be done or not. It is a dispute as to whether planning is to be done centrally, by one authority for the whole economic system, or is to be divided among many individuals. Planning in the specific sense in which the term is used in contemporary controversy necessarily means central planning—direction of the whole economic system according to one unified plan. Competition, on the other hand, means decentralized planning by many separate persons. The halfway house between the two, about which many people talk but which few like when they see it, is the delegation of planning to organized industries, or, in other words, monopolies.

Which of these systems is likely to be more efficient depends mainly on the question under which of them we can expect that fuller use will be made of the existing knowledge. This, in turn, depends on whether we are more likely to succeed in putting at the disposal of a single central authority all the knowledge which ought to be used but which is initially dispersed among many different individuals, or in conveying to the individuals such additional knowledge as they need in order to enable them to dovetail their plans with those of others.

3. It will at once be evident that on this point the position will be different with respect to different kinds of knowledge. The answer to our question will therefore largely turn on the relative importance of the different kinds of knowledge: those more likely to be at the disposal of particular individuals and those which we should with greater confidence expect to find in the possession of an authority made up of suitably chosen experts. If it is today so widely assumed that the latter will be in a better position, this is because one kind of knowledge, namely, scientific knowledge, occupies now so prominent a place in public imagination that we tend to forget that it is not the only kind that is relevant. It may be admitted that, as far as scientific knowledge is concerned, a body of suitably chosen experts may be in the best position to command all the best knowledge available—though this is of course merely shifting the difficulty to the problem of selecting the experts. What I wish to point out is that, even assuming that this problem can be readily solved, it is only a small part of the wider problem.

Today it is almost heresy to suggest that scientific knowledge is not the sum of all knowledge. But a little reflection will show that there is beyond question a body of very important but unorganized knowledge which cannot possibly be called scientific in the sense of knowledge of general rules: the knowledge of the particular circumstances of time and place. It is with respect to this that practically every individual has some advantage over all others because he possesses unique information of which beneficial use might be made, but of which use can be made only if the decisions depending on it are left to him or are made with his active cooperation. We need to remember only how much we have to learn in any occupation after we have completed our theoretical training, how big a part of our working life we spend learning particular jobs, and how valuable an asset in all walks of life is knowledge of people, of local conditions, and of special circumstances. To know of and put to use a machine not fully employed, or somebody's skill which could be better utilized, or to be aware of a surplus stock which can be drawn upon during an interruption of supplies, is socially quite as useful as the knowledge of better alternative techniques. The shipper who earns his living from using otherwise empty or half-filled journeys of tramp-steamers, or the estate agent whose knowledge is almost exclusively one of temporary opportunities, or the *arbitrageur* who gains from local differences of commodity prices—are all performing eminently useful functions based on special knowledge of circumstances of the fleeting moment not known to others.

It is a curious fact that this sort of knowledge should today be generally regarded with a kind of contempt and that anyone who by such knowledge gains an advantage over somebody better equipped with theoretical or technical knowledge is thought to have acted almost disreputably. To gain an advantage from better knowledge of facilities of communication or transport is sometimes regarded as almost dishonest, although it is quite as important that society make use of the best opportunities in this respect as in using the latest scientific discoveries. This prejudice has in a considerable measure affected the attitude toward commerce in general compared with that toward production. Even economists who regard themselves as definitely immune to the crude materialist fallacies of the past constantly commit the same mistake where activities directed toward the acquisition of such practical knowledge are concerned—apparently because in their scheme of things all such knowledge is supposed to be "given." The common idea now seems to be that all such knowledge should as a matter of course be readily at the command of everybody, and the reproach of irrationality leveled against the existing economic order is frequently based on the fact that it is not so available. This view disregards the fact that the method by which such knowledge can be made as widely available as possible is precisely the problem to which we have to find an answer.

4. If it is fashionable today to minimize the importance of the knowledge of the particular circumstances of time and place, that is closely connected with the smaller importance which is now attached to change as such. Indeed, there are few points on which the assumptions made (usually only implicitly) by the planners differ from those of their opponents as much as with regard to the significance and frequency of changes which will make substantial alterations of production plans necessary. Of course, if detailed economic plans could be laid down for fairly long periods in advance and then closely adhered to, so that no further economic decisions of importance would be required, the task of drawing up a comprehensive plan governing all economic activity would be much less formidable.

It is, perhaps, worth stressing that economic problems arise always and only in consequence of change. As long as things continue as before, or at least as they were expected to, there arise no new problems requiring a decision, no need to form a new plan. The belief that changes, or at least day-to-day adjustments, have become less important in modern times implies the contention that economic problems also have become less important. This belief in the decreasing importance of change is, for that reason, usually held by the same people who argue that the importance of economic considerations has been driven into the background by the growing importance of technological knowledge.

Is it true that, with the elaborate apparatus of modern production, economic decisions are required only at long intervals, as when a new factory is to be erected or a new process to be introduced? Is it true that, once a plant has been built, the rest is all more or less mechanical, determined by the character of the plant, and leaving little to be changed in adapting to the ever changing circumstances of the moment?

The fairly widespread belief in the affirmative is not, as far as I can ascertain, borne out by the practical experience of the businessman. In a competitive industry at any rate—and such an industry alone can serve as a test—the task of keeping cost from rising requires constant struggle, absorbing a great part of the energy of the manager. How easy it is for an inefficient manager to dissipate the differentials on which profitability rests and that it is possible, with the same technical facilities, to produce with a great variety of costs are among the commonplaces of business experience which do not seem to be equally familiar in the study of the economist. The very strength of the desire, constantly voiced by producers and engineers, to be allowed to proceed untrammeled by considerations of money costs, is eloquent testimony to the extent to which these factors enter into their daily work.

One reason why economists are increasingly apt to forget about the constant small changes which make up the whole economic picture is probably their growing preoccupation with statistical aggregates, which show a very much greater stability than the movements of the detail. The comparative stability of the aggregates cannot, however, be accounted for—as the statisticians occasionally seem to be inclined to do—by the "law of large numbers" or the mutual compensation of random changes. The number of elements with which we have to deal is not large enough for such accidental forces to produce stability. The continuous flow of goods and services is maintained by constant deliberate adjustments, by new dispositions made every day in the light of circumstances not known the day before, by B stepping in at once when A fails to deliver. Even the large and highly mechanized plant keeps going largely because of an environment upon which it can draw for all sorts of unexpected needs: tiles for its roof, stationery or its forms, and all the thousand and one kinds of equipment in which it cannot be self-contained and which the plans for the operation of the plant require to be readily available in the market.

This is, perhaps, also the point where I should briefly mention the fact that the sort of knowledge with which I have been concerned is knowledge of the kind which by its nature cannot enter into statistics and therefore cannot be conveyed to any central authority in statistical form. The statistics which such a central authority would have to use would have to be arrived at precisely by abstracting from minor differences between the things, by lumping together, as resources of one kind, items which differ as regards location, quality, and other particulars, in a way which may be very significant for the specific decision. It follows from this that central planning based on statistical information by its nature cannot take direct account of these circumstances of time and place and that the central planner will have to find some way or other in which the decisions depending on them can be left to the "man on the spot."

5. If we can agree that the economic problem of society is mainly one of rapid adaptation to changes in the particular circumstances of time and place, it would seem to follow that the ultimate decisions must be left to the people who are familiar with these circumstances, who know directly of the relevant changes and of the resources immediately available to meet them. We cannot expect that this problem will be solved by first communicating all this

knowledge to a central board which, after integrating all knowledge, issues its orders. We must solve it by some form of decentralization. But this answers only part of our problem. We need decentralization because only thus can we insure that the knowledge of the particular circumstances of time and place will be promptly used. But the "man on the spot" cannot decide solely on the basis of his limited but intimate knowledge of the facts of his immediate surroundings. There still remains the problem of communicating to him such further information as he needs to fit his decisions into the whole pattern of changes of the larger economic system.

How much knowledge does he need to do so successfully? Which of the events which happen beyond the horizon of his immediate knowledge are of relevance to his immediate decision, and how much of them need he know?

There is hardly anything that happens anywhere in the world that *might* not have an effect on the decision he ought to make. But he need not know of these events as such, nor of *all* their effects. It does not matter for him *why* at the particular moment more screws of one size than of another are wanted, *why* paper bags are more readily available than canvas bags, or *why* skilled labor, or particular machine tools, have for the moment become more difficult to obtain. All that is significant for him is *how much more or less* difficult to procure they have become compared with other things with which he is also concerned, or how much more or less urgently wanted are the alternative things he produces or uses. It is always a question of the relative importance of the particular things with which he is concerned, and the causes which alter their relative importance are of no interest to him beyond the effect on those concrete things of his own environment.

It is in this connection that what I have called the "economic calculus" (or the Pure Logic of Choice) helps us, at least by analogy, to see how this problem can be solved, and in fact is being solved, by the price system. Even the single controlling mind, in possession of all the data for some small, self-contained economic system, would not—every time some small adjustment in the allocation of resources had to be made—go explicitly through all the relations between ends and means which might possibly be affected. It is indeed the great contribution of the Pure Logic of Choice that it has demonstrated conclusively that even such a single mind could solve this kind of problem only by constructing and constantly using rates of equivalence (or "values," or "marginal rates of substitution"), that is, by attaching to each kind of scarce resource a numerical index which cannot be derived from any property possessed by that particular thing, but which reflects, or in which is condensed, its significance in view of the whole means-end structure. In any small change he will have to consider only these quantitative indices (or values) in which all the relevant information is concentrated; and, by adjusting the quantities one by one, he can appropriately rearrange his dispositions without having to solve the whole puzzle *ab initio* or without needing at any stage to survey it at once in all its ramifications.

Fundamentally, in a system in which the knowledge of the relevant facts is dispersed among many people, prices can act to coordinate the separate actions of different people in the same way as subjective values help the individual to coordinate the parts of his plan. It is worth contemplating for a moment a very simple and commonplace instance of the action of the price system to see what precisely it accomplishes. Assume that somewhere in the world a new opportunity for the use of some raw material, say, tin, has arisen, or that one of the sources of supply of tin has been eliminated, It does not matter for our purpose—and it is significant that it does not matter—which of these two causes has made tin more scarce. All that the users of tin need to know is that some of the tin they used to consume is now more profitably employed elsewhere and that, in consequence, they must economize tin. There is no need for the great majority of them even to know where the more urgent need has arisen, or in favor of what other needs they ought to husband the supply. If only some of them know directly of the new demand, and switch resources over to it, and if the people who are aware of the new gap thus created in turn fill it from still other sources, the effect will rapidly spread throughout the whole economic system and influence not only all the uses of tin but also those of its substitutes and the substitutes of these substitutes, the supply of all the things made of tin, and their substitutes, and so on; and all this without the great majority of those instrumental in bringing about these substitutions knowing anything at all about the original cause of these changes. The whole acts as one market, not because any of its members survey the whole field, but because their limited individual fields of vision sufficiently overlap so that through many intermediaries the relevant information is communicated to all. The mere fact that there is one price for any commodity—or rather that local prices are connected in a manner determined by the cost of transport, etc.— brings about the solution which (it is just conceptually possible) might have been arrived at by one single mind possessing all the information which in fact dispersed among all the people involved in the process.

6.   We must look at the price system as such a mechanism for communicating information if we want to understand its real function—a function which, of course, it fulfills less perfectly as prices grow more rigid. (Even when quoted prices have become quite rigid, however, the forces which would operate through changes in price still operate to a considerable extent through changes in the other terms of the contract.) The most significant fact about this system is the economy of knowledge with which it operates, or how little the individual participants need to know in order to be able to take the right action. In abbreviated form, by a kind of symbol, only the most essential information is passed on and passed on only to those concerned. It is more than a metaphor to describe the price system as a kind of machinery for registering change, or a system of telecommunications which enables individual producers to watch merely the movement of a few pointers, as an engineer might watch the hands of a few dials, in order to adjust their activities to changes of which they may never know more than is reflected in the price movement.

Of course, these adjustments are probably never "perfect" in the sense in which the economist conceives of them in his equilibrium analysis. But I fear that our theoretical habits of approaching the problem with the assumption of more or less perfect knowledge on the part of almost everyone has made us somewhat blind to the true function of the price mechanism and led us to apply rather misleading standards in judging its efficiency. The marvel is that in a case like that of a scarcity of one raw material, without an order being issued, without more than perhaps a handful of people knowing the cause, tens of thousands of people whose identity could not be ascertained by months of investigation, are made to use the material or its products more sparingly; that is, they move in the right direction. This is enough of a marvel even if, in a constantly changing world, not all will hit it off so perfectly that their profit rates will always be maintained at the same even or "normal" level.

I have deliberately used the word "marvel" to shock the reader out of the complacency with which we often take the working of this mechanism for granted. I am convinced that if it were the result of deliberate human design, and if the people guided by the price changes understood that their decisions have significance far beyond their immediate aim, this mechanism would have been acclaimed as one of the greatest triumphs of the human mind. Its misfortune is the double one that it is not the product of human design and that the people guided by it usually do not know why they are made to do what they do. But those who clamor for "conscious direction"—and who cannot believe that anything which has evolved without design (and even without our understanding it) should solve problems which we should not be able to solve consciously—should remember this: The problem is precisely how to extend the span of our utilization of resources beyond the span of the control of any one mind; and, therefore, how to dispense with the need of conscious control and how to provide inducements which will make the individuals do the desirable things without anyone having to tell them what to do.

The problem which we meet here is by no means peculiar to economics but arises in connection with nearly all truly social phenomena, with language and with most of our cultural inheritance, and constitutes really the central theoretical problem of all social science. As Alfred Whitehead has said in another connection, "It is a profoundly erroneous truism, repeated by all copybooks and by eminent people when they are making speeches, that we should cultivate the habit of thinking what we are doing. The precise opposite is the case. Civilization advances by extending the number of important operations which we can perform without thinking about them." This is of profound significance in the social field. We make constant use of formulas, symbols, and rules whose meaning we do not understand and through the use of which we avail ourselves of the assistance of knowledge which individually we do not possess. We have developed these practices and institutions by building upon habits and institutions which have proved successful in their own sphere and which have in turn become the foundation of the civilization we have built up.

The price system is just one of those formations which man has learned to use (though he is still very far from having learned to make the best use of it) after he had stumbled upon it without understanding it. Through it not only a division of labor but also a coordinated utilization of resources based on an equally divided knowledge has become possible. The people who like to deride any suggestion that this may be so usually distort the argument by insinuating that it asserts that by some miracle just that sort of system has spontaneously grown up which is best suited to modern civilization. It is the other way round: man has been able to develop that division of labor on which our civilization is based because he happened to stumble upon a method which made it possible. Had he not done so, he might still have developed some other, altogether different, type of civilization, something like the "state" of the termite ants, or some other altogether unimaginable type. All that we can say is that nobody has yet succeeded in designing an alternative system in which certain features of the existing one can be preserved which are dear even to those who most violently assail it—such as particularly the extent to which the individual can choose his pursuits and consequently freely use his own knowledge and skill.

QUESTIONS FOR DISCUSSION

1   In Hayek's view what is the most productive and ethical way for a person to relate to others? Illustrate his view by considering rent control on apartments around a university area. Who benefits and who loses from this well-intentioned policy?
2   What is Hayek's basic criticism of economic planning? Can you see any uses for economic planning which Hayek may have neglected?
3   Why is the price system economical in the use of information and human intelligence?

John Maynard Keynes

CHAPTER 7

KEYNES AND THE KEYNESIANS

EDITOR'S INTRODUCTION

A contemporary of Joseph Schumpeter, **John Maynard Keynes** (1883-1946) was a thoroughly English neo-classical economist for most of his life. Keynes favored competition, stable money, and the use of market forces, though he was personally a left-wing Liberal, anti-nationalist, and cultural bohemian. It was only when market adjustments were too slow that Keynes recommended government intervention.[1] Out of this impatience to get capitalism working better came the distinct Keynesian perspective, which persists to this day within and beyond the English-speaking mainstream.

Like many economists of his era, Keynes doubted that aggregate demand would be adequate to absorb all the new production made possible by technical progress. Who would buy the autos, electrical appliances, rayon textiles, and other innovations which flooded the market after World War I? The working class did not have the incomes to do so, and the upper classes would not suffice. Population growth had slowed, meaning less demand for housing. What is more, automation would threaten the jobs of the working classes. To this fear of underconsumption, the traditional answer had been "Say's Law"; with flexible prices and interest rates, the flows of income from production would be enough to absorb any level of output, either as consumption or as investment at home or abroad. Money earned could, of course, be hoarded,

---

[1]For example, Keynes' well-known recommendation for protectionism in the early 1930s can be traced to his impatience with devaluation of the £ sterling in the circumstances of world depression. During normal times, Keynes was far from ignoring the role of the exchange rate in improving the trade balance, as he showed in his polemic on the gold standard, "The Economic Consequences of Mr. Churchill" (1925), reprinted in *Essays in Persuasion.*

but then the general price level would decline to the point where nominal wealth holders (e.g., owners of government bonds) would be willing to spend their capital gains. This mechanism for the restoration of full-employment equilibrium—called the "Pigou Effect," after a contemporary opponent of Keynes'—would supplement wage cuts as a way to employ all who wished to work at marginal productivity wages.

The theoretic impossibility of sustained involuntary unemployment can be seen in the usual labor market analysis common to English neo-classical writers, including the early Keynes. The supply of labor in response to real wage offers reflects individual choices about working or remaining at leisure; the supply price is the value of the leisure foregone at the margin by working an extra hour. Demand reflects the value to employers of workers' marginal productivity. Provided wages were flexible up or down, workers would be hired up to the point that their contribution to revenues just paid the competitive wage. If anyone remained unemployed, it was merely a sign that the wage commanded by the worker's abilities was insufficient for him or her. After all, everyone who works less than the physical maximum per week voluntarily chooses some "unemployment"—really, leisure.

Neo-Classical Macroeconomics in Keynes' Time

Should anything block the prompt adjustment of prices to any change in the environment—say minimum wage laws, stubborn labor unions, or stickiness in interest rates—then neo-classical writers like Irving Fisher and Knut Wicksell would foresee recession or unemployment. Accordingly, the conventional policy to deal with periodic trade cycles was monetary accommodation, lower interest rates on credit-worthy commercial paper, wage restraint, balanced budgets, and patience. Over the longer run, any expansion of the money stock beyond the "needs of trade" would have to be reabsorbed, lest there be inflation. With such a monetary policy, neo-classical economists believed that market forces would, if allowed to operate freely, push the economy to the maximum production consistent with its factor endowment and state of technology. Otherwise, the size of the money supply would have no role except to fix the nominal price level. Fiscal policy would have no role except to divide national income between public and various private uses. So macroeconomics hardly existed, nor did aggregate statistics. Employment and industrial output figures simply registered the (presumably equilibrium) outcome of microeconomic decisions.

What changed this was Keynes' impatient conviction[2] that conventional prescriptions had been adequate to eliminate the massive unemployment which characterized much of English interwar history. When a normal European downtown in the late 1920s developed into a worldwide financial panic by 1931, easy money, devaluation, government economies, and lower prices did

---

[2]Keynes was notoriously impatient and occasionally irresponsible, as well as clearly brilliant. Referring to the effects of monetary policy he wrote, "In the long run we are all dead." To be relevant, economic policy had to be prompt.

not seem to help. They even seemed to aggravate the pessimism and gloom. Nor did the neo-classical perspective seem to explain what had gone wrong.

Keynes' answer, published as *The General Theory of Employment, Interest and Money* (1936), excerpted below, was to show that social forces were blocking the prompt adjustment of prices in the markets for labor, commodities, and financial assets as required by neo-classical theory. In doing so, Keynes developed a new mode of macroeconomic analysis, which constitutes the Keynesian perspective. Keynes clearly considered the older English neo-classical economics a "special case" for which he was producing a more "general" one without the special assumption of market clearing and full employment.

Keynes' Perspective

(1) **Social Forces and the Fallacy of Composition.** While a competitive market for one particular type of labor may clear by bidding over the contractual wage, this would not necessarily be the case for the aggregate labor market. This illustrates the fallacy of composition: what is true for one individual may not be true for a group. One person can safely escape a crowded theater by running at the first smell of smoke, but an entire audience cannot, because people will interfere with and trample each other. Thus, the attempt of one type of worker to seek employment by bidding down wages may not affect others. In the aggregate, however, as nominal wages fall, so do prices, and the real wage may not fall far enough fast enough. Wage cuts can depress consumer and business confidence, hence discretionary spending. Furthermore, people will resist a cut in their own wages, fearing a *relative* deterioration in their own standard of living. If real wages could be cut uniformly, such as by a price increase, then Keynes believed that workers wouldn't necessarily reduce their supply of labor below demand. Moreover, falling prices would transfer wealth to passive rentiers and creditors and away from active investors.[3] Moderate inflation would have the reverse effect of enhancing the position of active investors, who Keynes considered essential. Such holistic thinking characterizes Keynesian thinking to this day, whereas neo-classical mainstream economists take the rational individual as their unit of analysis.

(2) **Expectations.** The demand for investment goods derives from the hope for future profit and the subjective evaluation of uncertainty.[4] Credit will be extended by banks or other lenders and taken up by businesses or other borrowers only when the "marginal efficiency of investment" (in ordinary terms, the rate of profit) exceeds the cost of finance, the interest rate on bonds. But these expectations are unpredictable, even irrational, given the irreducible

---

[3]J. M. Keynes, "Social Consequences of Changes in the Value of Money" (1923).

[4]Keynes' earliest work on probability introduced the distinction between risk, in which known probabilities can be entered into decision-making formulae, and uncertainty, which is not objectively quantifiable.

uncertainty of the future.[5] "Animal spirits," emotional speculation, and habitual commitments have as much to do with investment booms, thought Keynes, as any systematic appreciation of the future. In particular, if easy money pushed bond prices close to historic highs, market players might resist any further fall in interest rates by absorbing any monetary influx into idle balances or hoards (the "liquidity trap").

Businesses and consumers act in large part by habitual responses, disregarding the long-run consequences of their actions. Consumers would expend some fixed proportion of their current disposable incomes, Keynes held, depending on their place in the income distribution and the expectation that future incomes will continue about as they have in the past. Such a psychology leads to the aggregate consumption function, $C = f(Y)$. Hence savings, too, depend on disposable income, as well as on interest rates. In uncertain times attempts to save more by consuming less could lead to lower aggregate demand unless investment demand exactly replaced consumption foregone. Over the short run reduced demand and the consequent pileup of inventory stocks could lead businessmen to cut production plans in preference to an immediate cut in prices. If the production cutbacks reinforced one another, a general recession would come about.

(3) **Disequilibria.** Owing to these uncertainties, supply may exceed demand for important resources or ranges of goods and services for a fairly long period of time. Of course, institutional factors such as long-term contracts or government regulations (e.g., a fixed exchange rate) needed for equity or stability may also prevent market clearing. If underlying data—tastes, investment opportunities, technologies—shift faster than prices do in important markets, then no equilibrium is to be expected. As noted above, Keynes believed investment demand would be particularly volatile, depending as it does on expected future profits, together with the cost of capital, as determined in unpredictable stock and bond markets.

Taking some of these new elements various theorists have produced explicit models predicting the effects of behavior or policy shifts. This one is due to **John Hicks** and to **Alvin Hansen**, the prominent American followers of Keynes who did so much to make his teaching acceptable to American economists just before World War II.[6] Keynes endorsed the model, even though it reduces the differences between his new theory and those of

---

[5] Expectations might be "adaptive"—i.e., conventionally based on recent experience—but they would not be calculable or "rational," as the term is used by the "new classical economists," for whom expectations are unbiased forecasts emerging from a fully defined and agreed stochastic model with known probabilities of future events. "The hypothesis of a calculable future leads to a wrong interpretation of the principles of behavior which the need for action compels us to adopt, and to an underestimation of the concealed factors of utter doubt, precariousness, hope, and fear." *Quarterly Journal of Economics* (1937), as reprinted in *The Collected Works of John Maynard Keynes,* vol. XIV ("The General Theory and After"), ed. by Donald Moggridge (London: Macmillan, 1973), p. 122.

[6] Alvin Hansen, *A Guide to Keynes* (New York: McGraw-Hill, 1953); John Hicks, "Mr. Keynes and the 'Classics': A Suggested Interpretation," *Econometrica* 5 (1937), pp. 147-159.

neo-classical writers to differences over the shape of crucial behavior relations. Whether shifts in these originate in the private economy or from the monetary authorities is an additional major difference between Keynesians and monetarist neo-classical writers, as Franco Modigliani emphasizes.

FIGURE 7-1
Aggregate Demand in Commodity Markets

$AD = C(Y) + I(Y,r)$ with Y the real national income, at fixed prices (P), and r the real interest rate. (Government demand and net exports are ignored.)
Demand for real money-balances, $M/P = L(r,Y)$
Supply of money, $Ms = Ms(r)$

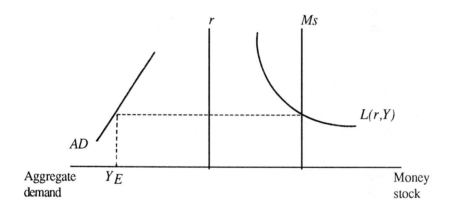

FIGURE 7-2
Equilibrium National Output

In the famous $IS\text{-}LM$ diagram, Y_E is the "equilibrium" output level at which both commodity market $(AD=AS)$ and financial market (demand and supply for money and bonds) are in equilibrium.

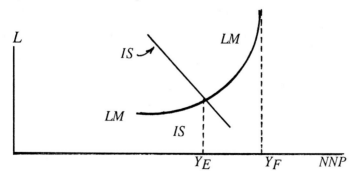

FIGURE 7-3
The Aggregate Labor Market

Supply of labor, $L_S = L_S(w/P)$
Demand for labor, $L_d = L_d(w/P; Y_E)$

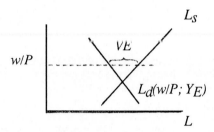

With fixed wate (w) and price level (P), the demand for labor at the equilibrium national output (Y_E) would be lower than voluntary supply, leaving involuntary unemployment (VE).

America's "Neo-Keynesians"

Among the contemporary American economists influenced by Keynes are Paul Samuelson, James Tobin, Robert Solow, and Franco Modigliani—all Nobel Prize winners for Economic Science. All these men would also consider themselves neo-classical economists[7] for some purposes and have endeavored to reintegrate some of Keynes' insights into the mainstream. In his influential textbook *Economics,* Samuelson (1915-   ) laid out what he called the "neo-classical synthesis": Keynesian aggregate demand was relevant to under-employment situations, but neo-classical analysis remained appropriate for full-employment or inflationary situations. **Robert Solow's** (1924-   ) famous growth model was neo-classical, but his analysis of unemployment and the budget deficit is admittedly Keynesian. None of these "neo-Keynesians" have attempted to include all the innovative elements of the Keynesian perspective into their macroeconomic theories, as have the more radical "post-Keynesians."

The Anglo-Italian and American "Post-Keynesians"

The greatest radical Keynesian was **Joan Robinson** (1903-1983). Her *The Accumulation of Capital* (1956) tried to construct a dynamic Keynesian growth model, and she always stressed the similarity of Marxian and Keynesian social insights into economic behavior. In her last years Mrs. Robinson rejected equilibrium economics, to which she had contributed her well-known *Imperfect Competition* (1933), and pursued an evolutionary theory which would not

---

[7]Arjo Klamer, *Conversations with Economists* (Totowa, New Jersey: Rowman & Allanheld, 1984), pp. 101, 131, 114, 121.

depend on comparative statics and Walrasian general equilibrium. Because of their fuller adoption of what we have identified above as the "Keynesian" perspective, Mrs. Robinson and her associates at Cambridge University claim the title "true Keynesians." Other economists who have pursued similar directions in the United Kingdom are **Michael Kalecki** (1899-1970), **Nicholas Kaldor** (1908-   ), and **Luigi Pasinetti** (1930-   ). In the United States the *Journal of Post-Keynesian Economics* contains articles by leading American post-Keynesians, such as **Hyman P. Minsky** (1919-   ), **Sidney Weintraub** (1922-   ), and **Paul Davidson** (1930-   ).

What characterizes the "post-Keynesian" paradigm at this early point in its development, besides a thorough rejection of neo-classical macroeconomics, is (1) an unwillingness to believe the economy has a *long-run* equilibrium, (2) their linking of the growth rate of the economy to its functional distribution of income, and (3) the view that conflict over the distribution of income and institutional arrangements of the credit markets cause inflation, rather than some exogenous increase in the stock of money.[8] For example, the "financial Keynesian" Hyman Minsky of Washington University believes that the stability of the mixed capitalist economy is threatened by the gradual erosion of liquidity among corporations. Following Kalecki, Minsky believes that profits and the ability to meet financial commitments depend on the continued willingness to invest, as well as the willingness of the government to serve as lender of last resort.[9]

READING 16

John Maynard Keynes (1883-1946), son of a prominent mathematical statistician at Cambridge, was an Englishman of many talents, interests, and involvements. Like many other English economists, he was a student of Alfred Marshall's. Early in his career, Keynes concerned himself with colonial finance and the Versailles settlement of World War I. His journalistic articles on the gold standard, employment policies, and protectionism were vigorous, articulate, and influential. As bursar of King's College, Cambridge, he successfully managed its finances. He was active in the Royal Economic Society and served as editor of the *Economic Journal* for many years. At the same time he was one of the most brilliant teachers of economic theory at Cambridge. Prominent in the avant-garde Bloomsbury group, his interest in high culture was a life-long activity. After World War II and until his death, he strove to restore a liberal international order based on stable exchange rates and such institutions as the International Monetary Fund. For his devoted service to his country, he was made Lord Keynes just before his death. The excerpts which follow illustrate his captivating and learned writing style.

---

[8]Alfred S. Eichner, ed., *A Guide to Post-Keynesian Economics* (White Plains: M. E. Sharpe, 1978). It has not been possible to include a representative and authoritative article from this new perspective.

[9]Hyman P. Minsky, *Can "It" Happen Again? Essays on Instability and Finance* (Armonk, New York: M. E. Sharpe, 1982).

The General Theory of Employment, Interest and Money*

John Maynard Keynes

Chapter 1. The General Theory

I have called this book the *General Theory of Employment, Interest and Money,* placing the emphasis on the prefix *general*. The object of such a title is to contrast the character of my arguments and conclusions with those of the *classical*[10] theory of the subject, upon which I was brought up and which dominates the economic thought, both practical and theoretical, of the governing and academic classes of this generation, as it has for a hundred years past. I shall argue that the postulates of the classical theory are applicable to a special case only and not to the general case, the situation which it assumes being a limiting point of the possible positions of equilibrium. Moreover, the characteristics of the special case assumed by the classical theory happen not to be those of the economic society in which we actually live, with the result that its teaching is misleading and disastrous if we attempt to apply it to the facts of experience. . . .

Chapter 3. The Principle of Effective Demand

I. . . . It is sometimes convenient, when we are looking at it from the entrepreneur's standpoint, to call the aggregate income (i.e., factor cost *plus* profit) resulting from a given amount of employment the *proceeds* of that employment. On the other hand, the aggregate supply price of the output of a given amount of employment is the expectation of proceeds which will just make it worth the while of the entrepreneurs to give that employment.

It follows that in a given situation of technique, resources and factor cost per unit of employment, the amount of employment, both in each individual firm and industry and in the aggregate, depends on the amount of the proceeds which the entrepreneurs expect to receive from the corresponding output. For entrepreneurs will endeavour to fix the amount of employment at the level which they expect to maximize the excess of the proceeds over the factor cost.

Let Z be the aggregate supply price of the output from employing N men, the relationship between Z and N being written $Z = \phi(N)$, which can be called

---

Source: Excerpted from *The Collected Writings of John Maynard Keynes,* vol. 7, *The General Theory of Employment, Interest and Money* (London: Macmillan, 1973). Copyright © The Royal Economic Society, 1973. Reprinted with the permission of Cambridge University Press.

10·The classical economists' was a name invented by Marx to cover Ricardo and James Mill and their *predecessors,* that is to say for the founders of the theory which culminated in the Ricardian economics. I have become accustomed, perhaps perpetrating a solecism, to include in 'the classical school' the *followers* of Ricardo, those, that is to say, who adopted and perfected the theory of the Ricardian economics, including (for example), J. S. Mill, Marshall, Edgeworth and Prof. Pigou. [Footnote in original.]

the *aggregate supply function*. Similarly, let D be the proceeds which entre-preneurs expect to receive from the employment of N men, the relationship between D and N being written $D = f(N)$, which can be called the *aggregate demand function*.

Now if for a given value of N the expected proceeds are greater than the aggregate supply price, i.e., if D is greater than Z, there will be an incentive to entrepreneurs to increase employment beyond N, and if necessary, to raise costs by competing with one another for the factors of production, up to the value of N for which Z has become equal to D. Thus the volume of employment is given by the point of intersection between the aggregate demand function and the aggregate supply function; for it is at this point that the entrepreneurs' expectation of profits will be maximized. The value of D at the point of the aggregate demand function, where it is intersected by the aggregate supply function, will be called *the effective demand*. Since this is the substance of the General Theory of Employment, which it will be our object to expound, the succeeding chapters will be largely occupied with examining the various factors upon which these two functions depend.

The classical doctrine, on the other hand, which used to be expressed cate-gorically in the statement that 'Supply creates its own Demand' [Say's Law] and continued to underlie all orthodox economic theory, involves a special assumption as to the relationship between these two functions. For 'Supply creates its own Demand' must mean that $f(N)$ and $\phi(N)$ are equal for all values of N, i.e., for all levels of output and employment; and that when there is an increase in Z $(= \phi(N))$ corresponding to an increase in N, $D = f(N))$ neces-sarily increases by the same amount as Z. The classical theory assumes, in other words, that the aggregate demand price (or proceeds) always accommo-dates itself to the aggregate supply price; so that, whatever the value of N may be, the proceeds D assume a value equal to the aggregate supply price Z which corresponds to N. That is to say, effective demand, instead of having a unique equilibrium value, is an infinite range of values all equally admissible; and the amount of employment is indeterminate except in so far as the marginal dis-utility of labor sets an upper limit.

If this were true, competition between entrepreneurs would always lead to an expansion of employment up to the point at which the supply of output as a whole ceases to be elastic, i.e., where a further increase in the value of the effective demand will no longer be accompanied by any increase in output. Evidently this amounts to the same thing as full employment. . . .

II. We shall assume that the money-wage and other factor costs are constant per unit of labor employed. But this simplification, with which we shall dispense later, is introduced solely to facilitate the exposition. The essential character of the argument is precisely the same whether or not money-wages, etc., are liable to change.

The outline of our theory can be expressed as follows. When employment increases, aggregate real income is increased. The psychology of the community is such that when aggregate real income is increased aggregate consumption is increased, but not by so much as income. Hence employers would make a loss if the whole of the increased employment were to be devoted to satisfying the increased demand for immediate consumption. Thus, to justify any given amount of employment there must be an amount of current investment sufficient to absorb the excess of total output over what the community chooses to consume when employment is at the given level. For unless there is this amount of investment, the receipts of the entrepreneur will be less than is required to induce them to offer the given amount of employment. It follows, therefore, that, given what we shall call the community's propensity to consume, the equilibrium level of employment, i.e., the level at which there is no inducement to employers as a whole either to expand or to contract employment, will depend on the amount of current investment. The amount of current investment will depend, in turn, on what we shall call the inducement to invest; and the inducement to invest will be found to depend on the relation between the schedule of the marginal efficiency of capital and the complex of rates of interest on loans of various maturities and risks.

Thus, given the propensity to consume and the rate of new investment, there will be only one level of employment consistent with equilibrium; since any other level will lead to inequality between the aggregate supply price of output as a whole and its aggregate demand price. This level cannot be *greater* than full employment, i.e., the real wage cannot be less than the marginal disutility of labor. But there is no reason in general for expecting it to be equal to full employment. The effective demand associated with full employment is a special case, only realized when the propensity to consume and the inducement to invest stand in a particular relationship to one another. This particular relationship, which corresponds to the assumptions of the classical theory, is in a sense an optimum relationship. But it can only exist when, by accident or design, current investment provides an amount of demand just equal to the excess of the aggregate supply price of the output resulting from full employment over what the community will choose to spend on consumption when it is fully employed. . . .

For every value of N there is a corresponding marginal productivity of labor in the wage-goods industries; and it is this which determines the real wage . . . N cannot exceed the value which reduces the real wage to equality with the marginal disutility of labor. . . .

Thus the volume of employment is not determined by the marginal disutility of labor measured in terms of real wages, except in so far as the supply of labor available at a given real wage sets a *maximum* level to employment. The propensity to consume and the rate of new investment determine between them the volume of employment, and the volume of employment is uniquely related to a given level of real wages—not the other way round. If the propensity to consume and the rate of new investment result in a deficient effective demand, the actual level of employment will fall short of the supply of labor potentially available at the existing real wage, and the equilibrium real wage will be *greater* than the marginal disutility of the equilibrium level of employment.

This analysis supplies us with an explanation of the paradox of poverty in the midst of plenty. For the mere existence of an insufficiency of effective demand may, and often will, bring the increase of employment to a standstill before a level of full employment has been reached. The insufficiency of effective demand will inhibit the process of production in spite of the fact that the marginal product of labor still exceeds in value the marginal disutility of employment.

Moreover, the richer the community, the wider will tend to be the gap between its actual and its potential production; and therefore the more obvious and outrageous the defects of the economic system. For a poor community will be prone to consume by far the greater part of its output, so that a very modest measure of investment will be sufficient to provide full employment; whereas a wealthy community will have to discover much ampler opportunities for investment if the saving propensities of its wealthier members are to be compatible with the employment of its poorer members. If in a potentially wealthy community the inducement to invest is weak, then, in spite of its potential wealth, the working of the principle of effective demand will compel it to reduce its actual output, until, in spite of its potential wealth, it has become so poor that its surplus over its consumption is sufficiently diminished to correspond to the weakness of the inducement to invest.

But worse still. Not only is the marginal propensity to consume weaker in a wealthy community, but, owing to its accumulation of capital being already larger, the opportunities for further investment are less attractive unless the rate of interest falls at a sufficiently rapid rate. . . .

Chapter 5. Expectation as Determining Output and Employment

. . . The behavior of each individual firm in deciding its daily[11] output will be determined by its *short-term expectations*—expectations as to the cost of output on various possible scales and expectations as to the sale-proceeds of this output; though, in the case of additions to capital equipment and even of sales to distributors, these short-term expectations will largely depend on the long-term (or medium-term) expectations of other parties. It is upon these various expectations that the amount of employment which the firms offer will depend. The *actually realized* results of the production and sale of output will only be relevant to employment in so far as they cause a modification of subsequent expectations. Nor, on the other hand, are the original expectations relevant, which led the firm to acquire the capital equipment and the stock of intermediate products and half-finished materials with which it finds itself at the time when it has to decide the next day's output. Thus, on each and every occasion of such a decision, the decision will be made, with reference indeed to this equipment and stock, but in the light of the *current* expectations of *prospective* costs and sale-proceeds.

Now, in general, a *change* in expectations (whether short-term or long-term) will only produce its full effect on employment over a considerable period. . . . Suppose that the change is of such a character that the new long-period employment will be greater than the old. Now, as a rule, it will only be the rate of input which will be much affected at the beginning, that is to say, the volume of work on the earlier stages of new processes of production, whilst the output of consumption-goods and the amount of employment on the later stages of processes which were started before the change will remain

---

[11]*Daily* here stands for the shortest interval after which the firm is free to revise its decision as to how much employment to offer. It is, so to speak, the minimum effective unit of economic time. [Footnote in original.]

much the same as before. In so far as there were stocks of partly finished goods, this conclusion may be modified; though it is likely to remain true that the initial increase in employment will be modest. As, however, the days pass by, employment will gradually increase. Moreover, it is easy to conceive of conditions which will cause it to increase at some stage to a *higher* level than the new long-period employment. For the process of building up capital to satisfy the new state of expectation may lead to more employment and also to more current consumption than will occur when the long-period position has been reached. Thus the change in expectation may lead to a gradual crescendo in the level of employment, rising to a peak and then declining to the new long-period level. The same thing may occur even if the new long-period level is the *same* as the old, if the change represents a change in the direction of consumption which renders certain existing processes and their equipment obsolete. Or again, if the new long-period employment is less than the old, the level of employment during the transition may fall for a time *below* what the new long-period level is going to be. Thus a mere change in expectation is capable of producing an oscillation of the same kind of shape as a cyclical movement, in the course of working itself out. . . .

Although output and employment are determined by the producer's short-term expectations and not by past results, the most recent results usually play a predominant part in determining what these expectations are. It would be too complicated to work out the expectations *de novo* whenever a productive process was being started; and it would, moreover, be a waste of time since a large part of the circumstances usually continue substantially unchanged from one day to the next. Accordingly, it is sensible for producers to base their expectations on the assumption that the most recently realized results will continue except in so far as there are definite reasons for expecting a change. . . .

Chapter 11. The Marginal Efficiency of Capital

When a man buys an investment or capital-asset, he purchases the right to the series of prospective returns, which he expects to obtain from selling its output, after deducting the running expenses of obtaining that output, during the life of the asset. This series of annuities $Q_1, Q_2, \ldots Q_n$ it is convenient to call the *prospective yield* of the investment.

Over against the prospective yield of the investment we have the *supply price* of the capital asset, meaning by this, not the market-price at which an asset of the type in question can actually be purchased in the market, but the price which would just induce a manufacturer newly to produce an additional unit of such assets, i.e. what is sometimes called its *replacement cost*. The relation between the prospective yield of a capital asset and its supply price or replacement cost, i.e. the relation between the prospective yield of one more unit of that type of capital and the cost of producing that unit, furnishes us with the *marginal efficiency of capital* of that type. More precisely, I define the marginal efficiency of capital as being equal that rate of discount which would make the present value of the series of annuities given by the returns expected from the capital-asset during its life just equal to its supply price. This gives us the marginal efficiencies of particular types of capital-assets. The greatest of these marginal efficiencies can then be regarded as the marginal efficiency of capital in general. . . .

If there is an increased investment in any given type of capital during any period of time, the marginal efficiency of that type of capital will diminish as the investment in it is increased, partly because the prospective yield will fall as the supply of that type of capital is increased, and partly because, as a rule, pressure on the facilities for producing that type of capital will cause its supply price to increase; the second of these factors being usually the more important in producing equilibrium in the short run, but the longer the period in view the more does the first factor take its place. . . . We can then aggregate these schedules for all the different types of capital, so as to provide a schedule relating the rate of aggregate investment to the corresponding marginal efficiency of capital in general which that rate of investment will establish. We shall call this the investment demand schedule; or, alternatively, the schedule of the marginal efficiency of capital.

Now it is obvious that the actual rate of current investment will be pushed to the point where there is no longer any class of capital-asset of which the marginal efficiency exceeds the current rate of interest. In other words, the rate of investment will be pushed to the point on the investment demand-schedule where the marginal efficiency of capital in general is equal to the market rate of interest. . . .

It follows that the inducement to invest depends partly on the investment demand-schedule and partly on the rate of interest. . . . We must ascertain the rate of interest from some other source, and only then can we value the asset by 'capitalizing' its prospective yield. . . .

III. The most important confusion concerning the meaning and signifi- cance of the marginal efficiency of capital has ensued on the failure to see that it depends on the *prospective* yield of capital, and not merely on its current yield. This can be best illustrated by pointing out the effect on the marginal efficiency of capital of an expectation of changes in the prospective cost of production, whether these changes are expected to come from changes in labor cost, i.e. in the wage-unit, or from inventions and new technique. The output from equipment produced today will have to compete, in the course of its life, with the output from equipment produced subsequently, perhaps at a lower labor cost, perhaps by an improved technique, which is content with a lower price for its output and will be increased in quantity until the price of its output has fallen to the lower figure with which it is content. Moreover, the entrepreneur's profit (in terms of money) from equipment, old or new, will be reduced, if all output comes to be produced more cheaply. In so far as such developments are foreseen as probable, or even as possible, the marginal efficiency of capital produced today is appropriately diminished.

This is the factor through which the expectation of changes in the value of money influences the volume of current output. The expectation of a fall in the value of money stimulates investment, and hence employment generally, because it raises the schedule of the marginal efficiency of capital, i.e. the investment demand-schedule; and the expectation of a rise in the value of money is depressing, because it lowers the schedule of the marginal efficiency of capital. . . .

The prices of *existing* assets will always adjust themselves to changes in expectation concerning the prospective value of money. The significance of such changes in expectation lies in their effect on the readiness to produce net assets through their reaction on the marginal efficiency of capital. The stimulating effect of the expectation of higher prices is due, not to its raising the rate of interest (that would be a paradoxical way of stimulating output—in so far as the rate of interest rises, the stimulating effect is to that extent offset), but to its raising the marginal efficiency of a given stock of capital. *If* the rate of interest were to rise *pari passu* with the marginal efficiency of capital, there would be no stimulating effect from the expectation of rising prices. For the stimulus to output depends on the marginal efficiency of a given stock of capital rising *relatively* to the rate of interest. . . .

Two types of risk affect the volume of investment which have not commonly been distinguished, but which it is important to distinguish. The first is the entrepreneur's or borrower's risk and arises out of doubts in his own mind as to the probability of his actually earning the prospective yield for which he hopes. If a man is venturing his own money, this is the only risk which is relevant.

But where a system of borrowing and lending exists, by which I mean the granting of loans with a margin of real or personal security, a second type of risk is relevant which we may call the lender's risk. This may be due either to moral hazard, i.e., voluntary default or other means of escape, possibly lawful, from the fulfillment of the obligation, or to the possible insufficiency of the margin of security, i.e. involuntary default due to the disappointment of expectation. A third source of risk might be added, namely, a possible adverse change in the value of the monetary standard which renders a money-loan to this extent less secure than a real asset; though all or most of this should be already reflected, and therefore absorbed, in the price of durable real assets.

Now the first type of risk is, in a sense, a real social cost, though susceptible to diminution by averaging as well as by an increased accuracy of foresight. The second, however, is a pure addition to the cost of investment which would not exist if the borrower and lender were the same person. Moreover, it involves in part a duplication of a proportion of the entrepreneur's risk, which is added *twice* to the pure rate of interest to give the minimum prospective yield which will induce the investment. For if a venture is a risky one, the borrower will require a wider margin between his expectation of yield and the rate of interest at which he will think it worth his while to borrow; whilst the very same reason will lead the lender to require a wider margin between what he charges and the pure rate of interest in order to induce him to lend (except where the borrower is so strong and wealthy that he is in a position to offer an exceptional margin of security). The hope of a very favorable outcome, which may balance the risk in the mind of the borrower, is not available to solace the lender.

This duplication of allowance for a portion of the risk has not hitherto been emphasized, so far as I am aware; but it may be important in certain circumstances. During a boom the popular estimation of the magnitude of both these risks, both borrower's risk and lender's risk, is apt to become unusually and imprudently low.

Chapter 12.   The State of Long-Term Expectation

The considerations upon which expectations of prospective yields are based are partly existing facts which we can assume to be known more or less for certain, and partly future events which can only be forecasted with more or less confidence. Amongst the first may be mentioned the existing stock of various types of capital-assets and of capital-assets in general and the strength of the existing consumers' demand for goods which require for their efficient production a relatively larger assistance from capital. Amongst the latter are future changes in the type and quantity of the stock of capital-assets and in the tastes of the consumer, the strength of effective demand from time to time during the life of the investment under consideration, and the changes in the wage-unit in terms of money which may occur during its life. We may sum up the state of psychological expectation which covers the latter as being the *state of long-term expectation;* as distinguished from the short-term expectation upon the basis of which a producer estimates what he will get for a product when it is finished if he decides to begin producing it today with the existing plant. . . .

It would be foolish, in forming our expectations, to attach great weight to matters which are very uncertain. It is reasonable, therefore, to be guided to a considerable degree by the facts about which we feel somewhat confident, even though they may be less decisively relevant to the issue than other facts about which our knowledge is vague and scanty. For this reason the facts of the existing situation enter, in a sense disproportionately, into the formation of our long-term expectations; our usual practice being to take the existing situation and to project it into the future, modified only to the extent that we have more or less definite reasons for expecting a change.

The state of long-term expectation, upon which our decisions are based, does not solely depend, therefore, on the most probable forecast we can make. It also depends on the *confidence* with which we make this forecast—on how highly we rate the likelihood of our best forecast turning out quite wrong. If we expect large changes but are very uncertain as to what precise form these changes will take, then our confidence will be weak.

The *state of confidence,* as they term it, is a matter to which practical men always pay the closest and most anxious attention. . . . There is, however, not much to be said about the state of confidence *a priori.* Our conclusions must mainly depend upon the actual observation of markets and business psychology. . . .

The outstanding fact is the extreme precariousness of the basis of knowledge on which our estimates of prospective yield have to be made. Our knowledge of the factors which will govern the yield of an investment some years hence is usually very slight and often negligible. If we speak frankly, we have to admit that our basis of knowledge for estimating the yield ten years hence of a railway, a copper mine, a textile factory, the goodwill of a patent medicine, an Atlantic liner, a building in the City of London amounts to little and sometimes to nothing; or even five years hence. In fact, those who seriously attempt to make any such estimate are often so much in the minority that their behavior does not govern the market.

In former times, when enterprises were mainly owned by those who undertook them or by their friends and associates, investment depended on a sufficient supply of individuals of sanguine temperament and constructive impulses who embarked on business as a way of life, not really relying on a precise calculation of prospective profit. The affair was partly a lottery, though with the ultimate result largely governed by whether the abilities and character of the managers were above or below the average. Some would fail and some would succeed. But even after the event no one would know whether the average results in terms of the sums invested had exceeded, equalled or fallen short of the prevailing rate of interest; though, if we exclude the exploitation of natural resources and monopolies, it is probable that the actual average results of investments, even during periods of progress and prosperity, have disappointed the hopes which prompted them. Business men play a mixed game of skill and chance, the average results of which to the players are not known by those who take a hand. If human nature felt no temptation to take a chance, no satisfaction (profit apart) in constructing a factory, a railway, a mine or a farm, there might not be much investment merely as a result of cold calculation.

Decisions to invest in private business of the old-fashioned type were, however, decisions largely irrevocable, not only for the community as a whole, but also for the individual. With the separation between ownership and management which prevails today and with the development of organized investment markets, a new factor of great importance has entered in, which sometimes facilitates investment but sometimes adds greatly to the instability of the system. In the absence of security markets, there is no object in frequently attempting to revalue an investment to which we are committed. But the Stock Exchange revalues many investments every day and the revaluations give a frequent opportunity to the individual (though not to the community as a whole) to revise his commitments. It is as though a farmer, having tapped his barometer after breakfast, could decide to remove his capital from the farming business between 10 and 11 in the morning and reconsider whether he should return to it later in the week. But the daily revaluations of the Stock Exchange, though they are primarily made to facilitate transfers of old investments between one individual and another, inevitably exert a decisive influence on the rate of current investment. For there is no sense in building up a new enterprise at a cost greater than that at which a similar existing enterprise can be purchased; whilst there is an inducement to spend on a new project what may seem an extravagant sum, if it can be floated off on the Stock Exchange at an immediate profit. Thus certain classes of investment are governed by the average expectation of those who deal on the Stock Exchange as revealed in the price of shares, rather than by the genuine expectations of the professional entrepreneur. How then are these highly significant daily, even hourly, revaluations of existing investments carried out in practice? . . .

As a result of the gradual increase in the proportion of the equity in the community's aggregate capital investment which is owned by persons who do not manage and have no special knowledge of the circumstances, either actual or prospective, of the business in question, the element of real knowledge in the valuable of investments by those who own them or contemplate purchasing them has seriously declined.

Day-to-day fluctuations in the profits of existing investments, which are obviously of an ephemeral and non-significant character, tend to have an altogether excessive, and even an absurd, influence on the market. It is said, for example, that the shares of American companies which manufacture ice tend to sell at a higher price in summer when their profits are seasonally high than in winter when no one wants ice. . . .

A conventional valuation which is established as the outcome of the mass psychology of a large number of ignorant individuals is liable to change violently as the result of a sudden fluctuation of opinion due to factors which do not really make much difference to the prospective yield; since there will be no strong roots of conviction to hold it steady. In abnormal times in particular, when the hypothesis of an indefinite continuance of the existing state of affairs is less plausible than usual even though there are no express grounds to anticipate a definite change, the market will be subject to waves of optimistic and pessimistic sentiment, which are unreasoning and yet in a sense legitimate where no solid basis exists for a reasonable calculation.

But there is one feature in particular which deserves our attention. It might have been supposed that competition between expert professionals, possessing judgment and knowledge beyond that of the average private investor, would correct the vagaries of the ignorant individual left to himself. It happens, however, that the energies and skill of the professional investor and speculator are mainly occupied otherwise. For most of these persons are, in fact, largely concerned, not with making superior long-term forecasts of the probable yield of an investment over its whole life, but with foreseeing changes in the conventional basis of valuation a short time ahead of the general public. They are concerned, not with what an investment is really worth to a man who buys it 'for keeps', but with what the market will value it at, under the influence of mass psychology, three months or a year hence. Moreover, this behavior is not the outcome of a wrong-headed propensity. It is an inevitable result of an investment market organized along the lines described. For it is not sensible to pay 25 for an investment of which you believe the prospective yield to justify a value of 30, if you also believe that the market will value it at 20 three months hence.

Thus the professional investor is forced to concern himself with the anticipation of impending changes, in the news or in the atmosphere, of the kind by which experience shows that the mass psychology of the market is most influenced. This is the inevitable result of investment markets organized with a view to so-called 'liquidity'. Of the maxims of orthodox finance none, surely, is more anti-social than the fetish of liquidity, the doctrine that it is a positive virtue on the part of investment institutions to concentrate their resources upon the holding of 'liquid' securities. It forgets that there is no such thing as liquidity of investment for the community as a whole. The social object of skilled investment should be to defeat the dark forces of time and ignorance which envelop our future. The actual, private object of the most skilled investment today is 'to beat the gun', as the Americans so well express it, to outwit the crowd, and to pass the bad, or depreciating, half-crown to the other fellow.

This battle of wits to anticipate the basis of conventional valuation a few months hence, rather than the prospective yield of an investment over a long term of years, does not even require gulls amongst the public to feed the maws of the professional;—it can be played by professionals amongst themselves. Nor is it necessary that anyone should keep his simple faith in the conventional basis of valuation having any genuine long-term validity. For it is, so to speak, a game of Snap, of Old Maid, of Musical Chairs—a pastime in which he is victor who says Snap neither too soon nor too late, who passed the Old Maid to his neighbor before the game is over, who secures a chair for himself when the music stops. These games can be played with zest and enjoyment, though all the players know that it is the Old Maid which is circulating, or that when the music stops some of the players will find themselves unseated.

Or, to change the metaphor slightly, professional investment may be likened to those newspaper competitions in which the competitors have to pick out the six prettiest faces from a hundred photographs, the prize being awarded to the competitor whose choice most nearly corresponds to the average preferences of the competitors as a whole; so that each competitor has to pick, not those faces which he himself finds prettiest, but those which he thinks likeliest to catch the fancy of the other competitors, all of whom are looking at the problem from the same point of view. It is not a case of choosing those which, to the best of one's judgment, are really the prettiest, nor even those which average opinion genuinely thinks the prettiest. We have reached the third degree where we devote our intelligences to anticipating what average opinion expects the average opinion to be. And there are some, I believe, who practice the fourth, fifth and higher degrees.

If the reader interjects that there must surely be large profits to be gained from the other players in the long run by a skilled individual who, unperturbed by the prevailing pastime, continues to purchase investments on the best genuine long-term expectations he can frame, he must be answered, first of all, that there are, indeed, such serious-minded individuals and that it makes a vast difference to an investment market whether or not they predominate in their influence over the game-players. But we must also add that there are several factors which jeopardize the predominance of such individuals in modern investment markets. Investment based on genuine long-term expectation is so difficult today as to be scarcely practicable. He who attempts it must surely lead much more laborious days and run greater risks than he who tries to guess better than the crowd how the crowd will behave; and, given equal intelligence, he may make more disastrous mistakes. There is no clear evidence from experience that the investment policy which is socially advantageous coincides with that which is most profitable. It needs more intelligence to defeat the forces of time and our ignorance of the future than to beat the gun. Moreover, life is not long enough;—human nature desires quick results, there is a peculiar zest in making money quickly, and remoter gains are discounted by the average man at a very high rate. The game of professional investment is intolerably boring and overexacting to anyone who is entirely exempt from the gambling instinct; whilst he who has it must pay to this propensity the appropriate toll. Furthermore, an investor who proposes to ignore near-term market fluctuations needs greater resources for safety and must not operate on so large a scale, if at all, with borrowed money—a further reason for the higher return from the pastime to a given stock of intelligence and resources. Finally it is the long-term investor, he who most promotes the public interest, who will in practice come in for most criticism, wherever investment funds are managed by committees or boards or banks. For it is in the essence of his behavior that he should be eccentric, unconventional and rash in the eyes of average opinion. If he is successful, that will only confirm the general belief in his rashness; and if in the short run he is unsuccessful, which is very likely, he will not receive much mercy. Worldly wisdom teaches that it is better for reputation to fail conventionally than to succeed unconventionally.

So far we have had chiefly in mind the state of confidence of the speculator or speculative investor himself and may have seemed to be tacitly assuming that, if he himself is satisfied with the prospects, he has unlimited command over money at the market rate of interest. This is, of course, not the case. Thus we must also take account of the other facet of the state of confidence, namely, the confidence of the lending institutions towards those who seek to borrow from them, sometimes described as the state of credit. A collapse in the price of equities, which has had disastrous reactions on the marginal efficiency of capital, may have been due to the weakening either of speculative confidence or of the state of credit. But whereas the weakening of either is enough to cause a collapse, recovery requires the revival of both. For whilst the weakening of credit is sufficient to bring about a collapse, its strengthening, though a necessary condition of recovery, is not a sufficient condition. . . .

Speculators may do no harm as bubbles on a steady stream of enterprise. But the position is serious when enterprise becomes the bubble on a whirlpool of speculation. When the capital development of a country becomes a by-product of the activities of a casino, the job is likely to be ill-done. The measure of success attained by Wall Street, regarded as an institution of which the proper social purpose is to direct new investment into the most profitable channels in terms of future yield, cannot be claimed as one of the outstanding triumphs of *laissez-faire* capitalism—which is not surprising, if I am right in thinking that the best brains of Wall Street have been in fact directed towards a different object.

These tendencies are a scarcely avoidable outcome of our having successfully organized 'liquid' investment markets. . . . For the fact that each individual investor flatters himself that his commitment is 'liquid' (though this cannot be true for all investors collectively) calms his nerves and makes him much more willing to run a risk. If individual purchases of investments were rendered illiquid, this might seriously impede new investment, so long as *alternative ways* in which to hold his savings are available to the individual. This is the dilemma. So long as it is open to the individual to employ his wealth in hoarding or lending *money,* the alternative of purchasing actual capital assets cannot be rendered sufficiently attractive (especially to the man who does not manage the capital assets and knows very little about them), except by organizing markets wherein these assets can be easily realized for money. . . .

Even apart from the instability due to speculation, there is the instability due to the characteristic of human nature that a large proportion of our positive activities depend on spontaneous optimism rather than on a mathematical expectation, whether moral or hedonistic or economic. Most, probably, of our decisions to do something positive, the full consequences of which will be drawn out over many days to come, can only be taken as a result of animal spirits—of a spontaneous urge to action rather than inaction, and not as the outcome of a weighted average of quantitative benefits multiplied by quantitative probabilities. Enterprise only pretends to itself to be mainly actuated by the statements in its own prospectus, however candid and sincere. Only a little more than an expedition to the South Pole, is it based on an exact calculation of benefits to come. Thus if the animal spirits are dimmed and the spontaneous optimism falters, leaving us to depend on nothing but a mathematical expectation, enterprise will fade and die;—though fears of loss may have a basis no more reasonable than hopes of profit had before.

It is safe to say that enterprise which depends on hopes stretching into the future benefits the community as a whole. But individual initiative will only be adequate when reasonable calculation is supplemented and supported by animal spirits, so that the thought of ultimate loss which often overtakes pioneers, as experience undoubtedly tells us and them, is put aside as a healthy man puts aside the expectation of death.

This means, unfortunately, not only that slumps and depressions are exaggerated in degree, but that economic prosperity is excessively dependent on a political and social atmosphere which is congenial to the average business man. If the fear of a Labour government or a New Deal depresses enterprise, this need not be the result either of a reasonable calculation or of a plot with political intent;—it is the mere consequence of upsetting the delicate balance of spontaneous optimism. In estimating the prospects of investment, we must have regard, therefore, to the nerves and hysteria and even the digestions and reactions to the weather of those upon whose spontaneous activity it largely depends. . . .

For my own part I am now somewhat skeptical of the success of a merely monetary policy directed towards influencing the rate of interest. I expect to see the State, which is in a position to calculate the marginal efficiency of capital goods on long views and on the basis of the general social advantage, taking an ever greater responsibility for directly organizing investment; since it seems likely that the fluctuations in the market estimation of the marginal efficiency of different types of capital, calculated on the principles I have described above, will be too great to be offset by any practicable changes in the rate of interest. . . .

Chapter 18. The General Theory of Employment Restated

. . . There will be an inducement to push the rate of new investment to the point which forces the supply-price of each type of capital-asset to a figure which, taken in conjunction with its prospective yield, brings the marginal efficiency of capital in general to approximate equality with the rate of interest. That is to say, the physical conditions of supply in the capital-goods industries, the state of confidence concerning the prospective yield, the psychological attitude to liquidity and the quantity of money (preferably calculated in terms of wage-units) determine, between them, the rate of new investment

But an increase (or decrease) in the rate of investment will have to carry with it an increase (or decrease) in the rate of consumption; because the behavior of the public is, in general, of such a character that they are only willing to widen (or narrow) the gap between their income and their consumption if their income is being increased (or diminished). That is to say, changes in the rate of consumption are, in general, *in the same direction* (though smaller in amount) as changes in the rate of income. The relation between the increment of consumption which has to accompany a given increment of saving is given by the marginal propensity to consume. The ratio, thus determined, between an increment of investment and the corresponding increment of aggregate income, both measured in wage-units, is given by the investment multiplier.

Finally, if we assume (as a first approximation) that the employment multiplier is equal to the investment multiplier, we can, by applying the multiplier to the increment (or decrement) in the rate of investment brought about by the factors first described, infer the increment of employment.

An increment (or decrement) of employment is liable, however, to raise (or lower) the schedule of liquidity-preference,[12] there being three ways in which it will tend to increase the demand for money, inasmuch as the value of output will rise when employment increases even if the wage-unit and prices (in terms of the wage-unit) are unchanged, but, in addition, the wage-unit itself will tend to rise as employment improves, and the increase in output will be accompanied by a rise of prices (in terms of the wage-unit) owing to increasing cost in the short period. . . .

It is an outstanding characteristic of the economic system in which we live that, whilst it is subject to severe fluctuations in respect of output and employment, it is not violently unstable. Indeed it seems capable of remaining in a chronic condition of sub-normal activity for a considerable period without any marked tendency either towards recovery or towards complete collapse. Moreover, the evidence indicates that full, or even approximately full, employment is of rare and short-lived occurrence. Fluctuations may start briskly but seem to wear themselves out before they have proceeded to great extremes, and an intermediate situation which is neither desperate nor satisfactory is our normal lot. It is upon the fact that fluctuations tend to wear themselves out before proceeding to extremes and eventually to reverse themselves, that the theory of business cycles having a regular phase has been founded. The same thing is true of prices, which, in response to an initiating cause of disturbance, seem to be able to find a level at which they can remain, for the time being, moderately stable.

Now, since these facts of experience do not follow of logical necessity, one must suppose that the environment and the psychological propensities of the modern world must be of such a character as to produce these results. It is, therefore, useful to consider what hypothetical psychological propensities would lead to a stable system; and, then, whether these propensities can be plausibly ascribed, on our general knowledge of contemporary human nature, to the world in which we live.

---

[12]A person's liquidity preference is defined by Keynes as "a schedule of the amounts of his resources, valued in terms of money or of wage-units, which he will wish to retain in the form of money," normally related to the volume of transactions and, inversely, to the rate of interest. [See *General Theory,* chapter 13]

The conditions of stability which the foregoing analysis suggests to us as capable of explaining the observed results are the following:

(i) The marginal propensity to consume is such that, when the output of a given community increases (or decreases) because more (or less) employment is being applied to its capital equipment, the multiplier relating the two is greater than unity but not very large.

(ii) When there is a change in the prospective yield of capital or in the rate of interest, the schedule of the marginal efficiency of capital will be such that the change in new investment will not be in great disproportion to the change in the former; i.e. moderate changes in the prospective yield of capital or in the rate of interest will not be associated with very great changes in the rate of investment.

(iii) When there is a change in employment, money-wages tend to change in the same direction as, but not in great disproportion to, the change in employment; i.e. moderate changes in employment are not associated with very great changes in money-wages. This is a condition of the stability of prices rather than of employment.

(iv) We may add a fourth condition, which provides not so much for the stability of the system as for the tendency of a fluctuation in one direction to reverse itself in due course; namely, that a rate of investment, higher (or lower) than prevailed formerly, begins to react unfavorably (or favorably) on the marginal efficiency of capital if it is continued for a period which, measured in years, is not very large.

(i) Our first condition of stability, namely that the multiplier, whilst greater than unity, is not very great, is highly plausible as a psychological characteristic of human nature. As real income increases, both the pressure of present needs diminishes and the margin over the established standard of life is increased; and as real income diminishes the opposite is true. Thus it is natural—at any rate on the average of the community—that current consumption should be expanded when employment increases, but by less than the full increment of real income; and that it should be diminished when employment diminishes, but by less than the full decrement of real income. Moreover, what is true of the average of individuals is likely to be also true of governments, especially in an age when a progressive increase of unemployment will usually force the state to provide relief out of borrowed funds. . . .

(ii) Our second condition provides that a moderate change in the prospective yield of capital-assets or in the rate of interest will not involve an indefinitely great change in the rate of investment. This is likely to be the case owing to the increasing cost of producing a greatly enlarged output from the existing equipment. If, indeed, we start from a position where there are very large surplus resources for the production of capital-assets, there may be considerable instability within a certain range; but this will cease to hold good as soon as the surplus is being largely utilized. . . .

(iii) Our third condition accords with our experience of human nature. For although the struggle for money-wages is, as we have pointed out above, essentially a struggle to maintain a high relative wage, this struggle is likely, as employment increases, to be intensified in each individual case both because the bargaining position of the worker is improved and because the diminished marginal utility of his age and his improved financial margin make him readier to run risks. Yet, all the same, these motives will operate within limits, and workers will not seek a much greater money-wage when employment improves or allow a very great reduction rather than suffer any unemployment at all.

But here again, whether or not this conclusion is plausible *a priori*, experience shows that some such psychological law must actually hold. For if competition between unemployed workers always led to a very great reduction of the money-wage, there would be a violent instability in the price-level. Moreover, there might be no position of stable equilibrium except in conditions consistent with full employment; since the wage-unit might have to fall without limit until it reached a point where the effect of the abundance of money in terms of the wage-unit on the rate of interest was sufficient to restore a level of full employment. At no other point could there be a resting-place.

(iv) Our fourth condition, which is a condition not so much of stability as of alternate recession and recovery, is merely based on the presumption that capital-assets are of various ages, wear out with time and are not all very long-lived; so that if the rate of investment falls below a certain minimum level, it is merely a question of time (failing large fluctuations in other factors) before the marginal efficiency of capital rises sufficiently to bring about a recovery of investment above this minimum. And similarly, of course, if investment rises to a higher figure than formerly, it is only a question of time before the marginal efficiency of capital falls sufficiently to bring about a recession unless there are compensating changes in other factors.

For this reason, even those degrees of recovery and recession, which can occur within the limitations set by our other conditions of stability, will be likely, if they persist for a sufficient length of time and are not interfered with by changes in the other factors, to cause a reverse movement in the opposite direction, until the same forces as before again reverse the direction.

Thus our four conditions together are adequate to explain the outstanding features of our actual experience;—namely, that we oscillate, avoiding the gravest extremes of fluctuation in employment and in prices in both directions, round an intermediate position appreciably below full employment and appreciably above the minimum employment a decline below which would endanger life. . . .

Chapter 22.   Notes on the Trade Cycle

If we examine the details of any actual instance of the trade cycle, we shall find that it is highly complex and that every element in our analysis will be required for its complete explanation. In particular we shall find that fluctuations in the propensity to consume, in the state of liquidity-preference, and in the marginal efficiency of capital have all played a part. But I suggest that the essential character of the trade cycle and, especially, the regularity of time-sequence and of duration which justifies us in calling it a *cycle,* is mainly due to the way in which the marginal efficiency of capital fluctuates. The trade cycle is best regarded, I think, as being occasioned by a cyclical change in the marginal efficiency of capital, though complicated and often aggravated by associated changes in the other significant short-period variables of the economic system. . . .

We have seen above that the marginal efficiency of capital depends, not only on the existing abundance or scarcity of capital-goods and the current cost of production of capital-goods, but also on current expectations as to the future yield of capital-goods. In the case of durable assets it is, therefore, natural and reasonable that expectations of the future should play a dominant part in determining the scale on which new investment is deemed advisable. But, as we have seen, the basis for such expectations is very precarious. Being based on shifting and unreliable evidence, they are subject to sudden and violent changes.

Now, we have been accustomed in explaining the 'crisis' to lay stress on the rising tendency of the rate of interest under the influence of the increased demand for money both for trade and speculative purposes. At times this factor may certainly play an aggravating and, occasionally perhaps, an initiating part. But I suggest that a more typical, and often the predominant, explanation of the crisis is, not primarily a rise in the rate of interest, but a sudden collapse in the marginal efficiency of capital.

The later stages of the boom are characterized by optimistic expectations as to the future yield of capital goods sufficiently strong to offset their growing abundance and their rising costs of production, and, probably, a rise in the rate of interest also. It is of the nature of organized investment markets, under the influence of purchasers largely ignorant of what they are buying and of speculators who are more concerned with forecasting the next shift of market sentiment than with a reasonable estimate of the future yield of capital-assets, that, when disillusion falls upon an over-optimistic and over-bought market, it should fall with sudden and even catastrophic force. Moreover, the dismay and uncertainty as to the future which accompanies a collapse in the marginal efficiency of capital naturally precipitates a sharp increase in liquidity-preference—hence a rise in the rate of interest. Thus the fact that a collapse in the marginal efficiency of capital tends to be associated with a rise in the rate of interest may seriously aggravate the decline in investment. But the essence of the situation is to be found, nevertheless, in the collapse in the marginal efficiency of capital, particularly in the case of those types of capital which have been contributing most to the previous phase of heavy new investment. Liquidity-preference, except those manifestations of it which are associated with increasing trade and speculation, does not increase until *after* the collapse in the marginal efficiency of capital.

It is this, indeed, which renders the slump so intractable. Later on, a decline in the rate of interest will be a great aid to recovery and, probably, a necessary condition of it. But, for the moment, the collapse in the marginal efficiency of capital may be so complete that no practicable reduction in the rate of interest will be enough. If a reduction in the rate of interest was capable of proving an effective remedy by itself, it might be possible to achieve a recovery without the elapse of any considerable interval of time and by means more or less directly under the control of the monetary authority. But, in fact, this is not usually the case; and it is not so easy to revive the marginal efficiency of capital, determined, as it is, by the uncontrollable and disobedient psychology of the business world. It is the return of confidence, to speak in ordinary language, which is so insusceptible to control in an economy of individualistic capitalism. This is the aspect of the slump which bankers and business men have been right in emphasizing, and which the economists who have put their faith in a 'purely monetary' remedy have underestimated.

This brings me to my point. The explanation of the *time-element* in the trade cycle, of the fact that an interval of time of a particular order of magnitude must usually elapse before recovery begins, is to be sought in the influences which govern the recovery of the marginal efficiency of capital. There are reasons, given firstly by the length of life of durable assets in relation to the normal rate of growth in a given epoch, and secondly by the carrying-costs of surplus stocks, why the duration of the downward movement should have an order of magnitude which is not fortuitous, which does not fluctuate between, say, one year this time and ten years next time, but which shows some regularity of habit between, let us say, three and five years. . . .

Unfortunately a serious fall in the marginal efficiency of capital also tends to affect adversely the propensity to consume. For it involves a severe decline in the market value of stock exchange equities. Now, on the class who take an active interest in their stock exchange investments, especially if they are employing borrowed funds, this naturally exerts a very depressing influence. These people are, perhaps, even more influenced in their readiness to spend by rises and falls in the value of their investments than by the state of their incomes. With a 'stock-minded' public as in the United States today, a rising stock market may be an almost essential condition of a satisfactory propensity to consume and this circumstance, generally overlooked until lately, obviously serves to aggravate still further the depressing effect of a decline in the marginal efficiency of capital. . . .

In conditions of *laissez-faire* the avoidance of wide fluctuations in employment may, therefore, prove impossible without a far-reaching change in the psychology of investment markets such as there is no reason to expect. I conclude that the duty of ordering the current volume of investment cannot safely be left in private hands.

READING 17

Economic Possibilities for our Grandchildren*

John Maynard Keynes

I. We are suffering just now from a bad attack of economic pessimism. It is common to hear people say that the epoch of enormous economic progress which characterized the nineteenth century is over; that the rapid improvement in the standard of life is now going to slow down—at any rate in Great Britain;

Source: First published in the *Nation and Athenaeum,* 11 and 18, October, 1930, reprinted in *Essays in Persuasion,* in vol. IX of *The Collected Works of John Maynard Keynes,* pp. 321-332. Reprinted with the permission of Cambridge University Press.

that a decline in prosperity is more likely than an improvement in the decade which lies ahead of us.

I believe that this is a wildly mistaken interpretation of what is happening to us. We are suffering, not from the rheumatics of old age, but from the growing-pains of over-rapid changes, from the painfulness of readjustment between one economic period and another. The increase of technical efficiency has been taking place faster than we can deal with the problem of labor absorption; the improvement in the standard of life has been a little quick; the banking and monetary system of the world has been preventing the rate of interest from falling as fast as equilibrium requires. And even so, the waste and confusion which ensue relate to not more than $7^1/2$ percent of the national income; we are muddling away one and sixpence in the £, and have only 28s 6d, when we might, if we were more sensible, have £1; yet, nevertheless, the 18s 6d mounts up to as much as the £1 would have been five or six years ago. We forget that in 1929 the physical output of the industry of Great Britain was greater than ever before, and that the net surplus of our foreign balance available for new foreign investment, after paying for all our imports, was greater last year than that of any other country, being indeed 50 per cent greater than the corresponding surplus of the United States. Or again—if it is to be a matter of comparisons—suppose that we were to reduce our wages by a half, repudiate four-fifths of the national debt, and hoard our surplus wealth in barren gold instead of lending it at 6 per cent or more, we should resemble the now much-envied France. But would it be an improvement?

The prevailing world depression, the enormous anomaly of unemployment in a world full of wants, the disastrous mistakes we have made, blind us to what is going on under the surface—to the true interpretation of the trend of things. For I predict that both of the two opposed errors of pessimism which now make so much noise in the world will be proved wrong in our own time—the pessimism of the revolutionaries who think that things are so bad that nothing can save us but violent change, and the pessimism of the reactionaries who consider the balance of our economic and social life so precarious that we must risk no experiments.

My purpose in this essay, however, is not to examine the present or the near future, but to disembarrass myself of short views and take wings into the future. What can we reasonably expect the level of our economic life to be a hundred years hence? What are the economic possibilities for our grandchildren?

From the earliest times of which we have record—back, say, to two thousand years before Christ—down to the beginning of the eighteenth century, there was no very great change in the standard of life of the average man living in the civilized centers of the earth. Ups and downs certainly. Visitations of plague, famine, and war. Golden intervals. But no progressive, violent change. Some periods perhaps 50 per cent better than others—at the utmost 100 per cent better—in the four thousand years which ended (say) in A.D. 1700.

This slow rate of progress, or lack of progress, was due to two reasons—to the remarkable absence of important technical improvements and to the failure of capital to accumulate.

The absence of important technical inventions between the prehistoric age and comparatively modern times is truly remarkable. Almost everything which really matters and which the world possessed at the commencement of the modern age was already known to man at the dawn of history. Language, the same domestic animals which we have today, wheat, barley, the vine and the olive, the plough, the wheel, the oar, the sail, leather, linen and cloth, bricks and pots, gold and silver, copper, tin, and lead—and iron was added to the list before 1000 B.C.—banking, statecraft, mathematics, astronomy, and religion. There is no record of when we first possessed these things.

At some epoch before the dawn of history—perhaps even in one of the comfortable intervals before the last ice age—there must have been an era of progress and invention comparable to that in which we live today. But through the greater part of recorded history there was nothing of the kind.

The modern age opened, I think, with the accumulation of capital which began in the sixteenth century. I believe—for reasons with which I must not encumber the present argument—that this was initially due to the rise of prices, and the profits to which that led, which resulted from the treasure of gold and silver which Spain brought from the New World into the Old. From that time until today the power of accumulation by compound interest, which seems to have been sleeping for many generations, was reborn and renewed its strength. And the power of compound interest over two hundred years is such as to stagger the imagination.

Let me give an illustration of this a sum which I have worked out. The value of Great Britain's foreign investments today is estimated at about £4,000 million. This yields us an income at the rate of about $6\frac{1}{2}$ per cent. Half of this we bring home and enjoy; the other half, namely, $3\frac{1}{4}$ per cent, we leave to accumulate abroad at compound interest. Something of this sort has now been going on for about 250 years.

For I trace the beginnings of British foreign investment to the treasure which Drake stole from Spain in 1580. In that year he returned to England bringing with him the prodigious spoils of the *Golden Hind*. Queen Elizabeth was a considerable shareholder in the syndicate which had financed the expedition. Out of her share she paid off the whole of England's foreign debt, balanced her budget, and found herself with about £40,000 in hand. This she invested in the Levant Company—which prospered. Out of the profits of the Levant Company, the East India Company was founded; and the profits of this great enterprise were the foundation of England's subsequent foreign investment. Now it happens that £40,000 accumulating at $3\frac{1}{4}$ per cent compound interest approximately corresponds to the actual volume of England's foreign investments at various dates, and would actually amount today to the total of £4,000 million which I have already quoted as being what our foreign investments now are. Thus, every £1 which Drake brought home in 1580 has now become £100,000. Such is the power of compound interest!

From the sixteenth century, with a cumulative crescendo after the eighteenth, the great age of science and technical inventions began, which since the beginning of the nineteenth century has been in full flood—coal, steam, electricity, petrol, steel, rubber, cotton, the chemical industries, automatic machinery and the methods of mass production, wireless, printing,

Newton, Darwin, and Einstein, and thousands of other things and men too famous and familiar to catalogue.

What is the result? In spite of an enormous growth in the population of the world, which it has been necessary to equip with houses and machines, the average standard of life in Europe and the United States has been raised, I think, about fourfold. The growth of capital has been on a scale which is far beyond a hundredfold of what any previous age had known. And from now on we need not expect so great an increase of population. . . .

For the moment the very rapidity of these changes is hurting us and bringing difficult problems to solve. Those countries are suffering relatively which are not in the vanguard of progress. We are being afflicted with a new disease of which some readers may not yet have heard the name, but of which they will hear a great deal in the years to come—namely, *technological unemployment.* This means unemployment due to our discovery of means of economizing the use of labor outrunning the pace at which we can find new uses for labor.

But this is only a temporary phase of maladjustment. All this means in the long run *that mankind is solving its economic problems.* I would predict that the standard of life in progressive countries one hundred years hence will be between four and eight times as high as it is today. There would be nothing surprising in this even in the light of our present knowledge. It would not be foolish to contemplate the possibility of a far greater progress still.

II. Let us, for the sake of argument, suppose that a hundred years hence we are all of us, on the average, eight times better off in the economic sense than we are today. Assuredly there need be nothing here to surprise us.

Now it is true that the needs of human beings may seem to be insatiable. But they fall into two classes—those needs which are absolute in the sense that we feel them whatever the situation of our fellow human beings may be, and those which are relative in the sense that we feel them only if their satisfaction lifts us above, makes us feel superior to, our fellows. Needs of the second class, those which satisfy the desire for superiority, may indeed be insatiable; for the higher the general level, the higher still are they. But this is not so true of the absolute needs—a point may soon be reached, much sooner perhaps than we all of us are aware of, when these needs are satisfied in the sense that we prefer to devote our further energies to non-economic purposes.

Now for my conclusion, which you will find, I think, to become more and more startling to the imagination the longer you think about it.

I draw the conclusion that, assuming no important wars and no important increase in population, the *economic problem* may be solved, or be at least within sight of solution, within a hundred years. This means that the economic problem is not—if we look into the future—*the permanent problem of the human race.*

Why, you may ask, is this so startling? It is startling because—if, instead of looking into the future, we look into the past—we find that the economic problem, the struggle for subsistence, always has been hitherto the primary, most pressing problem of the human race, but of the whole of the biological kingdom from the beginnings of life in its most primitive forms.

Thus we have been expressly evolved by nature—with all our impulses and deepest instincts—for the purpose of solving the economic problem. If the economic problem is solved, mankind will be deprived of its traditional purpose.

Will this be a benefit? If one believe at all in the real values of life, the prospect at least opens up the possibility of benefit. Yet I think with dread of the readjustment of the habits and instincts of the ordinary man, bred into him for countless generations, which he may be asked to discard within a few decades.

To use the language of today—must we not expect a general 'nervous breakdown'? We already have a little experience of what I mean—a nervous breakdown of the sort which is already common enough in England and the United States amongst the wives of the well-to-do classes, unfortunate women, many of them, who have been deprived by their wealth of their traditional tasks and occupations—who cannot find it sufficiently amusing, when deprived of the spur of economic necessity, to cook and clean and mend, yet are quite unable to find anything more amusing. . . .

Thus for the first time since his creation man will be faced with his real, his permanent problem—how to use his freedom from pressing economic cares, how to occupy his leisure, which science and compound interest will have won for him, to live wisely and agreeably and well.

The strenuous purposeful money-makers may carry all of us along with them into the lap of economic abundance. But it will be those peoples, who can keep alive, and cultivate into a fuller perfection, the art of life itself and do not sell themselves for the means of life, who will be able to enjoy the abundance when it comes.

Yet there is no country and no people, I think, who can look forward to the age of leisure and of abundance without a dread. For we have been trained too long to strive and not to enjoy. It is a fearful problem for the ordinary person, with no special talents, to occupy himself, especially if he no longer has roots in the soil or in custom or in the beloved conventions of a traditional society. To judge from the behavior and the achievements of the wealthy classes today in any quarter of the world, the outlook is very depressing! For these are, so to speak, our advance guard—those who are spying out the promised land for the rest of us and pitching their camp there. For they have most of them failed disastrously, so it seems to me—those who have an independent income but no associations or duties or ties—to solve the problem which has been set them.

I feel sure that with a little more experience we shall use the new-found bounty of nature quite differently from the way in which the rich use it today, and will map out for ourselves a plan of life quite otherwise than theirs.

For many ages to come the old Adam will be so strong in us that everyone will need to do *some* work if he is to be contented. We shall do more things for ourselves than is usual with the rich today, only too glad to have small duties and tasks and routines. But beyond this, we shall endeavor to spread the bread thin on the butter—to make what work there is still to be done to be as widely shared as possible. Three-hour shifts or a fifteen-hour week may put off the problem for a great while. For three hours a day is quite enough to satisfy the old Adam in most of us!

There are changes in other spheres too which we must expect to come. When the accumulation of wealth is no longer of high social importance, there will be great changes in the code of morals. We shall be able to rid ourselves of many of the pseudo-moral principles which have hag-ridden us for two hundred years, by which we have exalted some of the most distasteful of human qualities into the position of the highest virtues. We shall be able to afford to dare to assess the money-motive at its true value. The love of money as a possession—as distinguished from the love of money as a means to the enjoyments and realities of life—will be recognized for what it is, a somewhat disgusting morbidity, one of those semi-criminal, semi-pathological propensities which one hands over with a shudder to the specialists in mental disease. All kinds of social customs and economic practices, affecting the distribution of wealth and of economic reward and penalties, which we now maintain at all cost, however distasteful and unjust they may be in themselves, because they are tremendously useful in promoting the accumulation of capital, we shall then be free, at last, to discard.

Of course there will still be many people with intense, unsatisfied purposiveness who will blindly pursue wealth unless they can find some plausible substitute. But the rest of us will no longer be under any obligation to applaud and encourage them. For we shall inquire more curiously than is safe today into the true character of this 'purposiveness' with which in varying degrees Nature has endowed almost all of us. For purposiveness means that we are more concerned with the remote future results of our actions than with their own quality or their immediate effects on our own environment. The "purposive" man is always trying to secure a spurious and delusive immortality for his acts by pushing his interest in them forward into time. He does not love his cat, but his cat's kittens; nor, in truth, the kittens, but only the kittens' kittens, and so on forward for ever to the end of catdom. For him jam is not jam unless it is a case of jam tomorrow and never jam today. Thus by pushing his jam always forward into the future, he strives to secure for his act of boiling it an immortality. . . .

I see us free, therefore, to return to some of the most sure and certain principles of religion and traditional virtue—that avarice is a vice, that the exaction of usury is a misdemeanor, and the love of money is detestable, that those walk most truly in the paths of virtue and sane wisdom who take least thought for the morrow. We shall once more value ends above means and prefer the good to the useful. We shall honor those who can teach us how to pluck the hour and the day virtuously and well, the delightful people who are capable of taking direct enjoyment in things, the lilies of the field who toil not, neither do they spin.

But beware! The time for all this is not yet. For at least another hundred years we must pretend to ourselves and to every one that fair is foul and foul is fair; for foul is useful and fair is not. Avarice and usury and precaution must be our gods for a little longer still. For only they can lead us out of the tunnel of economic necessity into daylight.

I look forward, therefore, in days not so very remote, to the greatest change which has ever occurred in the material environment of life for human beings in the aggregate. But, of course, it will all happen gradually, not as a catastrophe. Indeed, it has already begun. The course of affairs will simply be that there will be ever larger and larger classes and groups of people from whom problems of economic necessity have been practically removed. The critical difference will be realized when this condition has become so general that the nature of one's duty to one's neighbor is changed. For it will remain reasonable to be economically purposive for others after it has ceased to be reasonable for oneself.

The *pace* at which we can reach our destination of economic bliss will be governed by four things—our power to control population, our determination to avoid wars and civil dissensions, our willingness to entrust to science the direction of those matters which are properly the concern of science, and the rate of accumulation as fixed by the margin between our production and our consumption; of which the last will easily look after itself given the first three.

Meanwhile there will be no harm in making mild preparations for our destiny, in encouraging, and experimenting in, the arts of life as well as the activities of purpose.

But, chiefly, do not let us overestimate the importance of the economic problem, or sacrifice to its supposed necessities other matters of greater and more permanent significance. It should be a matter for specialists—like dentistry. If economists could manage to get themselves thought of as humble, competent people, on a level with dentists, that would be splendid!

QUESTIONS FOR DISCUSSION

1   What is meant by a "general theory" and why is the (neo-) classical theory "special"? What rhetorical purpose is served by this distinction?
2   What is the "classical assumption"?
3   How is involuntary unemployment defined? How does it differ from voluntary unemployment?
4   How can expectations create cyclical movements in real variables?
5   What is the marginal efficiency of capital exactly? And what influences it?
6   Why is the modern stock market harmful to the economy, in Keynes' opinion? In light of events in 1987 and since, do you agree?
7   What forces will eventually overcome the stagnation of the economy?

READING 18

James Tobin (1918-   ), America's greatest neo-Keynesian, was a student of Alvin Hansen's at Harvard before World War II, and became professor at Yale in 1947. Among his "Keynesian" contributions are the development of the cost-of-capital *(Q)* theory of investment and inventory holdings, studies on the interest-elasticity of money demand, the effect of business cycles and stabilization policy on long-term growth, and his trenchant defense of incomes and pro-employment policies against neo-classical and "new classical" critics.

Inflation and Unemployment[*]

James Tobin

The world economy today is vastly different from the 1930's. . . . Economics is very different, too. Both the science and its subject have changed, and for the better, since World War II. But there are some notable constants. Unemployment and inflation still preoccupy and perplex economists, statesmen, journalists, housewives, and everyone else. The connection between them is the principal domestic economic burden of presidents and prime ministers, and the major area of controversy and ignorance in macroeconomics. . . .

I. The Meanings of Full Employment

Today, as thirty and forty years ago, economists debate how much unemployment is voluntary, how much involuntary; how much is a phenomenon of equilibrium, how much a symptom of disequilibrium; how much is compatible with competition, how much is to be blamed on monopolies, labor unions, and restrictive legislation; how much unemployment characterizes "full" employment.

Full employment—imagine macroeconomics deprived of the concept. But what is it? What is the proper employment goal of policies affecting aggregate demand? Zero unemployment in the monthly labor force survey? That outcome is so inconceivable outside of Switzerland that it is useless as a guide to policy. Any other numerical candidate, yes even 4 percent, is patently arbitrary without reference to basic criteria. Unemployment equal to vacancies? Measurement problems aside, this definition has the same straightforward appeal as zero unemployment, which it simply corrects for friction.

A concept of full employment more congenial to economic theory is labor market equilibrium, a volume of employment which is simultaneously the amount employers want to offer and the amount workers want to accept at prevailing wage rates and prices. Forty years ago theorists with confidence in markets could believe that full employment is whatever volume of employment the economy is moving toward, and that its achievement requires of the government nothing more than neutrality, and nothing less.

After Keynes challenged the classical notion of labor market equilibrium and the complacent view of policy to which it led, full employment came to mean maximum aggregate supply, the point at which expansion of aggregate demand could not further increase employment and output.

Full employment was also regarded as the economy's inflation threshold. With a deflationary gap, demand less than full employment supply, prices

[*]*Source:* Presidential Address delivered at the eighty-fourth meeting of the American Economic Association, New Orleans, Louisiana, December 28, 1971, excerpted from *American Economic Review* (March, 1972), pp. 1-18, by permission of the author and the Association. To conserve space, most references to related literature have had to be deleted.

would be declining or at worst constant. Expansion of aggregate demand short of full employment would cause at most a one-shot increase of prices. For continuing inflation, the textbooks told us, a necessary and sufficient condition was an inflationary gap, real aggregate demand in excess of feasible supply. The model was tailor-made for wartime inflation.

Postwar experience destroyed the identification of full employment with the economy's inflation threshold. The profession, the press, and the public discovered the "new inflation" of the 1950's, inflation without benefit of gap, labelled but scarcely illuminated by the term "cost-push." Subsequently the view of the world suggested by the Phillips curve merged demand-pull and cost-push inflation and blurred the distinction between them. This view contained no concept of full employment. In its place came the tradeoff, along which society supposedly can choose the least undesirable feasible combination of the evils of unemployment and inflation.

Many economists deny the existence of a durable Phillips tradeoff. Their numbers and influences are increasing. Some of them contend that there is only one rate of unemployment compatible with steady inflation, a "natural rate" consistent with any steady rate of change of prices, positive, zero, or negative. The natural rate is another full employment candidate, a policy target at least in the passive sense that monetary and fiscal policy makers are advised to eschew any numerical unemployment goal and to let the economy gravitate to this equilibrium. So we have come full circle. Full employment is once again nothing but the equilibrium reached by labor markets unaided and undistorted by governmental fine tuning.

In discussing these issues, I shall make the following points. First, an observed amount of unemployment is not revealed to be voluntary simply by the fact that money wage rates are constant, or rising, or even accelerating. I shall recall and extend Keynes's definition of involuntary unemployment and his explanation why workers may accept price inflation as a method of reducing real wages while rejecting money wage cuts. The second point is related. Involuntary unemployment is a disequilibrium phenomenon; the behavior, the persistence, of excess supplies of labor depend on how and how fast markets adjust to shocks, and on how large and how frequent the shocks are. Higher prices or faster inflation can diminish involuntary, disequilibrium unemployment, even though voluntary, equilibrium labor supply is entirely free of money illusion.

Third, various criteria of full employment coincide in a theoretical full stationary equilibrium, but diverge in persistent disequilibrium. These are (1) the natural rate of unemployment, the rate compatible with zero or some other constant inflation rate, (2) zero involuntary unemployment, (3) the rate of unemployment needed for optimal job search and placement, and (4) unemployment equal to job vacancies. The first criterion dictates higher unemployment than any of the rest. Instead of commending the natural rate as a target of employment policy, the other three criteria suggest less unemployment and more inflation. Therefore, fourth, there are real gains from additional employment, which must be weighed in the social balance against the costs of inflation. I shall conclude with a few remarks on this choice, and on the possibilities of improving the terms of the tradeoff.

II.   Keynesian and Classical Interpretations of Unemployment

To begin with the *General Theory* is not just the ritual piety economists of my generation owe the book that shaped their minds. Keynes's treatment of labor market equilibrium and disequilibrium in his first chapter is remarkably relevant today. Keynes attacked what he called the classical presumption that persistent unemployment is voluntary unemployment. The presumption he challenged is that in competitive labor markets actual employment and unemployment reveal workers' true preferences between work and alternative uses of time, the presumption that no one is fully or partially unemployed whose real wage per hour exceeds his marginal valuation of an hour of free time. Orthodox economists found the observed stickiness of money wages to be persuasive evidence that unemployment, even in the Great Depression, was voluntary. Keynes found decisive evidence against this inference in the willingness of workers to accept a larger volume of employment at a lower real wage resulting from an increase of prices.

Whenever unemployment could be reduced by expansion of aggregate demand, Keynes regarded it as involuntary. He expected expansion to raise prices and lower real wages, but this expectation is not crucial to his argument. Indeed, if it is possible to raise employment without reduction in the real wage, his case for calling the unemployment involuntary is strengthened.

But why is the money wage so stubborn if more labor is willingly available at the same or lower real wage? Consider first some answers Keynes did not give. He did not appeal to trade union monopolies or minimum wage laws. He was anxious, perhaps over-anxious, to meet his putative classical opponents on their home field, the competitive economy. He did not rely on any failure of workers to perceive what a rise in prices does to real wages. The unemployed take new jobs, the employed hold old ones, with eyes open. Otherwise, the new situation would be transient.

Instead, Keynes emphasized the institutional fact that wages are bargained and set in the monetary unit of account. Money wage rates are, to use an unKeynesian term, "administered prices." That is, they are not set and reset in daily auctions but posted and fixed for finite periods of time This observation led Keynes to his central explanation: Workers, individually and in groups, are more concerned with relative than absolute real wages. They may withdraw labor if their wages fall relatively to wages elsewhere, even though they would not withdraw any if real wages fall uniformly everywhere. Labor markets are decentralized, and there is no way money wages can fall in any one market without impairing the relative status of the workers there. A general rise in prices is a neutral and universal method of reducing real wages, the only method in a decentralized and uncontrolled economy. Inflation would not be needed, we may infer, if by government compulsion, economy-wide bargaining, or social compact, all money wage rates could be scaled down together. . . .

Keynes's explanation of money wage stickiness is plausible and realistic. But two related analytical issues have obscured the message. Can there be involuntary unemployment in an equilibrium, a proper, full-fledged neo-classical equilibrium? Does the labor supply behavior described by Keynes betray "money illusion"? Keynes gave a loud yes in answer to the first question, and this seems at first glance to compel an affirmative answer to the second.

An economic theorist can, of course, commit no greater crime than to assume money illusion. Comparative statics is a nonhistorical exercise, in which different price levels are to be viewed as alternative rather than sequential. Compare two situations that differ only in the scale of exogenous monetary variables; imagine, for example, that all such magnitudes are ten times as high in one situation as in the other. All equilibrium prices, including money wage rates, should differ in the same proportion, while all real magnitudes, including employment, should be the same in the two equilibria. To assume instead that workers' supply decisions vary with the price level is to say that they would behave differently if the unit of account were, and always had been, dimes instead of dollars. Surely Keynes should not be interpreted to attribute to anyone money illusion in this sense. He was not talking about so strict and static an equilibrium. . . .

What Keynes calls equilibrium should be viewed as persistent disequilibrium, and what appears to be comparative statics is really shrewd and incisive, if awkward, dynamic analysis. Involuntary unemployment means that labor markets are not in equilibrium. The resistance of money wage rates to excess supply is a feature of the adjustment process rather than a symptom of irrationality.

The other side of Keynes's story is that in depressions money wage deflation, even if it occurred more speedily, or especially if it occurred more speedily, would be at best a weak equilibrator and quite possibly a source of more unemployment rather than less. . . .

What relevance has this excursion into depression economics for contemporary problems of unemployment and wage inflation? The issues are remarkably similar, even though events and [A.W.] Phillips have shifted attention from levels to time rates of change of wages and prices. Phillips curve doctrine is in an important sense the postwar analogue of Keynesian wage and employment theory, while natural rate doctrine is the contemporary version of the classical position Keynes was opposing.

Phillips curve doctrine implies that lower unemployment can be purchased at the cost of faster inflation. Let us adapt Keynes's test for involuntary unemployment to the dynamic terms of contemporary discussion of inflation, wages, and unemployment. Suppose that the current rate of unemployment continues. Associated with it is a path of real wages, rising at the rate of productivity growth. Consider an alternative future, with unemployment at first declining to a rate one percentage point lower and then remaining constant at the lower rate. Associated with the lower unemployment alternative will be a second path of real wages. Eventually this real wage path will show, at least to first approximation, the same rate of increase as the first one, the rate of productivity growth. But the paths may differ because of the transitional effects of increasing the rate of employment. The growth of real wages will be retarded in the short run if additional employment lowers labor's marginal productivity. In any case, the test question is whether with full information about the two alternatives labor would accept the second one—whether, in other words, the additional employment would be willingly supplied along the second real wage path If the answer is affirmative, then that one percentage point of unemployment is involuntary.

For Keynes's reasons, a negative answer cannot necessarily be inferred from failure of money wage rates to fall or even decelerate. Actual unemployment and the real wage path associated with it are not necessarily an equilibrium. Rigidities in the path of money wage rates can be explained by workers' preoccupation with relative wages and the absence of any central economy-wide mechanism for altering all money wages together.

According to the natural rate hypothesis, there is just one rate of unemployment compatible with steady wage and price inflation, and this is in the long run compatible with any constant rate of change of prices, positive, zero, or negative. Only at the natural rate of unemployment are workers content with current and prospective real wages, content to have their real wages rise at the rate of growth of productivity. Along the feasible path of real wages they would not wish to accept any larger volume of employment. Lower unemployment, therefore, can arise only from economy-wide excess demand for labor and must generate a gap between real wages desired and real wages earned. The gap evokes increases of money wages designed to raise real wages faster than productivity. But this intention is always frustrated, the gap is never closed, money wages and prices accelerate. By symmetrical argument, unemployment above the natural rate signifies excess supply in labor markets and ever accelerating deflation. Older classical economists regarded constancy of money wage rates as indicative of full employment equilibrium, at which the allocation of time between work and other pursuits is revealed as voluntary and optimal. Their successors make the same claims for the natural rate of unemployment, except that in the equilibrium money wages are not necessarily constant but growing at the rate of productivity gain plus the experienced and expected rate of inflation of prices.

III. Is Zero-Inflation Unemployment Voluntary and Optimal?

There are, then, two conflicting interpretations of the welfare value of employment in excess of the level consistent with price stability. One is that additional employment does not produce enough to compensate workers for the value of other uses of their time. The fact that it generates inflation is taken as prima facie evidence of a welfare loss. The alternative view, which I shall argue, is that the responses of money wages and prices to changes in aggregate demand reflect mechanics of adjustment, institutional constraints, and relative wage patterns and reveal nothing in particular about individual or social valuations of unemployed time vis-à-vis the wages of employment. . . .

Empirically the proposition that in the United States the zero-inflation rate of unemployment reflects voluntary and efficient job-seeking activity strains credulity. If there were a natural rate of unemployment in the United States, what would it be? It is hard to say because virtually all econometric Phillips curves allow for a whole menu of steady inflation rates. But estimates constrained to produce a vertical long-run Phillips curve suggest a natural rate between 5 and 6 percent of the labor force.

So let us consider some of the features of an overall unemployment rate of 5 to 6 percent. First, about 40 percent of accessions in manufacturing are rehires rather than new hires. Temporarily laid off by their employers, these workers had been awaiting recall and were scarcely engaged in voluntary search activity. Their unemployment is as much a deadweight loss as the disguised unemployment of redundant workers on payrolls. This number declines to 25-30 percent when unemployment is 4 percent or below. Likewise, a 5-6 percent unemployment rate means that voluntary quits amount only to about a third of separations, layoffs to two-thirds. The propositions are reversed at low unemployment rates.

Second, the unemployment statistic is not an exhaustive count of those with time and incentive to search. An additional 3 percent of the labor force are involuntarily confined to part-time work, and another 3/4 of 1 percent are out of the labor force because they "could not find job" or "think no work available"—discouraged by market conditions rather than personal incapacities.

Third, with unemployment of 5-6 percent the number of reported vacancies is less than 1/2 of 1 percent. Vacancies appear to be understated relative to unemployment, but they rise to $1^1/_2$ percent when the unemployment rate is below 4 percent. At 5-6 percent unemployment, the economy is clearly capable of generating many more jobs with marginal productivity high enough so that people prefer them to leisure. The capital stock is no limitation, since 5-6 percent unemployment has been associated with more than 20 percent excess capacity. Moreover, when more jobs are created by expansion of demand, with or without inflation, labor force participation increases; this would hardly occur if the additional jobs were low in quality and productivity. . . .

In summary, labor markets characterized by 5-6 percent unemployment do not display the symptoms one would expect if the unemployment were voluntary search activity. Even if it were voluntary, search activity on such a large scale would surely be socially wasteful. The only reason anyone might regard so high an unemployment rate as an equilibrium and social optimum is that lower rates cause accelerating inflation. But this is almost tautological. The inferences of equilibrium and optimality would be more convincing if they were corroborated by direct evidence.

IV.   Why is There Inflation without Aggregate Excess Demand?

Zero-inflation unemployment is not wholly voluntary, not optimal, I might even say not natural. In other words, the economy has an inflationary bias: When labor markets provide as many jobs as there are willing workers, there is inflation, perhaps accelerating inflation. Why? . . .

One rationalization might be termed a theory of stochastic macroequilibrium: stochastic, because random intersectoral shocks keep individual labor markets in diverse states of disequilibrium; macroequilibrium, because the perpetual flux of particular markets produces fairly definite aggregate outcomes of unemployment and wages. . . .

It is an essential feature of the theory that economy-wide relations among employment, wages, and prices are aggregations of diverse outcomes in heterogeneous markets. The myth of macroeconomics is that relations among aggregates are enlarged analogues of relations among corresponding variables for individual household, firms, industries, markets. The myth is a harmless and useful simplification in many contexts, but sometimes it misses the essence of the phenomenon.

Unemployment is, in this model as in Keynes reinterpreted, a disequilibrium phenomenon. Money wages do not adjust rapidly enough to clear all labor markets every day. Excess supplies in labor markets take the form of unemployment, and excess demands the form of unfilled vacancies. At any moment, markets vary widely in excess demand or supply, and the economy as a whole shows both vacancies and unemployment.

The overall balance of vacancies and unemployment is determined by aggregate demand, and is therefore in principle subject to control by overall monetary and fiscal policy. Higher aggregate demand means fewer excess supply markets and more excess demand markets, accordingly less unemployment and more vacancies.

In any particular labor market, the rate of increase of money wages is the sum of two components, an equilibrium component and a disequilibrium component. The first is the rate at which the wage would increase were the market in equilibrium, with neither vacancies nor unemployment. The other component is a function of excess demand and supply—a monotonic function, positive for positive excess demand, zero for zero excess demand, nonpositive for excess supply. I begin with the disequilibrium component.

Of course the disequilibrium components are relevant only if disequilibria persist. Why aren't they eliminated by the very adjustments they set in motion? Workers will move from excess supply markets to excess demand markets, and from low wage to high wage markets. Unless they overshoot, these movements are equilibrating. The theory therefore requires that new disequilibria are always arising. Aggregate demand may be stable, but beneath its stability is never-ending flux: new products, new processes, new tastes and fashions, new developments of land and natural resources, obsolescent industries and declining areas.

The overlap of vacancies and unemployment—say, the sum of the two for any given difference between them—is a measure of the heterogeneity or dispersion of individual markets. The amount of dispersion depends directly on the size of those shocks of demand and technology that keep markets in perpetual disequilibrium, and inversely on the responsive mobility of labor. The one increases, the other diminishes the frictional component of unemployment, that is, the number of unfilled vacancies coexisting with any given unemployment rate.

A central assumption of the theory is that the functions relating wage change to excess demand or supply are non-linear, specifically that unemployment retards money wages less than vacancies accelerate them. Nonlinearity in the response of wages to excess demand has several important implications. First, it helps to explain the characteristic observed curvature of the Phillips curve. Each successive increment of unemployment has less effect in reducing the rate of inflation. Linear wage response, on the other hand, would mean a linear Phillips relation.

Second, given the overall state of aggregate demand, economy-wide vacancies less unemployment, wage inflation will be greater the larger the variance among markets in excess demand and supply. As a number of recent empirical studies have confirmed, dispersion is inflationary. Of course, the rate of wage inflation will depend not only on the overall dispersion of excess demands and supplies across markets but also on the particular markets where the excess supplies and demands happen to fall. An unlucky random drawing might put the excess demands in highly responsive markets and the excess supplies in especially unresponsive ones.

Third, the nonlinearity is an explanation of inflationary bias, in the following sense. Even when aggregate vacancies are at most equal to unemployment, the average disequilibrium component will be positive. Full employment in the sense of equality of vacancies and unemployment is not compatible with price stability. Zero inflation requires unemployment in excess of vacancies.

Criteria that coincide in full long-run equilibrium—zero inflation and zero aggregate excess demand—diverge in stochastic macro-equilibrium. Full long-range equilibrium in all markets would show no unemployment, no vacancies, no unanticipated inflation. But with unending sectoral flux, zero excess demand spells inflation and zero inflation spells net excess supply, unemployment in excess of vacancies. In these circumstances neither criterion can be justified simply because it is a property of full long-run equilibrium. Both criteria automatically allow for frictional unemployment incident to the required movements of workers between markets; the no-inflation criterion requires enough additional unemployment to wipe out inflationary bias.

I turn now to the equilibrium component, the rate of wage increase in a market with neither excess demand nor excess supply. It is reasonable to suppose that the equilibrium component depends on the trend of wages of comparable labor elsewhere. A "competitive wage," one that reflects relevant trends fully, is what employers will offer if they wish to maintain their share of the volume of employment. This will happen where the rate of growth of marginal revenue product—the compound of productivity increase and price inflation— is the same as the trend in wages. But in some markets the equilibrium wage will be rising faster, and in others slower, than the economy-wide wage trend.

A "natural rate" result follows if actual wage increases feed fully into the equilibrium components of future age increases. There will be acceleration whenever the non-linear disequilibrium effects are on average positive, and steady inflation, that is stochastically steady inflation, only at unemployment rates high enough to make the disequilibrium effects wash out. Phillips tradeoffs exist in the short run, and the time it takes for them to evaporate depends on the lengths of the lags with which today's actual wage gains become tomorrow's standards.

A rather minor modification may preserve Phillips tradeoffs in the long run. Suppose there is a floor on wage change in excess supply markets, independent of the amount of excess supply and of the past history of wages and prices. Suppose, for example, that wage change is never negative; it is either zero or what the response function says, whichever is algebraically larger. So long as there are markets where this floor is effective, there can be determinate rates of economy-wide wage inflation for various levels of aggregate demand. Markets at the floor do not increase their contributions to aggregate wage inflation when overall demand is raised. Nor is their contribution escalated to actual wage experience. But the frequency of such markets diminishes, it is true, both with overall demand and with inflation. The floor phenomenon can preserve a Phillips tradeoff within limits, but one that becomes ever more fragile and vanishes as greater demand pressure removes markets from contact with the zero floor. The model implies a long-run Phillips curve that is very flat for high unemployment and becomes vertical at a critically low rate of unemployment.

These implications seem plausible and even realistic. It will be objected, however, that any permanent floor independent of general wage and price history and expectation must indicate money illusion. The answer is that the floor need not be permanent in any single market. It could give way to wage reduction when enough unemployment has persisted long enough. But with stochastic intersectoral shifts of demand, markets are always exchanging roles, and there can always be some markets, not always the same ones, at the floor.

This model avoids the empirically questionable implication of the usual natural rate hypothesis that unemployment rates only slightly higher than the critical rate will trigger ever-accelerating deflation. Phillips curves seem to be pretty flat at high rates of unemployment. During the great contraction of 1930-33, wage rates were slow to give way even in the face of massive unemployment and substantial deflation in consumer prices. Finally in 1932 and 1933 money wage rates fell more sharply, in response to prolonged unemployment, layoffs, shutdowns, and to threats and fears of more of the same.

I have gone through this example to make the point that irrationality, in the sense that meaningless differences in money values *permanently* affect individual behavior, is not logically necessary for the existence of a long-run Phillips tradeoff. In full long-run equilibrium in all markets, employment and unemployment would be independent of the levels and rates of change of money wage rates and prices. But this is not an equilibrium that the system ever approaches. The economy is in perpetual sectoral disequilibrium even when it has settled into a stochastic macro-equilibrium. . . .

Why are the wage and salary rates of employed workers so insensitive to the availability of potential replacements? One reason is that the employer makes some explicit or implicit commitments in putting a worker on the payroll in the first place. The employee expects that his wages and terms of employment will steadily improve, certainly never retrogress. He expects that the employer will pay him the rate prevailing for persons of comparable skill, occupation, experience, and seniority. He expects such commitments in return for his own investments in the job; arrangements for residence, transportation, and personal life involve set-up costs which will be wasted if the job turns sour. The market for labor services is not like a market for fresh produce where the entire current supply is auctioned daily. It is more like a rental housing market, in which most existing tenancies are the continuations of long-term relationships governed by contracts or less formal understandings.

Employers and workers alike regard the wages of comparable labor elsewhere as a standard, but what determines those reference wages? There is not even an auction where workers and employers unbound by existing relationships and commitments meet and determine a market-clearing wage. If such markets existed, they would provide competitively determined guides for negotiated and administered wages, just as stock exchange prices are reference points for stock transactions elsewhere. In labor markets the reverse is closer to the truth. Wage rates for existing employees set the standards for new employees, too.

The equilibrium components of wage increases, it has been argued, depend on past wage increases throughout the economy. In those theoretical and econometric models of inflation where labor markets are aggregated into a single market, this relationship is expressed as an autoregressive equation of fixed structure: current wage increase depends on past wage increases. The same description applies when past wage increases enter indirectly, mediated by price inflation and productivity change. The process of mutual inter-dependence of market wages is a good deal more complex and less mechanical than these aggregated models suggest.

Reference standards for wages differ from market to market. The equilibrium wage increase in each market will be some function of past wages in all markets, and perhaps of past prices too. But the function need not be the same in every market. Wages of workers contiguous in geography, industry, and skill will be heavily weighted. . . . Since wage decisions and negotiations occur infrequently, relative wage adjustments involve a lot of catching up and leap-frogging, and probably take a long time. . . .

A system in which only relative magnitudes matter has only a neutral equilibrium, from which it can be permanently displaced by random shocks. Even when a market is in equilibrium, it may outdo the recent wage increases in related markets. A shock of this kind, even though it is not repeated, raises permanently the steady state inflation rate. This is true cost-push—inflation generated neither by previous inflation nor by current excess demand. Shocks, of course, may be negative as well as positive. For example, upward pushes arising from adjustments in relative wage *levels* will be reversed when those adjustments are completed.

To the extent that one man's reference wages are another man's wages, there is something arbitrary and conventional, indeterminate and unstable, in the process of wage setting. In the same current market circumstances, the reference pattern might be 8 percent per year or 3 percent per year or zero, depending on the historical prelude. Market conditions, unemployment and vacancies and their distributions, shape history and alter reference patterns. But accidental circumstances affecting strategic wage settlements also cast a long shadow.

Price inflation, as previously observed, is a neutral method of making arbitrary money wage paths conform to the realities of productivity growth, neutral in preserving the structure of relative wages. If expansion of aggregate demand brings both more inflation and more employment, there need be no mystery why unemployed workers accept the new jobs, or why employed workers do not vacate theirs. They need not be victims of ignorance or inflation illusion. They genuinely want more work at feasible real wages, and they also want to maintain the relative status they regard as proper and just.

Guideposts could be in principle the functional equivalent of inflation, a neutral method of reconciling wage and productivity paths. The trick is to find a formula for mutual de-escalation which does not offend conceptions of relative equity. No one has devised a way of controlling average wage rates without intervening in the competitive struggle over relative wages. Inflation lets this struggle proceed and blindly, impartially, impersonally, and nonpolitically scales down all its outcomes. There are worse methods of resolving group rivalries and social conflict. . . .

QUESTIONS FOR DISCUSSION

1 Summarize Tobin's disequilibrium theory of unemployment. In the short run, what factors would be expected to increase the measured level of unemployment? What does Tobin say to those who insist that involuntary unemployment cannot exist in long-run equilibrium?
2 Why, according to Tobin, are we likely to have some inflation even when unemployment is quite low? What should be done about this? Do you agree?

READING 19

Another leading economist originally attracted by Keynes' explanation of the Depression is **Franco Modigliani** (1918-   ), once a refugee from Fascist Italy and now a professor at MIT. According to Modigliani, Keynes' permanent contribution was "the combination of wage rigidity (in the short run) and liquidity preference." Modigliani developed the finance side of Keynes' insights, establishing the conditions under which active monetary policy would be an effective stabilization tool. His "life cycle hypothesis" also developed the Keynesian consumption function and explained how the savings rate could remain stable over time, even though the marginal propensity to save appears to exceed the average propensity in time series, as well as cross-sections. The following article reviews some of Modigliani's differences with the neo-classical monetarists. These economists believe that flexible wages and interest rates would automatically stabilize the economy at full-employment levels. For Modigliani, as for other neo-Keynesians, the delays in learning about macroeconomic conditions, together with the existence of long-term contracts for labor and some raw materials, strengthen the case for automatic stabilizers and for fiscal and monetary interventions by the government.

The Monetarist Controversy or, Should We Forsake Stabilization Policies?*

Franco Modigliani

In recent years and especially since the onset of the current depression, the economics profession and the lay public have heard a great deal about the sharp conflict between "monetarists and Keynesians" or between "monetarists and fiscalists." The difference between the two "schools" is generally held to center on whether the money supply or fiscal variables are the major

*Source: Presidential Address delivered to the American Economic Association, Atlantic City, New Jersey, September 17, 1976, excerpted from American Economic Review, March, 1977, pp. 1-19, by permission of the author and the Association.

determinants of aggregate economic activity, and hence the most appropriate tool of stabilization policies.

My central theme is that this view is quite far from the truth, and that the issues involved are of far greater practical import. There are in reality no serious analytical disagreements between leading monetarists and leading non-monetarists. Milton Friedman was once quoted as saying, "We are all Keynesians, now," and I am quite prepared to reciprocate that "we are all monetarists"—if by monetarism is meant assigning to the stock of money a major role in determining output and prices. Indeed, the list of those who have long been monetarists in this sense is quite extensive, including among others John Maynard Keynes as well as myself. . . .

In reality the distinguishing feature of the monetarists school and the real issues of disagreement with nonmonetarists is not monetarism, but rather the role that should probably be assigned to stabilization policies. Nonmonetarists accept what I regard to be the fundamental practical message of *The General Theory,* that a private enterprise economy using an intangible money *needs* to be stabilized, *can* be stabilized and threfore *should* be stabilized by appropriate monetary and fiscal policies. Monetarists by contrast take the view that there is no serious need to stabilize the economy; that even if there were a need, it could not be done, for stabilization policies would be more likely to increase than to decrease instability; and, at least some monetarists would, I believe, go so far as to hold that, even in the unlikely event that stabilization policies could on balance prove beneficial, the government should not be trusted with the necessary power.

What has led me to address this controversy is the recent spread of mone-tarism, both in a simplistic, superficial form and in the form of growing influence on the practical conduct of economic policy, which influence, I shall argue presently, has played at least some role in the economic upheavals of the last three years. . . .

I.   The Keynesian Case for Stabilization Policies

A. The General Theory. Keynes' novel conclusion about the need for stabilization policies . . . resulted from the interaction of a basic contribution to traditional monetary theory—liquidity preference—and an unorthodox hypothesis about the working of the labor market—complete downward rigidity of wages.

Because of liquidity preference, a change in aggregate demand, which may be broadly defined as any event that results in a change in the market clearing or equilibrium rate of interest, will produce a corresponding change in the real demand for money or velocity of circulation, and hence in the real stock of money needed at full employment. As long as wages are perfectly flexible, even with a constant nominal supply, full employment could and would be maintained by a change of wages and prices as needed to produce the required change in the real money supply—though even in this case, stability of the price level would require a countercyclical monetary policy. But under the Keynesian wage assumption the classical adjustment through prices can occur only in the case of an increased demand. In the case of a decline, instead, wage rigidity prevents the necessary increase in the real money supply and the concomitant required fall in interest rates. Hence, if the nominal money supply is constant, the initial equilibrium must give way to a new stable one, characterized by lower output and by an involuntary reduction in employment, so labeled because it does not result from a shift in notional demand and supply schedules in terms of real wages, but only from an insufficient real money supply. The nature of this equilibrium is elegantly captured by the Hicksian *IS-LM* paradigm, which to our generation of economists has become almost as familiar as the demand-supply paradigm was to earlier ones.

This analysis implied that a fixed money supply far from insuring approximately stability of prices and output, as held by the traditional view, would result in a rather unstable economy, alternating between periods of protracted unemployment and stagnation, and bursts of inflation. The extent of downward instability would depend in part on the size of the exogenous shocks to demand and in part on the strength of what may be called the Hicksian mechanism. By this I mean the extent to which a shift in *IS*, through its interaction with *LM*, results in some decline in interest rates and thus in a change in income which is smaller than the original shift. The stabilizing power of this mechanism is controlled by various parameters of the system. In particular, the economy will be more unstable the greater the interest elasticity of demand for money, and the smaller the interest responsiveness of aggregate demand. Finally, a large multiplier is also destabilizing in that it implies a larger shift in *IS* for a given shock.

However, the instability could be readily counteracted by appropriate stabilization policies. Monetary policy could change the nominal supply of money so as to *accommodate* the change in real demand resulting from shocks in aggregate demand. Fiscal policy, through expenditure and taxes, could *offset* these shocks, making full employment consistent with the initial nominal money stocks. In general, both monetary and fiscal policies could be used in combination. But because of a perceived uncertainty in the response of demand to changes in interest rates, and because changes in interest rates through monetary policy could meet difficulties and substantial delays related to expectations (so-called liquidity traps), fiscal policy was regarded as having some advantages. . . .

II. The Monetarists' Attack

The monetarists' attack on Keynesianism was directed from the very beginning not at the Keynesian framework as such, but at whether it really implied a need for stabilization. It rested on a radically different empirical assessment of the value of the parameters controlling the stabilizing power of the Hicksian mechanism and of the magnitude and duration of response to shocks, given a stable money supply. And this different assessment in turn was felt to justify a radical downgrading of the *practical relevance* of the Keynesian framework as distinguished from its *analytical validity*.

Liquidity preference was a fine contribution to monetary theory but in practice the responsiveness of the demand for money and hence of velocity, to interest rates, far from being unmanageably large, was so small that according to a well-known paper by Milton Friedman,[13] it could not even be detected empirically. On the other hand, the effect of interest rates on aggregate demand was large and by no means limited to the traditional fixed investments but quite pervasive. The difficulty of detecting it empirically resulted from focusing on a narrow range of measured market rates and from the fact that while the aggregate could be counted on to respond, the response of individual components might not be stable. Finally Friedman's celebrated contribution to the theory of the consumption function . . . and my own work on the life cycle hypothesis . . . implied a very high short-run marginal propensity to save in response to transient disturbances to income and hence a small short term multiplier.

All this justified the conclusion that (i) though demand shocks might qualitatively work along the lines described by Keynes, the Hicks mechanism is so strong that their impact would be *small* and *transient,* provided the stock of money was kept on a steady growth path; (ii) fiscal policy actions, like other demand shocks, would have *minor* and *transitory* effects on demand, while changes in money would produce *large* and *permanent* effects on money income; and, therefore, (iii) the observed instability of the economy, which was anyway proving moderate as the postwar period unfolded, was most likely the result of the unstable growth of money, be it due to misguided endeavors to stabilize income or to the pursuit of other targets, which were either irrelevant, or in the case of balance of payment goals, should have been made irrelevant by abandoning fixed exchanges.

But the most serious challenge came in Friedman's 1968 Presidential Address. . . . Its basic message was that, despite appearances, wages were in reality perfectly flexible and there was accordingly no involuntary unemployment. The evidence to the contrary, including the Phillips curve, was but a statistical illusion resulting from failure to differentiate between price changes and *unexpected* price changes.

Friedman starts out by reviving the Keynesian notion that, at any point of time, there exists a unique full-employment rate which he labels the "natural rate." An unanticipated fall in demand in Friedman's competitive world leads firms to reduce prices and also output and employment along the short-run marginal cost curve—unless the nominal wage declines together with prices. But workers, failing to judge correctly the current and prospective fall in prices, misinterpret the reduction of nominal wages as a cut in *real* wages. Hence, assuming a positively sloped supply function, they reduce the supply of labor. As a result, the effective real wage rises to the point where the resulting decline in the demand for labor matches the reduced supply. Thus, output falls not because of the decline in demand but because of the entirely voluntary reduction in the supply of labor, in response to erroneous perceptions. Furthermore, the fall in employment can only be temporary, as expectations must soon catch up with the facts, at least in the absence of new shocks. The very same mechanism works in the case of an increase in demand, so that the responsiveness of wages and prices is the same on either side of the natural rate.

---

[13]"The Demand for Money: Some Theoretical and Empirical Results," in Milton Friedman, *The Optimum Quantity of Money, and Other Essays* (Chicago: Aldine, 1969).

The upshot is that Friedman's model also implies a Phillips-type relation between inflation, employment or unemployment, and past inflation, provided the latter variable is interpreted as a reasonable proxy for expected inflation. But it turns the standard explanation on its head: instead of (excess) employment causing inflation, it is (the unexpected component of) the rate of inflation that causes excess employment.

One very basic implication of Friedman's model is that the coefficient of price expectations could be precisely unity. This specification implies that whatever the shape of the short-run Phillips curve—a shape determined by the relation between expected and actual price changes, and by the elasticity of labor supply with respect to the perceived real wage—the long-run curve *must be vertical*. . . .

III.   How Valid is the Monetarist Case?

In setting out the counterattack it is convenient to start with the monetarists' model of price and wage behavior. . . . The proposition that other things equal, and given time enough, the economy will eventually adjust to any indefinitely maintained stock of money . . . can be derived from a variety of models and, in any event, is of very little practical significance. What is unacceptable, because inconsistent with both micro and macro evidence, is the specific monetarist model set out above and its implication that all unemployment is a voluntary, fleeting response to transitory misperceptions. . . . Equally serious objections apply to Friedman's modeling of the commodity market as a perfectly competitive one—so that the real wage rate is continuously equated to the short-run marginal product of labor—and to his treatment of labor as a homogenous commodity traded in an auction market, so that, at the going wage, there never is any excess demand by firms of excess supply by workers. The inadequacies of this model as a useful formalization of present day Western economies are so numerous that only a few of the major ones can be mentioned here.

Friedman's view of unemployment as a voluntary reduction in labor supply could at best provide an explanation of variations in labor force—and then only under the questionable assumption that the supply function has a significantly positive slope—but cannot readily account for changes in unemployment. Furthermore, it cannot be reconciled with the well-known fact that *rising* unemployment is accompanied by a fall, not by a *rise* in quits, nor with the role played by temporary layoffs. . . . His competitive model of the commodity market, accepted also in *The General Theory*, implies that changes in real wages, adjusted for long-run productivity trend, should be significantly negatively correlated with cyclical changes in employment and output and with changes in money wages. . . . This conclusion was rejected by some eighty years of British experience and . . . in more recent tests for the United States and Canada. Similar tests of my own, using quarterly data, provide striking confirmation that for the last two decades from the end of the Korean War until 1973, the association of trend adjusted real compensations of the private non-farm sector with either employment or the change in nominal compensation is prevailingly positive and very significantly so.

This evidence can, instead, be accounted for by the oligopolistic pricing model—according to which price is determined by *long-run* minimum average cost up to the mark-up reflecting entry-preventing considerations . . . coupled with some lags in the adjustment of prices to cost. This model implies that firms respond to a change in demand by endeavoring to adjust output and employment, without significant changes in prices relative to wages; and their initial impact not on wages but rather on unemployment by way of layoffs and recalls and through changes in the level of vacancies, and hence on the length of average search time.

If, in the process, vacancies rise above a critical level, or "natural rate," firms will endeavor to reduce them by outbidding each other, thereby raising the rate of change of wages. Thus, as long as jobs and vacancies remain above, and unemployment remains below, some critical level which might be labeled the "noninflationary rate," . . . wages and prices will tend to accelerate. If, on the other hand, jobs fall below, and unemployment rises above, the non-inflationary rate, firms finding that vacancies are less than optimal—in the limit the unemployed queuing outside the gate will fill them instantly—will have an incentive to reduce their relative wage offer. But in this case, in which too much labor is looking for too few jobs, the trend toward a sustained decline in the rate of growth of wages is likely to be even weaker than the corresponding acceleration when too many jobs are bidding for too few people. The main reason is the nonhomogeneity of labor. By far the largest and more valuable source of labor supply to a firm consists of those already employed who are not readily interchangeable with the unemployed and, in contrast with them, are concerned with protecting their earnings and not with reestablishing full employment. For these reasons, and because the first to quit are likely to be the best workers, a reduction of the labor force can, within limits, be accomplished more economically, not by reducing wages to generate enough quits, but by firing, or, when possible, by layoffs which insure access to a trained labor force when demand recovers. More generally, the inducement to reduce relative wages to eliminate the excess supply is moderated by the effect that such a reduction would have on quits and costly turnover, even when the resulting vacancies can be readily filled from the ranks of the unemployed. Equally relevant are the consequences in terms of loss of morale and good will. . . . Thus, while there will be some tendency for the rate of change of wages to fall, the more so the larger the unemployment—at least in an economy like the United States where there are no overpowering centralized unions—that tendency is severely damped. . . .

In any event, what is really important for practical purposes, is not the long-run equilibrium relation as such, but the speed with which it is approached. Both the model sketched out and the empirical evidence suggest that the process of acceleration or deceleration of wages when unemployment differs from the noninflationary rate will have more nearly the character of a crawl than of a gallop. It will suffice to recall in this connection that there was excess demand pressure in the United States at least from 1965 to mid-1970, and during that period the growth of inflation was from 1.5 to only about 5.5 percent per year. And the response to the excess supply pressure from mid-1970 to early 1973, and from late 1974 to date [1976] was equally sluggish.

There remains to consider the monetarists' initial criticism of Keynesianism, to wit, that even without high wage flexibility, the system's response to demand shocks is small and short-lived, thanks to the power of the Hicksian mechanism. Here it must be acknowledged that every one of the monetarists' criticisms of early, simple-minded Keynesianism has proved in considerable measure correct. . . . Both theoretical and empirical work, reflected in part in econometric models, have largely vindicated the monetarist contention that interest effects on demand are pervasive and substantial. . . .

There is, therefore, substantial agreement that in the United States the Hicksian mechanism is fairly effective in limiting the effect of shocks, and that the response of wages and prices to excess demand or supply will also work *gradually* toward eliminating largely, if not totally, any effect on employment. But in the view of nonmonetarists, the evidence overwhelmingly supports the conclusion that . . . the wheels of the offsetting mechanism grind slowly. To be sure, . . . the rise in short-term rates gets promptly into play and heftily, given the low money demand elasticity; but most expenditures depend on long-term rates, which generally respond but gradually, and the demand response is generally also gradual. Furthermore, while this response is building up, multiplier and accelerator mechanisms work toward amplifying the shock. Finally, the classical mechanism—the change in real money supply through prices—has an even longer lag because of the sluggish response of wages to excess demand. . . .

From the theory and evidence reviewed, we must then conclude that opting for a constant rate of growth of the nominal money supply can result in a stable economy only in the absence of significant exogenous shocks. But obviously the economy has been and will continue to be exposed to many significant shocks, coming from such things as war and peace, and other large changes in government expenditure, foreign trade, agriculture, technological progress, population shifts, and what not. The clearest evidence on the importance of such shocks is provided by our postwar record with its six recessions. . . .

IV. The Record of Stabilization Policies: Stabilizing or Destabilizing

. . . The reduced severity of fluctuations might in part reflect structural changes in the economy and the effect of stronger built-in stabilizers, inspired, of course, by the Keynesian analysis. Furthermore, the greater stability in the United States, and in other industrialized countries, are obviously not independent events. . . . Part of the credit for the greater stability should go to the conscious and on balance, successful endeavor at stabilizing the economy. . . .

VI. Conclusion

To summarize, the monetarists have made a valid and most valuable contribution in establishing that our economy is far less unstable than the early Keynesians pictured it and in rehabilitating the role of money as a determinant of aggregate demand. They are wrong, however, in going as far as asserting that the economy is sufficiently shock-proof that stabilization policies are not needed. They have also made an important contribution in pointing out that such policies might in fact prove destabilizing. This criticism has had a salutary effect on reassessing what stabilization policies can and should do, and on trimming down fine-tuning ambitions. But their contention that postwar fluctuations resulted from an unstable money growth or that stabilization policies decreased rather than increased stability just does not stand up to an impartial examination of the postwar record of the United States and other industrialized countries. Up to 1974, these policies have helped to keep the economy reasonably stable by historical standards, even though one can certainly point to some occasional failures.

The serious deterioration in economic stability since 1973 must be attributed in the first place to the novel nature of the shocks that hit us, namely supply shocks. Even the best possible aggregate demand management cannot offset such shocks without a lot of unemployment together with a lot of inflation. But, in addition, demand management was far from the best. This failure must be attributed in good measure to the fact that we had little experience or even an adequate conceptual framework to deal with such shocks: but at least from my reading of the record, it was also the result of failure to use stabilization policies, including too slavish adherence to the monetarists' constant money growth prescription.

We must, therefore, categorically reject the monetarist appeal to turn back the clock forty years by discarding the basic message of *The General Theory*. We should instead concentrate our efforts in an endeavor to make stabilization policies even more effective in the future than they have been in the past.

QUESTIONS FOR DISCUSSION

1   Using the Hicks-Hansen framework of Figures 7-1 and 7-2, could you capture the differences Modigliani thinks now exist between monetarists and non-monetarists?

2   Which elements of the Keynesian perspective do Modigliani and Tobin endorse? Which, if any, do they downplay? Do they introduce any elements not present in either Keynes or the neoclassical mainstream?

3   Look up the Presidential Address by Milton Friedman, the most prominent present-day monetarist, in the *American Economic Review,* March, 1968, and his Nobel Lecture, in the *Journal of Political Economy,* June, 1977. Formulate in a short paper Friedman's challenge to Keynesian and neo-Keynesian macroeconomics, including the notion of a Phillips curve. Do the answers by Tobin and Modigliani satisfy you? Can you imagine the response which Friedman might give?

Thorstein Veblen

CHAPTER 8

INSTITUTIONALISM AND NEO-INSTITUTIONALISM

EDITOR'S INTRODUCTION

Some of the perspectives in this book were presented and developed by a "school" of interacting economists. Previous chapters spoke of the "classical" English school of political economy or of the Austrian economists, many of whom studied with other members in Vienna. Some other perspectives were not self-conscious groups; particular practitioners often quarreled, when they knew about each other at all. The mercantilists, the Marxists, and neo-Keynesians are examples of such diverse groups of thinkers who nevertheless share certain preconceptions. As for the "institutionalists," there is little to unite all of the economists sometimes called by this name except a pronounced dissatisfaction with the neo-classical mainstream and especially its tolerance of the American *status quo*.[1] Indeed, at least one of today's most prominent institutionalist writers, **John Kenneth Galbraith** (1908-   ), denies being an "institutionalist" at all!

While institutionalism has been called the only native American school of thought, its progenitors were influenced by late 19th century German economists. **Thorstein Veblen** (1857-1929) and the early institutionalists adopted the German historical school's idea that economic theory should be related to the stage of development of the society, hence could not be deduced from univer-sal principles. **Gustav Schmoller** (1838-1917), an influential professor of that school, advocated government intervention to solve social problems. Two others related to this school, **Max Weber** (1864-1920) and **Werner Sombart** (1863-1941), emphasized the role of attitudes towards risk and entrepreneurship as crucial for the development of capitalism. All were

---

[1] As examples of this diversity, "institutionalists" **Wesley Clair Mitchell** (1874-1948) established the inductive, statistical study of business cycles just before World War I, while **John R. Commons** (1862-1945), the Wisconsin progressive, worked for labor law reform and wrote mostly in a descriptive and normative mode.

critical of English classical economies as over-simplified and too materialist and individualist in its assumptions.

Four Elements of the Institutionalist Perspective

From Veblen, the original "institutionalist" dissenter, to contemporary neo-institutionalists of the Association for Evolutionary Economists,[2] the institutionalist perspective may be identified as comprising four main principles:

(1) **Focus on the Institution as the Unit of Analysis.**[3] An institution may be defined as a "social arrangement regulating the relations of individuals and collective groups to each other."[4] Examples would be customs, rules, or laws which regulate the distribution of income, permissible competitive behavior, or how money is spent. While for some institutionalists, like **Karl Polanyi** (1886-1964), these social rules provided a desirable stability in the face of market flux, for Veblen they were often negative. Veblen typically portrayed customs and ceremonies as irrationally confining or misdirecting the instincts of "idle curiosity," workmanship, and parenthood, which he credited with stimulating technical progress. "Pecuniary canons of taste," wrote Veblen about one such negative institution, required a vast waste of money to establish the financial reputation of banks, business corporations, and persons. Money-oriented business practices designed to bolster stock values must lead to recessions and to a waste of what engineers create.[5]

The net result of the conflict between creativity and conservatism, between progressive instincts and restrictive social customs, cannot be predicted. But Veblen did believe that those follower countries would be likely to succeed who could copy the progressive technique of the leading countries without encumbering themselves with the wasteful commercial practices accompanying them. Obsolete capital stock and business forms, according to a well-known

---

[2]Founded by **Allan G. Gruchy** (1906-   ), whose *Contemporary Economic Thought* and *The Contribution of Neo-Institutional Economics* defend this perspective in modern economics. The organization publishes the *Journal of Economic Issues,* edited by Marc R. Tool. Tool also edited *An Instititutionalist Guide to Economics and Public Policy* (Armonk, N.Y.: M. E. Sharpe, 1984), which contains a fair sampling of neo-institutionalist thinking on major policy issues.

[3]As opposed to the state in mercantilism, the income recipients in classical models, the class in Marxism, or the spending unit in Keynesianism.

[4]Martin Bronfenbrenner, "Early American Leaders—Institutional and Critical Traditions," *American Economic Review,* December, 1985, pp. 13ff.

[5]*Theory of Business Enterprise* (1904) and *Engineers and the Price System* (1921). The attempt to defend inflated capital values by use of credit eventually leads to collapse. In normal times, businessmen must emphasize vendibility, rather than useful value, in their wares. Sales effort can overcome customer resistance to rather worthless goods. Galbraith made a similar point in *The Affluent Society* (1957).

book of Veblen's, were penalizing Great Britain for "taking the lead" in industrialization, allowing Germany to surge ahead.[6]

(2) Evolutionary Process. Like the survival of the fittest biological species in Darwinian evolution, economic institutions are cumulative results of heredity and experience in achieving human ends. Economic forms of life are also mutating in an unknown direction. The new forms may or may not survive, depending on power, as well as cooperation and human intelligence. Consequently, determinate equilibrium economic models like those of classical mechanics are hardly appropriate to describe evolving institutions. Empirical induction would be a more appropriate mode of investigation. Accordingly, zoology or anthropology provides a more promising exemplar for economists than does physical mechanics.

(3) Diverse Goals of Economic Activity. Evolving economic institutions can serve many goals, not simply the hedonistic or profit-maximizing ones usually assumed by the mainstream in their working models. Stability and relative status may be quite important in some circumstances.[7] Rules of fair dealing reduce transaction costs and therefore may make some efficient exchanges possible, as urged by John R. Commons.

(4) Essential Normative Orientation. Unlike neo-classical economists, who take individual choices as sovereign,[8] institutionalists usually take a utilitarian or "pragmatic" point of view. For Veblen—as for his contemporary, the pragmatist John Dewey—everyday function or use was the standard of value. Usefulness is judged by Veblen on "whether it serves to enhance human life on the whole . . . impersonally," as evaluated by dispassionate common sense. Judged by this standard, "conspicuous consumption" or ostentatious leisure is denounced as an attempt to gain honorific status by "invidious comparisons" with one's neighbors. "[T]he pervading . . . abiding test of good breeding is the requirement of a substantial and patent waste of time."[9] For instance, women of the upper classes are to display their men's distinction by their dress and behavior. They must, wrote Veblen derisively, be "infirmly delicate . . . hazardously slender." Note that Veblen's condemnation of feminine fashion was not based upon mere taste, but rather upon what would objectively enhance or impair the life of women.

With respect to public policy, the institutionalists' standard is democratic, not plutocratic. Property rights and the existing distribution of income are not

---

[6]*Imperial Germany and the Industrial Revolution* (1915).

[7]Karl Polanyi, *The Great Transformation* (Boston: Beacon Press, 1957). Veblen himself taught that stable prices would save managerial time and effort, while "normal" profits on all past investments, price leadership, and market sharing would help stabilize oligopolistic structures.

[8]While recognizing, as neo-classical welfare economists A. C. Pigou and **Abram Bergson** (1914-   ) always taught, that choices and underlying preferences may not reflect mature, informed satisfactions.

[9]*The Theory of the Leisure Class,* pp. 277, 288.

sacred. What the market supplies to those with the money to buy, therefore, is not necessarily what ought to be provided. Anyway, who can say what ought to be with any certainty? Since society is constantly evolving under the influence of technological change, policymakers cannot be certain that their interventions will work out well. Life, including public life, must be experimental, not an approximation to a Pareto or known social welfare optimum, as the neo-classical perspective has it.

With their strong aversion for the *laissez-faire* attitudes of the Gilded Age of robber barons and monopolies, the institutionalists often defended the consumer, worker, small business person, and farmer against the big "vested interests," such as the railroads, Standard Oil, and the military-industrial complex. With such enemies, institutionalists often found themselves allied with the Populist, Progressive, and Democratic parties in American politics. Institutionalists like J. R. Commons, Wilbur Cohen (one of the founders of the Social Security Administration), Rexford Tugwell and Gardiner Means (prominent New Dealers), and Leon Keyserling (chairman of the Council of Economic Advisers under President Harry S Truman) worked within Democratic administrations for progressive social causes and economic reforms like democratic planning. More technocratic than Marxist in outlook, institutionalists favored reform, rather than revolution. Despite some sympathy for Russian experiments, no important institutionalist ever became a Communist.

There are many parallels between the rhetoric and programs of Professors Veblen and Galbraith, despite the two generations separating them. Like Veblen, Galbraith (who worked for the Office of Price Administration during World War II) favored price controls as a way to control inflation in a market dominated by big price-makers.[10] Veblen called for world citizenship and free trade, while Galbraith has been a strong internationalist as Chairman of the Americans for Democratic Action and U.S. Ambassador to India under President John F. Kennedy, and has condemned the arms race and other ecological threats as the consequences of corporate irresponsibility. Despite criticism of big business, Galbraith has been skeptical of antitrust legislation as a real remedy to market power. He has preferred the "countervailing power" of unions or government purchasing agencies. For some defense industries, he has advised nationalization. Both Veblen and Galbraith often referred sarcastically to American universities. University administrators, whom Veblen labeled "captains of erudition," are mostly concerned to indoctrinate a new generation of businessmen, while according to Prof. Galbraith the "conventional wisdom" of neo-classical economics is really an ideology intended to justify big business privileges. Young academic economists, he has said, adopt the mainstream apparatus because it is convenient to present in class and because such conformity to reputable doctrine helps their careers.

Besides showing us how to debunk privilege, do the institutionalists have a research program? According to Veblen, classical economics was no longer in touch with reality. Galbraith has little patience for its neo-classical version. Indeed, Veblen did not hold out much hope for causal generalizations for the evolutionary social science he thought economics should become. Since

---

[10]In *The Theory of Price Control* (1952).

Veblen, institutionalists like Galbraith have tried to incorporate monopoly power, political influences, and modern psychological conceptions into their work.[11] Still, the relative lack of testable positive theories about contemporary economies derived from the institutionalist perspective must be considered a serious deficiency. Lacking quantifiable concepts and hypotheses, few institutional scholars do statistical work to confirm their theories.

READING 20

The son of well-to-do Norwegian-American farmers, **Thorstein Veblen** received an excellent education. Yet despite his brilliance and well-received books, he failed as an academic because of his unorthodox private life and dissenting views. Veblen's master-piece, *The Theory of the Leisure Class* (1899), from which this selection is excerpted, bitterly ridicules the money culture of the turn of the century.

The Theory of the Leisure Class

Thorstein Veblen

2. Pecuniary Emulation

In the sequence of cultural evolution the emergence of a leisure class coincides with the beginning of ownership. This is necessarily the case, for these two institutions result from the same set of economic forces. . . .

It is as elements of social structure—conventional facts—that leisure and ownership are matters of interest for the purpose in hand. A habitual neglect of work does not constitute a leisure class; neither does the mechanical fact of use and consumption constitute ownership. . . . The point in question is the origin and nature of a conventional leisure class on the one hand and the beginnings of individual ownership as a conventional right or equitable claim on the other hand. . . .

The early differentiation out of which the distinction between a leisure and a working class arises is a division maintained between men's and women's work in the lower stages of barbarism. Likewise the earliest form of ownership is an ownership of the women by the able-bodied men of the community. . . . The ownership of women begins in the lower barbarian stages of culture, apparently with the seizure of female captives. The original reason for the seizure and appropriation of women seems to have been their usefulness as trophies. The practice of seizing women from the enemy as trophies, gave rise to a form of ownership-marriage, resulting in a household with a male head. This was followed by an extension of slavery to other

---

[11]For several surveys of these efforts, from several unorthodox perspectives, see Benjamin Gilad and Stanley Kaish, eds., *Handbook of Behavioral Economics* (Greenwich, Connecticut: JAI Press, 1986).

captives and inferiors, besides women, and by an extension of ownership-marriage to other women than those seized from the enemy. The outcome of emulation under the circumstances of a predatory life, therefore, has been on the one hand a form of marriage resting on coercion, and on the other hand the custom of ownership. The two institutions are not distinguishable in the initial phase of their development; both arise from the desire of the successful men to put their prowess in evidence by exhibiting some durable result of their exploits. Both also minister to that propensity for mastery which pervades all predatory communities. From the ownership of women the concept of ownership extends itself to include the products of their industry, and so there arises the ownership of things as well as of persons.

In this way a consistent system of property in goods is gradually installed. And although in the latest stages of the development, the serviceability of goods for consumption has come to be the most obtrusive element of their value, still, wealth has by no means yet lost its utility as an honorific evidence of the owner's prepotence.

Wherever the institution of private property is found, even in a slightly developed form, the economic process bears the character of a struggle between men for the possession of goods. It has been customary in economic theory, and especially among those economists who adhere with least faltering to the body of modernized classical doctrines, to construe this struggle for wealth as being substantially a struggle for subsistence. Such is, no doubt, its character in large part during the earlier and less efficient phases of industry. Such is also its character in all cases where the "niggardliness of nature" is so strict as to afford but a scanty livelihood to the community in return for strenuous and unremitting application to the business of getting the means of subsistence. But in all progressing communities an advance is presently made beyond this early stage of technological development. Industrial efficiency is presently carried to such a pitch as to afford something appreciably more than a bare livelihood to those engaged in the industrial process. It has not been unusual for economic theory to speak of the further struggle for wealth on this new industrial basis as a competition for an increase of the comforts of life— primarily for an increase of the physical comforts which the consumption of goods affords.

The end of acquisition and accumulation is conventionally held to be the consumption of the goods accumulated—whether it is consumption directly by the owner of the goods or by the household attached to him and for this purpose identified with him in theory. This is at least felt to be the economically legitimate end of acquisition, which alone it is incumbent on the theory to take account of. Such consumption may of course be conceived to serve the consumer's physical wants—his physical comfort—or his so-called higher wants—spiritual, aesthetic, intellectual, or what not; the latter class of wants being served indirectly by an expenditure of goods, after the fashion familiar to all economic readers.

But it is only when taken in a sense far removed from its naive meaning that consumption of goods can be said to afford the incentive from which accumulation invariably proceeds. The motive that lies at the root of ownership is emulation; and the same motive of emulation continues active in the further development of the institution to which it has given rise and in the development of all those features of the social structure which this institution of ownership touches. The possession of wealth confers honor; it is an invidious distinction. . . . As regards those members and classes of the community who are chiefly concerned in the accumulation of wealth, the incentive of subsistence or of physical comfort never plays a considerable part. Ownership began and grew into a human institution on grounds unrelated to the subsistence minimum. The dominant incentive was from the outset the invidious distinction attaching to wealth, and, save temporarily and by exception, no other motive has usurped the primacy at any later stage of the development. . . .

Gradually, as industrial activity further displaces predatory activity in the community's everyday life and in men's habits of thought, accumulated property more and more replaces trophies of predatory exploit as the conventional exponent of prepotence and success. With the growth of settled industry, therefore, the possession of wealth gains in relative importance and effectiveness as a customary basis of repute and esteem. Not that esteem ceases to be awarded on the basis of other, more direct evidence of prowess; not that successful predatory aggression or warlike exploit ceases to call out the approval and admiration of the crowd, or to stir the envy of the less successful competitors; but the opportunities for gaining distinction by means of this direct manifestation of superior force grow less available both in scope and frequency. At the same time opportunities for industrial aggression, and for the accumulation of property by the quasi-peaceable methods of nomadic industry, increase in scope and availability. And it is even more to the point that property now becomes the most easily recognised evidence of a reputable degree of success. . . . By a further refinement, wealth acquired passively by transmission from ancestors or other antecedents presently becomes even more honorific than wealth acquired by the possessor's own effort; but this distinction belongs at a later stage in the evolution of the pecuniary culture and will be spoken of in its place. . . .

In order to stand well in the eyes of the community, it is necessary to come up to a certain, somewhat indefinite, conventional standard of wealth; just as in the earlier predatory stage it is necessary for the barbarian man to come up to the tribe's standard of physical endurance, cunning, and skill at arms. A certain standard of wealth in the one case, and of prowess in the other, is a necessary condition of reputability, and anything in excess of this normal amount is meritorious.

Those members of the community who fall short of this, somewhat indefinite, normal degree of prowess or of property suffer in the esteem of their fellowmen; and consequently they suffer also in their own esteem, since the usual basis of self-respect is the respect accorded by one's neighbors. Only individuals with an aberrant temperament can in the long run retain their self-esteem in the face of the disesteem of their fellows. Apparent exceptions to the rule are met with, especially among people with strong religious convictions. But these apparent exceptions are scarcely real exceptions, since such persons commonly fall back on the putative approbation of some super-natural witness of their deeds.

So soon as the possession of property becomes the basis of popular esteem, therefore, it becomes also a requisite to that complacency which we call self-respect. In any community where goods are held in severalty it is necessary, in order to his own peace of mind, that an individual should possess as large a portion of goods as others with whom he is accustomed to class himself; and it is extremely gratifying to possess something more than others. But as fast as a person makes new acquisitions, and becomes accustomed to the resulting new standard of wealth, the new standard forthwith ceases to afford appreciably greater satisfaction than the earlier standard did. The tendency in any case is constantly to make the present pecuniary standard the point of departure for a fresh increase of wealth; and this in turn gives rise to a new standard of sufficiency and a new pecuniary classification of one's self as compared with one's neighbors. So far as concerns the present question, the end sought by accumulation is to rank high in comparison with the rest of the community. . . . The invidious comparison can never become so favorable to the individual making it that he would not gladly rate himself still higher relatively to his competitors in the struggle for pecuniary reputability.

In the nature of the case, the desire for wealth can scarcely be satiated in any individual instance, and evidently a satiation of the average or general desire for wealth is out of the question. However widely, or equally, or "fairly," it may be distributed, no general increase of the community's wealth can make any approach to satiating this need, the ground of which is the desire of everyone to excel every one else in the accumulation of goods. . . .

Besides this, the power conferred by wealth also affords a motive to accumulation. That propensity for purposeful activity and that repugnance to all futility of effort which belong to man by virtue of his character as an agent do not desert him when he emerges from the naive communal culture where the dominant note of life is the unanalyzed and undifferentiated solidarity of the individual with the group with which his life is bound up. . . . The propensity changes only in the form of its expression and in the proximate objects to which it directs the man's activity. Under the regime of individual ownership the most available means of visibly achieving a purpose is that afforded by the acquisition and accumulation of goods; and as the self-regarding antithesis between man and man reaches fuller consciousness, the propensity for achievement—the instinct of workmanship—tends more and more to shape itself into a straining to excel others in pecuniary achievement. . . .

3. Conspicuous Leisure

For those for whom acquisition and emulation is possible only within the field of productive efficiency and thrift, the struggle for pecuniary reputability will in some measure work out in an increase of diligence and parsimony. . . . But certain secondary features of the cumulative process, yet to be spoken of, come in to very materially circumscribe and modify emulation in these directions among the pecuniarily inferior classes as well as among the superior class.

But it is otherwise with the superior pecuniary class, with which we are here immediately concerned. For this class also the incentive to diligence and thrift is not absent; but its action is so greatly qualified by the secondary demands of pecuniary emulation, that any inclination in this direction is practically overborne and any incentive to diligence tends to be of no effect. The most imperative of these secondary demands of emulation, as well as the one of widest scope, is the requirement of abstention from productive work. . . .

The archaic theoretical distinction between the base and the honorable in the manner of a man's life retains very much of its ancient force even to-day. So much so that there are few of the better class who are not possessed of an instinctive repugnance for the vulgar forms of labor. . . . From the days of the Greek philosophers to the present, a degree of leisure and of exemption from contact with such industrial processes as serve the immediate everyday purposes of human life has ever been recognized by thoughtful men as a prerequisite to a worthy or beautiful, or even a blameless, human life. . . .

The characteristic feature of leisure-class life is a conspicuous exemption from all useful employment.

The normal and characteristic occupations of the class in this mature phase of its life history are in form very much the same as in its earlier days. These occupations are government, war, sports, and devout observances. Persons unduly given to difficult theoretical niceties may hold that these occupations are still incidentally and indirectly "productive"; but it is to be noted as decisive of the question in hand that the ordinary and ostensible motive of the leisure class in engaging in these occupations is assuredly not an increase of wealth by productive effort. At this as at any other cultural stage, government and war are, at least in part, carried on for the pecuniary gain of those who engage in them; but it is gain obtained by the honorable method of seizure and conversion. These occupations are of the nature of predatory, not of productive, employment. . . .

But leisure in the narrower sense as distinct from exploit and from any ostensibly productive employment of effort on objects which are of no intrinsic use, does not commonly leave a material product. The criteria of a past performance of leisure therefore commonly take the form of "immaterial" goods. Such immaterial evidences of past leisure are quasi-scholarly or quasi-artistic accomplishments and a knowledge of processes and incidents which do not conduce directly to the furtherance of human life. So, for instance, in our time there is the knowledge of the dead languages and the occult sciences; of correct spelling; of syntax and prosody; of the various forms of domestic music and other household art; of the latest proprieties of dress, furniture, and equipage; of games, sports, and fancy-bred animals, such as dogs and race-horses. In all these branches of knowledge the initial motive from which their acquisition proceeded at the outset, and through which they first came into vogue, may have been something quite different from the wish to show that one's time had not been spent in industrial employment; but unless these accomplishments had approved themselves as serviceable evidence of an unproductive expenditure of time, they would not have survived and held their place as conventional accomplishments of the leisure class. . . .

4. Conspicuous Consumption

The utility of consumption as an evidence of wealth . . . is an adaptation to a new end, by a selective process, of a distinction previously existing and well established in men's habits of thought. . . .

In the nature of things, luxuries and the comforts of life belong to the leisure class. Under the tabu, certain victuals, and more particularly certain beverages, are strictly reserved for the use of the superior class.

The ceremonial differentiation of the dietary is best seen in the use of intoxicating beverages and narcotics. If these articles of consumption are costly, they are felt to be noble and honorific. Therefore the base classes, primarily the women, practice an enforced continence with respect to these stimulants, except in countries where they are obtainable at a very low cost. From archaic times down through all the length of the patriarchal regime it has been the office of the women to prepare and administer these luxuries, and it has been the prerequisite of the men of gentle birth and breeding to consume them. Drunkenness and the other pathological consequences of the free use of stimulants therefore tend in their turn to become honorific, as being a mark, at the second remove, of the superior status of those who are able to afford the indulgence. Infirmities induced by over-indulgence are among some peoples freely recognised as manly attributes. It has even happened that that name for certain diseased conditions of the body arising from such an origin has passed into everyday speech as a synonym for noble or "gentle." It is only at a relatively early stage of culture that the symptoms of expensive vice are conventionally accepted as marks of a superior status, and so tend to become virtues and command the deference of the community; but the reputability that attaches to certain expensive vices long retains so much of its force as to appreciably lessen the disapprobation visited upon the men of the wealthy or noble class for any excessive indulgence. The same invidious distinction adds force to the current disapproval of any indulgence of this kind on the part of women, minors, and inferiors. This invidious traditional distinction has not lost its force even among the more advanced peoples of today. Where the example set by the leisure class retains its imperative force in the regulation of the conventionalities, it is observable that the women still in great measure practice the same traditional continence with regard to stimulants. . . .

The greater abstinence of women is in some part due to an imperative conventionality; and this conventionality is, in a general way, strongest where the patriarchal tradition—the tradition that the woman is a chattel—has retained its hold in greatest vigour. In a sense which has been greatly qualified in scope and rigor, but which has by no means lost its meaning even yet, this tradition says that the woman, being a chattel, should consume only what is necessary to her sustenance, except so far as her further consumption contributes to the comfort or the good repute of her master. The consumption of luxuries, in the true sense, is a consumption directed to the comfort of the consumer himself, and is, therefore, a mark of the master. Any such consumption by others can take place only on a basis of sufferance. . . .

The quasi-peaceable gentleman of leisure, then, not only consumes of the staff of life beyond the minimum required for subsistence and physical efficiency, but his consumption also undergoes a specialization as regards the quality of the goods consumed. He consumes freely and of the best, in food, drink, narcotics, shelter, services, ornaments, apparel, weapons and accoutrements, amusements, amulets, and idols or divinities. . . .Since the consumption of these more excellent goods is an evidence of wealth, it becomes honorific; and conversely, the failure to consume in due quantity and quality becomes a mark of inferiority and demerit. This growth of punctilious discrimination as to qualitative excellence in eating, drinking, etc., presently affects not only the manner of life, but also the training and intellectual activity of the gentleman of leisure. He is no longer simply the successful, aggressive male—the man of strength, resource, and intrepidity. In order to avoid stultification he must also cultivate his tastes, for it now becomes incumbent on him to discriminate with some nicety between the noble and the ignoble in consumable goods. He becomes a connoisseur in creditable viands of various degrees of merit, in manly beverages and trinkets, in seemly apparel and architecture, in weapons, games, dancers, and the narcotics. This cultivation of the aesthetic faculty requires time and application, and the demands made upon the gentleman in this direction therefore tend to change his life of leisure into a more or less arduous application to the business of learning how to live a life of ostensible leisure in a becoming way. Closely related to the requirement that the gentleman must consume freely and of the right kind of goods, there is the requirement that he must know how to consume them in a seemly manner. His life of leisure must be conducted in due form. Hence arise good manners in the way pointed out in an earlier chapter. High-bred manners and ways of living are items of conformity to the norm of conspicuous leisure and conspicuous consumption.

Conspicuous consumption of valuable goods is a means of reputability to the gentleman of leisure. As wealth accumulates on his hands, his own unaided effort will not avail to sufficiently put his opulence in evidence by this method. The aid of friends and competitors is therefore brought in by resorting to the giving of valuable presents and expensive feasts and entertainments. . . .

From the foregoing survey of the growth of conspicuous leisure and consumption, it appears that the utility of both alike for the purposes of reputability lies in the element of waste that is common to both. In the one case it is a waste of time and effort, in the other it is a waste of goods. Both are methods of demonstrating the possession of wealth, and the two are conventionally accepted as equivalents. . . . The question is, which of the two methods will most effectively reach the persons whose convictions it is desired to affect. . . .

So long as the community or social group is small enough and compact enough to be effectually reached by common notoriety alone—that is to say, so long as the human environment to which the individual is required to adapt himself in respect of reputability is comprised within his sphere of personal acquaintance and neighborhood gossip—so long the one method is about as effective as the other. . . . But when the differentiation has gone farther and it becomes necessary to reach a wider human environment, consumption begins to hold over leisure as an ordinary means of decency. This is especially true during the later, peaceable economic stage. The means of communication and the mobility of the population now expose the individual to the observation of many persons who have no other means of judging of his reputability than the display of goods (and perhaps of breeding) which he is able to make while he is under their direct observation.

The modern organization of industry works in the same direction also by another line. The exigencies of the modern industrial system frequently place individuals and households in juxtaposition between whom there is little contact in any other sense than that of juxtaposition.   One's neighbors, mechanically speaking, often are socially not one's neighbors, or even acquaintances; and still their transient good opinion has a high degree of utility. The only practicable means of impressing one's pecuniary ability on these unsympathetic observers of one's everyday life is an unremitting demonstration of ability to pay. In the modern community there is also a more frequent attendance at large gatherings of people to whom one's everyday life is unknown; in such places as churches, theatres, ballrooms, hotels, parks, shops, and the like. In order to impress these transient observers, and to retain one's self-complacency under their observation, the signature of one's pecuniary strength should be written in characters which he who runs may read. It is evident, therefore, that the present trend of the development is in the direction of heightening the utility of conspicuous consumption as compared with leisure.

It is also noticeable that the serviceability of consumption as a means of repute, as well as the insistence on it as an element of decency, is at its best in those portions of the community where the human contact of the individual is widest and the mobility of the population is greatest. Conspicuous consumption claims a relatively larger portion of the income of the urban than of the rural population, and the claim is also more imperative. The result is that, in order to keep up a decent appearance, the former habitually live hand-to-mouth to a greater extent than the latter. So it comes, for instance, that the American farmer and his wife and daughters are notoriously less modish in their dress, as well as less urbane in their manners, than the city artisan's family with an equal income. It is not that the city population is by nature much more eager for the peculiar complacency that comes of a conspicuous consumption, nor has the rural population less regard for pecuniary decency.   But the provocation to this line of evidence, as well as its transient effectiveness, are more decided in the city. This method is therefore more readily resorted to, and in the struggle to outdo one another the city population push their normal standard of conspicuous consumption to a higher point, with the result that a relatively greater expenditure in this direction is required to indicate a given degree of pecuniary decency in the city. The requirement of conformity to this higher conventional standard becomes mandatory. The standard of decency is higher, class for class, and this requirement of decent appearance must be lived up to on pain of losing caste.

Consumption becomes a larger element in the standard of living in the city than in the country. Among the country population its place is to some extent taken by savings and home comforts known through the medium of neighborhood gossip sufficiently to serve the like general purpose of pecuniary repute.   These home comforts and the leisure indulged in—where the indulgence is found—are of course also in great part to be classed as items of conspicuous consumption; and much the same is to be said of the savings. The smaller amount of the savings laid by by the artisan class is no doubt due, in some measure, to the fact that in the case of the artisan the savings are a less effective means of advertisement, relative to the environment in which he is placed, than are the savings of the people living on farms and in the small villages. Among the latter, everybody's affairs, especially everybody's pecuniary status, are known to everybody else. Considered by itself simply—taken in the first degree—this added provocation to which the artisan and the urban laboring classes are exposed may not very seriously decrease the amount of savings; but in its cumulative action, through raising the standard of decent expenditure, its deterrent effect on the tendency to save cannot but be very great. . . .

[But] the instinct of workmanship . . . disposes men to look with favor upon productive efficiency and on whatever is of human use. It disposes them to deprecate waste of substance or effort. The instinct of workmanship is present in all men, and asserts itself even under very adverse circumstances. . . . In so far as it comes into conflict with the law of conspicuous waste, the instinct of workmanship expresses itself not so much in insistence on substantial usefulness as in an abiding sense of the odiousness and aesthetic impossibility of what is obviously futile. . . .

All extraneous considerations apart, those adults are but a vanishing minority today who harbour no inclination to the accomplishment of some end, or who are not impelled of their own motion to shape some object or fact or relation for human use. The propensity may in large measure be overborne by the more immediately constraining incentive to a reputable leisure and an avoidance of indecorous usefulness, and it may therefore work itself out in make-believe only; as for instance in "social duties," and in quasi-artistic or quasi-scholarly accomplishments, in the care and decoration of the house, in sewing-circle activity or dress reform, in proficiency at dress, cards, yachting, golf, and various sports. But the fact it may under stress of circumstances eventuate in inanities no more disproves the presence of the instinct than the reality of the brooding instinct is disproved by inducing a hen to sit on a nestful of china eggs. . . .

In the narrower sphere of vicarious leisure a similar change has gone forward. Instead of simply passing her time in visible idleness, as in the best days of the patriarchal regime, the housewife of the advanced peaceable stage applies herself assiduously to household cares. . . .

The use of the term "waste" is in one respect an unfortunate one. As used in the speech of everyday life the word carries an undertone of deprecation. It is here used for want of a better term that will adequately describe the same range of motives and of phenomena, and it is not to be taken in an odious sense, as implying an illegitimate expenditure of human products or of human life. In the view of economic theory the expenditure in question is no more and no less legitimate than any other expenditure. It is here called "waste" because this expenditure does not serve human life or human well-being on the whole, not because it is waste or misdirection of effort or expenditure as viewed from the standpoint of the individual consumer who chooses it. If he chooses it, that disposes of the question of its relative utility to him, as compared with other forms of consumption that would not be deprecated on account of their wastefulness. Whatever form of expenditure the consumer chooses, or whatever end he seeks in making his choice, has utility to him by virtue of his preference. . . . The popular reprobation of waste goes to say that in order to be at peace with himself the common man must be able to see in any and all human effort and human enjoyment an enhancement of life and well-being on the whole. In order to meet with unqualified approval, any economic fact must approve itself under the test of impersonal usefulness—usefulness as seen from the point of view of the generically human. Relative or competitive advantage of one individual in comparison with another does not satisfy the economic conscience, and therefore competitive expenditure has not the approval of this conscience. . . .

In strict accuracy nothing should be included under the head of conspicuous waste but such expenditure as is incurred on the ground of an invidious pecuniary comparison. . . . The indispensability of these things [dress, jewelry, etc.] after the habit and the convention have been formed, however, has little say in the classification of expenditures as waste or not waste in the technical meaning of the word. The test to which all expenditure must be brought in an attempt to decide that point is the question whether it serves directly to enhance human life on the whole—whether it furthers the life process taken impersonally. . . .

6. Pecuniary Canons of Taste

. . . So far as the economic interest enters into the constitution of beauty, it enters as a suggestion or expression of adequacy to a purpose, a manifest and readily inferable subservience to the life process. This expression of economic facility or economic serviceability in any object—what may be called the economic beauty of the object—is best served by neat and unambiguous suggestion of its office and its efficiency for the material ends of life.

On this ground, among objects of use the simple and unadorned article is aesthetically the best. But since the pecuniary canon of reputability rejects the inexpensive in articles appropriated to individual consumption, the satisfaction of our craving for beautiful things must be sought by way of compromise. The canons of beauty must be circumvented by some contrivance which will give evidence of a reputably wasteful expenditure, at the same time that it meets the demands of our critical sense of the useful and the beautiful, or at least meets the demand of some habit which has come to do duty in place of that sense. Such an auxiliary sense of taste is the sense of novelty; and this latter is helped out in its surrogateship by the curiosity with which men view ingenious and puzzling contrivances. Hence it comes that most objects alleged to be beautiful, and doing duty as such, show considerable ingenuity of design and are calculated to puzzle the beholder—to bewilder him with irrelevant suggestions and hints of the improbable—at the same time that they give evidence of an expenditure of labor in excess of what would give them their fullest efficiency for their ostensible economic end.

This process of selective adaptation of designs to the end of conspicuous waste, and the substitution of pecuniary beauty for aesthetic beauty, has been especially effective in the development of architecture. It would be extremely difficult to find a modern civilized residence or public building which can claim anything better than relative inoffensiveness in the eyes of any one who will dissociate the elements of beauty from those of honorific waste. The endless variety of fronts presented by the better class of tenements and apartment houses in our cities is an endless variety of architectural distress and of suggestions of expensive discomfort. Considered as objects of beauty, the dead walls of the sides and back of these structures, left untouched by the hands of the artist, are commonly the best feature of the building. . . .

While men may have set out with disapproving an inexpensive manner of living because it indicated inability to spend much, and so indicated a lack of pecuniary success, they end by falling into the habit of disapproving cheap things as being intrinsically dishonorable or unworthy because they are cheap. As time has gone on, each succeeding generation has received this tradition of meritorious expenditure from the generation before it, and has in its turn further elaborated and fortified the traditional canon of pecuniary reputability in goods consumed; until we have finally reached such a degree of conviction as to the unworthiness of all inexpensive things, that we have no longer any misgivings in formulating the maxim, "Cheap and nasty." So thoroughly has this habit of approving the expensive and disapproving the inexpensive been ingrained into our thinking that we instinctively insist upon at least some measure of wasteful expensiveness in all our consumption, even in the case of goods which are consumed in strict privacy and without the slightest thought of display. We all feel, sincerely and without misgiving, that we are the more lifted up in spirit for having, even in the privacy of our own household, eaten our daily meal by the help of hand-wrought silver utensils, from hand-painted china (often of dubious artistic value) laid on high-priced table linen. Any retrogression from the standard of living which we are accustomed to regard as worthy in this respect is felt to be a grievous violation of our human dignity. So, also, for the last dozen years candles have been a more pleasing source of light at dinner than any other. Candlelight is now softer, less distressing to well-bred eyes, than oil, gas, or electric light. The same could not have been said thirty years ago, when candles were, or recently had been, the cheapest available light for domestic use. Nor are candles even now found to give an acceptable or effective light for any other than a ceremonial illumination. . . .

QUESTIONS FOR DISCUSSION

1 Can you give any present-day examples of "conspicuous consumption" or "conspicuous leisure"? Can the motive for consumption be shown objectively? Would the demand curve for such an item look any different from an ordinary demand schedule?
2 Does Veblen give us a convincing reason for the subordination of women in the American society of his times? Can you give any others?

READING 21

John Kenneth Galbraith, born in rural Canada to Scots parents, graduated as an agricultural economist from the University of California at Berkeley and eventually became a professor at Harvard. Intermittently, he has been a journalist for *Fortune* magazine, a television commentator, public servant, and humorist. Influenced by Keynes, as well as theorists of monopolistic competition, Galbraith is perhaps the best known dissenting economist in America today.

Economics and the Public Purpose (1973), from which this excerpt is drawn, is the fourth in a line of books, beginning with *American Capitalism: The Concept of Counter-vailing Power* (1952), *The Affluent Society* (1958), and *The New Industrial State* (1967). According to these works, a "technostructure" of professional managers and their staffs dominate big business's strategic decisions. Because they have market power, corporate managers don't have to obey the untutored demands of consumers. Instead, they can manipulate those demands for their own ends.

What does the modern corporation seek? Provided a decent profit is assured to placate stockholders, the managers will seek sales growth and the consequent enlargement of the technostructure itself. The more people and places in the technostructure, the higher the salaries and the greater the prestige of top managers. To obtain greater growth and a secure market position, the corporation will not raise prices to the short-run profit-maximizing level because lower, and infrequently changed, prices make the corporation less vulnerable to competitive and political pressures. Non-price competitive tactics are a better way to increase market share.

Though the technostructure does possess the knowledge for control of the large corporate (or "planned") sector, it is prone to complacency and mediocrity. But the market sector outside is too powerless to provide much dynamism, absent aid from the government. Such aid was in fact successfully provided by the agricultural extension service in this country, Galbraith recalls, and could help small business, too.

Economics and the Public Purpose*

John Kenneth Galbraith

The large corporation is something new . . . a clear break with what is described by traditional doctrine.

The traditional economics assumes that economic institutions and the motivation of the people who comprise them change but slowly. As with physics or botany economic truth once established is largely immutable. This is agreeable but not so. Economic institutions change rather rapidly; the large corporation and its relations with the community and state are especially in flux. And with such change comes new information, new insight. In consequence the rate of obsolescence in economic knowledge is high. (p. x)

[T]he function of the economic system is no longer simple—at least for anyone wishing to see the reality of things. Partly the economic system serves

---

Source: Copyright © 1973 by John Kenneth Galbraith and reprinted by permission of Houghton Mifflin Company. Owing to space limitations, Galbraith's reform proposals have had to be omitted.

the individual. But partly it is now seen to serve the needs of its own organizations. General Motors exists to serve the public. But General Motors also serves itself as well or instead. Not many will find such a proposition radically in conflict with common sense. To quite a few it will seem trite. It is only remarkable in being at odds with the main thrust of economics as it is traditionally taught. A shrewder view does, in fact, accept what is trite. It seeks to identify the interests the great organizations pursue, how they conduct the pursuit and with what effect on the public. (3-4)

Cultivation of useful belief is particularly important because of the way power is exercised in the modern economic system. It consists, as noted, in inducing the individual to abandon the goals he would normally pursue and accept those of another person or organization. . . . Persuasion (in forms later to be examined) becomes the basic instrument for exercise of power. For this the existence of an image of economic life that is congenial to the organizations that are exercising power is vital. So is instruction that implants this image. It persuades people that the goals of organization are really their own. . . . (6)

The management of the private consumer is a task of no slight sophistication; the cost is considerable, and it uses some of the most expert and specialized talent to be found anywhere in the planning system. Its most obvious instrument is advertising. And the uniquely powerful instrument of advertising is television which allows of persuasive communication with virtually every user of goods and services and with no minimum requirement in effort, literacy or intelligence. . . . It makes extensive use of market research and testing to ascertain to what the consumer can be persuaded and by what means and what cost. . . . Modern innovation is more often to create a need that one had previously perceived. (137)

The power to influence the individual consumer is not, of course, plenary. It operates within the limits of cost. . . . What will have to be spent to win a given amount of custom for a particular soap will depend on what has been spent on that soap in the past and also on what has been spent by all soap manufacturers to establish the imperatives of a clean and odorless personality. (138)

People can be persuaded and scholars can persuade themselves that General Dynamics or General Motors is responding to the public will so long as the exercise of its power does not threaten public existence. When ability to survive the resulting arms competition or breathe the resulting air is in doubt, persuasion is less successful. Similarly, when houses and health care are unavailable and male deodorants are abundant, the notion of a benign response to public wants begins to buckle under the strain. . . .

In the case of weapons . . . the initiating decision is taken by the weapons firm and by the particular service for which the item is intended. The action is ratified by the President who, though not without power, is extensively a captive of the bureaucracy he heads. The Armed Services Committees of the Congress, staffed with reliable sycophants of the weapons firms and the services, accept all but automatically the decision so taken. . . . Members of both the public and private technostructures are served by growth and the consequent promotions, pay, prerequisites and power, and what expands one bureaucracy expands the other. Technical development . . . is particularly important both for the autonomy and growth of the public bureaucracy and for the supplying technostructure. . . . In the United States bureaucratic symbiosis reaches its highest state of development in the relation between the weapons firms and the Department of Defense and its constituent elements. Lockheed, Boeing, Grumman or General Dynamics can develop and build military aircraft. This serves their affirmative goal of growth with the concurrent reward to their technostructures. The public bureaucracy that is associated with research and development, contracting, contract supervision, operations and command is similarly rewarded by the development and possession of a new generation of planes. But bureaucratic symbiosis also works at a more elementary level. The technostructure of the weapons firm is a natural source of employment for those who have completed a career in (or otherwise exhausted the possibilities of) the public bureaucracy. Leadership in the Department of Defense, by the same token, is extensively in the hands of men recruited temporarily from senior positions in the technostructures of the weapons firms. Not only is this exchange rewarding to individuals, but it serves, more incidentally, to cement the symbiotic relationship. (143-144)

Organization develops very unevenly in the economic system. It reaches its greatest scale in communications and the automobile industry, its greatest technical complexity and most intimate relation to the state in the manufacture of weapons. In agriculture, housing construction, the service industries, the arts, the more uncomplicated forms of vice, the business firm remains relatively simple. With these differences go very great differences in power and consequent social effect. Ford, Shell, and Proctor & Gamble deploy much power. The individual farmer has no such power; the residential builder has very little. These differences, in turn, have much to do with how the economic system performs—and for whom. Here, rather more than in the original eccentricities of consumer or citizen taste, is the explanation for the high level of automobile, highway and weapons development, the low level of development in housing, health and nutrition. . . . [M]uch is clarified by dividing business organization between two classes, those that deploy the full range of the instruments of power—over prices, suppliers, consumers, the community and the government—and those that do not. . . . (9-10)

Technology—the development and application of scientific or systematic knowledge to practical tasks—is a central feature of modern economic development. It comes to bear on both products and services and on the processes by which these are made or rendered. Organization goes hand in hand with technical advance. Little use can be made of technology from the knowledge available to any one man; all but invariably its employment requires the shared knowledge of several or numerous specialists—in short, of an organization. . . . The capital that is now at risk and the organization that now exists must be paid for—are an overhead cost. It is incurred or persists whatever the level of output. This adds to the need to control intervening events. Things that might go wrong and jeopardize sales and therewith the return to capital or the revenue that is needed to pay for organization must be prevented from going wrong: things that need to go right must be made to go right.

In specific terms this means that prices must, if possible, be under control; that decisive costs must also be under control or so managed that adverse movements can be offset by the controlled prices; that effort must be made to ensure that the consumer responds favorably to the product; that if the state is the customer, it will remain committed to the product or its development; that other needed state action is arranged and any adverse government action prevented; that other uncertainties external to the firm are minimized and other external needs assured. In other words, the firm is required, with increasingly technical products and processes, increasing capital, a lengthening gestation period and an increasingly large and complex organization, to control or seek to control the social environment in which it functions. . . . (38-39)

The market, the traditional and revered mechanism, for such coordination [of production plans by different firms] does not work. . . . The contract, projecting the buyer's requirements for months and years—and specifying prices and terms—does ensure response. The firm's planning turns on prospective growth as the primary goal. From this, requirements are readily adduced. Along with similar information and guarantees from others the supplying firm is provided with the information required for *its* planning. It is then able to meet the needs of its customers in accordance with their schedule. . . . With increasing development and increasing technical complexity of products and the processes by which they are manufactured, this web of contracts continuously extends and thickens. . . . Business in the planning system, it can be said with only slight exaggeration, is mostly contract negotiation. (126-127)

When the task lends itself to organization, there is no set upper limit to the size of the firm . . . it can become very large. (82)

The need to control environment—to exclude untoward events— encourages much greater size [than the technically optimum]. The larger the firm, the larger it will be in its industry The greater, accordingly, will be its influence in setting prices and costs. And the greater, in general, will be its influence on consumers, the community and the state. . . .

As an organization acquires power, it uses that power, not surprisingly, to serve the ends of those involved. These ends—job security, pay, promotion, prestige, company plane and private washroom, the charm of collectively exercised power—are all strongly served by the growth of the enterprise. . . . (40)

Some qualifications are now in order—for the person who is resisting truth nothing is so convenient as the overstatement, which becomes a handle for assault on the whole proposition. Only in the largest corporations is the power of the technostructure plenary—only there has it worked itself fully to completion. And there, if the corporation is failing to make money, stockholders may be aroused—although individual stockholders will usually accept the cheaper option of selling out. Proxy battles in very large firms occur all but exclusively in those that are doing badly.

Also, as stockholders are dispersed by some forces, they are aggregated by others—notably by insurance companies, pension funds, mutual funds and banks. This does something to arrest the deterioration of the power of the stockholder. However the effect is easily exaggerated. The tradition of financial institutions in relation to management is usually passive. There is a sense of the danger of uninformed intervention. (87-88)

The basic strategy by which the technostructure protects its decision-making process from owners or creditors consists in ensuring a certain minimum (though not necessarily a low) level of earnings. Nothing else is so important. Given some basic level of earnings, stockholders are quiescent. They become aroused, either individually or collectively, only when earnings are poor or there are losses and dividends are omitted. . . . Among the hundred or so largest corporations (which account for the major share of all sales and assets) proxy battles, when earnings are good, are virtually unknown. This is another way of saying that the position of technostructure under these circumstances is invulnerable. (94)

[T]he growth of the firm also serves as does nothing else the direct pecuniary interest of the technostructure. In a firm that is static in size an individual's advancement awaits the death, disability or retirement of those above him in the hierarchy. Or it depends on his ability to displace them. And, as he may hope to displace others, others below will hope to displace him. . . . In a growing firm, in contrast, new jobs are created by expansion. Promotion ceases to be a zero sum game in which what one wins, another loses. All can advance. . . . And as sales, number of employees or the value of assets managed increase, so do salary, expense accounts, and the individual's claim to nonsalary income or privilege . . . employee obeisance and peer group homage. (100-101)

In the market system managers and workers continue to supply products and services at levels of remuneration that are below those for comparable talent in the planning system. . . . Equality is not the tendency between the planning and the market system; the basic tendency is to inequality. The figures affirm the expectation. In 1971, hourly compensation in durable goods manufacture, the part of manufacturing most strongly represented in the industrial system, averaged $3.80. In nondurable manufacturing, where (in apparel and other manufacture) is a substantial market component, it was $3.26. In services, which are strongly oriented to the market system, it was $2.99. In retail trade, where the market system also retains a strong foothold, it was $2.57. In agriculture, the industry most characteristic of the market system, it was $1.48. Were executive and entrepreneurial income included with that of wage labor, the difference would, of course, be greatly increased. (132)

The contribution of any subordinate individual or group to earnings is merged with that of many others. Under all circumstances, it is subjective. . . . In the case of growth, in contrast, the contribution is direct and visible. The sales figures of a new product, gadget or line are a datum even if their contribution to earnings is less clear. (101)

In all times, growth by acquisition is a wholly normal tendency of the planning system. Between 1948 and 1965—years that exclude the frantic mergers of the latter sixties—the 200 largest manufacturing corporations in the United States acquired 2692 other firms with total assets of $21.5 billion. These assets accounted for about one seventh of all growth in assets by these firms during this period. (105)

In the planning system the role of prices is greatly diminished. They are much more effectively under the control of the firm. . . . Prices may be less important than the energy, guile or resourcefulness with which the firm persuades the consumer or the government to want what it produces or by which it eliminates the possibility of choice. . . . What it now produces is the result of its past skill in winning government support for its research and development with resulting processes or products. (111-112)

To protect itself the firm must be able to increase prices in order to offset increases in labor costs that it cannot prevent. The firm must also control prices and customer and supplier response because technological development tends to make demand increasingly inelastic and markets increasingly erratic. . . . To release an increased supply of high-capacity computers for what they would bring would be unthinkable. The situation is similar with labor, materials and components. The market is a reliable source of unskilled labor which can always be had at or a little above the going wage. Specialized engineering talent is not similarly available on short notice in response to higher wages. Nor are esoteric materials or components. Instead of relying on higher wages or prices to procure labor, materials or components the firm must set wages, salaries and prices and then concentrate its energies on getting the requisite supply at these levels and prices. (113-114)

The power to set the price means that any other major firm in the industry—Ford or Chrysler in the case of automobiles or Bethlehem or Inland in the case of steel—can, by fixing a lower price, force an alteration in the level first established. This may happen. But there is also a general recognition that such action, should it lead to further and retributive action by the firm originally establishing the price, could lead to general price-cutting. This would mean a general loss of control. . . . The danger is recognized by all. In the planning system there is, accordingly, a convention that outlaws such behavior. It is almost perfectly enforced. No contract, no penalties and usually no communication are involved. There is only an acute recognition of the disadvantage of such competitive and retributive action for all participants. . . . (114-115)

Having established a generally satisfactory level of prices, the practice in most industries is to leave them unchanged for an appreciable period of time. . . . Such small danger as there may be of loss of control comes when prices are changed. Then misunderstanding of another firm's motives in cutting a price or refusing an increase opens the way, however slightly, to competitive price-cutting. To minimize the number of price changes is thus to minimize this risk. (117-118)

The elimination of price competition as part of the protective purposes of the technostructure does not similarly eliminate other forms of rivalry between firms. Competition in product development, advertising, salesmanship and public ingratiation continues. Unlike price competition the effects of such rivalry are limited. Price-cutting can plunge all firms into disastrous loss. Other forms of rivalry, although they can be expensive, have no similar potential for damage. On the contrary, . . . each firm's selling efforts do something to sell the products or services of the industry as a whole and to affirm the happiness which derives from consumption in general. (119)

The advertising of the individual automobile company seeks to win consumers from other makes. But the advertising of all together contributes to the conviction that happiness is associated with automobile ownership. Additionally, make and model apart, it persuades people that the contemporary tendencies in automobile physiognomy and decoration are desirable, that those of the past are obsolete, eccentric or otherwise unworthy. . . . More important, still, the aggregate of all such persuasion affirms in the most powerful possible manner that happiness is the result of the possession and use of goods and that, pro tanto, happiness will be enhanced in proportion as more goods are produced and consumed. (140)

One branch of neoclassical economics has long held that the advertising and persuasion in the typically oligopolistic industry is a purely wasteful exercise in aggression and defense. . . . Were this the case, steps would long ago have been taken to limit advertising outlays by common agreement. No law would have stood against this effort, for the cost to the industry and the waste for the public would have been solemnly and influentially cited and policy would thus have been accommodated to the needs of the planning system. (141)

Technology and organization allows of increasing productivity and falling costs. Of these the public approves. These firms set prices with a view to expanding sales—to growth. Of this, the antithesis of monopoly pricing, the public also approves. The neoclassical model describes an ill that does not exist because it assumes a purpose that is not pursued. And proof lies in the fact that the ill it describes provokes no grave public complaint. It is inconceivable that the public could be universally exploited without being aware of it. (120)

The function of the multinational corporation is . . . the accommodation of the technostructure to the peculiar uncertainties of international trade. . . . It accomplishes over a world of multiple national sovereignties what it first accomplishes within any one. It minimizes the need for tariffs, quotas, and embargoes to reduce uncertainty in national markets. And, needless to say, it is not peculiarly American. . . . The transnational corporation can produce or arrange production where costs are lowest. This advantage has been extensively and increasingly exploited, especially by American-based corporations, in recent years. (167-168)

The planning system, in the absence of state intervention, is inherently unstable. It is subject to recession or depression which is not self-limiting but which can become cumulative. And it is subject to inflation which is also persistent, not self-correcting. The consequences of recession and inflation in the planning system then overflow with profound and damaging effect on the market system. (179) As the savings decisions of the planning system are made by a comparatively small number of large corporations, so also are the decisions to invest. Large magnitudes are involved. And there is no mechanism by which the two sets of planning decisions . . . are matched. Not even the most ardent defender of the neoclassical system imagines that the market any longer serves—that interest rates fall as necessary to discourage excessive savings and to encourage insufficient investment so as to keep the two equal. Accordingly intentions to save can easily exceed intentions to investment. In consequence there can be a deficiency in demand. . . . Spending on the products of the planning system is extensively the result of persuasion. However effective this management, the resulting consumption is less reliable than that derived from individual discovery based on pressing need for food, shelter, medicine or clothing. When incomes in the planning system fall, people can cut their consumption far more readily than in the market system. Finally in the planning system . . . prices, being subject to the control of the firm, do not fall. And wages, being subject to the authority of the unions, cannot be reduced. Accordingly, when demand falls, there is no offsetting effect of added sales from lower prices. And there is no chance that the effect of lower wages will be offset by increased employment. The entire impact of their reduction in demand is on output and employment. (182-183)

In the planning system . . . an important purpose of this power [to set prices] is to allow wage costs to be passed on to the public. . . . When power is possessed by the technostructure, the decision is taken by men who do not themselves pay the cost. And since profits are not being maximized—since there is, in effect, an unused possibility for monopoly gain—it will frequently happen that by raising prices profits can be kept at their former level. To be sure, higher prices are inimical to growth. But in the short run growth will frequently be better served by uninterrupted production than by a nasty strike. In the longer run the support that is accorded by the state to aggregate demand is . . . an extension of the power of the planning system. It will thus be assumed, and correctly, that, should demand be insufficient to clear markets at the higher prices, the state will sooner or later take action to make up the deficiency. All of this means that, in the planning system, the normal tendency is to accede to the wage claims of unions. (187)

QUESTIONS FOR DISCUSSION

1　Which assumptions of mainstream economic theory is Galbraith challenging? (See list in chapter 5.) If he is right, how would that challenge the notion that a market economy best serves the material interests of consumers?

2　How would mainstream neo-classical or Marxist analysis explain some of the facts about the American economy which Galbraith uses to prove his points?

3　Do you see enough similarities between Galbraith and Veblen to class both as "institutionalists"?

AFTERWORD

The hope which has inspired this new approach to the history of economic thought is that readers will comprehend good economic writings better if they understand the perspectives which give structure to most of them. The assumptions, procedures, and normative consequences of articles written from a neo-classical perspective are different from those which neo-Marxists employ. Once you spot the perspective an unknown writer is employing, you can more easily understand the economist's logic, argument, rhetoric, and policy recommendations. You can anticipate the characteristic blind spots and weaknesses of each perspective as the basis for criticism.

If perspectives are unavoidably partial views open to criticism, can one write without a perspective? My implicit argument is that one cannot really think or write without some perspective, though great and deep thinkers will be more conscious of it than will others. All the great economists wrote from a definite theoretical perspective.

Can one write from more than one perspective? Though one cannot exclude this, mixing perspectives can easily lead to shallow eclecticism, as well as unperceived contradictions, unless both perspectives are clearly recognized and segregated. Occasionally, mixing neo-classical and Keynesian or neo-institutionalist thinking has been fruitful. Galbraith uses both Keynesian and institutionalist perspectives for different problems; Baran and Sweezy were influenced by Keynes, as well as by Marx. Modigliani employs neo-classical concepts, as well as Keynesian ones.

Perspectives are not different language families incomprehensible to each other. Advocates of one perspective can, if they are open-minded, appreciate the strengths of another. Different problems may yield to different theories or even different perspectives. Neo-classical economics performs well for problems of administration of a given market system, but neo-mercantilism and Keynesianism may be able to improve that performance. Marxism illumines the change of systems, but classical and neo-Malthusian writers also have a version of the future. Institutionalism has a well-developed normative sense, but so does libertarianism. Perspectives often directly oppose one another. Doing economics from more than one perspective, like speaking two or more languages at once, is a feat few will perform gracefully. For ordinary mortals, it's better to choose. This book is only a menu for choice, an invitation to master one or another economic language. The rest is up to you.